Standardizing Personal Data Protection

OXFORD DATA PROTECTION AND PRIVACY LAW

Series Editors
Christopher Kuner, Affiliated Professor of Law, University of Copenhagen
Graham Greenleaf, Honorary Professor, Macquarie University, Sydney, and Senior Researcher, AustLII

The aim of this series is to publish important and original books on legal issues of data protection and privacy. This includes many different areas of law, including comparative law, EU law, human rights law, international law, privacy on the Internet, and others. Prospective authors are welcome to submit proposals for the series, as outlined on the series website: global.oup.com/academic/content/series/o/oxford-data-protection-and-privacy-law-odppl/

RECENT TITLES IN THE SERIES

Data Privacy and Competition Law in the Age of Big Data
Unpacking the Interface Through Complexity Science
Samson Y. Esayas

Data Protection Law and Emotion
Damian Clifford

Governing Cross-Border Data Flows
Reconciling EU Data Protection and International Trade Law
Svetlana Yakovleva

Coherence between Data Protection and Competition Law in Digital Markets
Klaudia Majcher

Vulnerability and Data Protection Law
Gianclaudio Malgieri

Privacy and the Role of International Law in the Digital Age
Kinfe Yilma

Standardizing Personal Data Protection

IRENE KAMARA
Assistant Professor, Cybercrime Law and Human Rights, Tilburg Institute for Law, Technology and Society, Netherlands (the)

OXFORD
UNIVERSITY PRESS

OXFORD
UNIVERSITY PRESS

Great Clarendon Street, Oxford, OX2 6DP,
United Kingdom

Oxford University Press is a department of the University of Oxford.
It furthers the University's objective of excellence in research, scholarship,
and education by publishing worldwide. Oxford is a registered trade mark of
Oxford University Press in the UK and in certain other countries

Published in the United States of America by Oxford University Press
198 Madison Avenue, New York, NY 10016, United States of America

British Library Cataloguing in Publication Data

Data available

Library of Congress Control Number: 2024951458

ISBN 9780198893288

DOI: 10.1093/9780191997037.001.0001

Printed and bound by
CPI Group (UK) Ltd., Croydon, CR0 4YY

MIX
Paper | Supporting
responsible forestry
FSC® C013604

The manufacturer's authorised representative in the EU for product safety is
Oxford University Press España S.A. of El Parque Empresarial San Fernando de Henares,
Avenida de Castilla, 2 – 28830 Madrid (www.oup.es/en or
product.safety@oup.com). OUP España S.A. also acts as importer into Spain
of products made by the manufacturer.

Foreword

*By Mireille Hildebrandt**

When Irene Kamara invited me to write a short foreword, I could not resist. This book provides a much-needed and in-depth analysis of standardization in the context of EU data protection law, from a legal, a theoretical and an empirical perspective. Legal scholars tend to restrict themselves to doctrinal analyses of binding or 'hard' law, keeping their distance from other normative orderings, often called 'soft law', such as codes of conduct or certification. Soft law, in fact, is not law and not necessarily soft. It is not law as it has no legal effect and it is not necessarily soft as it depends on the power relationships that define interactions in the absence of actionable legal redress. Indeed, soft law may have an *indirect effect* on legal effect, for instance when it eases or obstructs compliance with the law. We can see this in previous attempts by the Interactive Advertising Bureau (IAB) in Europe to help their members to deploy dark patterns to secure 'consent' for the use of cookies.[1]

As Kamara explains, although standardization is often qualified as a kind of soft law, one can argue against that, because the technical standards that are integrated by big players basically define the playing field of those who depend on their cloud servers, global mobile infrastructure, tech platforms or operating systems. This is how a standard moves from having *a non-binding normative impact* on those who develop, provide, or deploy the relevant technologies to having *a(n) (f)actual impact* on those who engage with the technologies. The latter is due to the way that the implementation of a standard results in enabling or constraining those who develop, provide, deploy or *use* a standardized technology. Where the German legal and political philosopher Jellinek spoke of the 'normative force of the factual',[2] we could in turn speak of the (f)actual force of technical normativity, asserting that even if standards have no legal effect they may nevertheless decide whether the use of a technology will be compliant with data protection law. This

* Mireille Hildebrandt is a Research Professor of 'Interfacing Law and Technology' at the Faculty of Law and Criminology of Vrije Universiteit Brussels and Full Professor of 'Smart Environments, Data Protection and the Rule of Law' at the Science Faculty of Radboud University in the Netherlands. See https://lsts.research.vub.be/mireille-hildebrandt.

[1] Gunawan J, Santos C, and Kamara I, 'Redress for Dark Patterns Privacy Harms? A Case Study on Consent Interactions', in *Proceedings of the 2022 Symposium on Computer Science and Law*, CSLAW 2022 (New York, NY, USA: Association for Computing Machinery, 2022), 181–94, https://doi.org/10.1145/3511265.3550448.

[2] Hildebrandt M, 'Text-Driven Jurisdiction in Cyberspace' in Floinn MÓ and others (eds), *Transformations in Criminal Jurisdiction. Extraterritoriality and Enforcement* (Bloomsbury 2023), 56–57, https://www.bloomsbury.com/uk/transformations-in-criminal-jurisdiction-9781509954223/.

move will be particularly relevant in the context of generative AI, where big players like Microsoft, Google, Meta, Amazon and Anthropic may *de facto* define standards due to the market shares of their cloud service, search engine or social media platform and their impact in standardization bodies.

Kamara speaks of standardization as 'developing and establishing consensus-based technical specifications (standards)' which she further defines as 'a private normative ordering'. She discusses the technology-specific and -adaptive nature of standardization, and the cross-jurisdictional effectiveness and the flexibility this entails compared to legislation. This relates to what she calls the bottom-up development of standards, involving those who are meant to implement them, and the voluntary nature of such implementation—suggesting this may increase the uptake and impact of standards. At the same time, these characteristics raise a lot of flags about the democratic legitimacy of standardization, especially where legal effect is directly or indirectly attributed by the EU legislature and/or where standardization has a (f)actual effect on the fundamental right to data protection, which is at the core of this book.

By combining a doctrinal analysis, paying keen attention to the relevant case law of the Court of Justice of the EU and decisions of EU regulators, with a theoretical framework based on a specific type of legal pluralism and that of transnational private regulation (TPR), complemented with an empirical study, this book will contribute to a better understanding to what is at stake. It does this by unfolding how products, systems and processes develop and interact as a consequence of standardization and what this means for the fundamental right to data protection. This book should be 'at hand' on the desk of legislatures, courts, regulators, law firms and those who advocate for the fundamental right to data protection, making sure they are well informed of the relevant details and aware of what is at stake.

Preface

When I first started exploring the regulatory power of technical standards more than a decade ago, and pursued studying data protection through the lens of private regulation, I did not imagine that this fascinating journey would lead to a dual PhD, several studies, projects, publications, and this book. Standardization is a highly complex and sophisticated system of self-regulation, where private and public interests, politics, and diverse agendas are intertwined with a drive for innovation, excellence, and efficiency. Technical standards, usually twenty-page long documents, produced under technocratic processes, very often shape, and even determine many aspects of our daily lives from ergonomics to product safety. This is why studying technical standardization in relation to a fundamental right, the right to protection of personal data, is important. Because technical standards, on the one hand offer answers as to how to implement data protection on the ground, but on the other hand standards are private regulation. Who develops those technical standards therefore and how, matters in that the legitimacy of technical standardization frames the role and boundaries of technical standards in support of the data protection law.

This book has benefited from the guidance and feedback of many scholars and practitioners, and mainly my PhD supervisors Eleni Kosta, Paul De Hert, and Kees Stuurman, and also Ronald Leenes. Thanks to Mireille Hildebrandt for the foreword to this book. I would like to thank the members of the PhD jury, Panos Delimatsis, Joris van Hoboken, Chris Hoofnagle, Andeas Mitrakas, and Vanessa Mak. My colleagues and friends at the Tilburg Institute for Law, Technology, and Society (TILT) at Tilburg Law School, and the Law, Science, Technology, and Society (LSTS) Research group at the Law and Criminology department of the Vrije Universiteit Brussel. My understanding of standardization has been enriched by my participation at the NEN Technical Committee on Privacy and Security, and several European and national projects, conferences such as the ETSI Security week, and the time spent at the CEN CENELEC Management Centre.

I would also like to thank Peter Daniell and Matthew Williams from OUP for the excellent collaboration, as well as Christopher Kuner and Graham Greenleaf, the editors of the series.

Last but not least, thank you to my parents, Pavlos and Dina, my sister Paola, Liana, Joyce, my partner Ernst, and my babies Paul and Danae for all the love and support.

Amoni, 4 August 2024
Irene Kamara

Contents

Table of Cases

ECtHR

CJEU AND GENERAL COURT

NATIONAL COURTS

UK

Abbreviations

Accreditation Regulation	Regulation 765/2008
AI	Artificial Intelligence
AI Act	Regulation 2024/1689
AIOTI	Alliance for Internet of Things
ANEC	European Consumer Association for Standardization
ANSI	American Standards Association
APEC	Asia-Pacific Economic Cooperation
ASA	American Standards Association
B2B	Business to Business
BCR	Binding Corporate Rules
CBPR	Cross-Border Privacy Rules
CCPA	California Consumer Privacy Act
CEN	European Committee for Standardisation
CENELEC	European Committee for Electrotechnical Standardization
CFREU	Charter of Fundamental Rights of the European Union
CJEU	Court of Justice of the European Union
COPPA	Children's Online Privacy Protection Act (US)
COPOLCO ISO	Committee for Consumer Policy of the International Organization for Standardization
CSA	Code Model Code for the Protection of Personal Information
CRA	Cyber Resilience Act 2847/2024
CWA	CEN Workshop Agreement
DNT	Do Not Track W3C technical specification
DPA	Data Protection Authority
DPO	Data Protection Officer
ECHR	European Convention on Human Rights
ECOS	Environmental Coalition on Standards
ECtHR	European Court of Human Rights
EDPB	European Data Protection Board
EDPS	European Data Protection Supervisor
EN	European standard
ePrivacy	Privacy of electronic communications
ESOs	European Standardization Organisations (CEN, CENELEC, ETSI)
ETSI	European Telecommunications Standards Institute
EU	European Union
FTC	Federal Trade Commission
GDPR	General Data Protection Regulation 679/2016
IAB	Interactive Advertising Bureau

ICT	Information Communication Technology
IEC	International Electrotechnical Commission
IEEE	Institute of Electrical and Electronics Engineers
IETF	Internet Engineering Task Force
IMS	Identity Management System
IoT	Internet of Things
IPSE	Initiative for Privacy Standardization in Europe
ISA	International Society for Automation
ISO	International Organization for Standardization
ISSS	Information Society Standardization System
ITU	International Telecommunication Union
JCT 1	Joint Technical Committee 1 of ISO and IEC
NAB	National Accreditation Body per Regulation 765/2008
NEN	Dutch Standardization Institute
NIS	Network and Information Security Directive 1148/2016
NIS2	Network and Information Security Directive 2555/2022
NIST	National Institute for Standards and Technology (US)
NLF	New Legislative Framework
OASIS	Organization for the Advancement of Structured Information Standards
OECD	Organisation for Economic Co-operation and Development
P3P	Privacy Preferences Platform
PET	Privacy Enhancing Technologies
PII	Personally Identifiable Information
PIMS	Privacy Information Management Systems
PIPEDA	Personal Information Protection and Electronic Documents Act 2000 (Canada)
PMS	Privacy Management Systems
prEN	draft European standard
PNR	Passenger Name Record data
RAPEX	Rapid Alert system for dangerous products
RED	Radio Equipment Directive 2014/53/EU
SMEs	Small and Medium Enterprises
SOTA	State of the art
SSO	Standard setting organization
TC13	Technical Committee CEN-CLC/TC13 on Cybersecurity and Data Protection
TC Cyber	ETSI Technical Committee Cyber Security
TEU	Treaty on European Union
TFEU	Treaty on the Functioning of the European Union
TPR	Transnational Private Regulation
UCCP	Unfair Contract Commercial Practices Directive 2005/29/EC
W3C	Word Wide Web Forum
WG5	CEN/CLC/JTC13/WG5
WP29	Article 29 Data Protection Working Party
WS/DPP	CEN/ISSS Workshop Data Protection and Privacy

1

Two Worlds Converging in 2015

Standardization and Data Protection

1.1 The 2015 Data Protection Standardization Request

In 2015, the European Commission requested the European Standardization Organizations develop standards in support of the right to protection of personal data as enshrined in art 8 of the CFREU and art 16 TFEU and protected in the EU secondary legislation.[1] The request was delivered in the form of a Commission Implementing Decision and was based on an earlier Communication on Security Industrial Policy that identified standards as a means to address privacy concerns in the design of security technologies.[2] The 2015 standardization request provided:

> In order to address these issues [ethical concerns, notably privacy issues, in the context of security products], the Commission aims to encourage the integration of "Privacy by Design" and "Privacy by Default" concepts at the early stages of the design and development and production processes of security technologies by means of voluntary European standards.

The 2015 standardization request by the Commission inaugurated the 'mandated' standardization activity in the field of data protection at European level.[3] The European Standardization Organizations ('ESOs'), namely CEN, CENELEC, and

[1] According to art 1 of the Regulation 1025/2012, a standard is 'a technical specification, adopted by a recognised standardization body, for repeated or continuous application, with which compliance is not compulsory, and which is one of the following: (a) 'international standard' means a standard adopted by an international standardization body; (b) 'European standard' means a standard adopted by a European standardization organization; (c) 'harmonised standard' means a European standard adopted on the basis of a request made by the Commission for the application of Union harmonization legislation; (d) 'national standard' means a standard adopted by a national standardization body.' Regulation 1025/2012/EU (hereafter 'Standardization Regulation' or 'Regulation 1025/2012').

[2] European Commission, Communication from the Commission to the European Parliament, the Council and the European Economic and Social Committee Security Industrial Policy Action Plan for an innovative and competitive Security Industry, COM/2012/0417 final.

[3] There already was a prior standardization request in 2008, which however did not request the development of specific technical standards on data protection, but guidelines. See European Commission, Standardization Mandate to the European Standardization Organizations in the field of Information and Communications Technologies applied to Radio Frequency Identification (RFID) and Systems, M 436, December 2008.

Standardizing Personal Data Protection. Irene Kamara, Oxford University Press. © Irene Kamara 2025.
DOI: 10.1093/9780191997037.003.0001

ETSI, established a new Working Group with the aim to carry out the request and develop the new standards. The standardization request in the field of data protection was aligned with the EU regulator's standpoint that standards can support Union legislation and address major societal challenges.[4]

Standards in the fields of data protection and privacy however had already been on the radar of the EU policy makers before the 2015 standardization request. In fact, standards were part of the debate during the reform of the EU data protection legislation since its very beginning.[5] The Commission Communication that launched the legal reform of the Data Protection Directive stressed the importance of coherence between the legal framework on data protection and international technical standards with the aim to ensure a consistent and practical implementation of data protection rules.[6] The Commission had undertaken at the time to follow *inter alia* the development of international technical standards to ensure that they usefully complemented the legal rules and to 'ensure operational and effective implementation of the key data protection requirements'.[7] In addition, technical standards for the protection of personal data were linked to the EU enlargement policy and its ambition to provide a benchmark for third countries in regulating personal data.[8]

The national data protection authorities of the EU Member States and their former common advisory group, the WP29, have also referred to standardization in numerous opinions and guidelines on the interpretation and application of EU data protection law. In the Opinion on a cloud computing code of conduct, the WP29 encouraged the implementation of standards for cloud computing, especially related to interoperability, portability, and security.[9] Similar references in opinions dating back to 2005 stand out on the topics of risk assessment,[10] information and transparency in relation to RFID,[11] anonymization,[12] and other data protection related issues.

[4] Recitals 25 and 19 respectively Regulation 1025/2012.

[5] European Commission, A comprehensive approach on personal data protection in the European Union, OJ C181/01.

[6] Directive 95/46/EC of the European Parliament and of the Council of 24 October 1995 on the protection of individuals with regard to the processing of personal data and on the free movement of such data, OJ L281/31 (hereafter 'Data Protection Directive' or 'Directive 95/46/EC').

[7] European Commission, A comprehensive approach on personal data protection in the European Union, COM(2010) 609 final, OJ C181/01 (hereafter Commission 'COM(2010) 609').

[8] COM(2010) 609 (n 7).

[9] WP29, Opinion 02/2015 on C-SIG Code of Conduct on Cloud Computing, 2588/15/EN WP232, 22 September 2015.

[10] WP29, Opinion 5/2010 on the Industry Proposal for a Privacy and Data Protection Impact Assessment Framework for RFID Applications, WP175, July 2010.

[11] WP29, Working Document on data protection issues related to RFID technology WP105, January 2005.

[12] WP29, Opinion 05/2014 on Anonymisation Techniques, WP216, April 2014.

1.2 The Roots of the Convergence: Technological Challenges in Effective Protection

The unusual 'marriage' of technical standardization with the fundamental right to protection of personal data was part of the modernization of data protection legislation and the search for tools to address effectiveness problems of data protection law. The introduction of the concept of standards in data protection policy and law is rooted in a reported weakness of the former legislative framework in the Union to fully address the complexity and challenges posed to data protection by unprecedented technological developments.[13] Such developments and their challenges to data protection law have been flagged by scholars and policy makers since the mid 1990's,[14] and were one of the reasons that spurred legislative reform of the Union data protection law in the first place.[15] A 2010 Commission Communication pointed at the elaborate way data were collected in a non-transparent and often non-detectable manner, and the processing and use of such data to infer conclusions about individuals. The Communication highlighted the scale of collection, the sharing of information by individuals on social networks—also called 'prosumers'–, as implicating factors that intensify the need for control over one's own personal data.[16] Further, the admittedly broad scope of EU data protection law, which has been characterized as the 'law of everything'[17] enlarges the number of entities with a duty to comply with Union data protection legislation.

The loss of control over personal data and the lack of effective protection of the individual in general, is illustrated in the example of Internet of Things (IoT). 'Smart homes' embedded with grid sensors which provide an accurate image of the activity, habits, and schedules of its residents, and visitors. In the IoT environment, personal assistants using AI are increasingly part of the problem. A study conducted on personal assistants such as Alexa, Siri and Google Assistant, showed that these devices may be mistakenly activated up to nineteen times a day and record

[13] While technical standards in data protection law are a novel coupling in the Union, this is not the case with other jurisdictions. In the US for example, the Computer Security Act of 1987 (Public Law 100-235) assigned responsibility to the National Institute of Standards and Technology (NIST) to develop computer security guidelines and standards. Madsen W, *Handbook of personal data protection* (Maxmillan Publishers, 1992), 136.

[14] See among many the reports of the Berlin Group of that period, a working group of the International Conference of Data Protection and Privacy Commissioners, https://www.datenschutz-berlin.de/datenschutz/zusammenarbeit-und-gremien/ [accessed 20 September 2023]. And later writings on this matter: Read among many: Norwegian Data Protection Authority 'Big Data – privacy principles under pressure' (2013) https://www.datatilsynet.no/globalassets/global/english/big-data-engelsk-web.pdf [accessed 20 September 2023].

[15] Recital 6 GDPR.

[16] COM(2010) 609 (n 7) 2.

[17] Purtova N, 'The Law of Everything. Broad Concept of Personal Data and Future of EU Data Protection Law' (2018) 10 Law, Innovation and Technology, 40; Read also Brkan M, 'The Unstoppable Expansion of the EU Fundamental Right to Data Protection: Little shop of horrors?' (2016) 23 Maastricht Journal of European and Comparative Law, 812.

private conversations without the knowledge of the discussants.[18] Personal assistants may not only collect the content of discussions or any other information from the regular use of the devices, but are also reported to go far beyond that. Amazon has received a patent for Alexa's emotional intelligence technology, which detects users' physical, emotional, and behavioural states.[19] Data derived from sources such as sensors, cameras, and personal assistants are combined and analysed for purposes relating to improvement of services, but also more importantly advertisements from the service providers known to the individuals or unknown third parties,[20] or more problematic purposes such as manipulation and deception.[21]

The AI personal assistant example illustrates a range of issues pertaining to autonomy, independence, control over personal data, and the adverse conditions for exercising substantive data protection rights such as the rights to information, access, rectification, and erasure of personal data. In some cases, those issues stem from the intentional use of such technologies. Ineffective exercise of rights or limitations to independence and informational self-determination are foreseen and sometimes considered an accepted risk by those entities implementing the technologies. In some other cases, the severity of the impacts of using one or the other technology are, mistakenly and negligently unaccounted for. These are companies that have limited resources or are less interested in making value out of acquired data. In theory, a negligent behaviour may be prevented with instruments that focus on guidance and awareness, of course those will not work for companies who act *mala fide*.[22] The acknowledgment however that some infringements may be attributed to the complexity of obligations, is relevant for considering regulatory instruments additional to legislation.

Independently of the intentions behind the behaviour of companies collecting and using data in a manner incompatible with the wishes of the individuals, there are two substantial factors. First is that some technologies do not only enable an infringing behaviour, such as covert cross-website or cross-device tracking of

[18] O' Flaherty, Kate 'Amazon, Apple, Google Eavesdropping: Should You Ditch Your Smart Speaker?' (26 February 2020), Forbes. https://www.forbes.com/sites/kateoflahertyuk/2020/02/26/new-amazon-apple-google-eavesdropping-threat-should-you-quit-your-smart-speaker/[accessed 20 September 2023].

[19] Sarnoff, Peter 'A new Amazon patent reveals Alexa could become emotionally intelligent' (17 October 2018), Business Insider, See https://www.businessinsider.com/amazon-patent-alexa-emotional-intelligence-2018-10 [accessed 20 September 2023]. This is done with the detection of audible cues in the voice, such as the tone of a voice or a cough, and the combination of such cues with other information about the user such as age, location and purchase history. Read on Emotional Artificial Intelligence Clifford D, *Data Protection Law and Emotion* (Oxford University Press 2024).

[20] The acquired data are shared with or accessed by law enforcement agencies, see the case https://www.washingtonpost.com/technology/2019/11/02/police-think-amazons-alexa-may-have-information-fatal-stabbing-case/ [accessed 20 September 2020].

[21] Confessore N, 'Cambridge Analytica and Facebook: The scandal and the fallout so far.' *The New York Times* 4 (2018); Burkell Jand Regan PM, 'Voter preferences, voter manipulation, voter analytics: policy options for less surveillance and more autonomy.' *Internet Policy Review* 8, no 4 (2019): 1–24.

[22] The General Data Protection Regulation however imposes a strict liability regime.

Internet users,[23] but play a more active role in the actual infringing behaviour such as prompting it, when for example their design is such that collects unnecessary personal data by default or sorts data based on the prohibited grounds of race or gender, which eventually might lead to discriminatory treatment of individuals or groups of people.[24] Second is, infringements are facilitated by the *de facto* existing power asymmetries. As in other fields of law, e.g. consumer law with the concept of 'vulnerable consumer' used to determine misleading commercial practices, the individual in data protection is most often at a vulnerable position due to lack of knowledge or expertise or the lack of effective redress mechanisms,[25] and needs enhanced protection.[26]

The effective protection of the individual against such risks may take many forms such as placing the individual at the centre of legislation, or creating a framework of safeguards which by design protect the vulnerable individual from making uninformed self-harming choices.[27] In fact, the GDPR places *control* at the centre of the legislative reform, together with fairness and accountability[28] even though it is reported to not (yet) fully achieve its goals, especially the one of enhancing individual control.[29] Those are eminent and recurring issues of design of (legal) regulation.

Traditionally, the EU primarily resorts to legislation to regulate such challenges,[30] as shown also with the 2012 data protection reform. In the case of data

[23] See for example Federal Trade Commission, 'Cross-Device Tracking' FTC Staff Report (2017) urging entities with direct consumer-facing relationships and those engaging in cross-device tracking to be transparent about their data collection and use practices. https://www.ftc.gov/system/files/documents/reports/cross-device-tracking-federal-trade-commission-staff-report-january-2017/ftc_cross-device_tracking_report_1-23-17.pdf [accessed 20 September 2023].

[24] For example Tucker I, 'A white mask worked better: Why algorithms are not colour blind.'" *The Guardian* 28 (2017); Buolamwini J and Gebru T, 'Gender shades: Intersectional accuracy disparities in commercial gender classification' in *Conference on fairness, accountability and transparency* (2018) 77–91.

[25] See art 5(3) Unfair Commercial Practices Directive. Read also: González Fuster G, 'How uninformed is the average data subject? a quest for benchmarks in EU personal data protection' (2014) 19 IDP. Revista de Internet, Derecho y Política, 92.

[26] See, among many, Mak V, 'Standards of Protection: In Search of the "Average Consumer" of EU Law in the Proposal for a Consumer Rights Directive' (2011) 19 European Review of Private Law, 25.

[27] For example Malgieri and Niklas have proposed a layered approach to the concept of vulnerability of data subjects, which allows tailored safeguards and institutional interventions to the risks occurred. See Malgieri G and Niklas J, 'Vulnerable Data Subjects' (2020) 37 Computer Law & Security Review 105415. Read on vulnerability in data protection law: Malgieri G, *Vulnerability and Data Protection Law* (Oxford University Press 2023).

[28] Recital 7 GDPR. Lynskey identifies an instrumental and conceptual role of 'control' in data protection law, and argues that 'individual control should be explicitly recognized as a facet of the right to data protection.' Lynskey O, *The Foundations of EU Data Protection Law* (Oxford University Press 2015) (hereafter Lynskey *The Foundations of EU Data Protection Law*), 228ff.

[29] Van Ooijen I and Vrabec HU, 'Does the GDPR Enhance Consumers' Control over Personal Data? An Analysis from a Behavioural Perspective' (2018) 42 Journal of Consumer Policy, 105ff.

[30] The European Commission's regulatory fitness and performance programme (REFIT), which is part of the Better Regulation agenda, and the Impact Assessments (IA), are policy instruments that aim to reduce the overreliance to legislation, when other measures can be taken. Research however shows

protection, legislation backed with enforcement, and redress mechanisms is better suited for the protection of a fundamental right. In parallel however, the need for additional supportive regulatory tools was manifested by both the 2015 Commission standardization request, discussed earlier, and the text of the Proposal for the GDPR, which included a considerable number of references to various regulation tools, including standardization.

Scholarship on the need for complementary instruments has preceded the introduction of standardization in the data protection field. From a non-European perspective, Bennet and Mulligan have argued that 'law is necessary, but not sufficient. It needs to be supplemented by other policy instruments, fashioned and implemented within a policy network.'[31] The authors have argued that privacy codes of conduct are a useful policy tool, within the context of a strong regulatory framework, creating baseline requirements for companies and empowering enforcement. Further, Bennett has reasoned that due to the lack of resources, data protection authorities need surrogates, 'including a complicated array of private sector actors with different levels of competence and independence' such as standard-setting organizations.[32] From an EU standpoint, Dumortier and Goemans have explained that the effectiveness of data protection legislation relies on its implementation mechanisms and instruments that can facilitate the compliance process with the legal obligations laid down in the data protection law.[33] On the issue of control of individuals over their personal data, Lynskey has argued that subjective rights must be complemented by 'an architecture which bolsters individual control over personal data in order to deliver partial privacy self-management'.[34] In a similar vein, Van Ooijen and Vrabec found that the GDPR has taken steps in addressing threats to individual control and effective protection, but remaining deficiencies 'may be mitigated by self-regulatory instruments'.[35] Various additional reasons have stirred scholarship and policy makers towards the direction of complementary instruments, and specifically, standardization, which is the focus of this book.

that those two instruments are often in practice used to legitimize a decision for legal intervention. Meuwese has found that Impact Assessments may be used to silence discussions on alternative regulatory options. Meuwese A, *Impact assessment in EU lawmaking* (Kluwer Law International 2008), 272.

[31] Bennett C and Mulligan DK, 'The Governance of Privacy Through Codes of Conduct: International Lessons for U.S. Privacy Policy' [2012] SSRN Electronic Journal.

[32] Bennett CJ, 'International privacy standards: Can accountability ever be adequate?' [2010] Privacy Laws &Business International Newsletter, 21.

[33] Dumortier J and Goenmans C, 'Data Privacy and Standardization' Discussion Paper prepared for the CEN/ISSS Open Seminar on Data Protection (2000).

[34] Lynskey, *The Foundations of EU Data Protection Law* (n 28) 257.

[35] van Ooijen I, and Vrabec HU, 'Does the GDPR Enhance Consumers' Control Over Personal Data? An Analysis from a Behavioural Perspective.' Journal of consumer policy 42, no 1 (2019) 91–107.

1.3 The Many Faces of Standardization and the Not So New Coupling of Standards and Union Law

Standard-setting, meaning 'developing and establishing consensus-based technical specifications (standards)', has been studied by a multitude of disciplines in different contexts such as political science, law (international trade law, global administrative law, European public and private law), legal and regulation theories, in addition to technical disciplines.[36] The versatility of standards reflects the multi-faceted and evolving nature of the concept and of the standard-setting activity.

While a full study of the various facets of the concept of standards is beyond the scope of the book, four preliminary remarks are relevant. The multi-faceted concept of standards[37] demonstrates different qualities which are relevant to challenges following the deployment of various disruptive technologies and the broad scope of the Union data protection law discussed above.

First, standards are a flexible regulatory instrument. The element of flexibility relates to the speedier development processes of standards in relation to law-making processes. Standards may be *technology-specific* and *technology-adaptive*.[38] This flexibility explains the potential of standardization for types of regulation with both legal and technical requirements.[39] Brownsword explains that for new technologies, 'regulation needs to incorporate a degree of flexibility or openendedness, wherever possible adopt "technologically neutral" strategies, that regulation should be interpreted purposively, and that soft law or light regulation might sometimes work better than hard or hard-wired confining law.'[40]

Second, the *bottom-up development process* of standards, namely from the intended users instead of (only) the legislature is another characteristic.[41] Standards developed bottom-up are reported to have higher chances of accommodating the reality and practices on the ground in place of a top-down imposed political

[36] See overview in Mariolina E and Cauffman C, 'The Legitimacy of Standardization as Regulatory Technique in the EU: A Cross-sector and Multi-level Analysis: An Introduction' in Mariolina E and Kauffman C (eds.) in *The Legitimacy of Standardization as a Regulatory Technique* (Edward Elgar Publishing, 2020) (hereafter Eliantonio and Cauffman, 'An Introduction').

[37] The terms 'technical standards' and 'standards' in the meaning of Regulation 1025/2012 are used interchangeably. 'Legal standards' are referred to as such throughout the book.

[38] An example is information security standards, such as the Common Criteria, which are updated according to new information security risks. The Protection Profiles based on the Common Criteria standards, which define security problems, threats, security objectives and provide for IT security requirements. See for example the Protection Profile on Encrypted Storage Device 2012, https://www.commoncriteriaportal.org/files/ppfiles/FMV-PP-ESD.pdf [accessed 20 September 2023]

[39] Busch C, 'Towards a New Approach in European Consumer Law: Standardisation and Co-Regulation in the Digital Single Market' (2016) 5J. Eur. Consumer & Mkt., 197.

[40] Brownsword R, 'What the world needs now: Techno-regulation, human rights and human dignity.' *Global governance and the quest for justice*, (Hart Publishing 2004), 203.

[41] Peters A, Förster T and Koechlin L, 'Towards Non-State Actors as Effective, Legitimate, and Accountable Standard Setters,' in Peters A and others, *Non-State Actors as Standard Setters* (Cambridge University Press 2009), 579–610.

agenda. The collective expertise and best practices shared by the participants of the technical committees are qualities hardly met in the top-down development of policies or other instruments.

Third, in principle, the use of standards in the EU is *voluntary*. Thus, even when standards are linked to EU law and developed at the request of the legislature, they are in theory of a non-binding nature. However, one should keep in mind that there are different types of standards, which in turn have different characteristics. A content-based distinction is between standards that pertain to organizational matters, prescription of controls and requirements on the one hand (such as management and product safety standards), and standards related to ICT.[42] Even though, neither is formally binding in EU law, the use of the latter is more often of a *de facto* mandatory nature by web service providers or online platform providers in order to provide access to a service. When regulating *online* privacy for example, Mifsud Bonnici argues that the use of technical standards is inevitable.[43]

Finally, standards are *not constrained by jurisdiction borders*. Especially when standards are independent of regional or national laws, which is often the case for example with the international standards of the ISO, they have a transnational character. Such standards may be adopted and conformed with by any organization worldwide.[44]

Many of the characteristics of standardization are appealing for the Union policy makers and legislature, which have notably used standards to support public policy and legislation in a range of fields, elevating standardization to a sort of regulatory technique.[45] Prominent examples are the EU cybersecurity laws, and the New Approach Directives.[46] The latter rely strongly on standardization to specify technical aspects, since the Directives only provide for essential requirements to be met by products.[47] The New Approach legislation and consequently the European harmonized standards developed in support of the Directives focus on issues such as safety and health. In addition, standardization has been a common tool for the implementation of the environmental policy and legislation of the

[42] The second category of standards is linked to the discussions of regulating technology via technology, otherwise commonly coined as 'techno-regulation'. Read further: Bronwen M and Yeung K *An introduction to law and regulation: Text and materials* (CUP, 2007); Leenes R, 'Framing Techno-Regulation: An Exploration of State and Non-State Regulation by Technology' (2011) 5 Legisprudence, 143.

[43] Bonnici JPM, *Self-Regulation in Cyberspace* (TMC Asser Press 2008), 146ff.

[44] ibid (n 44), 136. On the competition of national markets to set global (ICT) standards, read: Winn JK, 'Globalization and Standards: the Logic of Two-Level Games,' (2009) 5 I/S: A Journal of Law and Policy for the Information Society, 185.

[45] Eliantonio and Cauffman, 'An Introduction' (n 36).

[46] See Network and Information Security Directive (NIS) 2016/1148/EU art 19, the Cybersecurity Act 881/2019 art 8; the revised NIS Directive (EU) 2022/2555/EU art 25.

[47] Bremer explains that the US uses differently the term 'essential requirements' which refers to ANSI's due process requirements for American National Standards. Bremer ES, 'Government Use of Standards in the United States and Abroad,' in Contreras JL (ed), *The Cambridge Handbook of Technical Standardization Law* (Cambridge University Press 2019).

Union.[48] The use of standards for supporting public policy goals and legislation has been growing throughout the decades and largely serve today the Union legislators and policy makers' agenda.

1.4 The Ambiguous Introduction in the General Data Protection Regulation

Returning to the reform of the general EU data protection law and the coupling of standards with the revised law in 2016, various endorsements to standards materialized in proposed legal provisions.[49] Two issues mark the post-GDPR era in relation to standards. The first is the very introduction of the concept of standards in the reformed law. The GDPR explicitly refers to standards on several occasions such as standards for certification, data protection seals, and marks,[50] and the right to object to processing[51] with the use of automated means using technical specifications.

The second issue is that despite the multiple policy endorsements, the legislator was hesitant to formalize in-depth and extensively the relationship of (technical) standards and the reformed secondary EU data protection law. The 2012 Commission proposal for the GDPR[52] and the 2014 European Parliament First

[48] Examples are Directive 2000/60/EC of the European Parliament and of the Council of 23 October 2000 establishing a framework for Community action in the field of water policy (Water Framework Directive); Directive 2009/29/EC of the European Parliament and of the Council of 23 April 2009 amending Directive 2003/87/EC so as to improve and extend the greenhouse gas emission allowance trading scheme of the Community; The Energy and Climate package; Sustainable Consumption, Production and Industry Action Plan, COM(2008) 397 final of 16 July 2008; Directive 2008/50/EC of the European Parliament and of the Council of 21 May 2008 on ambient air quality and cleaner air for Europe (Air Quality Directive); Directive 2010/75/EU of the European Parliament and of the Council of 24 November 2010 on industrial emissions (integrated pollution prevention and control) (Industrial Emissions Directive); Directive 2001/81/EC of the European Parliament and the Council on National Emission Ceilings for certain pollutants (NEC Directive); Directive 94/63/EC on the control of volatile organic compound (VOC) emissions resulting from the storage of petrol and its distribution from terminals to service stations; Directive 2006/21/EC on the management of waste from extractive industries and amending directive 2004/35/EC ('extractive waste') https://www.cen.eu/work/areas/env/Pages/default.aspx [accessed 20 September 2023], and a considerable number of standardization requests from the European Commission to the European Standardization Organizations to develop standards related to the environment, such as the Mandate M/514 under Directive 2010/75/EU for a European standard method to determine fugitive and diffuse emissions of volatile organic compounds (VOC) from certain industrial sources to the atmosphere.

[49] The General Data Protection Regulation replaced Directive 95/46/EC. For an overview of the GDPR, read further: De Hert P and Papakonstantinou V, 'The New General Data Protection Regulation: Still a Sound System for the Protection of Individuals?' (2016) 32 Computer Law & Security Review, 179; Mitrou L, 'The General Data Protection Regulation: A Law for the Digital Age?' in Synodinou T-E and others, EU Internet Law: Regulation and Enforcement (Springer 2017), 19ff.

[50] GDPR art 43(9).

[51] GDPR art 21(5).

[52] European Commission, Proposal for a Regulation of the European Parliament and of the Council on the protection of individuals with regard to the processing of personal data and on the free movement of such data (General Data Protection Regulation), COM (2012) 11 final, 25 January 2012

Reading[53] included notably more explicit references to standards such as for example in relation to data portability, and data protection by design and by default, which did not survive the Parliament and Council negotiations, and were eventually omitted in the final version of the GDPR.[54] In addition, as regards the quality of references to standards in the GDPR text, standards appear in the final text of the GDPR in a cloud of ambiguity. The role of standards in relation to the aims of the data protection law is assumed, but not spelled out. There is ambiguity as per the utility, legal effects, parties developing standards, types of standards, and further conditions of use and conformity. The 2017 proposed ePrivacy Regulation follows a similar approach when it comes to the quality of references; as regards the topics of references, those relate to standardized icons and provision of user's consent via technical settings.[55]

Despite standardization being broadly used in other fields of Union law, such as safety, health, and environment, the final text of data protection law did not fully endorse the coupling of standards and data protection. One could argue that further 'formalization' of the relationship via EU data protection secondary legislation is not necessary due to the existing general legal framework on standardization, the Standardization Regulation 1025/2012 ('Standardization Regulation'). However, issues of subject matter of standardization (what can be standardized), how and what role technical standards may have in relation to the right to protection of personal data are (naturally) not addressed in the Standardization Regulation. Furthermore, the Standardization Regulation provides only a general framework of principles and procedures. Senden argues that even if the Standardization Regulation 'has put some safeguards in place, the question remains whether these standards are sufficient, given the fact that harmonised standards are gaining EU public nature and are akin to the Commission's exercise of implementing powers'.[56] Similar arguments are made also for standards, which are increasingly assigned *de facto* legal effects in relation to EU legislation.[57] The legitimacy of

[53] European Parliament legislative resolution of 12 March 2014 on the proposal for a regulation of the European Parliament and of the Council on the protection of individuals with regard to the processing of personal data and on the free movement of such data (General Data Protection Regulation) (COM(2012)0011 - C7-0025/2012 - 2012/0011(COD)).

[54] Kamara I, 'Co-regulation in EU personal data protection: the case of technical standards and the privacy by design standardisation 'mandate' (2017) 8 European Journal of Law and Technology.

[55] European Commission, Proposal for a Regulation of the European Parliament and of the Council concerning the respect for private life and the protection of personal data in electronic communications and repealing Directive 2002/58/EC (Regulation on Privacy and Electronic Communications), COM/2017/010 final, January 2017/03 (Proposal for ePrivacy Regulation).

[56] Senden L, 'The Constitutional Fit of European Standardization Put to the Test' (2017) 44 Legal Issues of Economic Integration, 337 (hereafter Senden, 'The Constitutional Fit'). See chapter 5 in this book.

[57] The area of electronic identification and trust services offers an example: The Commission Implementing Decision 2016/650 enlists a number of international and European technical standards for the security assessment of information technology products. According to art 29(2) of the Electronic Identification Regulation (eIDAS Regulation), where a qualified electronic signature creation device meets the technical standards, there is a presumption of compliance with the requirements laid down in the eIDAS Regulation; Regulation 910/2014/EU of the European Parliament and of the Council of

standard-development processes, quality of and accessibility to standards have been debated in legal scholarship.[58]

1.5 Conceptual Framework and Aim

1.5.1 Objectives of the Book

The developments described in the previous sections give rise to questions of the normative and implementation nature regarding the development and use of standards in support of the regulation of the right to protection of personal data. The policy endorsements, the hesitant inclusion in the Union data protection law, the 2015 Commission standardization request coupled with the prominent and largely unanswered issues of safeguards and boundaries of the standard-setting activity in the field of data protection, point at the need for a legal study on the concept of standards in EU data protection legislation, and the use of standardization as an emerging regulatory technique in data protection.

In response to challenges to effective protection of the individual and loss of control over one's personal data due to technological developments that allow for processing of vast amounts of personal data and the broad scope of EU data protection law, the book assesses whether standards offer a solution to the problems data protection legislation is facing, and the extent to which standards may provide answers to those problems. The aim of this book is, in other words, to explore and analyse to what extent standards may have a role in protecting the individual's fundamental right to personal data protection by supplementing the Union data protection legislation.

The working hypothesis of the book is that standards can play a supportive role, as proposed by multiple policy documents,[59] hinted at in the text of the data protection law, and advocated by standards-development organizations and experts outlined in this Chapter. The extent to which standards may supplement the Union data protection law reveals an exploratory and a normative aspect. The exploratory aspect aims at identifying the role of standards in regulating the right to protection of personal data through the lens of the data protection law itself and

23 July 2014 on electronic identification and trust services for electronic transactions in the internal market and repealing Directive 1999/93/EC.

[58] See, among many, Van Gestel R and Micklitz H-W, 'European Integration through Standardization: How Judicial Review Is Breaking down the Club House of Private Standardization Bodies' (2013) 50 Common Market Law Review, 145.

[59] Among many, Senden, 'The Constitutional Fit' (n 57) 340. See also for example Commission Communication, A Strategic Vision for European Standards: Moving Forward to Enhance and Accelerate the Sustainable Growth of the European Economy by 2020, COM 2011/311 final; Article 29 Data Protection Working Party, Opinion 05/2014 on Anonymisation Techniques WP216 (2014).

the activity of standard-setting organizations. Thus, the aim of the exploratory aspect is to identify any 'added value'; what standards have to offer to *supplement* the data protection law vis-à-vis the power imbalances, ineffective protection and control over personal data. Second, the normative aspect aims at responding to the question on whether standards *should* have a role to play in this field. The normative aspect thus relates to the conditions and constraints under which standards may support the law in protecting the right to personal data protection, informed *inter alia* by the fundamental rights nature of data protection and the embedded safeguards in standard-setting.

The book explores the legal framework for standards in the Union, why there is a need for recognition of standards by the Union public regulator, how standards become part of binding and non-binding Union law, and how standardization functions as a regulatory technique to serve Union law goals. The book also explores principles and safeguards, how data protection standards emerged and evolved, in what data protection related topics standardization organizations direct their activities, and how and to what extent the Union secondary data protection law works as a legal basis for standardization.

1.5.2 Theoretical Lenses: Legal Pluralism and Transnational Private Regulation

The research essentially concerns the regulation[60] of the protection of a fundamental right. Further, it concerns the intersection and interaction of private regulation (standards) and public regulation (Union data protection primary and secondary law). As regards data protection, the fundamental rights nature of the right to protection of personal data is the compass for the analysis of the field of personal data protection. The secondary data protection legal framework is treated as giving expression to primarily the right to protection of personal data.[61] While the data protection secondary law is serving other purposes as well, such as the protection of rights and freedoms in general, the book focuses mainly on the right to protection of personal data. Next, notwithstanding the significant role of national law for the emergence and formulation of the right,[62] this study focuses mainly

[60] For the term 'regulation' the definition by Black is used, 'sustained and focused attempts to change the behavior of others in order to address a collective problem or attain an identified end or ends, usually through a combination of rules or norms and some means for their implementation and enforcement, which can be legal or non-legal.' Black J, 'Constructing and Contesting Legitimacy and Accountability in Polycentric Regulatory Regimes' (2008) 2 Regulation & Governance, 137 (hereafter Black, 'Constructing and contesting legitimacy').

[61] Muir E, 'The Fundamental Rights Implications of EU Legislation: Some Constitutional Challenges' (2014) 51 Common Market Law Review, 226ff.

[62] González Fuster G, *The emergence of personal data protection as a fundamental right of the EU* vol 16 (Springer 2014), 55ff.

on its EU expression. This is due to the very development of the right as an EU fundamental right by its inclusion in the CFREU and the TFEU, and the harmonized protection in the EU secondary legislation with the General Data Protection Regulation and the (proposal) for ePrivacy Regulation.[63] Studies of other jurisdictions (eg US) provide further insights into this matter.

As regards standards, the book is largely associated with the discipline which Schepel identified as 'standards law'.[64] 'Standards law' explores how legal systems deal with standards, how they use them, how they regulate them. This study is specifically concerned with such questions in relation to the EU legal order and EU data protection law.

The supplementary functions of standards to Union data protection law and the boundaries are studied in the light of the actors in data protection (regulatees and beneficiaries), but also the actors (co-)developing standards and the environment and processes which produce those instruments. The basis of this book is thus comprised of three components underlying the analysis:[65]

i. the interaction of standardization and the Union legal order at a *systemic* level
ii. the collaboration of the *actors* ie standardization bodies and the Union public regulator in the field of data protection
iii. the interaction of the *instruments*, standards and Union (data protection) law, and in specific standards in support to Union data protection law

Next to studying the EU law on standardization, the interaction of standardization and the Union legal order is examined through the lens of legal pluralism. Legal pluralism illustrates the dynamic interconnections between normative orders and offers answers on the autonomy of standardization bodies and the freedom to collaborate in the development of technical standards, and the voluntary nature of standards.[66] Legal pluralism explains in other words why standardization has its own standing, which interacts with the law (complies with it, supports, etc.), but its existence is not dependent on the Union public regulator.[67] Adapting von Benda-Beckman's words, legal pluralism is a starting point for describing and analysing

[63] The criterion for the selection of these two legal instruments as secondary data protection legislation is their legal basis on art 16 TFEU (ex 286 TEC). Consolidated versions of the Treaty on European Union and the Treaty on the Functioning of the European Union, Official Journal C326/1,.

[64] Schepel H, *The Constitution of Private Governance: Product Standards in the Regulation of Integrating Markets* (Hart Publishing 2005).

[65] See Calliess G-P, and Peer Z, *Rough Consensus and Running Code: A Theory of Transnational Private Law* (Hart Publishing 2010).

[66] In the same vein, Mifsud Bonnici used legal pluralism as the theoretical basis for her research on Self-regulation on the Internet Bonnici JPM, *Self-Regulation in Cyberspace* (TMC Asser Press 2008), 9ff.

[67] DaviesM, 'Legal Pluralism' in Cane P and Kritzer H (eds), *The Oxford Handbook of Empirical Legal Research* (OUP 2012) (hereafter Davies, 'Legal pluralism'); Von Benda-Beckmann F, 'Who's Afraid of Legal Pluralism?' (2002) 34 The Journal of Legal Pluralism and Unofficial Law, 37.

a complex empirical situation. One aspect of this complex situation is that Union policy and legislation uses standards that are extra-legal, the outcome of a process outside the law-making taking place in the Union. When standards of a private nature are supporting public policy or law, some sort of recognition by the Union legal order needs to exist to legitimize their use. The recognition and integration in the Union public order comes in different forms such as by direct reference in legislation. The book thus approaches standardization as a (semi-) autonomous normative ordering[68] through the lens of such Union recognition rules towards standardization. This angle has been characterized as *juristic*[69] or else *ordered* legal pluralism, which while it allows for some autonomy in private rule-making, it entails that forms of non-state law need to be recognized[70] by state law. This type of pluralism stands between a legal monism approach which would regard standards as fully subject to the Union legal order and a strong pluralistic approach, which would imply the absence of any hierarchy between standards and the Union legislation.[71] Juristic or ordered legal pluralism is most suitable for the questions the book seeks to answer, which concern the *supplementary role* of standardization to Union data protection legislation. Further, from a pragmatic standpoint, standardization organizations active in the broader field of data protection often show a tendency to subject their activity to the hierarchy of the Union (data protection) law. The tendency is, for example, shown by the intentional alignment (or at least the effort towards alignment) of the various international and European standards with the requirements of the Union data protection law.[72]

Regulation theory sheds light on the different degrees of cooperation between standardization organizations and the Union public regulator when standards are adopted for Union public policy and legislation. The regulatory perspective offered by Transnational Private Regulation (TPR)[73] complements the theoretical

[68] See analysis in chapter 4, section 4.1.1 in this book.

[69] See further Griffiths J, 'What Is Legal Pluralism?' (1986) 18 The Journal of Legal Pluralism and Unofficial Law, 1 (hereafter Griffiths, 'What is legal pluralism'). As Davies describes it, 'this form of pluralism is pluralistic in the sense that differences in legal heritage are reflected in "law" and it is juristic because it is a form of pluralism acknowledged by law and lawyers' in Davies 'Legal pluralism' (n 67), 12.

[70] This is an external type of recognition. See Michaels R, 'Law and Recognition – Towards a Relational Concept of Law,' in Roughan N and Halpin A (eds), *Pursuit of Pluralist Jurisprudence* (CUP 2017), 97.

[71] On the distinction between ordered and strong legal pluralism read: Mak V, *Legal Pluralism in European Contract Law* (Oxford University Press 2020), 203ff.

[72] One such example is the ISO/IEC 27701 standard which includes an annex explaining how its controls correspond to the legal requirements of the EU General Data Protection Regulation. See case study 2 in Chapter 8 in this book.

[73] On standards qualifying as TPR, see an overview Verbruggen P and Paiement P, 'Transnational private regulation' Oxford Bibliographies in Political Science (2017); Büthe T and Mattli W, 'Standards for Global Markets: Domestic and International Institutions,' in Enderlein H, Wälti S, Zürn M (eds.) *Handbook on Multi-level Governance* (Edward Elgar Publishing 2010); Scott C, Cafaggi F and Senden L, 'The Conceptual and Constitutional Challenge of Transnational Private Regulation' (2011) 38 Journal of Law and Society, 1 (hereafter Scott and others 'The conceptual and constitutional challenge').

framework of the book.[74] While legal pluralism offers the bigger picture, that is the systemic interaction of standardization and the Union legal order, the TPR, which is an expression of legal pluralism,[75] allows one to zoom in to aspects such as the private law nature of the standardization organizations, the voluntary character of standards, the need for recognition rules and legitimization, and the difficulties with regard to standards being subject to judicial scrutiny.[76] As Caffaggi has explained, private regulation in the Union has been developing with a complementarity to public regulation.[77] In fact, TPR is very often described as self-regulation or co-regulation, depending on the degree of participation of the public regulator in the TPR.[78] The private nature of standardization organizations together with their autonomy are maintained even when those organizations develop standards that serve public policy goals.

The use of legal pluralism and TPR as a theoretical framework as regards standardization, alongside the doctrinal analysis of the Union standardization related legislation, does not only embed this research in the state of the art,[79] and explains underlying rationales that are not explicit in the legislation (for example why standardization bodies according to the Standardization Regulation are allowed to

[74] The meaning of Transnational Private Regulation is 'body of rules, practices and processes, created primarily by private actors, firms, NGOs, independent experts like technical standard-setters and epistemic communities, either exercising autonomous regulatory power or implementing delegated power, conferred by international law or by national legislation'. Cafaggi F, 'New foundations of transnational private regulation' Journal of law and society 38, no 1 (2011): 20–49, 20. The use of TPR is compatible with the juristic legal pluralism in this book, as it ultimately uses the state as a point of reference to deploy arguments around the role of regulators and regulation instruments such as standards. Similarily juristic legal pluralism implies recognition of the ordering and its rules and outcomes by the public regulator and legislation.

[75] Cafaggi F, 'A comparative analysis of transnational private regulation: legitimacy, quality, effectiveness and enforcement' EUI Department of Law Research Paper 2014/145 (2014).

[76] It is very often the case that the boundaries between public and private are not as straightforward: private organizations exercise public power, or engage in partnerships with public authorities (Public Private Partnerships). This is especially the case for standardization with the involvement of public regulator (eg the European Commission) that is often characterized as private-public. See Senden L, Kica, E Klinger K, and Hiemstra MI 'Mapping Self-and Co-regulation Approaches in the EU Context": Explorative Study for the European Commission, DG Connect.' (2015), 35ff. In this book a narrow approach to the concept of State is adopted, namely as 'State' is considered any institution/ body established and operating under public law, and not occasionally subject to public law. The focus thus is mainly on the European Union, acting via its formal institutions thus those regulators with a legal mandate. See Black, 'Constructing and contesting legitimacy'(n 61) p.139. On the public/private law divide: Rosenfeld, Michel. 'Rethinking the boundaries between public law and private law for the twenty first century: An introduction.' International journal of constitutional law 11, no. 1 (2013): 125-128. While the distinction between public and private rule is not binary as explained, the 'private regulation' approach places the emphasis on the private nature of standardization activity, which reflects all those aspects that are important for the research question of this book (voluntary nature of standards, etc.).

[77] Cafaggi F and Janczuk A, 'Private regulation and legal integration: The European example.' (2010) 12 Business and Politics, 1.

[78] Cassese S, D'Alterio E and De Bellis M, 'The Enforcement of Transnational Private Regulation: A Fictitious Oxymoron' in Cafaggi F (ed), *Enforcement of Transnational Regulation* (Edward Elgar Publishing 2012).

[79] Taekema S, 'Theoretical and Normative Frameworks for Legal Research: Putting Theory into Practice' [2018] Law and Method.

reject a standardization request from the European Commission), but also offers normative direction and informs the structure of this book. One example is that TPR is often subject to criticism due to the engagement of private regulators for solving societal problems, which gives rise to legitimacy issues.[80] A related example concerns the tendency of transnational private regulation to adopt a technocratic problem-solving approach,[81] which raises questions of inclusion and interest representation. Those criticisms drew attention to the need to explore questions of legitimacy of standard-setting in this book.[82]

Legal pluralism and TPR imply a working hypothesis that standards induce normative underpinnings in personal data protection. Despite their voluntary nature, standards are usually not free from normative effects. When standards elucidate controls and requirements based on legislation, standard drafters propose optimal ways or best practices to implement the legal requirements. In doing so, they enjoy a form of discretion in relation to the proposed technical specifications and in particular, the technical means to achieve the goal prescribed in the law.

1.5.3 Analytical Tools and Methods

1.5.3.1 Technology

Technology has a dominant role in this research, but this research is not about technology *per se* or how a specific technology poses challenges to the right to protection of personal data.[83] Instead of seeing technologies in their singularity, the book rather uses the effects of technologies on the right to data protection. Thus, the book takes applications of technology as a starting point. In doing so, there is the assumption that technologies, especially those with a disruptive potential, have some common characteristics in the manner in which they cause the disruption: this could be the speed in which they do it, the effect of challenging legal concepts and the applicability of the law.[84] According to Brownsword, technological

[80] Graz J-C, and Nölke A, 'The limits of transnational private governance' in Guzzini S and Neumann I (eds), *The diffusion of power in global governance: International political economy meets Foucault* (Springer 2012), 118ff.

[81] ibid.

[82] Other points of criticism concern the challenge the pluralism of TPR regimes places on them having similar potential for achieving legitimacy Scott and others, 'The conceptual and constitutional challenge' (n 73).

[83] There is already rich literature on the topic, which is referred to in the book by means of example and to illustrate arguments and counter-arguments. Read among many: Pagallo U, Durante M, and Monteleone S, 'What Is New with the Internet of Things in Privacy and Data Protection? Four Legal Challenges on Sharing and Control in IoT.' in *Data Protection and Privacy:(In) visibilities and Infrastructures* (Springer, Cham, 2017) 59–78; Tene O, and Polonetsky J, 'Big data for all: Privacy and user control in the age of analytics' Nw. J. Tech. & Intell. Prop. 11 (2012): xxvii; Rubinstein IS, 'Big Data: The End of Privacy or a New Beginning?' (2013) 3 International Data Privacy Law, 74.

[84] Disruptive technology in plain terms is defined as 'a new technology that completely changes the way things are done.' https://dictionary-cambridge-org.tilburguniversity.idm.oclc.org/dictionary/english/disruptive-technology [accessed 20 September 2023].

change causes regulatory disconnection between the law and the technologies it regulates.[85] Although data protection law aims at regulating data processing rather than technologies as such, it indirectly regulates technologies to the extent they are involved in the processing of personal data. Technology-related examples are used throughout the book—only insofar as necessary—to highlight impacts on the regulation of the right to protection of personal data and to further identify whether standardization can, in relation to the right to data protection, accommodate technology-specific challenges.

1.5.3.2 Substantive and procedural legitimacy

While it is undisputed that standards are not laws, and thus they are not subject to formalities of public law instruments, they do bear effects and may sometimes be of a *de facto* binding nature.[86] Criticism of using private regulation instruments such as standards for public policy objectives stems from the nature of standardization as a semi-autonomous ordering,[87] which from a regulatory perspective essentially boils down to standardization bodies largely regulating their own activity. Concerns are heightened due to the power asymmetries and the vulnerability of data subjects, and the dominance of corporate interests over consumer or other societal interests in the standardization process.[88] The use of standards in legislation, as a prime example of standards used for public policy objectives, raises questions of legitimacy[89] of standardization organizations (SDOs) in this private regulatory role, and normative questions on whether standards *should* be adopted and used for the regulation of personal data. Legitimacy of standardization organizations as private regulators adopting technical standards has been broadly studied.[90] In this book, the definition provided by Black is adopted, 'whether or not an institution or organization is perceived as having a "right to govern" both by those it

[85] Brownsword R, *Rights, regulation, and the technological revolution* (Oxford University Press 2008).

[86] See Chapter 3, section 3.3 in this book.

[87] Chapter 4, section 4.1.1 in this book.

[88] Medzmariashvili M, *Regulating European Standardisation through Law: The Interplay between Harmonised European Standards and EU Law* (Doctoral dissertation, Lund University, 2019), 199ff.

[89] See discussion on types of legitimacy aspects for SSOs, as identified by Baron and others, in Legitimacy based on consent of affected parties, market forces, democratic legitimacy, procedural legitimacy, and expertise legitimacy ('technocratic models'). Baron J, Contreras JL, Husovec M, and others 'Making the Rules: The Governance of Standard Development Organizations and their Policies on Intellectual Property Rights.' JRC Science for Policy Report, (2019) (hereafter Baron and others 'Making the rules').

[90] Among many: Schepel H, *The Constitution of Private Governance: Product Standards in the Regulation of Integrating Markets* (Hart Publishing 2005); Eliantonio M, and Cauffman C, 'The Legitimacy of Standardization as a Regulatory Technique in the EU–A Cross-disciplinary and Multi-level Analysis: An Introduction' in Eliantonio and Cauffman (eds)*The Legitimacy of Standardization as a Regulatory Technique* (Edward Elgar Publishing, 2020).

seeks to govern and those on behalf of whom it purports to govern.'[91] A common distinction of types of legitimacy when studying standardization is input and output legitimacy. Input (process) legitimacy, relates to the conditions of standardization process eg who sets the agenda for new standards, who participates in the standard making process, how decisions are made, and others. 'Output (result) legitimacy', relates to the quality and accessibility of the result of the standardization process, namely the standard.[92] Schmidt coined the notion of 'throughput legitimacy'. For Schmidt, 'input legitimacy' relates to citizen's participation and governing elites' responsiveness, throughput legitimacy relates to the quality of the governance processes, including their 'efficacy, accountability, transparency, inclusiveness and openness to interest consultation', and output legitimacy to effectiveness and performance.[93] Another close distinction is between 'procedural legitimacy' and 'substantive legitimacy'; where the former focuses on the 'source and nature of the process validating a regime,' and the latter focuses on the 'content and purpose'.[94] Senden and van den Brink have further explained that substantive legitimacy relates to aspects such as consistency and precision of the limits regulators are expected to operate, while procedural legitimacy deals with issues such as rules of decision-making, participation, decisions being justifiable and open to judicial review.[95] Simply put, by Brownsword and Goodwin, substantive legitimacy concerns questions of 'what', procedural legitimacy focuses on the 'who' and the 'how'.[96] Baron et al. have argued that procedure is one potential source of legitimacy, ensuring that the outcome is legitimate.[97] The analysis in this book on standardization in the area of personal data protection follows the substantive/procedural legitimacy demarcation, where substantive legitimacy examines the legal basis and alignment with the law, and procedural legitimacy examines procedural safeguards in both the standardization process and after standards have been adopted.

[91] Black, 'Constructing and contesting legitimacy'(n 60).

[92] Weiler JHH, 'In the Face of Crisis: Input Legitimacy, Output Legitimacy and the Political Messianism of European Integration' (2012) 34 Journal of European Integration, 825; Scharpf FW, *Governing in Europe: Effective and democratic?* (OUP 1999).

[93] Schmidt VA, 'Is There a Deficit of Throughput Legitimacy in the EU?' [2019] Critical Reflections on Constitutional Democracy in the European Union 127. See also Schmidt VA, 'Democracy and Legitimacy in the European Union Revisited: Input, Output and 'Throughput'' (2012) 61 Political Studies 2. Although there are no red lines over the boundaries of the types of legitimacy, those offer useful background and context to legal discussions.

[94] Barnard, Frederick M, 'Democratic legitimacy: plural values and political power'vol 34, McGill-Queen's Press-MQUP, 2001, 27.

[95] Senden L and Van den Brink T, 'Checks and Balances of Soft EU Rule-Making.' Policy Department C: Citizens' Rights and Constitutional Affairs (2012).

[96] Brownsword R and Goodwin M.A 'A Look at Procedural Legitimacy: The Role of Public Participation in Technology Regulation' in Brownsword R and Goodwin M.A. (eds), *Law and the Technologies of the Twenty-First Century* (CUP 2012), 246.

[97] Other sources include consent of affected parties, market forces, expertise and democracy. Baron et al. 'Making the rules' (n 89).

1.5.3.3 Methods

The book uses a mix of methods. Doctrinal method is used in the book to systematically analyse the EU data protection legislation (GDPR, Directive 2002/58/EC, Proposal for ePrivacy Regulation), its principles, and the relevant case law of the CJEU. The book also analyses the EU legislation relevant to standardization, such as the New Approach legislation, the Standardization Regulation and Regulation 768/2008, and case law of the CJEU. The analysis for this book includes tracing of legal precedent and legislative interpretation[98] and looking at law together with the 'problems, the policies, and the processes that constitute the context of their operation.'[99] This choice is firstly due to the aim of the study to examine the interaction of a private regulation instrument used in public law context, and in relation to fundamental rights. Second, much of the activity that informs or even drives legislative choices relevant to the study is taking place at policy or other level.[100] Literature review is used for interpretative purposes and understanding and reflecting upon the broader debates surrounding the topic of this book such as the role of private actors in public regulation, legitimacy issues and safeguards in standardization in the field of data protection. Lastly, the book engages in empirical qualitative legal research[101] through document analysis[102] (standards), systematically presenting the emergence and evolution of standards relevant to data protection and analysing a selection of existing standards in data protection. Moreover, studying multiple standards allows to explore different types of standards against different areas of data protection law, where support with other instruments seems necessary or useful.

The selection of the specific standards rests on three criteria. First is the scope of those standards and their normative or informative references that point at the GDPR or the ePrivacy legislation. Second is the endorsement or acknowledgment of those standards by data protection authorities.[103] Third is the diversity in types of standards, that is an international standard, a European harmonized standard,

[98] Gawas VM., 'Doctrinal Legal research method as a guiding principle in reforming the law and legal system towards the research development',
International Journal of Law, vol 3, issue 5, September 2017, 128–130.

[99] Baxi U, McCrudden C, and Paliwala A, eds *Law's Ethical, Global and Theoretical Contexts: Essays in Honour of William Twining* (CUP, 2015).

[100] For instance the standardization activity at ISO is a private activity, not bound in principle by national or regional legislation.

[101] By empirical legal research in this context, 'involves the systematic collection of information ("data") and its analysis according to some generally accepted method'" Cane P and Kritzer H, *The Oxford Handbook of Empirical Legal Research* (OUP 2012), 5.

[102] Webley L, 'Qualitative approaches to empirical legal research' in Cane P and Kritzer HM (eds), *The Oxford handbook of empirical legal research* (OUP 2010), 926.

[103] See for example the CNIL reference to the ISO/IEC 27701 standard, see IAPP 'CNIL Stresses Importance of ISO 27701 for Global Data Protection Compliance' https://www.huntonprivacyblog.com/2020/04/06/cnil-stresses-importance-of-iso-27701-for-global-data-protection-compliance/ [accessed 20 September 2023]; the European Data Protection Supervisor preliminary opinion on data protection by design and by default p16 which refers to the standard being developed on the basis of the Commission standardization request (that is the EN 17529). See EDPS 'Opinion 5/2018. Preliminary Opinion on privacy by design' (31 May 2018) and the WP29 opinion proposing to make the Do Not

and a market-based 'standard'.[104] The analysis of existing standards demonstrates how rules apply on the ground and offers a 'reality check' to the findings of the theoretical and legal analysis.[105]

1.6 Perspective

The book focuses on a *supplementary* role of standardization to data protection law, which entails that the book does not explore whether standards should replace the law or similar questions, which, to my view, are issues already solved in relevant scholarship.[106] Hard law should be the main regulatory instrument for the protection and expression of a fundamental right. Especially in the case of personal data protection, the requirement for an independent supervisory authority,[107] and art 16(2) TFEU[108] do not cast any doubt on this matter.

Track specification mandatory. See WP29 'Opinion 01/2017 on the Proposed Regulation for the ePrivacy Regulation (2002/58/EC)' WP247 (2017) 17.

[104] The reason for using multiple criteria, beyond the fact that the standard itself refers to the EU data protection law, is dual: first, non-harmonized European standards and international standards as a matter of practice avoid being tied to and referring to legislation (see Guidance on drafting normative reference of European standards https://boss.cen.eu/reference%20material/Guidancedoc/Pages/NormRef.aspx [accessed 20 September 2023]). So even if those standards are developed taking into account some laws, they will rarely refer to them in the final text. This means that a number of relevant to study standards have been excluded. Second, despite the lack of reference to legislation (which might even be for reasons of timing: the law was adopted after the standard was published), it is often the case that standards are used in retrospect in practice for guidance, compliance, or other function, in relation to some law. For example the Dutch standard NEN 7510 was not developed with the GDPR in mind, neither does it refer to it, but it was used by the Dutch data protection authority as a benchmark to assess appropriate measures in line with art 32 GDPR.

[105] The author's understanding of the analysed standards and relevant debates was enriched by following the public mailing list of W3C Tracking Working Group since 2016 and since April 2020 the meetings of the Technical Committee on Cybersecurity and Data Protection (Cybersecurity & Gegevensbescherming) of the Dutch Standardization body NEN, which is participating (mirror committee) in the Technical Committees of ISO/IEC and CEN CENELEC that developed the studied standards.

[106] See Simitis '[...] self-regulation does not suffice, as with automated data retrieval. In its opinion on informational self-determination, the German Federal Constitutional Court has purposely underscored the indispensability of mandatory legislative measures. Self-regulation is not a genuine alternative to the legislature's intervention, even if, as with Facebook, users are fully informed and expressly asked to update their privacy settings. At best, self-regulation can help to *supplement legislation*' [emphasis added]. Simitis S 'Privacy—An Endless Debate?' (2010) California law review, 1989, 2004; Papakonstantinou in discussing the limitations of self-regulation in protecting privacy '[...] only self-regulation in the sense of *the cooperative state* could operate beneficially, for the short-term, within the Information Society context[...]' [emphasis added]. Papakonstantinou V, *Self-Regulation and the Protection of Privacy* (Nomos Baden-Baden, 2001) 157. Learning from the US example, see Hoofnagle CJ, 'Privacy Self-Regulation: A Decade of Disappointment,' in Winn J (ed), *Consumer Protection in the Age of the 'Information Economy* (Routledge 2006); Gellman R and Dixon P, 'Failures of Privacy Self-Regulation in the United States,' in Wright D and De Hert P, (eds.), *Enforcing Privacy: Regulatory, Legal and Technological Approaches* (Springer 2016).

[107] CFREU art 8(3).

[108] TFEU art 16(2) provides: 'The European Parliament and the Council, acting in accordance with the ordinary legislative procedure, shall lay down the rules relating to the protection of individuals with

The book does not explore as such a conflicting relationship between standardization and data protection law, where standards would intentionally prescribe norms or guidance to circumvent the requirements of data protection law.[109] However, this issue is not completely untackled. The matter on whether standards prescribe norms compatible to the EU data protection law norms and follow data protection safeguards and align with legal requirements is a matter of enquiry addressed in this book. Conflicts between standards are not examined either, but broader side-issues such as legal uncertainty or confusion from the multitude of data protection standards, are touched upon where relevant.

As regards the analysis of existing standards should be acknowledged, in that the analysis does not claim to offer empirical generalization. The analysis of standards is *context-dependent*, and provides empirical insights in the framework they are presented.

1.7 Scientific Contribution of the Book

This book aspires to contribute to data protection as a field of Union law, by exploring standards as a private regulation instrument to supplement data protection law and in extension protect the fundamental right of Art. 8 CFREU. The research unveils strengths and limitations of EU data protection as hard law, and shows how a non-binding private regulation instrument may facilitate the achievement of legislative goals and under which conditions and limitations. The research extends the scholarship on self-regulation instruments in EU data protection law and offers a detailed in-depth analysis of the promises and pitfalls of standardization as private regulation in the field.

Further, the research combines legal analysis with legal empirical research insights by analysing existing (technical) standards, internal regulations and statutes of international and European standardization organizations. This analysis offers a reality check and further delineates the findings of the legal analysis.

The book secondarily also aims at contributing to the field of standardization or 'standards law' by looking at data protection as a field of application of standardization in support of Union law. This aspect allows for future further comparative

regard to the processing of personal data by Union institutions, bodies, offices and agencies, and by the Member States when carrying out activities which fall within the scope of Union law, and the rules relating to the free movement of such data. Compliance with these rules shall be subject to the control of independent authorities.'

[109] See for example the antagonistic relationship between the deliberations of participants in Transnational Private Regulation human rights standardization for transnational corporations. Ryngaert C 'Transnational private regulation and human rights: The limitations of stateless law and the re-entry of the state 'in Letnar Cernic J and Van Ho T (eds), *Direct human rights obligations of multinational corporations* (Wolf Legal Publishers, Nijmegen 2015).

analysis of data protection with other fields such as cybersecurity, AI, health, environment and safety.

1.8 Structure of the Book

The book comprises of nine chapters. Following the Introduction chapter, Chapter 2 studies the emergence and evolution of existing standards in data protection, starting from the first concrete initiatives in mid 1990's, to the coordinated efforts in 2000s, until the structured and focused standard-setting in the field that takes place after the adoption of the GDPR. This Chapter explains how standardization bodies have grown to view data protection as a standardization field. Chapter 3 revolves around the concept of a technical standard. The Chapter analyses key legal instruments to determine the characteristics of the concept of standards in EU law, as well as the US approach. It further examines the evolution of standardization in support of Union policy and legislation. The Chapter also clarifies the relationship of standards with other private regulation instruments such as certifications and codes of conduct. The fourth Chapter offers the theoretical framework of the book. Standardization is viewed through the lens of legal pluralism as a private normative ordering. Having analysed why standardization is a semi-autonomous ordering and why standards are extra-legal, the Chapter introduces the mechanisms of integration of standards in the EU public order. The Chapter also presents how standards are developed at international and European standardization organizations, but also informal fora and consortia. The fifth Chapter delves into the legal basis of standardization in the field of data protection. The Chapter provides the analytical framework on functions of standards in relation to public regulation, and more specifically in the context of the EU data protection law. The Chapter further analyses the GDPR and ePrivacy legislation as bases for standardization. Chapter 6 turns to the US and explores the California Consumer Privacy Act and the Children's Online Privacy Protection Rule, two significant initiatives in the US legal order that have instigated the creation and use of standards to further support the implementation of those laws. Chapter 7 addresses procedural legitimacy, namely to which extent standardization is equipped to avoid legitimacy concerns in relation to private regulation instruments, such as lack of transparency. Chapter 8 presents three case studies by testing in terms of substantive and procedural legitimacy two technical standards and one technical specification, data protection by design, international data transfers, and online tracking. Chapter 9 concludes the book by reflecting on the findings and providing insights for further research.

2
The Global Emergence and Evolution of Data Protection Standards

2.1 The Early Data Protection Standardization Initiatives: From Canada to the EU

The general shift in the scope and fields of standardization in the post-WW II era set the foundations for the appearance of the first proposals for adoption of data protection standards. At the same time, the rising significance of protecting and regulating the use of personal data as demonstrated through the adoption of international instruments and regional laws, technological innovation and the subsequent increased collection, use, and flows of data, and the employment of standards as a public policy tool in domains such as product safety, also had an effect on the appearance of the first data protection standards. This section tracks the rationale, specific circumstances and scope of the first data protection standards.

2.1.1 The Canadian Model Code Standard of 1995

The first coordinated standardization effort in the field of data protection was the Model Code for the Protection of Personal Information (CSA Code) adopted as Canadian Standard 1996.[1]

The preparatory works for the CSA Code started in 1993. The Canadian Standards Association (CSA), a non-for-profit private sector organization, hosted the discussions of the Technical Committee on Privacy for the drafting of a code for the management of personal information by public and private sector organizations in Canada. The CSA Code was finalized in September 1995 and was formally adopted as the Canadian standard in March 1996.[2]

In its introduction, the CSA Code stresses the two reasons that necessitated its development. First, the creation, processing, and exchange of information in the

[1] Canadian Standards Association, Model Code for the Protection of Personal Information, approved by Standards Council of Canada, CAN/CSA-830-96, March 1996, ISSN 0317-5669 (hereafter 'CSA Code').

[2] Bennett CJ, 'Un historique de la normalisation dans le domaine de protection de la vie privée: document d' information', Background paper prepared for the Canadian Standards Council, 2007 (hereafter Bennett 'Un historique de la normalisation'). http://www.colinbennett.ca/Recent%20publications/Background%20Paper%201%20FR.pdf [accessed 20 August 2024].

Standardizing Personal Data Protection. Irene Kamara, Oxford University Press. © Irene Kamara 2025.
DOI: 10.1093/9780191997037.003.0002

global economy and second, concerns raised by the use of the technologies underlying the 'information economy' with regard to the 'rights of individuals to control the use and exchange of personal information'.[3] Thus what the Code calls as the need for 'protection of privacy rights'[4] –due to the increased data flows and the weakening of individuals' control over their personal information- lies at the heart of the first data protection standard. Further, the lack of federal privacy legislation for the private sector inevitably played a role in creating the grounds for the adoption of a data protection standard: a standard was a means for the industry to participate in rule-setting in a direct-manner and with consensus-based procedures, instead of anticipating top-down imposed privacy legislation.[5] For the regulator, participation in the development of the Code offered the possibility to influence the content of the rules to which the industry was willing to be voluntary subjected. Contentwise, the text of the CSA Code provides[6] it is based on the OECD Guidelines on the Protection of Privacy and Transborder Flows of Personal Data of 1980, to which Canada adhered in 1984.[7] In addition, the Code is said to have been influenced by the EU Data Protection Directive, especially the need for an adequate level of protection for transfers to non-EU Member States.[8] The standard adopted a flexible implementation approach. Organizations could tailor the Code according to their needs, by a) defining how they subscribe to its principles, b) developing an organization-specific code, and c) modifying the commentary, following each principle, to provide specific examples relevant to the organization. Organizations however could not cherry-pick principles and requirements.[9]

[3] CSA Code, 8.

[4] The CSA Code defines as personal information 'information about an identifiable individual that is recorded in any form'. CSA Model Code, 1.

[5] Canada introduced the first Federal Law, the Privacy Act (Privacy Act, R.S.C., 1985, c. P-21) and Access to Information Act (Access to Information Act, R.S.C., 1985, c. A-1) in 1985. Before that, in 1977, the first federal public sector privacy protection was established in the Canadian Human Rights Act. Bernal-Castillero M, 'Canada's Federal Privacy Laws', Library of Parliament Research Publications, https://lop.parl.ca/Content/LOP/ResearchPublications/2007-44-e.htm [accessed 20 September 2023]. However, with the exception of Quebec, Bennett has explained that protection of privacy in the private sector was not subject to a privacy law. Bennett CJ, 'Arguments for the Standardization of Privacy Protection Policy: Canadian Initiatives and American and International Responses' (1997) 14 Government Information Quarterly, 351 (hereafter Bennett, 'Arguments for the standardization of privacy protection policy').

[6] CSA Model Code, 8.

[7] OECD. 'OECD Guidelines on the Protection of Privacy and Transborder Flows of Personal Data.' (1980). Read further: Howard PP, 'Privacy restrictions on transnational data flows: A comparison of the Council of Europe draft convention and OECD guidelines.' Jurimetrics 21, no 4 (1981): 405–420; Kirby M, 'The History, Achievement and Future of the 1980 OECD Guidelines on Privacy' (2010) 1 International Data Privacy Law, 6. It should be noted however, that the CSA Code does not adopt the basic terminology (personal data, controller, processor) of neither the OECD Guidelines nor the EU Data Protection Directive and does not replicate the text of those instruments.

[8] Bennett and Raab explain that the CSA Code was based on the data protection legislation of Ontario and Quebec, alongside with the emerging European Union Data Protection Directive (especially in relation to arts 25 and 27 of Codes of Conduct) and the OECD Guidelines. Bennett CJ, and Raab C, 'The Adequacy of Privacy: The European Union Data Protection Directive and the North American Response' (1997) 13 The Information Society, 245.

[9] Bennett, 'Arguments for the standardization of privacy protection policy' (n 5).

The CSA Quality Management Institute (QMI) developed an assurance programme for the CSA Code aimed at providing assurance that organizations follow the standard. As Bennett explains, private sector organizations had several reasons to implement the CSA Code.[10] Some of them were using privacy protection as competitive advantage; other reasons were the avoidance of adverse publicity, but also the possibility to refer to the standard in a contract between private companies or government and for private companies to verify the level of protection of the counterparty. Furthermore, the potential enforcement of international contracts in the case of transborder flows originating from the Union could be another potential benefit. Despite arguments to make the CSA Code a legal requirement for organizations of both a public and private nature, the standard was voluntary.[11] Voluntary nature in this context means that organizations were free to choose to decide to adopt and follow the standard. However, once an organization decided to follow the CSA Code, a set of obligations were generated by such a decision. The CSA Code was appraised by the regulator as an innovative effort, despite its lack of enforcement mechanisms.[12] Several years later, in 2000, the Personal Information Protection and Electronic Documents Act (PIPEDA), the federal privacy law for private-sector organizations in the course of commercial activity was adopted.[13] PIPEDA realized the vision of the former Privacy Commissioner of Canada for a law incorporating the CSA Code. PIPEDA refers to the principles of the CSA Code in its Appendix and requires their adoption from the organizations subject to the law, which *essentially* made compliance with the CSA Code mandatory.

2.1.2 International Initiatives

Shortly after the CSA Privacy Committee started working on drafting the CSA Code, the international standardization community drew interest in

[10] ibid.

[11] The Privacy Commissioner of Canada, Bruce Philips, in its Annual Report 1994-1995, called for legislated 'standards' for the private sector instead of leaving privacy protection to the 'whim of the marketplace'. The Commissioner proposed to supplement the Privacy Act with provisions tailored to the private sector, such as the CSA Code or to directly make the observance of the CSA standard a legal obligation supported by a 'system of independent oversight'. The Commissioner noted that the CSA standard is a set of privacy rules that enjoys acceptance at federal and provincial level but is in need of 'teeth'. The Commissioner acknowledges that 'the greatest significance of the CSA Code may lie, not in its proposed form as a voluntary code for business, but in its embodiment into national framework legislation—a national standard of privacy protection against which all sectors can be held accountable.' Office of the Privacy Commissioner of Canada, 'Annual Report to Parliament 1994-1995', Canada Communications Group, (1995), https://www.priv.gc.ca/en/opc-actions-and-decisions/ar_index/02_04_03/ [accessed 20 September 2023]

[12] Office of the Privacy Commissioner of Canada, 'Annual Report to Parliament 1994-1995', Canada Communications Group, (1995).

[13] Personal Information Protection and Electronic Documents Act, S.C. 2000, c. 5 http://laws-lois.justice.gc.ca/PDF/P-8.6.pdf [accessed 20 September 2023]

data protection and privacy. Two initiatives stand out in this period. The first is the standardization proposal of the Committee for Consumer Policy of the International Organization for Standardization (COPOLCO ISO), which despite not being fruitful, launched the discussions for data protection related standards with ISO. The second is the World Wide Web Consortium (W3C) Privacy Preference Platform standard (P3P). The P3P standard was an Internet standard, developed by W3C - the organization that sets standards for the World Wide Web - and gained recognition by the privacy community, as discussed in the following sections.

2.1.2.1 Standards proposals at ISO, but no published standards

In 1994, COPOLCO adopted a Resolution to establish a Working Group with the task to assess whether standardization should be launched with respect to the protection of personal data and privacy. The starting point for the task would be the Canadian CSA Code, while it was also reported that the EU Data Protection Directive would influence the discussions and potentially the content of an international standard on privacy and/or data protection.[14] In 1996, the Working Group recommended the development of an ISO standard on privacy and data protection. The ISO General Council accepted the recommendation asserting that the rapid technological advances and the expansion of electronic communications and subsequently of databases demanded international norms for the protection of personal information.[15] The Technical Management Board established an *ad hoc* advisory group, which gave a positive recommendation in 1998 for the initiation of the work. However, several participant organizations were reported to have voiced concerns about how a privacy standard could impose 'significant burden on the global economy, especially if it were to lead to a program for third-party audits'.[16] The *ad hoc* advisory group was dissolved in 1999. Later the same year, standardization organizations discussed the possibility of developing other instruments, instead of a 'fully-fledged standard'.[17]

Several reasons seem to have led to the postponement of further developments for an ISO privacy standard at the time. The existence of data protection or privacy-related national/federal or regional legislation in some countries and the absence of such privacy laws in other countries played a significant role. Standards organizations from jurisdictions such as the US, with sectoral and limited in scope federal privacy laws were reluctant to start negotiating standards-drafting with

[14] CEN/ISSS Initiative on Privacy Standardization in Europe (IPSE), Final Report, (2002) p.10, https://danskprivacynet.files.wordpress.com/2008/06/ipse_finalreport1.pdf [accessed 20 September 2023] (hereafter 'IPSE report').

[15] Bennett 'Un historique de la normalisation' (n 2).

[16] Standards Council of Canada, Annual Report 1997-1998, (1998) http://publications.gc.ca/collections/Collection/P28-5-1998E.pdf [accessed 20 September 2023].

[17] Bennett CJ, 'An International Standard for Privacy Protection,' Proceedings of the tenth conference on Computers, freedom and privacy: challenging the assumptions (ACM 2000).

other standardization bodies coming from stricter legal regimes.[18] A fully-fledged privacy standard would entail for the members of the standardization bodies—the interests of which the standardization bodies represent– more obligations, than those the US-based organizations were *legally required* to implement by their national and regional laws. This was potentially *contra* the interests of those organizations, as pointed out by ANSI.[19] At the same time, standards organizations from the EU, which already had in place national laws implementing the Data Protection Directive or Canada, which was preparing its national privacy act (PIPEDA), were in favour of developing an international privacy (or data processing/protection) standard. Such an international privacy standard would help organizations with the management of privacy and data processing aspects, and would demonstrate to commercial counterparts the adequacy of the measures in processing personal data.[20] Even though, a potential international standard developed by ISO would by definition be of voluntary nature, it would create *de minimis* a reputational advantage for the organizations deciding to adopt it. In parallel, once the standard was published nothing would potentially prevent national legislators from referring to the standard, either informally in policy opinions or in legislation, as happened with PIPEDA and the CSA Code.[21]

2.1.2.2 International fora and technical specifications: the P3P standard

In 1997, the W3C started working on a platform that aimed to give control to Internet users over their personal data while browsing the Internet. According to Cranor, one of the originators of the idea for the Privacy Preferences Platform (P3P), P3P was designed to offer transparency regarding privacy policies of

[18] Taking the example of the US discussed in the text, we see that there were federal privacy laws and laws with privacy-related provisions (see Privacy Protection Act of 1980 (Public Law 95-540)). However, they were sectoral laws with very specific– if not limited–scope, unlike the Data Protection Directive 95/46/EC.

[19] See comments in the Standards Council of Canada, Annual Report 1997-1998, (1998) http://publications.gc.ca/collections/Collection/P28-5-1998E.pdf [accessed 20 September 2023]. Similarly, the IPSE Report (2002) states that 'efforts in ISO itself to address this issue have met with opposition from some members, taking their cue from industry pressure'. Section 4.7 IPSE Report (n 14).

[20] Data Protection Directive 95/46/EC. The PIPEDA was already introduced in 1998 as Bill C-54, but the House of Parliament failed to take final action before its recess, so the Act was re-introduced in 1999 as Bill C-6. See King E and Fuson J H, 'An overview of Canadian Privacy Law for Pharmaceutical and Device Manufacturers Operating in Canada' (2005) 57 Food and Drug Law Journal, 205.

[21] It should be noted that sector-specific Technical Committees undertook initiatives and eventually developed privacy-related sectoral standards, such as the ISO 22307/2008, which describe the components of privacy impact assessments for the financial services sector. Other Technical Committees on information technology undertook to publish a standard on a Privacy Framework, but without the draft being approved as a formal international standard. This is the ISO/IEC (PAS) Draft International Standard (DIS) 20886 for a Privacy Framework. The draft standard was based on a Privacy Framework developed by International Security, Trust, and Privacy Alliance (ISTPA), an industry-led initiative http://emoglen.law.columbia.edu/LIS/archive/cyber-440archive/cyber-archive/privacy-legis/ISTPA-FrameworkWhitePaper013101.pdf [accessed 20 September 2023]. See criticism Kosta E and Stuurman K, 'Technical Standards and the Draft General Data Protection Regulation,' in Delimatsis P (ed), *The Law, Economics and Politics of International Standardisation* (CUP 2015), 440ff.

websites and technically enable the communication of users' privacy preferences to the websites.[22] Web browsers would automatically retrieve the P3P policies of the websites and compare them to the privacy preferences of the users. A P3P policy shared with the Internet user included several elements providing information on the practices of the website owner, such as the type of collected data, the way data was collected, data retention policy, and whether the data would be shared with third parties and the possibility for opt-in or opt-out for the user. P3P policies were designed to be read by computers in machine-readable formats. Upon a website visit, the user would receive notifications about whether the privacy policies of the given website were matching their privacy preferences.[23] The work on P3P was concluded in 2002 with a formal W3C Recommendation,[24] which was withdrawn after over a decade.[25] While reasons for its withdrawal are not known, these can vary from the obsolescence of the technology and P3P mechanism, low engagement and use rates from the industry,[26] and new W3C initiatives have been developed since then.[27]

2.1.2.3 Standardization initiatives in the Asia-Pacific region

Several initiatives stand out in the Asia-Pacific region in this period. The Japanese Standards Association has been active in information security and quality management systems. One initiative inspired by the CSA Code was the Japanese management standard published in 2001. The Japanese Industry Privacy standard was developed by the Japanese Standards Association through discussions with the Industrial Standards Committee. The aim of the standard was to prescribe requirements for management of personal information handled by business entities.[28] The association also provides certification services based on the ISO/IEC 27001.

[22] Lorrie Faith Cranor 'P3P', (2013) Presentation https://cups.cs.cmu.edu/courses/pplt-fa13/slides/131010p3p.pdf [accessed 20 September 2023]. See the last version available was the W3C, The Platform for Privacy Preferences 1.1 (P3 P1.1) Specification, W3C Working Group Note 13 November 2006 (Retired 30 August 2018).

[23] World Wide Web, 'An introduction to P3P' (2000), https://www.w3.org/P3P/introduction.html [accessed 20 September 2023].

[24] The standards developed by W3C are called Recommendations, and usually are specifications about the world wide web. Read more about the procedure of adoption of a W3C Recommendation:https://www.w3.org/Consortium/Process/Process-19991111/process.html#Recs [accessed 20 September 2023].

[25] The Recommendation was withdrawn as obsolete on 30 August 2018 and has been inactive since then. The Internet Explorer browser that was still supporting P3P 1.0 until its withdrawal, issued an announcement advising website owners to avoid deploying P3P Policies. See https://msdn.microsoft.com/en-us/ie/mt146424(v = vs.94) [accessed 20 September 2023].

[26] The low adoption rate by the industry was confirmed by the International Working Group on Data Protection in Telecommunications (Berlin group) in its working paper on Web-tracking and privacy (2013). International Working Group on Data Protection in Telecommunications, 'Working Paper on Web Tracking and Privacy: Respect for context, transparency and control remains essential' (2013).

[27] See W3C Do Not Track Recommendations, 214ff.

[28] Yasunori F and others, 'Personal Data Sensitivity in Japan' (2017) 1 The ORBIT Journal, 3ff. See Japanese Privacy Mark JIS Q 15001:1999 'Personal information protection management systems - requirements' (updated in 2006 and 2017).

In the area of privacy and data security certification, the Japanese Privacy Mark System was established by JIPDEC and is based on the Japanese technical standard providing requirements for Personal information protection management systems.[29] Australia and New Zealand joined forces to adopt several ISO/IEC standards on information security and implementation guidance, such as the Code of Practice for Information Security Management Systems.[30] China followed a state-centric approach, developing a national standards strategy, while keeping an eye out for international developments.[31] China's activities were more oriented towards information technology, than privacy. In 2005, the APEC published the Privacy Framework, an effort to provide a 'tool in encouraging the development of appropriate information privacy protections and ensuring the free flow of information in the Asia Pacific region'.[32] A few years later, the APEC developed the Cross-Border Privacy Rules (CBPR) System that enables data transfers among the signatories. Both initiatives established some baseline principles and rules for the APEC members, however they were criticized for their lack of comprehensiveness and effectiveness.[33]

2.1.3 European Standards Organizations: First Explorative Steps

Since the international standardization efforts were not successful at ISO, the European Standards Organizations (ESOs) started exploring the possibility of developing European standards in the field of data protection.

Two years after the publication of the Data Protection Directive, CEN created a committee to work on information and ICT. The CEN/ISSS (Information Society Standardization System) included Technical Committees and open workshops, which were a less formal environment, in the sense that participation to the workshops did not require CEN membership.[34] The outcome of the CEN/ISSS workshops would be the development of informal European standards deliverables, the CEN Workshop Agreements.[35] Among the main subject areas of CEN/ISSS

[29] JIS Q 15001 Personal Information Protection Management System—Requirements.

[30] AS/NZS ISO/IEC 17799:2001.

[31] Suttmeier RP, Yao X, and Zixiang Tan A, 'Standards of power? Technology, institutions, and politics in the development of China's national standards strategy.' (2009) Geopolitics, History, and International Relations, 46.

[32] APEC Privacy Framework (2005), 3.

[33] Greenleaf G, and Waters N, 'APEC's CBPRs in Operation for Two Years: Low Take-Up, and Credibility Issues' Privacy Laws & Business International Report, 129.

[34] See information on CEN/ISSS http://ec.europa.eu/idabc/en/document/6990.html [accessed 20 September 2023].

[35] CEN Workshop Agreements (CWA) are informal standards developed and approved in CEN Workshops, the direct participation in which is open to interested parties. https://www.cen.eu/work/products/CWA/Pages/default.aspx [accessed 20 September 2023].

were technology support and public interest, which included Data Protection and Privacy.[36]

The efforts were supported by the Union regulator. The Commission engaged in a dialogue with stakeholders in 1999 in order to identify the need and usefulness of data protection technical standards following the New Approach paradigm.[37] Under the New Approach the European Commission had the power to issue mandates towards the ESOs to develop harmonized standards specifying essential requirements prescribed in the New Approach Directives. Since the outcome of this dialogue did not provide clear answers, the Commission issued a mandate for the ESOs to identify their role in data protection standardization.

2.1.3.1 The 1999 European Commission Mandate/289

With the Mandate 289 the Commission requested the ESOs to explore their role in support of the Data Protection Directive 95/46/EC.[38] The mandated work consisted in the development of an open platform on data protection and privacy as a basis for international cooperation, the identification of the role of the standards community in support of the requirements set by the Directive, and the assessment of relevant work performed by international and European standard-setting organizations. The Commission, aware of the difficulty for agreement on a common approach with regard to the development of a data protection standard in ISO, opted for a careful approach in requesting the ESOs to 'explore the role of standards' instead of requesting the development of standards. Despite not directly requesting standards, the mandate hints at the potential areas in which standards could develop in support of the Data Protection Directive.

The mandate refers to three main aspects of the Directive where standards bodies could support the legal framework. First, the codes of conduct in line with art 27 of the Data Protection Directive (DPD). The Commission identified a role for ESOs to develop guidance for complementing and specifying the provisions of the Directive for specific sectors. Such codes of conduct would be assessed by the WP29 for their requirements and added value. Second, the mandate identified the principle of data minimization (art 6 DPD), as essential for the development of Privacy Enhancing Technologies (PET) and similar technologies. The potential

[36] See presentation of CEN/ISSS in W3C in the framework of COPRAS (Cooperation Platform for Research & Standards) in 2004. https://www.w3.org/2004/copras/meetings/ist2004/041116_CEN_Introduction.pdf [accessed 20 September 2023].

[37] Winn JK, 'Technical Standards as Data Protection Regulation,' Reinventing Data Protection? Gutwirth S and others, Reinventing Data Protection? (Springer 2009).

[38] European Commission, Mandate addressed to CEN, CENELEC and ETSI Mandate addressed to CEN, CENELEC and ETSI in support of the European Directive on the protection of individuals with regard to the processing of personal data and the free movement of such data, Mandate/289, (1999) (hereafter Mandate/289). http://ec.europa.eu/growth/tools-databases/mandates/index.cfm?fuseaction = search.detail&id = 167 [accessed 20 September 2023].

role of the ESO would be to test and validate technology-specific solutions against the legal requirements of the Data Protection Directive. Third, the mandate points to cross-border transfers to non-EU countries. Due to the diversity of legal protections of personal data around the world, the Data Protection Directive required that the data could be transferred to another country only if that other country guaranteed an adequate level of protection.[39] The mandate states the role of *international* standards is in minimizing the differences among data protection regimes and in this manner facilitating the implementation of the Directive.[40] The Mandate/289 also refers to the Canadian and Japanese examples that are inspired by what the Commission called as 'a good basis for adequacy protection', namely the OECD Guidelines.[41]

2.1.3.2 The Initiative for Privacy Standardization in Europe

The Mandate/289 was accepted by the ESOs.[42] CEN established the Initiative for Privacy Standardization in Europe (IPSE) under the CEN/ISSS, a platform with representatives from industry, civil society, the regulator—including the European Commission and the Dutch Data Protection Authority–with a common interest in data protection standardization. IPSE held a number of open meetings, and delivered a final report, responding to the questions raised by the European Commission in the standardization mandate. During the meetings, there were two main factions; the supporters of moving ahead with a formal European *privacy* standard and the opposition in favour of awaiting developments within ISO.[43]

The final IPSE report considered the discussions held during the meetings and largely a study conducted by Dumortier and Goemans for CEN/ISSS, but showed hesitation in incorporating the proposed recommendations.[44] Dumortier and Goemans had proposed to start with a general data protection standard which would set out practical operational steps for organizations to comply with the Data Protection Directive. The study also recommended the launch of a series of sector-specific initiatives in the healthcare sector, human resources management, or electronic commerce.

The IPSE report demonstrated the diversity in the visions and aims of the different stakeholder groups. The IPSE report proposed several action areas, some of them demanding immediate action, and some long term-planning. What is

[39] Directive 95/46/EC Art 25

[40] Mandate /289, 2.

[41] OECD Guidelines on the Protection of Privacy and Transborder Flows of Personal Data (23 September 1980).

[42] Resolution BT 50/2000 (9TC/MG: item 2.2.1), applicable as of 19 September 2000.

[43] See Annex E of IPSE Report, Report of the Second Open Meeting: 'Could Standardization Aid Privacy? Paris, 27 September 2001. This however was somehow a circular argument, since in the ISO the discussions were not successful due to strong opposition from some standardization organizations and the *ad hoc* advisory committee was already dissolved in 1999.

[44] Dumortier J, Goemans C, 'Data Privacy and Standardization. Discussion paper prepared for the CEN/ISSS Open Seminar on Data Protection', (2000) (hereafter 'IPSE Report').

striking in the report is the disagreement of industry on the one hand and consumer associations, together with academics, on the other hand, on the development of data protection management standards. The report recommended the *avoidance* of initiation of management standards in data protection, 'especially in the sense of those involving a formal certification'.[45] The rationale for this negative recommendation was the lack of immediate industry demand for such a standard, despite the requests of consumer and other associations such as the (former) European Information and Communications Technology Industry Association.[46] The IPSE group characterized a European management standard in data protection field 'premature'. Points of criticism towards developing such a standard were mostly of an economical and administrative nature: the high audit costs that would bring,according to the Report, an unfair burden on businesses, the difficulty of eaching an agreement for such a standard, the weaknesses of quality management standards in other fields and the inflexibility of the monitoring of compliance systems.[47] In addition, companies saw the standard as a burden on top of their obligation to comply with the legal framework on data protection. Contra-arguments (thus, in favour of a management standard) were from a consumer perspective, the possibility of independent audits, the support of data transfers through the creation of a common understanding of expectations, best practices, and required diligence.

The IPSE, considering the possibility offered by art 27 Data Protection Directive on voluntary codes of conduct,[48] decided to recommend a 'softer' standard on best practices instead of an auditable formal management standard. A standard proposing 'best practices' would be applicable across sectors and would aim to assist companies to benefit from a pool of best practices. Further, a best practice type of standard was envisioned to also contribute to the harmonization of national law implementing the Directive, similar to art 27 Codes of Conduct. Other recommendations revolved around the topics of developing standard contractual clauses and terms by extending the work of the Commission, creating a data protection auditing practice inventory, and conducting a survey of web-seals.

2.1.3.3 First informal data protection European 'standards'

Following the publication of the IPSE Report, CEN/ISSS established the CEN/ISSS Workshop Data Protection and Privacy ('WS/DPP') in 2003 to carry out the

[45] IPSE Report (Recommendation 2).

[46] Today the EICTA is renamed to DIGITALEUROPE. See http://www.digitaleurope.org/Welcome [accessed 20 September 2023]

[47] Quality management standards such as the ISO 9001, which are today broadly adopted in the private and public sector, were not yet as popular.

[48] Data Protection Directive art 27(1) read 'The Member States and the Commission shall encourage the drawing up of codes of conduct intended to contribute to the proper implementation of the national provisions adopted by the Member States pursuant to this Directive, taking account of the specific features of the various sectors.'

recommendations set out by IPSE. As with the IPSE Report, the aim of the WS/DPP was to help organizations comply with the Data Protection Directive. The group identified the following working areas:

1. best practices and guidance, which would include best practices for data controllers and a generic set of contractual clauses
2. the assessment of data protection in practice, in particular in relation to auditing practices in the area of data protection
3. Web seals and technology impact analysis
4. measures to improve awareness.[49]

CEN wanted to keep the standardization activity as open to the relevant stakeholders as allowed by the CEN statutes. The selection of the type of standardization deliverables, one of CEN Workshop Agreements ('CWA'), as opposed to formal European Standards, reflects the wish for openness, since there are no strict CEN membership requirements for participation in the CWA development process. In addition, a CWA is an informal standard, which is not referenced in legislation or procurement.

The first CWA was the inventory of Data Protection Auditing Practices, both from public authorities, such as the Dutch DPA, and the industry[50]. The rationale was that data protection audits assist organizations to identify non-compliance issues and ensure compliance with data protection requirements. Interestingly, the CWA suggests that a *management* audit would be useful to be standardized at EU level, in helping organizations determine whether activities, which involve personal data processing are carried out in line with the organization's policies and whether processing meets the legal requirements of the Data Protection Directive.[51]

Based on the work of the Audit Inventory, the group of experts later developed a baseline audit framework inspired by the Data Protection Directive requirements.[52]

[49] CEN/ISSS Workshop Data Protection and Privacy, 'Business plan for CEN/ISSS Workshop Data Protection and Privacy' v. 2 (adopted in 2003).

[50] The CWA defines an audit as 'a systematic and independent examination with the objective to give assurance.' The difference of an audit from self-assessment, according to the CWA, is the independence of the (external or internal) auditor in the case of an audit. On the contrary, a self-assessment can be performed by a line manager, a process owner, or other that is not bound by the obligation of independence. It should also be noted that the above definition of 'audit' avoids naming the *object* of examination. CEN Workshop Agreement Inventory of Data Protection Auditing Practices, CWA 15262 (2005).

[51] CWA 15262:2005 (n 51), 31. The CWA distinguishes data protection management audits from product audits, which are defined as the process of auditing products 'in order to assess whether the product can be used in ways compliant to data protection regulation' and system development audits, which are defined as 'the process of developing an application used to process personal data is audited in order to assess whether data protection aspects where considered adequately so the end product can or is used in ways compliant to data protection regulation.'

[52] CEN Workshop Agreement, CWA 15499-1 Personal Data Protection Audit Framework (EU Directive EC 95/46) - Part I: Baseline Framework and CWA 15499-2 Part II: Checklists, questionnaires and templates for users of the framework - The protection of Personal Data in the EU (2005).

Beyond the audit-related CWAs, the WS/DPP came up with a CWA analysing Privacy Protection Technologies, namely PET, Privacy Management Systems (PMS), and Identity Management Systems (IMS) and the need for their standardization.[53] Lastly, the Workshop followed IPSE's recommendation on standardizing contractual clauses, and developed a generic standard contract form for art 17 Directive obligations (data security).[54] The contract form was developed for data controllers that are established in the Union and conduct business with data processors or other third parties to which the Directive applied.

These CEN Workshop Agreements are the first *informal* standardization deliverables in the Union in the field of data protection. They all related to the legal framework that existed at that time, the Data Protection Directive, either by aiming to help organizations comply with their legal obligations in general, or by providing insights on issues relating to how technology challenges the protection of personal data and how standardized technology could provide solutions, such as PET. The fact that this was a first endeavour, representing –or at least aspiring to represent diverse interests is reflected in several aspects of these informal standards: the depth of the analysis, the generic recommendations, the effort to create documents with broad acceptance. Nonetheless, one can identify value as well, in terms of placing data protection in the European standardization agenda and raising awareness about data protection aspects to industry. The CEN/ISSS also offered a platform of direct interaction of industry and consumer associations, under the observation of regulators. This interaction and the need for agreement on a common set of recommendations in the IPSE Report brought to the surface deeper problems, but also very specific issues—such as the disagreement on the data protection management standard—that would be valuable for the later generation of data protection standardization activity.

2.2 Intensification of Data Standardization Activity: 2010–2024

Following the hesitant initiatives in the period from 1990 until 2009, the new period from 2010 onwards sees more systematic and coordinated efforts. Overall, this period is marked by developments mainly at Union and international level, and to a lesser extent at national level:[55] the European Commission standardization request to the ESOs to develop a privacy by design standard, the establishment

[53] CEN Workshop Agreement, CWA 15263 Analysis of Privacy Protection Technologies, Privacy-Enhancing Technologies (PET), Privacy Management Systems (PMS) and Identity Management systems (IMS), the Drivers thereof and the need for standardization (2005).

[54] CEN Workshop Agreement, CWA 15292 Standard form contract to assist compliance with obligations imposed by article 17 of the Data Protection Directive 95/46/EC (2005).

[55] A notable exception of a national standard developed in this period is the UK BS 10012 Personal Information Management national standard.

of a Technical Committee at CEN on data protection and a range of international standards touching upon data processing and data protection aspects. The developments should not be seen autonomously in terms of rationale and context. Regional legislative developments, such as the data protection legislation reform in the EU that started in 2009, the 'constitutionalization' of the right to protection of personal data in the Union with the Lisbon Treaty, as well the Snowden revelations on illegal access and misuse of personal data by public and private actors in 2013,[56] matured the circumstances for action, among others, in the standardization field.

2.2.1 International Bodies and Consortia

The international standardization community started gaining strong interest in data protection related standards. This happened mainly following a sectoral approach, which had already slowly been developing since the ISO efforts for privacy management standards failed. The main ISO Technical Committee working on standards with a broader relevance to data protection is the Joint Technical Committee 1 of ISO and IEC (JTC 1) on standardization in the field of information technology, and in particular, its subcommittee working on IT Security Techniques (ISO/IEC JTC 1/SC 27). The subcommittee is developing standards with a focus on information security, touching upon *privacy* issues.

The activity of ISO/IEC JTC 1/SC 27 ranges from standards such as the ISO/IEC 29100:2011 providing a privacy framework, and principles for information technology, standards providing guidance such as the Guidelines for privacy impact assessment, and sector-specific standards on cloud computing, big data, Internet of Things, and smart cities.[57] Data protection and privacy were treated a subset of information technology and IT security techniques. This decision was perhaps a matter of convenience for organizational reasons in terms of standards development, however, raises several questions. First, to what extent the standards developed by this Technical Committee indeed concern only the information security domain. In other words, has ISO/IEC been developing data protection standards under the label of information security because standards have a

[56] See, among many, MacAskill E, Dance G, 'Files Decoded NSA. Edward Snowden's surveillance revelations explained' *The Guardian* 1 (2013).

[57] For example the ISO/IEC 27018: 2014 Information technology - Security techniques - Code of practice for protection of personally identifiable information (PII) in public clouds acting as PII processors was also developed as belonging to the scope of the Security Techniques sub-committee. Other Committees developing standards with privacy or data protection aspects include the TC on cryptography ISO TC 307—SG3—Security and Privacy. Standards developed by the TC include digital signatures (ISO/IEC 14888), entity authentication (ISO/IEC 9798), timestamping (ISO/IEC 18014), the ISO TC/215 working on health informatics. Standards developed by this TC include the ISO/TS 17975: 2015 on health informatics and principles & data requirements for consent in the collection, use, or disclosure of personal health information; ISO/TR 18638: 2017 on health informatics and guidance on health information privacy education in healthcare organizations.

prominent role to play in data protection only in terms of information technology and security techniques in comparison to other topics? Or do the standards of the ISO/IEC JTC 1 SC 27 WG5 have a broader scope, but are labelled as information security for other reasons, such as to overcome the prior reluctance of some ISO and IEC members to establish a committee working mainly on privacy and data protection standards? Certainly, information technology and security are eminent areas of data protection standardization due to the intensity of data collection by information technologies and the immense need for protection of personal data in terms of physical and cyber security.[58] Yet, the possibility of opting for data protection standards under the information technology label, for reasons that relate to the previous opposition can neither be excluded.

Examining for example the ISO/IEC 29100 standard,[59] one may notice a description of actors and roles, privacy safeguarding requirements and privacy principles, which refer to 'information and communication technology' (ICT) systems in a generic manner. The standard additionally provides that the privacy safeguarding requirements are complementary to legal requirements for the protection of Personally Identifiable Information (PII), without limiting its scope to the security requirements of such legislation. Several privacy or data protection standards of the JTC 1 SC27 follow the same example and in this way, they seem to go beyond the scope of the subcommittee's work, focusing only on security techniques.

After several years of handling privacy and PII as a subset of information security or as a side issue for cross-cutting technologies, in 2018, ISO established a new Committee on Privacy. The Committee was established following a proposal from COPOLCO, the ISO association for Consumer Policy. The ISO/PC 317 on consumer protection and privacy by design for consumer goods and services, the secretariat of which is held by the British Standards Institute, has already developed a standard on consumer policy and privacy by design.[60] The aim of the standard is to 'allow goods and services providers to address all the lifecycle issues of privacy by design, so that consumers can have greater confidence in their purchases and take back control over the use of their data'.[61]

Beyond the ISO and IEC work, other international standards organizations and consortia started working in the field, but with more targeted and limited activities. The W3C developed two Recommendations on the topic of online tracking, namely the Tracking Preference Expression Recommendation and the Do Not

[58] See also arts 5(1)(f) and 32 GDPR which show the significance of data security for data protection.
[59] The 2011 version of the ISO/IEC 29100 standard was updated in 2024.
[60] Read further on the webpage of the Committee: https://www.iso.org/committee/6935430.html [accessed 20 September 2023].
[61] See ANSI-Accredited U.S. TAG to ISO/PC 317: Consumer protection: privacy by design for consumer goods and services: https://www.ansi.org/standards_activities/standards_boards_panels/PC317?menuid = 3 [accessed 20 September 2023]

Track specification (DNT).[62] The development of standards that may technically support user preferences on the processing of their personal data, demonstrates another aspect of standards in data protection, beyond the management standards. Next to the DNT specification, W3C has been working on a report aiming at mapping privacy and data protection related terms, including terminology of the GDPR, called Data Privacy Vocabulary. The W3C Report includes a vocabulary, thus the terms, and an ontology (relationships among terms) 'using semantic-web standards to represent concepts associated with privacy and data protection'.[63] Other initiatives of non-recognized SSOs and fora include the Privacy Management Reference Model and Methodology developed by OASIS,[64] which aims at providing a methodology for analysing privacy policies and their privacy requirements,[65] and the work of the Kantara initiative on user management access.[66]

2.2.2 European Standardization: New Technical Committees

In the Union, the reform of the legal framework on data protection certainly stirred the standardization activity. The 2012 proposal for a General Data Protection Regulation and the discussion preceding the proposal made substantial references to technical standards in support of the data protection legislation.[67] Furthermore,

[62] Tracking Preference Expression (DNT) reached the status of W3C Candidate Recommendation in 2015, today: Tracking Preference Expression (DNT) W3C Working Group Note 17 January 2019. Read further on DNT specification: Kamara I and Kosta E, 'Do Not Track initiatives: regaining the lost user control.' (2016) 6 International Data Privacy Law, 276, and case study in Chapter 8 in this book.

[63] See W3C DPV webpage https://www.w3.org/community/dpvcg/ and the Data Privacy Vocabulary (DPV). version 1, Final Community Group Report 05 December 2022 https://w3c.github.io/cg-reports/dpvcg/CG-FINAL-dpv-20221205/ [accessed 20 September 2023]. See also the GDPR extension of the W3C DPV: W3C, Data Privacy Vocabulary (DPV) version 1, Final Community Group Report 05 December 2022, W3C, DPV-GDPR: GDPR Extension for DPV version 1 Final Community Group Report 05 December 2022.

[64] OASIS is the Organization for the Advancement of Structured Information Standards, a global non-for-profit consortium. See OASIS, Privacy Management Reference Model and Methodology (PMRM) Version 1.0 Committee Specification 02, 17 May 2016 http://docs.oasis-open.org/pmrm/PMRM/v1.0/cs02/PMRM-v1.0-cs02.html [accessed 20 September 2023].

[65] Another interesting OASIS initiative was the OASIS Privacy by Design Documentation for Software Engineers (PbD-SE) TC, a Technical Committee which was however closed by the central OASIS administration without producing any technical work. https://www.oasis-open.org/committees/tc_home.php?wg_abbrev = pbd-se#announcements [accessed 20 September 2023].

[66] Kantara initiative User-Managed Access (UMA) 2.0 Grant for OAuth 2.0 Authorization, v.2 (2018), which includes privacy considerations https://docs.kantarainitiative.org/uma/wg/rec-oauth-uma-grant-2.0.html#priv-consid [accessed 20 September 2023]. The specification was highlighted by the Commission ICT Rolling Plan 2020 as relevant to ePrivacy legislation: 'designed to ensure the privacy of websites by giving web users a unified control point for authorising access to online personal data, content, and services, no matter where they are hosted.' European Commission, Rolling Plan for ICT Standardization 2020, 47.

[67] European Commission (2010) Communication from the Commission of 19 May 2010 to the European Parliament, the Council, the European Economic and Social Committee and the Committee of the Regions—A Digital Agenda for Europe [COM(2010) 245 final]; European Commission (2012) Proposal for a Regulation of the European Parliament and of the Council on the protection

the increased references to standards in several policy areas with impact on data protection, such as cloud computing, the Internet of Things, and Artificial Intelligence, in combination with the legislative reform, gave new incentives to standardization bodies to work on data protection.

The refocused attention of the European Standardization Organizations on the broader field of data protection, data management, information security led to the creation of new Technical Committees working on data protection issues. In 2017, the Technical Committee CEN-CLC/TC13 (TC 13) on Cybersecurity and Data Protection was created. The aim of TC13 has been to develop standards for a range of diverse topics such as data protection, information protection and security techniques with a focus on cybersecurity. According to the CEN and CENELEC Work Programme, the new Technical Committee aims at identifying and adopting existing standards in support of GDPR, the NIS and NIS2 Directives,[68] and the proposal for a Regulation on privacy and electronic communications,[69]and recently the Cyber Resilience Act.[70] The same year, the Technical Committee 8 on Privacy Management in Products and Services (TC) was also created at CEN and CENELEC. TC 8 aimed at exploring the possibility to adopt standards in the field with regard to privacy by design (taking over the work of Joint Working Group 8 on the Mandate 530), video surveillance, and biometric face recognition.[71] Shortly after their establishment, the groups were restructured. JTC13 is currently comprised of five Working Groups, one of which is the former TC 8 (now Working Group 5 on Privacy, Data Protection and Identity Management')[72] on data protection.[73] A concern, which follows the

of individuals with regard to the processing of personal data and on the free movement of such data (General Data Protection Regulation) COM (2012) 11 final—2012/0011 (COD).

[68] Directive (EU) 2016/1148 of the European Parliament and of the Council of 6 July 2016 concerning measures for a high common level of security of network and information systems across the Union, OJ L 194, 19.7.2016; Directive (EU) 2022/2555 of the European Parliament and of the Council of 14 December 2022 on measures for a high common level of cybersecurity across the Union, amending Regulation (EU) No 910/2014 and Directive (EU) 2018/1972, and repealing Directive (EU) 2016/1148 (NIS 2 Directive), *OJ L 333, 27.12.2022, p. 80–152.*

[69] Commission, Proposal for a Regulation of the European Parliament and of the Council concerning the respect for private life and the protection of personal data in electronic communications and repealing Directive 2002/58/EC (Regulation on Privacy and Electronic Communications), COM (2017) 10 final.

[70] Regulation (EU) 2024/2847 of the European Parliament and of the Council on horizontal cybersecurity requirements for products with digital elements and amending Regulations (EU) No. 168/2013 and (EU) No 2019/1020 and Directive (EU) 2020/1828 (Cyber Resilience Act), (CRA),

[71] Guarino A, 'New CEN-CENELEC Technical Committees for Infosec and Data Protection Standardization (TC8)', Presentation at CEN-CENELEC event with the topic 'Cybersecurity and Data Protection Standards in support of European Policy', 19th September 2017, https://www.enisa.europa.eu/events/enisa-cscg-2017/presentations/guarino [accessed 20 September 2023]

[72] See https://standards.cen.eu/dyn/www/f?p = 204:7:0::::FSP_ORG_ID:2273903&cs = 1BB28F0625D0C6BA121FBC4A04EC8ED55 [accessed 20 September 2023]

[73] The other Working Groups are: WG1 Advisory Group, WG2 Management systems and controls sets, WG3 Security Evaluation and assessment, WG4 Cybersecurity Services, WG6 Product Security. https://standards.cen.eu/dyn/www/f?p = CENWEB:7:0::::FSP_ORG_ID:2416754&cs = 140A091203C84C7307DB4D06AB289BE3E [accessed 20 September 2023]

absorption of TC8 from JTC13 under the cybersecurity umbrella, is that any differentiation of the underlying subject matters, namely personal data protection and cybersecurity, might be lost in between the lines, because data protection is structurally treated as part of cybersecurity. The JTC13 aims at both adopting relevant international standards as European standards, and additionally exploring the need for and developing European standards (*home-grown* standards).[74]

A couple of years after its establishment, the CEN/CLC/JTC13/WG5 ('WG5') undertook a series of initiatives to attempt to establish European standards in the field of data protection, in support of the GDPR. An example is a feasibility study on a standard in support of data protection certification in line with arts 42 and 43 GDPR.[75] Further, the WG5 adopted international standards as European standards, such as the international standards providing a general privacy framework EN ISO/IEC 29100:2024[76] and the international standard providing guidelines on privacy impact assessment.[77]

ETSI has not established a dedicated Technical Committee or Working Group on data protection, but develops standards and other standardization deliverables relevant to data protection in ETSI Technical Committee Cyber Security, which raises similar concerns about intermingling the distinct issues of personal data protection and cybersecurity (TC Cyber).[78]

2.3 Classification of Data Protection Standards: Horizontal and Vertical Standards

The activity of international and European standardization organizations in the broader fields of privacy, data protection, and information security revealed the development of specific categories of standards.[79] This is partially due to the

[74] The adoption of ISO/IEC standards as European standards is possible because of the bilateral agreements of CEN with ISO, and CENELEC with IEC. See Agreement on technical co-operation between ISO and CEN (Vienna Agreement), Version 3.3 (2001) and Agreement on IEC-CENELEC Agreement on Common planning of new work and parallel voting (Frankfurt Agreement) (2016), which was preceded by the Dresden Agreement of 1996 and the Lugano Agreement of 1991. https://standards.cen.eu/dyn/www/f?p = 204:29:0::::FSP_ORG_ID,FSP_LANG_ID:2307986,25&cs = 1F4A71C19873519CC81C4B2C031CF3CF5#1 [accessed 20 September 2023].

[75] UNINFO - Feasibility study for standardization in support of article 42 of the GDPR European Data Protection Seal candidate scheme, CEN/CLC/JTC 8 N 164.

[76] EN ISO/IEC 29100:2024 Information technology - Security techniques - Privacy framework.

[77] EN ISO/IEC 29134:2020, Information technology - Security techniques - Guidelines for privacy impact assessment.

[78] See website of TC Cyber https://portal.etsi.org/tb.aspx?TBID = 824&subTB = 824 [accessed 20 September 2023].

[79] The presentation of the categories follows the ENISA study (2019) on 'Guidance and gaps analysis for European standardization: Privacy standards in the information security context', carried out by the author, together with standardization experts in international and European standardization bodies (hereafter ENISA 'Study 2019'). Similar categorization of ISO standards was suggested by De Hert and Papakonstantinou who proposed vertical data privacy-specific, and vertical data, privacy-related, horizontal privacy-related. De Hert P and Papakonstantinou V, 'Three scenarios for international

competences of Technical Committees that undertake to propose and draft those standards, but also the market needs which the relevant standards aim to satisfy. This section presents an overview by distinguishing standards in the broader field as horizontal or sector specific. Those standards also fall in the general classifications[80] on the basis of their requirements (performance-based and design-based standards) or their auditability and certifiability (requirements versus best practices standards). Requirements in performance-based standards in brief describe 'what a product must be able to do', while design-based standards describe characteristics of eg a product.[81] Standards may often be a mix of both types, containing both design and performance requirements.[82] In practice, standard setters show a preference to performance requirements in standards, which offers more flexibility to the addressees of the standards by not prescribing in the text of the standard the means to achieve the necessary result (performance).[83] Data protection standards are almost always performance-based standards,[84] while specifications by non-recognized standardization bodies may be either of the two types.[85]

One type of horizontal data protection standard is the *framework* (otherwise called fundamental) standard, which aims at providing a framework on a given topic or else a common language.

A prominent example is the privacy framework standard ISO/IEC 29100, which aims at helping companies define roles of actors in relation to the processing of personal information and provides a common terminology and an overview of privacy principles.[86] Another example is the standard ISO/IEC 20546, which by providing big-data related terminology and key data characteristics aspires to offer an overview of the field of big data, a terminological foundation for big data-related standards and an improved understanding of the area.[87] These horizontal standards are sometimes used as a point of reference in guidance from data protection authorities, especially when the data protection legislation does not specify

governance of data privacy: towards an international data privacy organization, preferably a UN agency.' (2013) 9 ISJLP, 296.

[80] Read further on classification of standards De Vries HJ, *Standardization: A Business Approach to the Role of National Standardization Organizations* (Springer 1999), 159ff.

[81] Schepel H, *The Constitution of Private Governance: Product Standards in the Regulation of Integrating Markets* (Hart Publishing 2005), 3ff.

[82] ISO, ISO Publication on Good Standardization Practices (2019) edn 1, 25.

[83] ibid, 59. As highlighted by ISO however, not all requirements can be expressed as performance based, when describing for instance dimensions of a product for compatibility within larger products.

[84] For a critical analysis of *performance-based regulation* in general, including standardization, read Coglianese C, 'The limits of performance-based regulation.' (2016) 50 U. Mich. JL Reform, 525.

[85] The Do Not Track specification is for example a *design-based* specification.

[86] ISO/IEC 29100:2024 Information technology – Security techniques – Privacy framework.

[87] ISO/IEC 20546:2019 Information technology—Big Data – Overview and Vocabulary.

the definition of a term.[88] Those references in the EDPB or DPA guidelines and opinions carry informational and guidance value.

Next, there are *information technology or information security focused standards with a privacy or data protection relevance*, due to the information security competence of the drafting Technical Committees. These type of standards usually address an issue that is relevant from a personal data protection perspective, without referring or aiming as such to address privacy or personal data protection. These may further be subdivided as security evaluation[89] and security implementation standards.[90]

Third, there are *data protection focused standards*, which place data protection at the core of their controls and guidance. These may be broadly further classified as management standards, guidance and codes of practice, and standards on the technical implementation aspects of data protection and/or privacy standards.[91] A management standard is the ISO/IEC 27701 providing requirements and controls on Privacy Information Management Systems (PIMS).[92] The standard is part of the information security international standards (27xxx series) of ISO and IEC. Specifically the standard is considered an extension of two other existing standards, namely the ISO/IEC 27001, which is a well-known information security management system standard,[93] and the ISO/IEC 27002,[94] which is a code of practice based on the ISO/IEC 27001. While the 27002 is not certifiable, the ISO/IEC 27701 can be used as a basis for conformity assessment in conjunction with ISO/IEC 27001 standard.[95] An example of a code of practice standard is the ISO/IEC 29151 standard, which is a code of practice providing controls for protection of Personally Identifable Information (PII).[96] The standard is addressed to controllers and establishes controls and guidelines for implementing controls 'to meet the requirements identified by a risk and impact assessment related to the protection of PII'.[97]

[88] Article 29 Data Protection Working Party 'Guidelines on Data Protection Impact Assessment (DPIA) and determining whether processing is "likely to result in a high risk' for the purposes of Regulation 2016/679" (2017) WP 248 rev.01.

[89] An example is the ISO/IEC 19608:2018 standard based on the well-know IT security evaluation framework Common Criteria. The standard provides guidance for developing 'security and privacy functional requirements based on ISO/IEC 15408.'

[90] ENISA Study 2019 (n 79), 16ff.

[91] ENISA Study 2019 (n 79) 12f.

[92] The ISO/IEC 27701:2019 defines PIMS as 'information security management system which addresses the protection of privacy as potentially affected by the processing of PII.' See Clause 3.2.

[93] ISO/IEC 27001:2022 Information technology—Security techniques—Information security management systems—Requirements. See statement from OneTrust that more than 60.000 companies have been certified against ISO/IEC 27001 https://www.onetrust.com/company/news/press-releases/onetrust-achieves-worlds-first-iso-27701/ [accessed 20 September 2023].

[94] ISO/IEC 27002:2013 Information technology—Security techniques—Code of practice for information security controls.

[95] Introduction 0.1 ISO/IEC 27701.

[96] ISO/IEC 29151:2017 Information technology—Security techniques—Code of practice for personally identifiable information protection.

[97] ibid.

The standard is a collaboration among ISO, IEC, and ITU.[98] Since ISO/IEC 29151 is a code of practice it is not certifiable.

In the last subgroup of technical implementations, one encounters standards that provide guidance or requirements on specific technical measures to achieve certain protection goals or focus on specific techniques. For example, the ISO/IEC 20889 provides a mapping of de-identification techniques.[99] The ISO/IEC online privacy notices and consent standard, which outlines in detail the conditions for privacy notices and the provision of informed and freely given consent, together with examples of user interfaces and consent receipts records.[100]

As regards sectoral standards, CEN and CENELEC enlist a broad range of Technical Committees, working on specific sectors with some relevance to data protection and cybersecurity.[101] Those include Technical Committees on Personal identification devices,[102] Intelligent Transport Systems,[103] and Biometrics.[104] Another case of sectoral standards, are those that build on horizontal standards. The ITU-T for example developed a Recommendation which specifies how an international standard applies to the telecommunication sector.[105]

2.4 Synthesis

This Chapter has traced the emergence of the first standards relating to data protection in the 1990s and explored the evolution of the field from the first hesitant steps in the efforts of the international standardization bodies to the rapidly growing standardization field today. The first standards were influenced by the principles and rights established in international instruments such as the OECD Guidelines and the CoE Convention 108.[106] At ISO, data protection was first put

[98] The same text is published as ITU Recommendation 'X.1058: Information technology – Security techniques – Code of practice for personally identifiable information protection'.

[99] ISO/IEC 20889:2018 'Privacy enhancing data de-identification terminology and classification of techniques.'

[100] ISO/IEC 29184:2020 Information technology—Online privacy notices and consent.

[101] See https://www.cen.eu/work/Sectors/Digital_society/Pages/Cybersecurity.aspx [accessed 20 September 2023]

[102] CEN/TC 224 Personal identification and related personal devices with secure element, systems, operations and privacy in a multi sectorial environment.

[103] CEN/TC 278 Intelligent transport systems. The TC has published a Technical Report on Privacy Aspects of Intelligent Transport Systems. CEN/TR 16742:2014 'Intelligent transport systems - Privacy aspects in ITS standards and systems in Europe.'

[104] CEN/TC 224/WG 18—Biometrics. The TC has published a Technical Specification on Biometric in Automated Border Control. CEN/TS 16634:2014 'Personal identification - Recommendations for using biometrics in European Automated Border Control.'

[105] The horizontal international standard was co-developed by ISO, IEC, and ITU-T. Recommendation ITU-T X.1058 (2017)/ISO/IEC 29151:2017, Information technology—Security techniques—Code of practice for personally identifiable information protection. The ITU-T sectoral standard is the ITU-T X.1058—Supplement on code of practice for personally identifiable information (PII) protection for telecommunication organizations.

[106] OECD 'OECD Guidelines on the Protection of Privacy and Transborder Flows of Personal Data.' (1980); Council of Europe Convention for the Protection of Individuals with regard to Automatic Processing of Personal Data, ETS No 108, 'Convention 108' (1981).

forward as an area for standardization by COPOLCO, the Committee responsible for consumer matters, but later became an issue of interesting to other committees with a more prominent information security character. The pre-law and post-law functions of standards seems to have played a role in the slow take-up in the international standardization bodies. Some of the national standardization bodies like the European ones already had legislation in place and favoured a post-law function of standardization, while others with no legislation in place showed concern for a pre-law function of standardization that would invoke legislative rules or more stringent rules than the ones in place. Such debates were not shared by the international fora and consortia developing technical specifications. The W3C for example started working on the Privacy Preferences Platform.

The ESOs established a committee on information and communication technologies. Some years later at the initiative of the Commission, the IPSE was established to further explore the standardization areas relevant to data protection. Similar to the debates at the international standardization bodies, there were disagreements among participant standardization bodies about stronger or weaker action. The debate was whether there should be management standards, which are auditable and certifiable, and thus more demanding, or softer forms such as best practices standards and informal standards such as CEN Workshop Agreements, with the latter being the preferred route.

In 2011, ISO and IEC adopted the privacy framework standard, which launched a new era for standardization in the field. Since then, ISO and IEC have been particularly active developing information security standards, which address data protection and privacy aspects. The European Standardization Organizations started to work more intensively in the field after the 2015 Commission standardization request to develop standards on privacy and data protection. Since then, CEN and CENELEC established dedicated committees working on data protection, while ETSI assigns the work mainly to TC Cyber. International fora and consortia such as the W3C, OASIS, IEEE, IETF, have also been active in developing technical specifications in the field.

Existing data protection standards may be categorized as horizontal and vertical standards. Horizontal standards are further divided in three categories: framework standards, standards on information security with a data protection relevance, and data protection focused standards. Those standards in terms of content range from management systems, quality management, to general frameworks providing terminology and common vocabularies, and ICT specifications. The purposes are also very diverse: from compliance with legal requirements, organizational and technical measures, methodologies for risk assessment and impact assessment, internal audits, certification, facilitating user choices and communicating preferences.

3

The Concept of a 'Technical Standard'

3.1 History and Origins of Standardization for EU Policy and Law Goals

3.1.1 The Shift in the Standardization Identity and the New Approach

Technical standards emerged from the need for coordination, interoperability, and efficiency in the production of goods. Beniger, quoting Durkheim, describes the emergence of standards as 'the need for coordination of function that accompanies differentiation and specialization in any system'.[1] The first modern standards were developed early in the 20th century.[2] The automotive industry had no consensus over the properties (size and materials) of essential components, such as wheels and bolts,[3] which resulted in high costs of production. Railway integration and electro-technical compatibility were also among the first standardization fields.[4] Standards initially developed within enterprises to improve performance, but slowly started to be developed at an inter-enterprise level as association standards, and later also in a more formalized manner through industry collaboration in the framework of standard-setting organizations.

Globalization and the need for common 'standardized' ways of doing things gave a boost to the role of organizations that were originally aimed at having a rather technical character;[5] that is, as Murphy and Yates explained, to develop specifications *inter alia* for nuts, bolts, and screws.[6] Alongside with shaping, or at least influencing, production and consumption, standardization bodies also shaped their own new identity. The standardization activity of standardization

[1] Beniger J, *The Control Revolution: Technological and Economic Origins of the Information Society* (Harvard University Press 2009), 11.

[2] Modern standards are the standards developed after the standardization organizations were established in the 20th century. See overview of the history of standardization: Yates J and Murphy CN, *Engineering Rules: Global Standard Setting since 1880* (JHU Press 2019).

[3] Olshan MA, 'Standards-Making Organizations and the Rationalization of American Life' (1993) 34 The Sociological Quarterly, 319.

[4] ibid.

[5] Hallstrom KT, *Organizing International Standardization: ISO and the IASC in Quest of Authority* (Edward Elgar Publishing 2004).

[6] Murphy CN and Yates J, *The International Organization for Standardization (ISO): Global Governance Through Voluntary Consensus* (Routledge 2009), 20.

Standardizing Personal Data Protection. Irene Kamara, Oxford University Press. © Irene Kamara 2025.
DOI: 10.1093/9780191997037.003.0003

bodies after WW II expanded to less 'traditional' domains. Standards became pertinent to technology, instead of having a merely technical character. The American Standards Association (ASA, today: ANSI) for example in its first years of establishment focused its work on mining, engineering, construction, and worker safety.[7] Occupational safety and household technology were the primary focus in 1930s, while during WWII the Association shifted its activity on standards that supported the war efforts. After the end of the WW II, ANSI started expanding its activity in growing technology areas including information technology.[8] In 1987 ANSI assumed the secretariat of the newly established joint technical committee of the international standard-setting organizations ISO and IEC on information technology. Similarly at international level, in the post-WW II period until 1989, the ISO established technical committees with topics ranging from safety to energy use.[9]

Standardization expanded in non-strictly technical fields such as quality management.[10] Technical committees working on the new fields of standardization work coexisted with the committees working on, what was considered until that time, traditional standardization fields. The establishment of new technical committees working in atypical fields has not been the only change. As expected, the content and scope of standards also changed. As Benoliel notes in the context of the later developed cyberspace standards, there has been a shift from technical standards to standards that regulate user behaviour.[11] Although the activity went beyond merely regulating user behaviour, to prescription of infrastructure requirements and other aspects, Benoliel's remark illustrates the shift of standardization activity to a broader range of subjects.

The new standardization activity stood out due to its updated scope in regulating user behaviour, alongside prescribing technical specifications. Some of these new types of standards, impact, or in other ways relate, to values that are deemed to be worthy of higher protection, because they safeguard collective or individual 'goods' or address societal challenges such as public health, environment,

[7] Source is the infographic for the celebration of hundred years since its foundation in 1918. https://share.ansi.org/Shared%20Documents/News%20and%20Publications/Brochures/ANSI-centennial-timeline.pdf [accessed 20 September 2023].

[8] ANSI worked as a coordinating body representing the interest of its members, the several standardization bodies in the US. Garcia DL, 'Standard Setting in the United States: Public and Private Sector Roles' (1992) 43 Journal of the American Society for Information Science, 535.

[9] ISO was founded in the form known today in 1947 and is a result of joined forces of the previously established International Federation of the National Standardising Associations and the United Nations Standards Coordinating Committee (UNSCC). Examples of technical committees are the fire safety ISO/TC 92 in 1958, the personal safety ISO/TC 94 in 1959, the thermal performance and energy use in the built environment ISO/TC 163 in 1975, the financial services ISO/TC 68 in 1972 and the solar energy ISO/TC 180 in 1980.

[10] ISO 9001 Quality management systems—Requirements, https://www.iso.org/standard/62085.html?browse = tc (accessed 20 September 2023).

[11] Benoliel D, 'Technological Standards, Inc.: Rethinking Cyberspace Regulatory Epistemology' (2004) 92 California Law Review, 1069.

and confidentiality of communications.[12] The broadening of the scope of standards and a generally perceived contribution of standards in achieving goals such as interoperability, together with the high acceptance rates from industry, were noticed by public regulators, who slowly started treating standards as a regulatory tool to achieve public policy aims. In the 1980s standards started explicitly being employed as an instrument to support Union legislation under the New Approach framework.[13] The New Approach introduced a framework of using technical standards to achieve results pre-determined in legislation. The underlying aim for developing the new framework was to reduce barriers in trade and facilitate the free movement of goods and the establishment of the Common Market within the Union. The precursor to the New Approach was according to Schepel the 1983 Information Directive.[14] The Directive, among other things, had launched a procedure according to which the European Commission could—after the opinion of a Standing Committee—issue a standardization request to the ESOs to develop European standards.[15] In 1985, the Council Resolution established the New Approach to technical harmonization and standards.[16] The New Approach has been characterized as an innovative regulatory technique, as it managed to accelerate legislative activity.[17] The role of harmonizing technical specifications, the agreement on which was the delay factor for the adoption of the relevant laws, was left to the private, non-for-profit bodies, the ESOs.[18]

The New Approach, which is used broadly by the Commission today,[19] entails that harmonization legislation limits its role in the adoption of only *essential*

[12] CFREU art 37 provides: 'A high level of environmental protection and the improvement of the quality of the environment must be integrated into the policies of the Union and ensured in accordance with the principle of sustainable development.' The ISO Technical Committees on Air Quality (ISO/TC 146), Water Quality (ISO/TC 147), and Environmental management (ISO/TC 207) provide an example of standardization activity in the field of environmental protection; Universal Declaration of Human Rights 1948 (art 12), CRFEU (art 8), ECHR (art 8).

[13] The Old Approach signalled *inter alia* a lack of confidence or trust in standardization systems. Read further on the 'Old Approach'. Read further Commission notice The Blue Guide' on the implementation of EU product rules 2022/C 247/01, C/2022/3637, OJ C247/1,6 (hereafter Commission, 'Blue Guide').

[14] Directive 83/189/EEC laying down a procedure for the provision of information in the field of technical regulations and standards [1983] OJ L109/8; Schepel H, 'The New Approach to the New Approach: The Juridification of Harmonized Standards in EU Law' (2013) 20 Maastricht Journal of European and Comparative Law, 523ff. (hereafter Schepel, 'The New Approach to the New Approach').

[15] Directive 83/189/EEC art 6.

[16] Council Resolution of 7 May 1985 on a New Approach to Technical Harmonization and Standards, OJ C136/1, (hereafter 'New Approach').

[17] Joerges C, Schepel H, and Vos E, 'The law's problems with the involvement of non-governmental actors in Europe's legislative processes: the case of standardisation under the "new approach"' Working Paper, EUI LAW, 1999/09 (1999).

[18] There was also the possibility stated in the Council Resolution that harmonized standards would be developed by other bodies, than CEN/CENELEC, but such harmonized standards would be submitted for approval by CEN/CENELEC. See also for a critical perspective: Schepel, 'The New Approach to the New Approach' (n 14), 521–533.

[19] See for example art 27 Regulation (EU) 2024/2847 of the European Parliament and of the Council of 23 October 2024 on horizontal cybersecurity requirements for products with digital elements and amending Regulations (EU) No 168/2013 and (EU) 2019/1020 and Directive (EU) 2020/1828 (Cyber

requirements[20] to which 'all products placed on the market must conform in order to benefit from freedom of movement within the Community'.[21] The development of specifications according to the needs of the industry, with the aim to facilitate the development of products conforming to the essential requirements provided by the relevant legislation is assigned to the ESOs. The essential requirements need to provide legally binding obligations, but also be written in a manner that enables manufacturers to assess the conformity of their products to those requirements.[22]

Conforming to harmonized European standards is not *de lege lata* mandatory, as with any other technical standard.[23] Conforming to harmonized standards has several benefits over other ways to demonstrate conformity to the requirements of the law. The most significant benefit is that following such harmonized European standards confers a *presumption of conformity* with the *essential* legal requirements.[24] The presumption of conformity is explicitly provided for in the New Approach legislation. The presumption is reversible, since a product enjoying a presumed conformity with the legal requirements, could be proved to be non-compliant. Further, in case the persons that bear the duty to comply with those Directives opt for other ways to demonstrate their compliance, they bear the burden of proof to do so. Standards developed in line with a standardization request from the Commission and based on a New Approach law, if they are found (after their development) by the European Commission[25] to align with the harmonization legislation are published in the Official Journal of the Union and obtain the status of harmonized standards. Those harmonized standards start conferring the presumption of conformity from the publication of their reference in the OJ, unless stated otherwise.[26]

Resilience Act) OJ L/1 (CRA) and art 41 Regulation (EU) 2024/1689 of the European Parliament and of the Council of 13 June 2024 laying down harmonized rules on artificial intelligence and amending Regulations (EC) No 300/2008, (EU) No 167/2013, (EU) No 168/2013, (EU) 2018/858, (EU) 2018/1139, and (EU) 2019/2144 and Directives 2014/90/EU, (EU) 2016/797, and (EU) 2020/1828 (Artificial Intelligence Act) OJ L/1 (AI Act).

[20] Annex I, Chapter R3, Article R8, Decision no 768/2008/EC of the European Parliament and of the Council.

[21] Commission 'Technical harmonization and standards: a New Approach' (1) COM(85)19 (P/85/12).

[22] Recital 11 Decision 768/2008. The essential requirements have been criticized for not being autonomous and self-executing, in that they require specification by the harmonized standards. Schepel H, *The Constitution of Private Governance: Product Standards in the Regulation of Integrating Markets* (Hart Publishing 2005), 255 (hereafter Schepel, *The Constitution of Private Governance*).

[23] New Approach (n 16) Annex II.

[24] For an overview of the New Approach framework, see Pelkmans J, 'The New Approach to Technical Harmonization and Standardization' (1987) 25 JCMS, 249; Schepel, *The Constitution of Private Governance* (n 22).

[25] Standardization Regulation art 10(6).

[26] See for example Notes under the Table of the harmonized standards in line with the Machinery Directive: Commission communication in the framework of the implementation of the Directive 2006/42/EC of the European Parliament and of the Council of 17 May 2006 on machinery, and amending Directive 95/16/EC (recast)(Publication of titles and references of harmonized standards under the directive).

The 1985 New Approach framework was updated with the introduction of the 2008 New Legislative Framework (NLF).[27] The NLF aimed at removing remaining obstacles to the free circulation of products focusing on issues such as the introduction of a horizontal framework for accreditation, common definitions, and general principles for the common mark, the CE marking. These harmonized standards are developed on the basis of requests from the Commission to the ESOs,[28] in line with the Standardization Regulation.[29] Finally, the Standardization Regulation provides the power to the European Parliament and the Member States to dispute the publication of the references in the Official Journal via the process of formal objection and ask the Commission to draft a Commission Decision in order to prevent or remove the presumption of conformity.[30] While the process is the same for the requests for all harmonized standards[31] based on the New Approach and those based on other laws or policies,[32] there is a considerable difference between the two: standards, which are not based on New Approach Directives or another law that explicitly provides a presumption of conformity, do not confer a presumption of conformity with the law to the entities conforming to them.

[27] Regulation (EC) No 765/2008 of the European Parliament and of the Council of 9 July 2008 setting out the requirements for accreditation and market surveillance relating to the marketing of products and repealing Regulation (EEC) No 339/93 OJ L218/30. Decision No 768/2008/EC of the European Parliament and of the Council of 9 July 2008 on a common framework for the marketing of products, and repealing Council Decision 93/465/EEC OJ L218/82, and the Regulation (EU) 2019/1020 of the European Parliament and of the Council of 20 June 2019 on market surveillance and compliance of products and amending Directive 2004/42/EC and Regulations (EC) No 765/2008 and (EU) No 305/2011 PE/45/2019/REV/1 OJ L169/1.

[28] See art 2(1)(c) Standardization Regulation: a harmonized standard is defined as a 'European standard adopted on the basis of a request made by the Commission for the application of Union harmonization legislation.'

[29] Standardization Regulation art 10.

[30] Standardization Regulation art 11. Read further: Commission, 'Blue Guide' (n 13), 41ff.

[31] The structure of Art 10 is admittedly confusing, since there is no information on the requested standards that do not offer a presumption of conformity effect of the New Approach harmonised standards. Those 'other' requested standards may also be called harmonised (but without the effects of the New Approach standards) based on Union harmonization law. The definition of a 'harmonised standard' ('harmonised standard means a European standard adopted on the basis of a request made by the Commission for the application of Union harmonization legislation'), it is so broadly written that requested standards based on any harmonization legislation of the Union (that is in one of the harmonised areas), may be classified as harmonised standards. Notably, the prominent elements that give the special status and effects to a New Approach harmonised standard ('essential requirements' and 'presumption of conformity') are not part of the definition of a 'harmonised standard' but provided for in the relevant New Approach laws: Art. 28 Transitional Provisions of the Standardization Regulation, which clarifies that the presumption of conformity is provided by the New Approach law ('In Union acts that provide for a presumption of conformity with essential requirements through the application of harmonised standards ') and the Model Directive in the Annex of the Council Resolution of 7 May 1985 on a new approach to technical harmonization and standards OJ C 136, 4.6.1985.

[32] Those requests are admittedly understudied in literature, since most scholars focus on the New Approach standards. But they are very relevant to data protection, since there is already one such standardization request (M/530). Van Leeuwen has noted the distinction Van Leeuwen B, *European Standardisation of Services and Its Impact on Private Law: Paradoxes of Convergence* (Bloomsbury Publishing 2017). Also, Schepel refers to the harmonised standards outside the New Approach as 'normal' harmonised standards. Schepel, *The Constitution of Private Governance* (n 22), 236 fn. 55.

The introduction of the innovative New Approach gave rise to mixed reactions. On the one hand, it was welcomed as a forward-looking manner of leveraging the expertise from private organizations and accelerating rule-making processes. On the other hand, the adoption of the New Approach caused the reactions of scholars opposed to the entrustment of tasks pertaining to the achievement of legislative goals to private actors ie the standardization bodies.[33] Despite the critical voices, the New Approach cemented the use of standards for serving public policy goals.[34]

3.1.2 Public Policy Goals and Societal Needs beyond the New Approach

While the New Approach model is still in use, the European public regulator expressed plans for a broader role for standards in assisting with the implementation and effectiveness of Union policies and law. The role of standards and standardization as a means to meet specific needs of the European market has been explicitly acknowledged by the Council, which has urged the Commission to examine the usefulness of applying the New Approach model to other sectors, as a means of 'improving and simplifying legislation wherever possible'.[35] In 2004, the Commission published a Communication on the role of European standards in the framework of European policies and legislation. The underlying rationale was that standards can improve the free movement of goods and services by enhancing intra-EU competitiveness. European standardization would be tasked, according to the Commission, to 'respond properly to the market needs, in particular those of the industry'.[36] The engagement of standardization for achieving harmonization and the market objectives was largely related to efforts to 'Europeanize' public policy issues in the Union,[37] and to prevent barriers to the Single Market.[38] In particular, often standards have been studied in relation to enforcement barriers to the Single Market and how they contribute to the elimination of technical or administrative restrictions by reducing costs resulting from regulatory heterogeneity among Member States.[39]

[33] Commission, 'Blue Guide' (n 13), 1–152.

[34] Specific issues pertaining to types of references of standards (direct/indirect, dated/non-dated), the act of publication of standards in the Official Journal in the EU are further discussed in Chapter 4 section 4.3 in this book.

[35] Council Resolution of 28 October 1999 on the role of standardization in Europe, OJ C141/1, May 2000, para 10.

[36] European Commission, Communication on the role of European standardization in the framework of European policies and legislation, COM (2004) 674 final, 3.

[37] Chowdhury N and Wessel RA, 'Conceptualising Multilevel Regulation in the EU: A Legal Translation of Multilevel Governance?' (2012) 18 European Law Journal, 335.

[38] Pelkmans J and De Brito A, Enforcement in the EU single market, Centre for European Policy Studies (2012).

[39] ibid.

With the re-launch of the debate on the Internal market in the framework of the Europe 2020 strategy, standards came to the spotlight in relation to the Digital Single Market.[40] Standards were put forward as a means to 'signal and verify compliance with the legal framework',[41] as enablers of user-friendly interfaces,[42] interoperable services,[43]and IT security measures.[44] Beyond the support of the above market related goals, another theme that emerged from the 2004 Commission Communication is standardization in support of *societal needs*. The Commission suggested that standardization could support environmental and consumer protection policies, security and accessibility for disabled and elderly people.[45]

Among several fields, data protection as a standardization field started appearing modestly in policy documents around the same period. In 2009, the European Commission issued a Communication announcing key priority issues for making the European Union an area of freedom, security, and justice.[46] The Communication announced *inter alia* a plan to establish a comprehensive personal data protection scheme and a European certification scheme for 'privacy aware' technologies.[47] In addition, the Commission stressed the need for the contribution of the Union to the development of international standards in data protection.[48] In June 2011, in its Communication on the strategic vision for European standards, the European Commission reinstated its position that standards are a tool to support European policies and legislation.[49] In that context, standards were

[40] European Commission, 'Communication from the Commission to the European Parliament, the Council, the European Economic and Social Committee and the committee of the Regions: Unleashing the Potential of Cloud Computing in Europe' COM (2012) 529 final.

[41] ibid 3

[42] ibid 4.

[43] ibid 8.

[44] ibid 8. At the same time, the Cloud Strategy Communication identifies that the proliferation of standards impedes the use of standardization as a tool to enhance user trust. The Communication therefore proposed a key action with the aim to 'cut through the jungle of standards', namely to create a framework for promoting existing standards suitable for the Commission's policy goals outlined in the Cloud strategy. Read on the topic: Gleeson NC and Walden I, 'It's a Jungle Out There?: Cloud Computing, Standards and the Law' (2014) 5 European Journal of Law and Technology, 2.

[45] European Commission, Communication on the role of European standardization in the framework of European policies and legislation, COM (2004) 674 final, 7. In relation to the environment, in his report on the Single Market Strategy, Mario Monty, stated that the need to use the full potential for a single market of energy requires 'delivering a stable regulatory framework [...] and proactive use of standardization to promote innovative green products and technologies'. Monti M, 'A New Strategy for the Single Market: At the Service of Europe's Economy and Society: Report to the President of the European Commission José Manuel Barroso by Mario Monti' European Union (2010).

[46] Commission of the European Communities, 'Communication from the Commission to the European Parliament and the Council. An area of freedom, security and justice serving the citizen', COM (2009) 262 final, June 2009 (hereafter COM (2009) 262).

[47] ibid.

[48] COM (2009) 262 (n 46), June 2009, Annex 'Priority Issues', 30.

[49] European Commission 'Communication from the Commission to the European Parliament, the Council and the European Economic and Social Committee. A strategic vision for European standards: Moving forward to enhance and accelerate the sustainable growth of the European economy by 2020' COM (2011) 311 final, June 2011, 4ff (hereafter COM (2011) 311).

presented as embodying a potential to support the Union policy for protection of personal data and privacy of individuals.[50]

3.1.3 Standards *in* Union Legislation and as *Alternative to* Legislation: Better Regulation

Following the vision for a broader role of standards, as expressed by the Commission, there is an increasing rate of references of the Union policy makers and legislators to standardization as an instrument to support Union rule-making in a considerable number of fields,[51] such as environmental legislation.[52] The 'support' of standards to Union laws manifests itself often in terms of implementation, harmonization, and efficiency. In the 2016 NIS Directive, standardization of security requirements and the conformity of the regulatees with such standards was proclaimed as a manner to 'ensure a high level of security of network and information systems at Union level'[53] and promote 'convergent implementation' of legal obligations.[54] The AI Act provides that 'standardization should play a key role to provide technical solutions to providers to ensure compliance with this Regulation.'[55] The regulator often assigns to standards a harmonization role and a public policy goal, such as the achievement of high information security level in NIS and NIS2. Similar approaches with a dual role attributed to standardization are followed by other Union laws, such as the electronic identification and trust services (eIDAS) Regulation.[56]

Next, the EU Better Regulation programme, which is an effort of the Commission to improve its policymaking covering the whole policy cycle from planning to enforcement, provides a good example of a Commission strategy institutionalizing the adoption of non-legislative measures in place of legislation. The Better Regulation programme sought to diversify the sources of rules in the

[50] COM (2011) 311 final, June 2011, 9 and COM (2010) 609 final.

[51] The increase of references to standardization as an instrument to support public policies or legislation is not unique to the European Union context, but also present in other regions or countries globally. See ISO/IEC 'Using and referencing ISO and IEC standards to support public policy' 2014, 37f.

[52] See for example Annex VI of Directive 2008/50/EC of the European Parliament and of the Council of 21 May 2008 on ambient air quality and cleaner air for Europe [2008] OJ L152/1, as amended by Commission Directive (EU 2015/1480) consolidated text available; Directive 2004/107/EC of the European Parliament and of the Council of 15 December 2004 relating to arsenic, cadmium, mercury, nickel and polycyclic aromatic hydrocarbons in ambient air OJ L023 26.1.2005, as amended by Regulation (EC) 219/2009 and Commission Directive 2015/1480.

[53] Directive (EU) 2016/1148 of the European Parliament and of the Council of 6 July 2016 concerning measures for a high common level of security of network and information systems across the Union, [2016] OJ L194/1, Recital (66) (hereafter NIS).

[54] NIS art 19.

[55] Recital 121 AI Act.

[56] Regulation No 910/2014 of the European Parliament and of the Council of 23 July 2014 on electronic identification and trust services for electronic transactions in the internal market and repealing Directive 1999/93/EC, [2014] L257/73.

Union,[57] taking into account the Interinstitutional Agreement on Better Law-Making and its considerations about regulation mechanisms alternative to legal instruments.[58] The Better Regulation programme requires that the Commission performs an Impact Assessment (IA) before proposing new legislation. Among the several components of the IA, the type of legislative or non-legislative action needs to be assessed and justified.

The Better Regulation Guidelines advise the Commission to consider 'the widest range of policy alternatives both in terms of content and instruments', including policy instruments such as non-regulatory alternatives, market-based solutions, and international standards.[59] The Commission therefore needs, in line with the principles of subsidiarity and proportionality, to consider whether a non-legislative measure may achieve the same goal as the proposed new legislation. Standardization is therefore routinely assessed in the framework of impact assessments as a self-regulation[60] and co-regulation action, alternative to legislation.[61] In practice, studies show that alternative to legislation measures are rarely adopted in this framework,[62] despite such possibility being offered by the Better Regulation framework. Independently of the plausibility of the reasons for this (such as the lack of conceptual clarity when it comes to the use of alternative forms of regulation),[63] one should keep in mind that the EU regulator shows a preference for incorporating the alternative mechanisms in its policy and law-making, and in this manner, regulate them, rather than the opposite, as shall be seen in the next Section on the main EU legal instrument on standardization.[64]

[57] Verbruggen P, 'Private Regulation in EU Better Regulation': Past performance and future promises (2017) 19 European Journal of Law Reform, 121.

[58] European Parliament, Council and Commission, Interinstitutional Agreement on Better Law Making, 2003/C 321/01, OJ C 321, 31 December 2003.

[59] In fact, the Guidelines state the IA Report needs to list the reasons for 'any divergence from international standards' European Commission, Commission Staff Working Document, Better Regulation Guidelines, SWS (2017) 350, 22ff.

[60] In the context of the Inter-institutional Agreement, self-regulation is defined as 'the possibility for economic operators, the social partners, non-governmental organizations or associations to adopt amongst themselves and for themselves common guidelines at European level (particularly codes of practice or sectoral agreements)'. European Commission, European Parliament and Council, Inter-Institutional Agreement on Better Lawmaking [2003] OJ C 321/01.

[61] Meuwese explains that Impact Assessments have been conceptualized both as (1) soft constitutional law, which while not being legally binding, it may lead to some practical effect or influence behaviour, and (2) partial meta-regulatory regime. See Meuwese A, *Impact Assessment in EU Law Making* (A.C.M.,2008), 275. See also relevant Kamara I, 'Co-regulation in EU Personal Data Protection: The Case of Technical Standards and the Privacy by Design Standardization "Mandate"' (2017) 8(1) European Journal of Law and Technology1 ; Hirsch D, 'The Law and Policy of Online Privacy: Regulation, Self-regulation, or Co-regulation' (2010) 34 Seattle University Law Review, 439.

[62] van den Hoogen T and Nowak T, 'The Emergence and Use of Self-Regulation in the European Decision-Making Process: Does It Make a Difference?' (2010) 4 Legisprudence, 343.

[63] Meuwese A and Senden L, 'European Impact Assessment And The Choice Of Alternative Regulatory Instruments,' in Verschuuren J (ed), *The Impact of Legislation* (Brill | Nijhoff 2009), 154.

[64] Read further on the incorporation of standards in the Union legal order by means of reference in Chapter 4 section 4.3.1 in this book.

In short, following the orientation of standardization bodies standards towards additional new fields, standardization started having a more prominent role in the public agenda of the Union policy makers. Standards associated with New Approach Directives are given the heavy task of translating legal requirements to technical controls. In other cases, standards are assigned roles of cementing abstract policy or legal goals. From a regulatory perspective, standardization entered the realm of Impact Assessments of the Commission's legislative initiatives, and needs to be considered as an alternative measure next to the adoption of legislative measures. Further, areas of public and societal interest such as environment and consumer protection entered the public regulators' radar as standardization areas in support of Union law, with personal data protection being one of those areas.

3.2 The EU Standardization Regulation

The general secondary law of EU standardization is Regulation 1025/2012 ('Standardization Regulation'), which entered into force in 2013, and harmonized and modernized the legislation of the Union regarding standardization. The reform of the EU standardization framework had already been initiated in late 2000s.[65] In 2009, the Commission expressed its intention to modernize ICT standardization in the EU,[66] *inter alia* to allow ICT specifications to be accommodated in the EU market. The former legal framework on standardization in the Union did not apply to ICT technical specifications in European legislation, policies, and public procurement. The Commission's White Paper suggested a series of safeguards for such ICT 'standards', such as openness, consensus, balanced participation, and transparency.[67] In its White Paper,[68] the Commission treated standards as a policy instrument, necessary in order to keep up with rapid technological developments.[69]

[65] The legal framework preceding the Regulation 1025/2012 comprised mainly of three legal instruments; namely the Directive 98/34/EC which laid down a procedure for the provision of information in the field of technical standards and regulations (the Directive had essentially codified the Directive 83/189 as amended), the Decision 1673/2006/EC laying down rules of European standardization, and the Council Decision 87/95/EEC. The Directive 98/34/EC was eventually replaced by the Directive 1535/2015.

[66] Commission of the European Communities, 'White Paper. Modernising ICT Standardization in the EU – The way forward', COM (2009) 324 final, July 2009 (hereafter COM (2009) 324).

[67] COM (2009) 324 (n 66), 4ff.

[68] This is confirmed in a later Communication, which emphasizes the need for reform of Union legislation on standardization to 'be adapted to new technologies'. European Commission, 'Communication from the Commission to the European Parliament, the Council, the Economic and Social Committee and the Committee of the Regions Single Market Act. Twelve levers to boost growth and strengthen confidence. Working together to create new growth.' COM (2011) 206 final, April 2011.

[69] Apart from the modernization of the EU approach to ICT standardization, other incentives to reform the legal framework on standardization included the acceleration of development of interoperable standards, the improvement of the way in which the European Standardization Organizations operate to 'leverage European and international standards for the long-term competitiveness of European industry', the improvement of the use of standards in public procurement, and the extension of EU

In response to the Commission' policies, the European Parliament published in 2010 a Report on the future of European Standardization.[70] The Parliament identified four main areas for improvement of the standardization system, namely the improvement of access to the standardization process, facilitation of access to standards, the enhancement of collaboration among EU Member States and their participation in the standardization activities of the European Standardization Organizations.[71] The Parliament called for a specific monitoring system, which would ensure the implementation of the principles and attributes. The Parliament also stressed the need for technical standards to adapt to challenges resulting from *inter alia* the evolution of technology.

In terms of data protection, the Future of European Standardization Report is one of the first EU policy documents to identify a link between technical standards and personal data protection.[72] The Parliament stressed that adapting ICT standardization policy to market and policy developments, would contribute to 'the development of standards in support of personal data protection'.[73] Despite the brief reference, the Report signalled personal data protection as a potential area of standardization in the Union. However, apart from the policy endorsements, there was no concrete legislative initiative at that point, nor explicit reference to a possible formalization of a legal relationship of technical standards and data protection legislation.

Following the ordinary legislative procedure,[74] the final text of the Regulation was published in 2012.[75] Regulation 1025/2012 is based on art 114 TFEU, which

standardization to services. European Commission, 'Communication from the Commission to the European Parliament, the Council, the Economic and Social Committee and the Committee of the Regions Single Market Act. Twelve levers to boost growth and strengthen confidence. Working together to create new growth.' COM (2011) 206 final, April 2011.

[70] European Parliament, 'Report on the Future of European Standardization', October 2010 (hereafter EP 'Future of Standardization Report').

[71] The Report proposed the introduction to the reformed legal framework of the principles of transparency, openness, impartiality, consensus, effectiveness, relevance and coherence, inspired by the WTO TBT Agreement and additional attributes such as neutrality, accountability, and availability.

[72] EP 'Future of Standardization Report' (n 70), 16.

[73] EP 'Future of Standardization Report' (n 70), 16.

[74] The European Commission published a Proposal for a Regulation on European Standardization in 2011. European Commission, 'Proposal for a Regulation of the European Parliament and of the Council on European Standardization and amending Council Directives 89/686/EEC and 93/15/EEC and Directives 94/9/EC, 94/25/EC, 95/16/EC, 97/23/EC, 98/34/EC, 2004/22/EC, 2007/23/EC, 2009/105/EC and 2009/23/EC of the European Parliament and the Council', COM (2011) 315 final. The choice of the instrument of a Regulation instead of a Directive, was justified by the need to establish a pan-European system for the creation of European Standards. Regulation (EU) 1025/2012 art 2. The direct applicability and direct effect of Regulations can avoid the uncertainty caused by incorrect or non-implementation of a directive. Rotondo E, 'The Legal Effect of EU Regulations' (2013) 29 Computer Law & Security Review, 437.

[75] In September 2012, the European Parliament on its first reading approved the Commission Proposal with amendments. Later the same year, the Council approved the European Parliament position on first reading.

concerns the power of European Parliament and the Council to adopt measures for approximation of laws, having as its objective the establishment and functioning of the Internal Market.[76] Article 114 TFEU does not confer on the EU a general competence to regulate all aspects of the functioning of the Internal Market, but only where there is a genuine link between the adopted measure and the removal of actual and potential obstacles in the Internal Market.[77] The choice of art 114 TFEU as legal basis resonates with the vision of the Union regulator to use standards for public policy goals and societal needs, such as product safety.[78] It also reflects the harmonization role of standards for the Internal Market. The choice of art 114 TFEU however also reinforces questions on a side effect of the adoption of the Standardization Regulation, which is the conferral to private standardization bodies of 'regulatory' or 'rule-making' powers.[79]

The Standardization Regulation aims at *full harmonization* in the field of standardization, in the sense that the Member States must implement the EU measures and are not allowed to adopt any measures that deviate or depart from the EU measures.[80] The Regulation addresses issues of transparency, accessibility to standards and stakeholder participation, which are all important aspects for the legitimacy of standardization activity. The Regulation also formalizes and codifies the European Commission standardization requests as a regulatory technique for the development of European standards in support of Union legislation and policies.[81] Following the intensive references to ICT standardization before the reform of the EU standardization legal framework, the Standardization Regulation

[76] The CJEU has provided that 'by using the words 'measures for the approximation' in art 114 TFEU, the authors of the Treaty intended to confer on the EU legislature a discretion, depending on the general context and the specific circumstances of the matter to be harmonized, as regards the method of approximation most appropriate for achieving the desired result, in particular in fields with complex technical features (see judgments in Case C-380/03 *Germany v Parliament* and Council, EU:C:2006:772, para 42, and Case C-270/12 *United Kingdom v Parliament and Council*, EU:C:2014:18, para 102). Judgment of 4 May 2016, Case C-358/14 *Poland v European Parliament*, EU: C: 2016: 323.

[77] Mańko R, 'EU Competence in Private Law: The Treaty Framework for a European Private Law and Challenges for Coherence' European Parliamentary Research Service (2015).

[78] TFEU art 114(3) provides: 'The Commission, in its proposals envisaged in paragraph 1 concerning health, safety, environmental protection and consumer protection, will take as a base a high level of protection, taking account in particular of any new development based on scientific facts. Within their respective powers, the European Parliament and the Council will also seek to achieve this objective.'

[79] Senden has characterized the use of art 114 TFEU as a basis for the Standardization Regulation as a 'weak and shallow legal foundation from a legitimacy perspective', even though she argues that the broader understanding of art 114 TFEU from a purely legal perspective can fit in the interpretation provided by the legislator and the CJEU. Senden L, 'The Constitutional Fit of European Standardization Put to the Test' (2017) 44 Legal Issues of Economic Integration, 345ff.

[80] Harmonization on the basis of art 114 TFEU may be full or partial harmonization. Read: Rafal M, 'EU competence in private law. The Treaty framework for a European private law and challenges for coherence' European Parliament, January 2015.

[81] Standardization Regulation arts 10–12.

regulates also standardization activity in the field of Information Communication Technologies vis-à-vis their use in public procurement.[82]

The Standardization Regulation was revised in 2022 with Regulation 2022/2480 to address decision-making and representation issues.[83] According to the EU legislator, when carrying out standardization requests, the internal decisions of ESOs must 'take into account the interests, policy objectives and values of the Union, as well as public interests in general'.[84] In a Communication released together with a proposal to amend the Standardization Regulation, the Commission expressed its concerns on ETSI's decision-making process, which allowed 'uneven power to corporate interests'.[85] To that end the Commission called upon the ESOs to address the 'uneven and intransparent representation of industrial interests and increasing the involvement of SMEs, civil society and users'.[86] Following the 2022 amendment, decisions and standardization work surrounding standardization requests to the ESOs may be carried out exclusively by 'representatives of the national standardization bodies within the competent decision-making body'.[87]

3.3 Legal Nature of Standards in the EU Law

3.3.1 The Definition of a Technical Standard

The Regulation offers a legal basis for regulating standardization activity in support of Union law and policies.[88] The definition of the concept of a *standard* is provided in art 1 Standardization Regulation.

According to the Standardization Regulation a *standard* is:

> *a technical specification, adopted by a recognised Standardization body, for repeated or continuous application, with which compliance is not compulsory, and which is one of the following:*

[82] The Regulation also includes Chapters on financing arrangements (ch V) and Delegated Acts (ch VI).

[83] Regulation (EU) 2022/2480 of the European Parliament and of the Council of 14 December 2022 amending Regulation (EU) No 1025/2012 as regards decisions of European standardization organizations concerning European standards and European standardization deliverables, [2022] OJ L323/1.

[84] Recital 4 Regulation 2022/2480.

[85] European Commission 'Communication from the Commission to the European Parliament, the Council, the European Economic and Social Committee and the Committee of the Regions, An EU Strategy on Standardization, Setting global standards in support of a resilient, green and digital EU single market' COM (2022) 31 final (hereafter COM (2022) 31). See also European Commission, 'Report from the Commission to the European Parliament and the Council on the implementation of the Regulation (EU) No 1025/2012 from 2016 to 2020', COM (2022) 30 final.

[86] COM (2022) 31 (n 85).

[87] Standardization Regulation art 2a.

[88] Standardization Regulation art 1(1).

(a) *'international standard' means a standard adopted by an international standardization body;*
(b) *'European standard' means a standard adopted by a European standardization organization;*
(c) *'harmonised standard' means a European standard adopted on the basis of a request made by the Commission for the application of Union harmonization legislation;*
(d) *'national standard' means a standard adopted by a national standardization body*[89]

A technical specification is a document that prescribes technical requirements to be fulfilled by a product, process, service, or system.[90] The specification may provide product or service characteristics—including levels of quality, performance, interoperability, production methods and processes.[91] This definition of a standard is in line with the definitions adopted by standards organizations such as the ISO[92] and the IEC.[93] The Standardization Regulation describes the aims of *technical specifications*—and by extension of standards–in art 2(4). Technical specifications may contain *inter alia* prescriptions of technical requirements and characteristics of products or services, regarding quality, performance, interoperability, environmental protection, health, or safety.[94] Thus, standards as technical specifications in the EU legal order are constrained by the above scopes, even though one could argue that the broad formulation thereof, is not setting overly limiting conditions on what may be included in a standard.[95]

[89] Standardization Regulation art 2(1).

[90] Other definitions of standards focus on their role in international governance—Nadvi and Waltring define a standard as a 'guide for behaviour and for judging behavior'. Nadvi K and Wältring F, 'Making Sense of Global Standards' in Schmitz H (ed), *Local Enterprises in the Global Economy: Issues of Governance and Upgrading* (Edward Elgar Pub 2004); Abbott KW and Snidal D, 'International "standards" and International Governance' (2001) 8 Journal of European Public Policy, 345.

[91] Standardization Regulation art 2(4).

[92] While the Standardization Regulation describes the *conditions*, the ISO definition also includes the *content and aim* of a standard According to ISO, a standard is 'an (international) document, established by consensus and approved by a recognized body, which provides, for common and repeated use, rules, guidelines or characteristics for activities or their results, aimed at the achievement of the optimum degree of order in a given context'. The definition is also accompanied by the note that 'standards should be based on the consolidated results of science, technology and experience, and aimed at the promotion of optimum community benefits'. ISO Guide 2:2004.

[93] According to the IEC international standards reflect 'agreements on the technical description of the characteristics to be fulfilled by a product, system, service, or object'. See IEC website: https://www.iec.ch/about/activities/?ref = menu (accessed 20 September 2023).

[94] Regulation 1025/2012 art 2(4) also refers to technical specifications in relation to production methods and processes for agricultural products (art 2(4b)) and methods and criteria for assessing the performance of construction products (art 2 (4d)).

[95] The definition of a standard of art 2(2) is the same for international, European harmonized or national standards.

3.3.2 Non-compulsory Compliance and *De Facto* Binding Standards

The non-compulsory compliance is the backbone of the concept of standards. The decision of an organization to conform[96] to a standard should be a *deliberate choice*. An organization therefore voluntarily decides to comply with a standard, for reasons other than an obligation.[97] While the term 'compulsory' usually relates to a legal obligation, the question arises whether only legislation could render compliance with a technical specification as compulsory, such as the excessive cost in case of a manufacturer following another solution or method than the one prescribed in the technical standard.

The question is what constitutes compulsory compliance and whether *compliance* with standards may become *de facto binding* by means other than incorporation in a binding private law instrument such as a contract.[98] This issue has gained attention in scholarship, especially in relation to standards destined to support legislation such as harmonized standards.[99] Schepel has explained that while compliance with standards is not formally 'mandatory', it is 'obviously a sensible idea to comply with them' for several reasons.[100] While an organization has the choice to demonstrate that it complies with legal requirements in another manner,

[96] To avoid confusion throughout the book the term 'compliance' is used in relation to legislation, while 'conformity' is used in relation to standards. In this section however the term compliance is also used in relation to standards, following the wording of art 2(1) of the Standardization Regulation.

[97] Reasons for the decision to conform to a standard could be that complying with a given standard is the optimal way of achieving a desired result, organizing processes and resources, or designing a product, system, or service. If compliance with a technical specification laid down in legislation is mandatory, then we speak of 'technical regulation'. A technical regulation is a law that lays down product characteristics or processes and production methods. In the Union, Directive 1535/2015 defines a technical regulation in the context of Information Society services as a 'technical specifications and other requirements or rules on services, including the relevant administrative provisions, the observance of which is compulsory, de jure or de facto, in the case of marketing, provision of a service, establishment of a service operator or use in a Member State or a major part thereof, as well as laws, regulations or administrative provisions of Member States, except those provided for in Article 7, prohibiting the manufacture, importation, marketing or use of a product or prohibiting the provision or use of a service, or establishment as a service provider'. Directive (EU) 2015/1535 of the European Parliament and of the Council of 9 September 2015 laying down a procedure for the provision of information in the field of technical regulations and of rules on Information Society services, [2015] OJ L241/1.

[98] The ISO and IEC even acknowledge in their internal regulations and rules the concept of 'mandatory standard'. The ISO/IEC Guide 2, a document that provides the standardization-related vocabulary used in the context of the ISO and IEC activities, defines as mandatory the standard 'the application of which is made compulsory by virtue of a general law or exclusive reference in a regulation'. Regulation 1025/2012 nonetheless, as analysed, does not consider those standards as mandatory. ISO/IEC Guide 2:2004 Standardization and related activities—General vocabulary. Section 11.4. An exclusive reference (as opposed to an indicative reference) is defined as a 'reference to standards that states that the only way to meet the relevant requirements of a technical regulation is to comply with the standard(s) referred to'. Section 11.3.1. of the ISO/IEC Guide 2: 2004.

[99] According to art 2(1)(c) Regulation 1025/2012 harmonized standard means 'a European standard adopted on the basis of a request made by the Commission for the application of Union harmonization legislation'

[100] Schepel H, 'Between Standards and Regulation' in Delimatsis P (ed), *The Law, Economics and Politics of International Standardisation* (Cambridge University Press 2015), 199–214 (hereafter Schepel 'Between Standards and Regulation').

conforming to the standard is usually the most cost-effective, and reliable way for an organization to prove its compliance.[101] In case the organization chooses to demonstrate compliance in another manner, it would need to prove that the 'alternative methods meet acceptable good standards of design', safety, and others.[102] As Van Gestel and Van Lochem frame it, often there is no opt-out.[103] Besides, oftentimes a standard is even endorsed by or developed following the instructions of the public regulator, as in the case of harmonized standards, which also impacts the deliberate *decision* of an organization to conform to a standard. In *Commission v. Belgium*,[104] the CJEU found that even if a Member State does not impose by means of legal obligation conformity of economic operators to national technical construction standards, the state still encourages contractors to choose construction products that follow those standards and marks, when it grants presumption of conformity with the legislation for construction products that follow the national standards and affix the national label.[105] The CJEU found that this behaviour did not only impact national operators, but also economic operators in other Member States with the intention to enter the Belgian market.[106] The CJEU specifically noted the manner that the national construction standards and relevant labels were promoted by the regulator *as offering the best protection for the user*, providing the developer with better guarantees of the quality of the products used and helping the contractor avoid risks related to the execution of the construction using products conforming to those national standards.[107]

In principle, standards as such have no *direct* binding effects, even though indirect or incidental effects cannot be excluded, when for example standards are incorporated in a contract between private parties.[108] If one accepts however, as

[101] Henson S and Reardon T, 'Private Agri-Food Standards: Implications for Food Policy and the Agri-Food System' (2005) 30 Food Policy, 241; Busch L and Bain C, 'New! Improved? The Transformation of the Global Agrifood System' (2004) 69 Rural Sociology, 321; Bernstein S and Hannah E, 'Non-State Global Standard Setting and the WTO: Legitimacy and the Need for Regulatory Space' (2008) 11 Journal of International Economic Law, 575.

[102] Schepel, 'Between Standards and Regulation' (n 100), 201.

[103] van Gestel R and van Lochem P, 'Private Standards as a Replacement for Public Lawmaking?' in Gamito MC and Micklitz HW (eds), *The Role of the EU in Transnational Legal Ordering* (Edward Elgar Publishing 2020), 32.

[104] CJEU, Judgment of 13 March 2008, Case C-227/06 *Commission v Kingdom of Belgium*, EU:C:2008:160 (available in French).

[105] C-227/06 (n 104) para 48.

[106] C-227/06 (n 104) para 50.

[107] C-227/06 (n 104) (own free translation). Original text (para 48): 'Ainsi, parmi les «avantages des produits de construction portant la marque 'BENOR' et 'ATG'», lesdits répertoires relèvent, notamment, que leur utilisation «constitue la meilleure protection de l'utilisateur», que «le maître d'ouvrage dispose d'une meilleure garantie de qualité des produits utilisés», que «l'auteur du projet peut consacrer son attention à la qualité d'exécution des ouvrages» et que «l'entrepreneur évite les risques liés à l'exécution des travaux de construction au moyen de produits de qualité inférieure». Ces mêmes répertoires indiquent, en conclusion que «les marques de conformité 'BENOR' et 'ATG' peuvent donc être considérées comme un maillon important dans le développement de l'assurance générale de la qualité dans la construction».'

[108] Gleeson NC and Walden I, 'It's a Jungle Out There? Cloud Computing, Standards and the Law' (2014) 5 European Journal of Law and Technology, 2; Stuurman K, 'Legal Aspects of Standardization

explained above, that there are cases, where standards are *de facto binding*, it follows that standards in those cases may bear direct effects.

In *EMC Development*, a Swedish cement company claimed that a European harmonized standard was of a *de facto binding nature*. The applicant relied on national legislation and the public procurement tender, which explicitly referred to the specific standard as a requirement, to argue, among other things, that the standard was in this manner imposed by the regulator and consequently dominated the market. The Court did not *ab initio* reject the idea that a European harmonized standard could be of a *de facto* binding nature. It did however provide that 'even if national regulations excluded products such as the applicant's by using specifications such as those which are included in the standard, the standard is not binding on account of its adoption by CEN'.[109] The Court in other words held that a standard adopted by a European standard-setting organization and being a European standard are not conditions that render on their own the nature of the standard as binding.[110]

In *Fra.bo*,[111] the CJEU ruled that European public law (art 28 EC) applies to standardization and certification activities by a private law body (DVWG),[112] when the national legislation considers the certified product as compliant with the national law'.[113] The Court found that even though there was an alternative means of proving compliance with the law, namely through verification by an appointed expert, the administrative difficulties associated with the alternative manner and the costs of the expert report, made the alternative procedure essentially of 'little or no practical use'.[114] As a result, almost all German consumers had purchased the products certified by the DVWG and in this manner the private certification body—despite not being financed by the state—in reality held the power to regulate entry into the German market of the products at issue in the proceedings.[115] Thus, while standards in this case were part of an activity between private law parties, they could have effects extending to a broader group of entities.

In *Public.Resource.Org*, the CJEU recognized that a harmonized standard may be mandatory. The case concerned the request made by Public.Resource.Org to the Commission to access specific harmonized technical standards on the basis of

of Information Technology and Telecommunications: An Overview' (1992) 8 Computer Law Security Review, 2; Micklitz H-W, '10. Soft Law, Technical Standards and European Private Law' in Eliantonio M, Korkea-aho E, and Mörth U (eds), *Research Handbook on Soft Law* (2023) 148.

[109] Judgment of the General Court of 12 May 2010, Case T-432/05 *EMC Development AB*, EU: T:2010:189, para 122.

[110] With regard to the '*de facto*' element, the applicant failed to prove his claims about market domination and lack of alternative means, and the action was dismissed.

[111] Judgment of 12 July 2012, Case C-171/11, *Fra.bo SpA*, EU:C:2012:453. De Vries SA, 'Balancing Fundamental Rights with Economic Freedoms According to the European Court of Justice' (2013) 9 Utrecht Law Review 169.

[112] Deutsche Vereinigung des Gas- und Wasserfaches eV.

[113] Case C-171/11, operative part.

[114] Case C-171/11, para 29.

[115] Case C-171/11, para 31.

the Regulation 1049/2001 on public access to documents of EU institutions. The CJEU in its ruling on appeal against the decision of the General Court found that although not generally mandatory, the specific harmonized European standards at hand, were 'manifestly mandatory'.[116] This effect was triggered by the fact that the relevant Regulation stipulated that standards adopted by CEN were to be used as test methods to demonstrate conformity with the requirements of that Regulation. In other words, as AG Medina stated referring to harmonized standards and the presumption of conformity:

> *To my mind, that clearly amounts to a situation where de facto all manufacturers or service providers will seek always to be in compliance with HTS because no rational manufacturer or service provider would be willing to expose themselves to huge commercial risk and to bear such a burden.*[117]

The CJEU cases show that there is no jurisprudence clearly supporting the argument for the general *de facto* binding nature of standards, but there is evidence of *de facto* binding effects. Thus, despite the definition of art 2(1) of the Standardization Regulation referring to non-compulsory compliance, standards should not without further consideration be regarded as not bearing direct legal effects. The complexity stems from the adoption of the variation of standards (national, international, European either harmonized, mandated, or other) and the surrounding conditions such as the diversity of references by the regulator to standards in binding and non-binding Union acts.[118]

3.3.3 Adopted by a *Recognized* Standardization Body

The Standardization Regulation requires a standard to be adopted by a *recognized* standardization body. The requirement for recognition of standardization bodies stems from the private nature of those bodies and the semi-autonomous nature of standardization, as discussed in the following Chapter.[119] Recognition is one of the means of the Union regulator to maintain control over who produces the extra-legal private norms introduced in the Union legal order. There is a notable absence of a definition of the meaning of a 'recognized standardization body', in the legal framework prior to the introduction of the Standardization Regulation.[120]

[116] Judgment of 5 March 2024, Case C-588/21 P, *Public.Resource.org v European Commission*, ECLI:EU:C:2024:201, para 75.

[117] Opinion of AG Medina of 22 June 2023, Case C-588/21 P *PublicResource.org*, ECLI:EU:C:2023:509, para 42. See also Kamara I, 'General Court EU: Commercial Interests Block the Right to Access European Harmonised Standards' (2022) 1 Journal of Standardisation 1.

[118] Read further Chapter 4 in this book.

[119] Read further Chapter 4 section 4.1 in this book.

[120] The Directive 83/189/EEC also referred to 'recognized standardizing body'. Council Directive 83/189/EEC of 28 March 1983 laying down a procedure for the provision of information in the field

The Standardization Regulation follows the approach of the previous regime; while not defining or enlisting the 'recognized standardization bodies' in its main text, it does designate in its Annex I CEN, CENELEC, and ETSI as the European Standardization Organizations. The reference in the Annex of the Regulation should be perceived as *recognition*, in the sense of art 2(1) of the Regulation. The Regulation defines as national standardization bodies, the bodies notified to the Commission by Member States, which the Commission publishes in the Official Journal.[121] The international standardization bodies listed are the ISO, the IEC and the ITU,[122] without any reference however to other notable standard-developing organizations such as the IEEE or the W3C,[123] and other bodies and consortia which have significant activity in the area of data protection.

The Standardization Regulation does not seem to use 'recognition' as a criterion that invites a broad interpretation. In fact, to prevent such interpretations that open the concept of 'recognized standardization bodies' to all kinds of fora and consortia, the Standardization Regulation explicitly provides for a limited number of standardization bodies allowed to adopt standards at national, European, and international level.[124] The Regulation adopts a restrictive approach as to who can

of technical standards and regulations [1983] OJ L109/8. The reference to recognized standardization bodies remained unspecified in other relevant subsequent legislation as in art 1(3), (4), (5) of Council Decision 87/95/EEC of 22 December 1986 on standardization in the field of information technology and telecommunications [1987] OJ L 036. In its Annex II, the Directive listed specific standardization bodies of the Member States, together with CEN and CENELEC. ETSI was added later with the Commission Decision of 15 July 1992 amending the lists of standards institutions annexed to Council Directive 89/189/EEC [1992] OJ L221/55. Several years later, the Directive 94/10/EC that amended the Directive 83/189/EEC, provided a list of the European Standardization Organizations in Annex I, and a list of the national standardization bodies of the Member States in its Annex II. Directive 94/10/EC of the European Parliament and the Council of 23 March 1994 materially amending for the second time Directive 83/189/EEC laying down a procedure for the provision of information in the field of technical standards and regulations [1994] OJ L100/30.

121 Standardization Regulation arts 2(10) and 27.

122 Recital (3) Regulation 1025/2012 and art 2(9).

123 The reference to '*recognised* bodies' is not uncommon in standardization. A similar reference to 'recognized standardization bodies' can be found in the definition of standards provided in the WTO Agreement on Technical Barriers to Trade (TBT), which provides that a standard is a document 'approved by a recognised body'. In the context of TBT agreement, the case US—Tuna II provided some clarity to the meaning of the term 'recognized body'. The Appellate Body found that recognition implies knowledge of the WTO Members that an international body is active in standardization; it avoided however to establish a set of criteria for recognition. Delimatsis P, Relevant International Standards" and "Recognised Standardisation Bodies" under the TBT Agreement,' in Delimatsis P (ed), *The Law, Economics and Politics of International Standardisation* (Cambridge University Press 2015). Appellate Body Report, United States—Measures Concerning the Importation, Marketing and Sale of Tuna and Tuna Products, WTO WT/DS381/AB/R (June 13, 2012).

124 Standardization Regulation art 2(1)(a) provides that international standards are adopted by an international standardization body and art 2(9) provides that an international standardization body means 'means the International Organization for Standardization (ISO), the International Electrotechnical Commission (IEC) and the International Telecommunication Union (ITU)'. Accordingly, art 2(1)(b) provides that European standards are adopted by a European standardization organization, and art 2(8) defines European standardization organizations as those organization referred to in Annex I of the Regulation, namely CEN, CENELEC, and ETSI. Finally, art 2(1)(d) defines a national standard as a 'standard adopted by a national standardization body', and art 2(10) defines a

de lege adopt technical specifications that qualify automatically as standards. For other organizations that develop technical specifications, such as consortia and fora, the Regulation provides the conditions for their deliverables to be recognized as standards, but not the organizations themselves to be routinely considered as 'recognized bodies' approving or adopting standards.

Informal 'standards' or else technical specifications from non-recognized standards development organizations may be *adopted* by recognized standards organizations, such as the ISO.[125] Since the EU Standardization Regulation requires that standards are adopted—instead of developed—by recognized standardization organizations, it should be accepted such specifications are also under the scope of a *standard* of art 2 of the Standardization Regulation, on the condition they fulfil the other conditions of art 2. This is particularly relevant in terms of legitimacy of standardization, since those other standards have not necessarily been developed observing the procedural safeguards of the Standardization Regulation or with the involvement of the public regulator.[126]

Regarding the legal nature of the standard-setting organizations, these may be established as either public or private law bodies.[127] The ESOs and the recognized international standardization bodies are private law bodies, and more specifically non-for-profit associations.[128] The varying legal nature of standardization bodies as private or public law organizations has raised a number of issues regarding

national standardization body as a 'a body notified to the Commission by a Member State' in line with art 27 of the Regulation.

[125] An example is the Portable Document Format (PDF), which was adopted as an ISO standard in 2008. ISO 32000-1:2008 Document management—Portable document format—Part 1: PDF 1.7.

[126] Read further in Chapter 7 section 7.3 in this book.

[127] A 2000 study identified five categories for national standardization bodies of EU Member States: a) Public bodies regulated by a general standards law, b) private bodies regulated by general standards law, c) private bodies with contractual relations to the state, where the contract does not imply a 'transfer of public powers' but codifies the conditions of collaboration, d) private bodies under indirect regulatory supervision (for example in the form of approval of the standardization body's by-laws by the state), and e) unregulated private bodies. See Schepel H and Falke J 'Legal aspects of standardization in the Member States of the EC and EFTA', Comparative Report (vol 1) 2000, 62ff.

[128] CEN is an international non-for-profit association (AISBL), governed by Belgian law. CEN 'The Statutes of CEN', July 2018, available: ftp://ftp.cencenelec.eu/CEN/AboutUs/Governance/Statutes/Statutes_CEN-EN.pdf (accessed 20 September 2023). CENELEC is also an international non-for-profit association registered in Belgium. ETSI is a non-for-profit association registered in France, ETSI 'ETSI Directives', v 47 (2023), 91. ISO defines itself as a non-governmental organization established in Switzerland https://www.iso.org/about-us.html [accessed 20 September 2023]. IEC defines itself as a non-for-profit quasi-governmental organization headquartered in Switzerland. https://www.iec.ch/about/profile/ (accessed 20 September 2023). According to the Swiss Federation however both ISO and IEC are quasi-governmental organizations with tax agreements with the state. See Swiss Federation 'The 43 organizations and secretariats in Switzerland', November 2018, available: https://www.eda.admin.ch/dam/mission-onu-omc-aele-geneve/en/documents/Tableau-des-OI_EN.pdf (accessed 20 September 2023). The ITU is an intergovernmental organization subject to Swiss law. 'Accord entre le Conseil fédéral suisse et l'Union internationale des télécommunications pour régler le statut juridique de cette organization en Suisse', July 1971, available: https://www.admin.ch/opc/fr/classified-compilation/19710186/index.html (accessed 20 September 2023).

both their legitimacy and transparency in the standards development process, but also, potentially the diverse quality of the developed national standards and the possibility of *judicial review* thereof. In *Fra.bo* in which the Court despite acknowledging the private law nature of the Deutsche Vereinigung des Gas -und Wasserfaches (DVGW), and the absence of any link to the Member State's public administration,[129] held that the private entity had the power 'to regulate the entry into the German market of products'[130] underlines this argument. The ruling illustrates that private law bodies may still be subject to regulations—in a broad sense—addressed to states due to the effects of their activities (in the case of Fra.bo by virtue of DVGW's authority to certify the specific products), independently of the legal nature of the entity.[131] With regard to the ESOs, in the CJEU seminal *James Elliot* case, the Court ruled that it is competent to deliver a preliminary ruling under art 267 TFEU over a harmonized standard, even though the European Standardization Organizations that developed the standard are not EU bodies or agencies and were not set up to perform specific EU tasks.[132] The Court found that a harmonized standard adopted on the basis of EU harmonization legislation, published in the Official Journal of the European Union 'forms part of EU law'.[133] The Court found thathas jurisdiction to interpret acts that 'are by their nature measures implementing or applying an act of EU law'.[134] This interpretation was justified by the very objective of art 267 TFEU to ensure that the interpretation of all provisions forming part of the EU legal system does not vary depending on the interpretation accorded to them by the various Member States.[135]

[129] There was no public financing, no influence of the Member State over the standardization and certification activities of the DVWG Judgment of 12 July 2012, *Fra.bo SpA v. Deutsche Vereinigung des Gas und Wasserfaches eV (DVGW) –TechnischWissenschaftlicher Verein*, C-171/11, EU:C:2012:453. Also read among many: Schepel, Harm. 'Case C-171/11 Fra. bo SpA v Deutsche Vereinigung des Gas- und Wasserfaches.' *European Review of Contract Law,* (2013) 9:2, 186-192; van de Kooij AC, "The Private Effect of the Free Movement of Goods: Examining Private-Law Bodies Activities under the Scope of Article 34 of the Treaty of the Functioning of the European Union" (2013) 40 Legal Issues of Economic Integration, 363; van Leeuwen B, "From Status to Impact, and the Role of National Legislation: The Application of Article 34 TFEU to a Private Certification Organisation in Fra.Bo" (2013) 4 European Journal of Risk Regulation, 405; van Harten H, and Nauta T, 'Towards horizontal direct effect for the free movement of goods? Comment on Fra. Bo.' (2013) 5 European law review, 677; Schepel, Harm. 'The New Approach to The New Approach: The Juridification of Harmonized Standards in EU Law.' (2013) 20(4) Maastricht Journal of European and Comparative Law, 521–33; Heyvaert V, 'The Transnationalization of Law: Rethinking Law Through Transnational Environmental Regulation' (2017) 6 Transnational Environmental Law 205.

[130] Case C-171/11, para 31.

[131] Case C-171/11, para 24. The ruling has been criticized as risking to open up standardization to complaints by individual manufacturers and thus risking a system paralysis and failing to increase the procedural integrity of European standardization. Schepel, Harm (2013), 533.

[132] Case C-613/14, *James Elliot,* EU:C:2016:821.

[133] Case C-613/14 *James Elliot,* para 40.

[134] Case C-613/14 *James Elliot,* para 34.

[135] See analysisin Megi Medzmariashvilli 'A harmonised European (technical) Standard-Provision of EU law! (Judgment in C-613.14 James Elliott Construction', European Law Blog (January 2017). See discussion on the judicial reviewability of standards in Chapter 7 section 7.5 in this book.

3.3.4 Repeated or Continuous Application

The repeated or continuous application as a property of a standard and a component of its definition strikes as unusual. The WTO TBT Agreement also stipulates that a standard is meant for 'common and repeated use',[136] but similar references to the application or use of standards are not found in the definitions of a standard coming from standardization bodies. Tracking the application of standards is neither in the scope of the work of standardization bodies, nor can it be assessed at the time of drafting the standard. Thus, the'repeated or continuous application', can only reflect the goal of the standardization body to develop standards aimed to be used by a broader audience throughout time.[137] The most appropriate interpretation of the phrase would then be that standards are developed with the aim to be sustainable over time.[138]

3.4 The Concept of 'Technical Standard' in the US

The US has a decentralized, largely sector-specific and market-based standardization system. Standards are developed by private non-for-profit organizations, consortia, professional and industry associations,[139] which are in principle not funded by the US state. There is no centralized authority coordinating the standardization activity.[140] Nevertheless, federal government agencies participate in technical committees and follow the developments in the standardization work in the country. According to the National Technology Transfer and Advancement Act (NTTA), federal agencies may use technical standards 'as a means to carry out policy objectives or activities determined by the agencies and departments'.[141]

[136] WTO: Agreement on Technical Barriers to Trade (Uruguay Round Agreement), Annex 1: Terms and their Definitions for the Purpose of this Agreement.

[137] This approach is supported by the Opinion of the Advocate General Wathelet in the Case C-170/13 where the AG interprets the definition of art 2 Regulation 1025/2012 as aiming to 'ensure the broadest possible application of the standard'. Opinion of 20 November 2014, Case C-170-13 *Huawei Technologies* v *ZTE*, EU: C: 2014:2391, fn 3.

[138] In practice, standardization bodies decide whether to withdraw or maintain a standard as active in the market. The decision is usually made by the members of the standardization body. See for example the ISO Rules for systematic review of ISO standards: ISO 'Guidance on the Systematic Review process in ISO', May 2017, available: https://www.iso.org/files/live/sites/isoorg/files/store/en/Guidance_systematic_review.pdf (accessed 20 September 2023).

[139] Read in more detail on the US standardization system in: Kanevskaia Whitaker O, *The Law and Practice of Global ICT Standardization* (Cambridge University Press 2023), 105.

[140] Bremer ES, 'Government Use of Standards in the United States and Abroad' in Contreras JL (ed), *The Cambridge Handbook of Technical Standardization Law: Further Intersections of Public and Private Law* (CUP, 2019), 32.

[141] NTTA, Section 12 Standards Conformity, (d).

In practice, technical standards may not only be informally followed by an agency, but also incorporated in legislation by means of reference.[142]

Technical standards may be used by federal agencies only if they are developed or adopted by 'voluntary consensus standards bodies'. In fact, the Office of Management and Budget (OMB) Circular Act A-119, stipulates that federal agencies must in principle use the available private technical standards, unless it is inconsistent with the law or impractical. Consequently, assuming that SDO are interested to have a public regulator following their standards as a best practice, the NTTA indirectly determines to some extent two elements of the standardization process in those private SDOs. The process thus must be voluntary and consensus based.

Technical standards, according to s 12(d)(4) NTTA, are defined as 'performance-based or design-specific technical specifications and related management systems practices.' The revision however of the OMB Circular Act A-119 in 1996, enriched the definition of technical standards, stipulating that technical standards means

> (1) Common and repeated use of rules, conditions, guidelines or characteristics for products or related processes and production methods, and related management systems practices. (2) The definition of terms; classification of components; delineation of procedures; specification of dimensions, materials, performance, designs, or operations; measurement of quality and quantity in describing materials, processes, products, systems, services, or practices; test methods and sampling procedures; or descriptions of fit and measurements of size or strength.

This definition is admittedly closer to the one provided in the Standardization Regulation. Further, the Circular Act A-119 clarifies the concept of voluntary consensus standards bodies, which entail bodies that in their standardization process abide by the principles of openness, balance, due process, consensus and have an appeals process in place. Lastly, consensus does not mean unanimity, but general agreement, following a procedure where comments and objections are 'considered using fair, impartial, open, and transparent processes.'[143]

Unlike the EU, the US legislation does not prescribe recognized bodies competent to adopt or develop technical standards, as long as the requirements of the Circular Act A-119 are met. An important actor in the US standardization system is the National Institute for Standards and Technology (NIST), which next to its

[142] Sheffner DJ, 'Integrating Technical Standards into Federal Regulations: Incorporation by Reference' in Contreras JL (ed), *The Cambridge Handbook of Technical Standardization Law: Further Intersections of Public and Private Law*, (CUP 2019) 110. Read further: Rossi J, 'Dynamic Incorporation of Federal Law' (2016) 77(2) Ohio State Law Journal, 457. Read also Coglianse (2023) 17.

[143] Those principles incorporated in the Circular Act A-119 (art 2(c)v) are the implementation of the WTO principles. See Baron, Justus and others, 'Making the Rules: The Governance of Standard Development Organizations and their Policies on Intellectual Property Rights' [2019] JRC Science for Policy Report 47.

role in receiving reports by federal agencies when they opt to develop their own technical standards, has a broad portfolio of its own standards, including data protection, privacy, and cybersecurity.[144]

3.5 The Relationship of European to National and International Standards, Technical Specifications, and Other Private Regulation Instruments

3.5.1 European v National Standards and the Standstill Principle

The Standardization Regulation identifies four types of standards, international, European, national and harmonized standards. These are not mutually exclusive categories. An international standard may also be adopted as a European standard; a European standard is also adopted as a national standard in all the Member States. While the national, European, and international standards are determined with territorial criteria vis-à-vis the standardization body that develops those standards, the fourth category of harmonized standards is different. The category of harmonized standards is a sub-category of European standards in that they are developed by the ESOs. Harmonized standards are developed upon the request of the Commission on the basis of harmonization legislation. When developed on the basis of the New Approach, harmonized standards offer to the organization that adopts them a presumption of compliance with the legislation on which they are based.[145]

European and national standards may be developed in parallel on tantamount subject matters.[146] In the case of harmonized standards however, national standards need to be 'completely in line' with the published harmonized standard.[147] The Standardization Regulation addresses the issue of conflicting European and national standards by imposing a *standstill* duty to national standards,[148] which essentially requires the national standardization bodies to withdraw their conflicting national standards.[149] The rationale of this implicit prioritization of

[144] See https://www.nist.gov/cybersecurity [accessed 10 April 2024].

[145] Recital 5 Standardization Regulation. In the same vein, Van Leeuwen further identifies two more categories of European standards in parallel to the harmonized standards. The European standards mandated by the European Commission in support of a policy or legislation (outside the New Approach) and the European Standards developed at the request of one of the national standardization organizations. Van Leeuwen Barend, *European Standardization of Services and its Impact on Private Law: Paradoxes of Convergence* (Hart Publishing 2017), 45.

[146] As explained, harmonized standards are a sub-category of European standards, and are not therefore examined separately in this section that seeks to explore potential hierarchies among national, European, and international standards.

[147] Standardization Regulation art 3(6).

[148] Recital 14 Standardization Regulation.

[149] A standstill principle is often applied in areas of Union law in relation to national law on the basis of art 92 TFEU. Klamert M, *The principle of loyalty in EU law* (Oxford University Press 2014), 175ff.

European (harmonized) standards over national ones lies with the aim of harmonized standards to support EU legislation. Once a national standard is not in line with the harmonized standard that fleshes out the technical requirements of the EU harmonized legislation, the national standard is also most likely in conflict with the relevant harmonized law itself. Thereby, the Standardization Regulation aims at eliminating possible impediments to the harmonization of the Internal Market, by granting a superior status to harmonized standards in relation to national ones.[150]

In practice, an application similar to the standstill principle is imposed to national bodies by the ESOs for every national standard that competes with a European one. While not foreseen in the Regulation for the case of non-harmonized standards, this usual practice stems from the internal regulations of the ESOs, to which national SSOs adhere with the admission of their membership to the ESOs.[151] The standstill policy of CEN and CENELEC, according to their internal regulations, requires the national members not to take any action during the preparation of a European standard or after it is approved, which could prejudice the harmonization intended. In particular, national SSOs are not allowed to publish a new or revised national standard that is not completely in line with a European standard.[152] The standstill principle in the case of conflicting national standards with European ones, serves the purpose of preventing confusion in the market.[153] After a European standard is published, national standardization bodies—members of CEN and CENELEC, are obliged to implement the standard nationally and assign it the status of a national standard.[154] Thus, maintaining any nationally developed conflicting standard would lead to a scenario that a national standardization body would be offering contradictory standards within its

[150] The previous legal framework on standards, Directive 83/189 as amended by Directive 88/182 and Directive 94/10, already provided a standstill obligation for technical regulations for Member States that were subject to the obligation to notify the European Commission of draft technical Regulations. Read more on the legislative history of the notification obligation and standstill principle in Weatherill S, 'Compulsory Notification of Draft Technical Regulations: The Contribution of Directive 83/189 to the Management of the Internal Market' (1996) 16 Yearbook of European Law, 129. With regard to the effect of omission of a notification to the Commission, the CIA case of the Court was of paramount importance, since the Court ruled that a failure to notify a technical regulation leads to uneforceability of the regulation against third parties in proceedings before national courts. See Judgment of 30 April 1996, Case C-194/94 *CIA Security International SA v Signalson SA and Securitel SPRL*, ECLI:EU:C:1996:172.

[151] See CEN-CENELEC website: https://boss.cen.eu/reference%20material/guidancedoc/pages/standstill.aspx (accessed 20 September 2023).

[152] CEN—CENELEC, Internal Regulations Part 2: Common Rules for Standardization Work, July 2023, 24.

[153] CEN and CENELEC define a conflicting national standard as a 'national standard with the same scope as an EN (and Harmonization Document for CENELEC) including requirements'. ibid 9.

[154] National implementation is the 'process of giving a CEN-CENELEC Publication the status of a national publication, identical in technical content and presentation (except translation) either by publication of an identical text or by endorsement'. ibid.

national market. Similar standstill rules are imposed by ETSI to its standardization body members.[155]

3.5.2 European v International Standards

Although a large number of European technical standards is developed by ESOs, technical standards in the fields of ICT, quality management and information security management, are usually 'imported' into the Union from international standardization bodies.

International standards developed by ISO and IEC often address overlapping fields and subject matters with European standards. CEN and CENELEC have established a collaboration with ISO and IEC aiming to avoid duplication of standardization work. The bilateral agreements between the standardization organizations, known as Vienna and Frankfurt Agreements,[156] allow each organization to adopt available publications from the other organization. In practice, CEN and CENELEC are most often adopting international standards developed at ISO and IEC.[157] The adoption is done either after the development of the international standard, or in parallel via coordinated procedures at the international standardization body and the European counterpart.

In terms of prioritization between international and European standards, in principle there is no explicit hierarchy derived from the Standardization Regulation. International and European standards operate under different regimes, rules, and leadership, and the only overarching relationship is their bilateral agreements. Nevertheless, those bilateral agreements stipulate the 'primacy' of international standards.[158]

The primacy of international standards over European standards is expressed with several clauses in the Vienna Agreement for example, such as the transfer of standardization work from CEN to ISO as a preferred mode of operation.[159]

[155] ETSI, ETSI Directives, v 47, 30 June 2023, 28. See also in relation to Information Society Services: Directive (EU) 2015/1535 of the European Parliament and of the Council of 9 September 2015 laying down a procedure for the provision of information in the field of technical regulations and of rules on Information Society services, [2015] OJ L241/1.

[156] ISO CEN, Agreement on Technical Co-operation between ISO and CEN (Vienna Agreement), 2001, codified, v. 3.3. and Agreement on IEC—CENELEC Agreement on Common planning of new work and parallel voting (Frankfurt Agreement) (2016), which was preceded by the Dresden Agreement of 1996 and the Lugano Agreement of 1991.

[157] According to CEN and CENELEC, 33% out of all CEN publications (:thus including other deliverables apart from standards, such as technical reports and workshop agreements) is identical to ISO publications, while 72% out of all CENELEC publications is identical to IEC publications. CEN-CENELEC 'Quarterly Statistical Pack. 2018 Q3', available: ftp://ftp.cencenelec.eu/EN/AboutUs/InFigures/CEN-CENELEC%20Quarterly%20Statistical%20Pack%20-%202018%20Q3.pdf (accessed 20 September 2023).

[158] ISO CEN, Agreement on Technical Co-operation between ISO and CEN (Vienna Agreement), 2001, codified, v 3.3, cl 2, p 1.

[159] ibid v 3.3, cl 2 p 2.

On the other hand, the stated primacy of international standards is not absolute. CEN and ISO acknowledge that the work of the two organizations cannot always be aligned. This is due to the 'particular needs' and interests at European level for a development of a specific European standard, for which there is no international interest.[160]

The relationship of international and European standards, and the subsequent work of international and European standardization organizations is not straightforward, and varies depending on the standard under development and its underlying rationale. This ambiguity is heightened in the case of ETSI European standards and the international standards developed by ISO and IEC, as the organizations collaborate *ad hoc* on a need basis.[161]

Substantially different is the relationship of the international standards developed by the International Telecommunications Union—the third *recognized* standardization body, alongside the ISO and the IEC—and European standards. The ITU develops international standards, the ITU-T Recommendations, which focus on defining how telecommunications networks operate and work together.[162] The ESOs participate in the standards development process of ITU-T Recommendations.[163] In the case of CEN and CENELEC, the interaction between European standards and the ITU-T Recommendations is not formalized. ETSI has signed a Memorandum of Understanding with ITU, which foresees the exchange of information and mutual participation in meetings between the two standardization organizations.[164] Therefore, one cannot speak of any statutory or contractual agreed primacy of one or the other, even though in terms of relevance for the European policy and legislation, the European standards, especially the *mandated* ones, are likely to be more fit for purpose.[165]

[160] ibid v 3.3, cl 2, p 1.

[161] ISO for example has achieved the status of liaison with a number of ETSI Technical Committees, on the basis of which ISO makes a technical contribution and actively participates (liaison type C), makes contributions for issues dealt with by ISO Technical Committees (liaison type B) or follows the development of the standardization work at ETSI, without contributing (liaison type B).

[162] The ITU-T Recommendations are non-binding and can be incorporated in national legislation. The ITU also includes two more branches: the ITU Development Sector and the ITU Radiocommunication Sector, alongside with the ITU Telecommunications Standardization Sector (ITU-T). For the purposes of this book, the focus is only on ITU-T.

[163] ETSI for example contributes to the work of ITU: https://www.etsi.org/about/what-we-do/global-collaboration (accessed 20 September 2023).

[164] ITU ETSI, Memorandum of Understanding, July 2012.

[165] It is worth mentioning that ISO, IEC, and ITU have also established bilateral inter-institutional collaboration that involves not only exchange of information and modes of participation in technical committees, but also granting standard access to the technical committees of the other organizations. See for collaboration between IEC and ITU: Agreement for Mutual Cooperation and Exchange of Documentation between the International Telecommunication Union and the International Electrotechnical Commission. October 2005, and for ISO and ITU: Agreement for Mutual Cooperation and Exchange of Documentation between the International Telecommunication Union and the International Organization for Standardization, August 2005.

3.5.3 International Technical Specifications by Non-recognized Bodies and Commission Specifications

International standardization consortia and fora, not listed in the Standardization Regulation as recognized bodies, develop specifications that present several benefits to companies that conform to them (market-based standardization), as for example oftentimes they standardize advanced proprietary technologies.[166] Especially the ICT sector specifications are commonly developed by industry consortia, rather than the recognized standardization organizations.[167] In data protection, several technical specifications with practical and technical advice and guidelines have been published by organizations such as the W3C and the IEEE.

International technical specifications adopted by non-recognized consortia and fora do not hold an equivalent status to European standards.[168] Such specifications are not subject to the rules of the Standardization Regulation and developed without observation of the principles and obligations established thereof.[169] The use of such specifications for Union policy purposes is nonetheless possible under certain conditions. Member States or the Commission may identify ICT technical specifications for reference in public procurement,[170] as long as those specifications meet requirements regarding their added value (for example they enjoy market acceptance),[171] their relationship with European standards (for example they do not conflict with ESOs publications),[172] their development process, maintenance (openness, consensus, transparency, neutrality, and other requirements),[173] and their quality and relevance.[174]

Despite the narrow scope of this provision in the Standardization Regulation being limited to public procurement, technical specifications, as an alternative to European standards, is gaining a momentum in the past years. This development is encountered in vertical legislation such as the AI Act, which refers to the power of the Commission to develop common specifications in the form of an implementing act.[175] This power comes into play under certain conditions,

[166] See Egyedi TM, 'Beyond Consortia, Beyond Standardisation? New Case Material and Policy Threads–Final Report for the European Commission' (2001).

[167] ILNAS and ANEC, Standards analysis. ICT Sector, Luxembourg, v 3 (2014) 155ff. Read also: Pohlmann TC, 'The Evolution of ICT Standards Consortia' (2014) 95 Communications & Strategies, Quarter, 17.

[168] Recital 31 Standardization Regulation.

[169] Read further on the discussion about the applicability of different frameworks imposing rules on consortia and fora: Kanevskaia Whitaker O, 'Disciplining Standard-Setting: Which Approach to Choose (If Any)?' TILEC Discussion Paper No 2017-036.

[170] Standardization Regulation art 13.

[171] Annex II (1) Standardization Regulation.

[172] Annex II (2) Standardization Regulation.

[173] Annex II (3)(a–c) & (4)(a–c) (e) Standardization Regulation.

[174] Annex II (4)(d), (f) Standardization Regulation.

[175] AI Act art 41.

including when the available European harmonized standards do not address fundamental rights concerns.[176]

3.5.4 Certification: Demonstrating Conformity to Standards

Certification is a third party attestation that a product, process, system or service conforms to a set of pre-determined requirements.[177] The attestation is provided by an independent third party, the certification body, which is tasked in assessing and evaluating the object of certification, be it product, process, system, or service. Usually, an organization applies for certification to a certification body voluntarily, unless mandatory certification is prescribed by law. The successful evaluation by the certification body leads to the awarding of the certification. This may be demonstrated with a certificate, a seal or a mark. Certification is broadly used in several domains such as information security, consumer goods, occupational health, and safety.[178]

The link of certification to standardization is twofold. First, standards serve as a basis for the assessment of the certification object. A certification body for example may use as a basis for the assessment of an information security system a technical standard, such as the ISO/IEC 27001.[179] The latter specifies requirements for 'establishing, implementing, maintaining and continually improving an information security management system within the context of the organization'. The certification body in this case uses the ISO/IEC 27001 to assess whether the information system under review provides sufficient information security safeguards. It is not necessary however that certification uses standards (or only standards) as a basis for evaluation. Legislation or other norms may also offer such substantive requirements or criteria. In addition, conformity to standards needs not necessarily be verified by a certification body. One should think of conformity to a standard as an internal activity of an organization implementing a set of controls and measures, while certification mainly aims at demonstrating to others (consumers, business partners, state, or other) that an organization has implemented those controls and safeguards, and offering some additional impact.[180]

The second link of standards to certification relates to the organization of the conformity assessment activity. Commonly, the assessment and evaluation

[176] AI Act art 41(a)(iii).

[177] ISO/IEC 17000: 2004—Conformity assessment vocabulary and general principles.

[178] Kamara I and De Hert P, 'Data Protection Certification in the EU: Possibilities, Actors and Building Blocks in a Reformed Landscape' in Rodrigues R and Papakonstantinou E (eds), *Privacy and Data Protection Seals* (TMC Asser Press 2018).

[179] ISO/IEC 27001:2013 Information technology—Security techniques—Information security management systems—Requirements.

[180] van Leeuwen Barend, *European Standardization of Services and its Impact on Private Law. Paradoxes of Convergence* (Hart Publishing, 2017) 203.

process of certification also conform to technical standards. These technical standards unlike the ones discussed earlier (eg information security standard) do not provide substantial requirements, but procedural requirements. They prescribe methods for assessment of results, requirements for complaints mechanisms, use of certificates and marks, personnel of the certification body requirements, and others. An example is the international standard ISO/IEC 17067, which provides a list of principles and requirements regarding certification of products, such as when a product is not conforming, handling of fraudulent claims of certification, outsourcing of the conformity assessment activities.[181]

3.5.5 Accreditation: 'Certifying the Certifiers'

Accreditation is aimed at ensuring that conformity assessment bodies, such as certification bodies, are suitable to perform conformity assessment activities.[182] In the Union, accreditation[183] is regulated by the Regulation 765/2008 (Accreditation Regulation), which aims at defining an overall framework of rules and principles and enhancing the operation of the substantive rules, already existing in national legislation.[184] The Accreditation Regulation establishes one competent non-for-profit National Accreditation Body (NAB) per Member State, tasked to perform competence assessments of conformity assessment bodies, when requested.[185] The role of the NAB is to ensure that the certification bodies, including those offering certification to harmonized standards, are independent and carry out assessments in an appropriate manner.[186] Thus, an accreditation by a NAB offers guarantees on the reliability of the certification process, and in turn conformity to standards.

There is both a direct and an indirect relation of standardization to accreditation. The direct link, similarly to certification, is that conformity standards often form the basis of and facilitate the accreditation process. The ISO/IEC 17021-1 international standard for example provides a set of requirements for bodies

[181] ISO/IEC 17067:2013 Conformity assessment—Fundamentals of product certification and guidelines for product certification schemes.

[182] Rodrigues R and others, 'The Future of Privacy Certification in Europe: An Exploration of Options Under Article 42 of the GDPR' International Review of Law, Computers & Technology, (2016) 30(3), 248–70.

[183] Regulation 765/2008 art 2(10) (Accreditation Regulation) defines accreditation as 'an attestation by a national accreditation body that a conformity assessment body meets the requirements set by harmonised standards and, where applicable, any additional requirements including those set out in relevant sectoral schemes, to carry out a specific conformity assessment activity'.

[184] Recital 3 Accreditation Regulation.

[185] Accreditation Regulation art 5(1).

[186] Accreditation Regulation art 8(10) specifies the open legal standard 'in an appropriate manner' meaning that 'unnecessary burdens are not imposed on undertakings and that due account is taken of the size of an undertaking, the sector in which it operates, its structure, the degree of complexity of the product technology in question and the mass or serial nature of the production process'.

providing audit and certification of management systems.[187] NABs can use this standard, together with any additional requirements necessary, to assess whether a certification body is competent to provide certification of management systems services. At the same time, specific international conformity assessment standards are designed and used for the peer evaluations of the NABs themselves.[188]

The second and indirect link of standardization and accreditation lies in an extra layer of reliability of accredited products. According to the Report on the implementation of the EU Accreditation Regulation, the accreditation process checking the technical capacity of conformity assessment bodies ensures reliable results in the conformity to standards assessment.[189] In practice, an accredited certification body is less prone to fraudulent practices such as issuing certification to standards without proper evaluation due to oversight by NAB. There is therefore a loose interconnection between the accredited conformity assessment body providing certification services and the reliability of the conformity to a standard.

3.5.6 Codes of Conduct

Codes of conduct or codes of practice are codified behavioural rules, drafted usually by an organization, a group of organizations, or a trade association. The aim of codes of conduct is self-organization, with rules of behaviour tailored to the needs of the organization, group of organizations—for example within the same sector– or the members of the trade association. Codes of conduct emerge where there is no applicable state-imposed regulation on a specific matter, or where there is need for specification of legal obligations in a sector or within a given organization.[190]

A 2001 study[191] conducted by the OECD found that labour issues, environmental stewardship, consumer protection, alongside the provision of information

[187] ISO/IEC 17021-1: 2015: Conformity assessment—Requirements for bodies providing audit and certification of management systems—Part 1: Requirements.

[188] Accreditation Regulation art 2(16) defines peer evaluation as 'a process for the assessment of a national accreditation body by other national accreditation bodies, carried out in accordance with the requirements of this Regulation, and, where applicable, additional sectoral technical specification'. An example of such a standard is the ISO/IEC 17011: 2017 international standards which provides requirements for accreditation bodies accrediting conformity assessment bodies.

[189] European Commission, Report from the Commission to the European Parliament, the Council and the European Economic and Social Committee on the implementation of Regulation (EC) No 765/2008 of the European Parliament and of the Council of 9 July 2008 setting out the requirements for accreditation and market surveillance relating to the marketing of products and repealing Regulation (EEC) No 339/93, COM (2017) 789 final, 2.

[190] There has been criticism that organizations, usually large global corporations, draft or adhere to codes of conduct in an effort to avoid regulation, namely to prevent the need for new state regulation in a given field. See among many: Jenkins R, 'Corporate Codes of Conduct: Self-Regulation in a Global Economy' United Nations Research Institute for Social Development, Paper Number 2 (2001).

[191] OECD 'Codes of Corporate Conduct: Expanded Review of their Contents', OECD Working Papers on International Investment, 2001/06, (2001) OECD Publishing, 8ff.

on the products and services, and protection of consumers' personal information.[192] The themes of codes of conduct therefore vary, mainly due to the absence of an overarching framework imposing specific content. Oftentimes however regional or national legislation refers to codes of conduct or assigns some sort of legal effect. In those cases, minimum content requirements such as aim, supervision mechanism, and sanctions are promulgated by the relevant law.[193]

Codes of conduct can be standardized, when for example they have proven to bring added value to the adhering organization (standardization of existing code of conduct) or when there is a new industry or consumer need to be addressed with a standardized code of conduct (development of a new code of conduct in the framework of a standardization process). A prominent example of such a Code of Conduct is the international standard ISO/IEC 27018, which aims at guiding public cloud computing service providers in addressing specific organizational and compliance risks.[194] The Code provides a 'high-level framework for the protection of personal information within information and communication technology systems'[195] and prescribes a set of issues to be addressed by an organization that processes personal information in the framework of implementing an information management system.[196] This example shows that standards and codes of conduct are different instruments, but not mutually exclusive. Codes of conduct can be adopted as formal standards and, in this manner, be vested with the effects of both instruments.

3.6 Synthesis

The growth of standardization over the years from a purely technical activity towards less or non-technical fields pushed standards in the agenda of the EU public regulator. Data protection appears in policy documents as a standardization area, alongside other areas, in the policy documents prepared in the drafting of the Standardization Regulation.

[192] ibid 15.

[193] This is the case the Codes of Conduct in Regulation 679/2016 in GDPR arts 40 and 41. Kamara I, 'Article 40 Commentary' in Kuner C, Bygrave LA, and Docksey C (eds), *The EU General Data Protection Regulation (GDPR): A Commentary* (OUP 2020); Kamara I,'Article 41 Commentary' in Kuner C, Bygrave LA, and Docksey C (eds), *The EU General Data Protection Regulation (GDPR): A Commentary* (OUP 2020).

[194] De Hert P, Papakonstantinou V, and Kamara I, 'The Cloud Computing Standard ISO/IEC 27018 through the Lens of the EU Legislation on Data Protection' (2016) 32 Computer Law & Security Review, 16 (hereafter De Hert and others, 'The cloud computing standard'), 16. See ISO/IEC 27018:2019 Information technology—Security techniques—Code of practice for protection of personally identifiable information (PII) in public clouds acting as PII processors.

[195] ISO/IEC 27018: 2019 Introduction.

[196] The standard refers to personally identifiable information (PII). De Hert and others, 'The Cloud Computing Standard' (n 194).

The concept of 'standard' is defined broadly in the Standardization Regulation in that it includes products, processes, services, or systems in any field within the competence of the Union legislator. Yet, the scope of the concept is constrained by the actors that develop and publish standards, that is 'recognized standardization bodies'. The Standardization Regulation acknowledges few national, European, and international bodies that adopt standards in the sense of the Regulation, excluding in this manner a broad variety of standardization consortia. Further, standards are voluntary. Conformity to a standard should be a non-compulsory decision of an organization. Nevertheless, practice shows that standards may be of a binding nature *de facto*, when the conditions are such that organizations do not essentially have a real alternative choice, as CJEU case law demonstrates. Similarly to the EU, US law speaks of voluntariness and consensus in standardization bodies and their decision-making processes. However, the entities that develop and adopt technical standards are not pre-determined in US law, and thus not as limited as the 'recognized bodies' in EU law.

Lastly, the variety of layers of adoption of standards at national, European, and international level, has pushed both the standardization organizations via inter-institutional bilateral agreements and European legislature in the form of the Standardization Regulation to establish hierarchy rules such as the standstill principle and the supremacy of international standards over European ones.

4
Incorporation of Technical Standards in Legal Orders

4.1 Incorporating Standards and Technical Specifications in a Legal Order: An Exploration of Theoretical Foundations of Standardization

4.1.1 Standardization as a Normative Ordering

Legal pluralism argues that 'non-state normative systems often co-exist with state law, sometimes competing with state law for authority over citizens'.[1] Pluralists do not necessarily acknowledge the dominance of state law in setting norms in a regulatory space or more generally a socio-political space. The argument made is that there are different sets of overlapping assertions in a given regulatory space. When defining this regulatory space as broadly as the global arena, the overlapping assertions may vary from state v state, state v international body, state v non-state entity.[2] In the EU, one can identify the Union law v Member States laws,[3] but also other forms of non-state law 'systems' co-existing with the state rule-settings.[4] Having as a starting point the reaction against legal monoism—primarily the state law—and the denunciation of the nationalization of laws,[5] legal pluralism draws a different narrative by acknowledging the different normative orderings and exploring possible interactions among those orderings. Legal pluralism offers a framework to explore their interactions, or more precisely—as Engle Merry explains—to 'delineate the dialectic mutually constitutive relation between state law and other

[1] Davies M 'Legal Pluralism' in Cane P and Kritzer H (eds), *The Oxford Handbook of Empirical Legal Research*, (OUP Oxford 2010) (hereafter Davies, 'Legal pluralism').

[2] Berman PS, 'The Evolution of Global Legal Pluralism' (2017) 42 GWU Law School Public Law Research Paper (hereafter Berman, 'The Evolution of Global Legal Pluralism').

[3] Depending on the pluralist theory adopted, Barber outlines two readings of the relationship of the Union legal order with the German legal order: the radical pluralist approach treats the two orders as distinct legal systems with their own rules of recognition, while the global pluralist approach posits one legal system with domestic legal orders as subsets contained in it. Barber NW, 'Legal Pluralism and the European Union' (2006) 12 European Law Journal, 306.

[4] Mak refers to the case law of the CJEU and private regulation such as contracting, self-regulation and co-regulation, including rule-making through standardization. Vanessa, Mak 'Pluralism in European Private Law' in *Cambridge Yearbook of European Legal Studies* 20 (2018): 202-232 (hereafter Mak, 'Pluralism in European Private Law').

[5] Michaels R, 'Global Legal Pluralism' (2009) 5 Annual Review of Law and Social Science, 244.

Standardizing Personal Data Protection. Irene Kamara, Oxford University Press. © Irene Kamara 2025.
DOI: 10.1093/9780191997037.003.0004

normative orders'.[6] Griffiths, one of the fathers of legal pluralism, emphasized the elements of normative heterogeneity and autonomy:

> *Legal pluralism refers to the normative heterogeneity attendant upon the fact that social action always takes place in a context of multiple, overlapping 'semi-autonomous social fields,' which it may be added, is in practice dynamic condition.*[7]

Although there are variations to the legal pluralist theories, there are arguably two main strands of legal pluralism, namely the one stemming from colonialism, and the ordinary or 'new' legal pluralism identified in any society.[8] The latter, which is relevant for this book, conceptualizes the complex and interactive relationship between official and unofficial forms of ordering. According to Engle Merry, this strand of legal pluralism instead of considering the influences between two separate entities, views 'plural forms of ordering as participating in the same social field'.[9] Before turning to the discussion on the types of interactions in more detail and the relationship of state law with other forms of ordering, it is important to make a few more observations, beginning with an explanation of when pluralism exists, by asking three main questions:

1. Is it plural?[10]
2. Is it an order or ordering?
3. Is it law?

Starting from the first question, plurality does not refer to the plural elements of the state law, be it on different levels (Member-State, Union, federal) or fields of law (criminal law, property law, contract law, other), as those levels are sub-sections of a single system.[11] As Davies asserts 'pluralism means, broadly speaking, that there is more than one classification, system, type, mode or form of law within a particular space'.[12] The frame of reference to determine what is pluralistic and what is not, is often considered in the context of the different systems themselves or a given territory. It has also been suggested that the frame of reference is the regulatee,[13] or

[6] Engle Merry S, 'Legal Pluralism' (1988) 22 Law & Society Review, 880 (hereafter Merry, 'Legal pluralism').

[7] Griffiths J, 'What Is Legal Pluralism?' (1986) 18 The Journal of Legal Pluralism and Unofficial Law, 1 (hereafter Griffiths, 'What is legal pluralism'), 38.

[8] Engle Merry, 'Legal pluralism' (n 6). For analysis of the strands see also Davies, 'Legal pluralism' (n 1).

[9] Engle Merry, 'Legal pluralism' (n 6), 873.

[10] As opposed to legal pluralism, legal diversity refers to special rules and procedures applicable to different types of transactions, or behaviours etc. See Griffiths, 'What is legal pluralism' (n 7),11.

[11] Davies, 'Legal pluralism' (n 1), 10.

[12] Davies, 'Legal pluralism' (n 1), 13.

[13] In the context of colonialism, Tamanaha explains that from the standpoint of the authority aiming at consolidating its legal rules, legal pluralism was a 'flaw to be rectified'. For the regulatees subject to legal pluralism however, it was a potential source of uncertainty, but also a possibility of 'resort to

else the subject of the rule(s)[14]. In this book, the regulated field, serves as the point of reference with a focus in the EU, to argue that standardization is a pluralistic approach to the Union primary and secondary data protection law. This perspective dually determines, both in terms of territory and subject matter, the approach followed in the book and narrows down the broad area of potentially co-existing discourses.

With regard to the second question on whether a specific form is an order (or ordering), it should be noted that the aim of the question is to distinguish any spontaneous form of social behaviour from a pluralist approach. Any form of ordering suffices, not necessarily a 'system'. Ordering implies a degree of organization, but which does not need to be comprehensive to the degree of a 'system'. Melissaris proposes a loose understanding of order (or else: institutionalization) in the form of legal discourses, which however still instigate some degree of commitment by the participating parties.[15] Many pluralists also attribute the element of autonomy, or at least semi-autonomy to a legal ordering,[16] meaning that the ordering or sphere is capable of generating rules and customs internally, but is also vulnerable to rules of other orderings, such as for example, state law. Davies argues that the element of semi-autonomy is useful also for determining the self-identity of the ordering, and its interconnectedness with other spheres.[17] Typical examples are the body of *lex mercatoria,* and indigenous law, which are considered to be enjoying a degree of autonomy to state law, but are not completely autonomous from it.

The third question ('is it law?') has been at the centre of debate about legal pluralism. One of the main criticisms against legal pluralism is the lack of a solid definition of the concept of *law*. Some pluralists adopt an over-expansive approach to what is law by concluding that law covers a continuum from state law to the 'vaguest forms of social control'.[18] This in turn leads to overly broad conceptualizations of law to the extent that everything may be considered as law. Another approach is an empirical one: Berman argues that pluralists should de-emphasize distinctions between norms, customs, law, and moral commands and focus instead on whether people in practice perceive such legal or quasi-legal commands to be binding and how these commands affect behaviours over time.[19] While this empirical approach

alternative legal regimes'. Tamanaha B Z, 'Understanding legal pluralism: past to present, local to global' (2008) 30 Sydney Law Review, 375 (hereafter Tamanaha, 'Understanding legal pluralism'), 385.

[14] Vanderlinden J, 'Return to Legal Pluralism: Twenty years later' (1989) 28 The Journal of Legal Pluralism and Unofficial Law, 149.

[15] Melissaris E, 'The More the Merrier? A New Take on Legal Pluralism' (2004) 13 Social & Legal Studies 57 (hereafter Melissaris, 'The more the merrier'), 74.

[16] Engle Merry, 'Legal pluralism' (n 6). According to Davies, Engle Merry coined the term 'semi-autonomous social field'.

[17] Davies, 'Legal pluralism' (n 1), 9.

[18] Woodman GR, 'Ideological Combat and Social Observation' (1998) 30 The Journal of Legal Pluralism and Unofficial Law, 21. Read further on the several approaches to defining 'law' in legal pluralism Tamanaha, 'Understanding legal pluralism' (n 13), 375ff.

[19] Berman, 'The Evolution of Global Legal Pluralism' (n 2), 154.

is not adopted by all pluralists, there is an agreement that it is not the task of legal pluralism theories to define law as a concept. More specifically, while there is pressure on pluralists to explain what they define as law, and in particular why non-state orderings should be considered as law, some pluralists reverse the question asking 'why not?'.[20] They argue that it is not possible to reach a common definition applicable to all expressions of legal pluralism—ranging from indigenous rules to private regulation and market codes of conduct—and that ultimately it is not necessary to construct a conception of law to frame legal pluralism.[21] The common element of the varying manifestations of law is that they share a claim to represent a legitimate normative authority,[22] but may not share other common characteristics, thus a conceptualization of 'law' would again lead to over-inclusive or overly limiting results.[23]

To further address the criticism, scholars have explored different conceptualizations of the underlying ideas of pluralism, such as normative pluralism, moving away the discussion in this manner from the dichotomy between law and non-law.[24] Although pluralists prefer referring to *legal* pluralism, as law implies a mandatory form of ordering,[25] many post-modern scholars avoid using 'law', reserving the term for *state law*, and use instead terms such as 'rule-generating fields' or normative orders (or orderings).[26] According to Twining, normative pluralism has the advantage that it can be applied to a variety of situations, such as institutionalized normative orders, discrete sets or systems of norms (such as the US Constitution), and looser aggregations of norms.[27]

In this book, since pluralism is used as the theoretical framework, the aim is to neither define what is law, nor make an argument that standards should be considered as law. It is true however that concepts such as standards may involve an element of normativity. Standardization generates rules and may imply a form of ordering, which despite not qualifying as law,[28] cannot be reduced either to merely executing Union law in all occasions.[29] Therefore, despite some conceptual weaknesses, pluralism still serves its purpose as a theoretical and analytical framework

20 Davies, 'Legal pluralism' (n 1), 16.

21 Tamanaha, 'Understanding legal pluralism' (n 13), 396.

22 Ibid.

23 For a critical overview of the different legal pluralism approaches read: Melissaris, 'The more the merrier' (n 15).

24 Other terms but with different meaning are regulatory pluralism and value pluralism.

25 Davies, 'Legal pluralism' (n 1), 16.

26 Moore for example refers to 'semi-autonomous social field'. Moore SF, 'Legal Pluralism as Omnium Gatherum' (2014) 10 FIU Law Review, 5.

27 Twining W, 'Normative and legal pluralism: a global perspective.' (2010) 20 Duke Journal of Comparative & International Law 473 (hereafter Twining, 'Normative and legal pluralism').

28 For the purposes of the book, unless specifically indicated otherwise or combined with another attribute ('soft', 'custom') by *law* is meant official 'state' legal institutions, including primary and secondary Union law. For binding and non-binding EU acts the term 'public regulation' is used.

29 The question of competition for prioritization is also not relevant, as the Union law has priority over other forms of normativity for the purposes of this book.

for this study.[30] In that sense, in the remaining part of the book, legal pluralism means plurality in terms of norms and orderings. The aim is to continue using pluralism as a framework, without interfering with the debate on conceptualization of law for the purposes of legal pluralism. In other words, the moderate working hypothesis that standardization is a sort of normative ordering suffices for the purposes of this book.

4.1.2 Standardization and Normativity: Implicit, Not Omni-present Relationship

Standards are often treated as a set of norms. The normative power of standards can be identified in several forms.[31] Certain standards are developed to specify how general legal rules apply to specific industry sectors.[32] Other standards with a normative character are standards aiming at shaping and regulating behaviour within an organization, independently of the existence of legal rules. In such cases, standards set rules on how actors should behave and prescribe policies, requirements, and methods to achieve the intended goal of each standard. Discussing the New Approach framework of standardization, Schepel has argued that 'standardization necessarily involves "political judgment" however carefully circumscribed the legal guidelines are'.[33] Standardization, according to Schepel, is not merely focused on technology—since law and technology do not occupy 'clearly separate spheres'–but 'involves normative value judgments that affect life and limb'.[34]

The normativity argument cannot however be generalized for all standards. Standardization bodies also develop standards of a solely technical nature, with a functional purpose to provide technical characteristics and methods.[35]

[30] As Tamanaha notes scholars who invoke legal pluralism need to be aware of the conceptual problem and its implications. Especially, for those that 'study legal pluralism as a social phenomenon, a useful caution is in order. One must avoid falling into either of two opposite errors: the first error is to think that state law matters above all else (as legal scholars sometimes assume); the second error is to think that other legal or normative systems are parallel to state law (as sociologists and anthropologists sometimes assume). In each social arena, particular official legal systems and normative systems must be examined on their own terms to see what their relations with other normative systems are, to observe their respective capacities to exert power, and to see how they are being utilised or responded to by individuals and groups'. Tamanaha, 'Understanding legal pluralism') (n 13), 410ff.

[31] Read also Teubner's view that comparable 'legal phenomena' such as corporate codes of conduct of multinational companies display normativity that does not remain in the realm of social norms, but may take on legal character under conditions. Teubner G, 'The corporate codes of multinationals: Company constitutions beyond corporate governance and co-determination' in Nickel R, *Conflict of Laws and Laws of Conflict in Europe and Beyond: Patterns of Supranational and Transnational Juridification* (Intersentia Uitgevers 2010).

[32] Mak, 'Pluralism in European Private Law' (n 4), 202.

[33] Schepel H, *The Constitution of Private Governance: Product Standards in the Regulation of Integrating Markets* (Hart Publishing 2005), 255–256.

[34] ibid.

[35] The ETSI European Standard on electromagnetic compatibility for example provides among others models for testing types of transmitters and methods of measuring conditions, parameters, and

Standards of a purely technical nature are usually encountered in areas of standardization that traditionally existed since the foundation of the standardization bodies. Modern fields dealing with emerging and new technologies also are in need of and often develop purely technical standards. Standards aimed at making devices interoperable, which in essence provide a catalogue of technical requirements cannot, in principle, be classified as normative rules in the sense discussed above. In some cases, even such technical standards however embed norms. The normative power of such otherwise purely technical standards can be extracted from the *purpose* of the standard as a whole, and its relative position in a market or policy area, and not by its particular provisions, which at first sight are prescribing technical specifications. An example is toy safety standardization. Toy safety belongs to the broader regulatory category of product safety, but due to its characteristic targeted user group being children, is subject to stricter legal requirements. In the Union, toy safety is regulated with secondary legislation, namely the Toy Safety Directive,[36] which mandates the specification of technical characteristics on how to construct safe toys to the ESO. Following the Toy Safety Directive, several European Standards have been developed such as the EN 71-1:2014 + A1:2018, which prescribes properties for safe toys. While at first sight, this standard would qualify as purely technical as it provides requirements for mechanical and physical properties of toys, one can identify normative elements in such a standard: the determination of what should be considered as a 'safe toy', the interpretation of the meaning of open legal standards of the Directive such as '*manufactured in such a way as to meet hygiene and cleanliness requirements in order to avoid any risk of infection, sickness or contamination*'[37] or the specification of what constitutes '*intended for use by*' according to the Toy Safety Directive[38] are elements that project normativity. Most importantly, by specifying and interpreting the above elements, the standard contributes to the formulation of –or at least influences–the toy safety policy in the Union and the manufacturers' behaviour in relation to their legal obligations.

Besides the quest for normativity in standards as such, there are other factors pointing to the direction of standardization being not a mere technical (non-normative) activity. The first factor is the type of actors participating in

limits of the tested devices. This standard has no normative elements. ETSI EN 302 537-1 V1.1.2 (2007-12), Electromagnetic compatibility and Radio Spectrum Matters (ERM); Short Range Devices (SRD); Ultra Low Power Medical Data Service Systems operating in the frequency range 401 MHz to 402 MHz and 405 MHz to 406 MHz; Part 1: Technical characteristics and test methods.

[36] The Directive has been amended by Commission's Directive 2012/7/EU, Commission's Regulation (EU) 681/2013, Commission's Directive 2014/79/EU, Commission's Directive 2014/81/EU, Commission's Directive 2014/84/EU.

[37] Annex II, Directive 2009/48/EC, as amended.

[38] Toy Safety Directive art 3(29) defines the term 'intended for use by' as meaning 'that a parent or supervisor shall reasonably be able to assume by virtue of the functions, dimensions and characteristics of a toy that it is intended for use by children of the stated age group'.

standards-development. Apart from industry, societal interests are often represented in the standard making process. Consumer and environmental associations are eager to participate in the development of standards. Organizations such as the Environmental Coalition on Standards (ECOS), which is a partner organization of the ESOs, funded by the EU to defend environmental interests in the standard-making process, show that standardization activity goes well beyond mere cataloguing of technical requirements. Mak has shown that the involvement of different 'lawmaking' actors, such as the EU legislature, the CJEU, national courts, and standard-setting organizations in the development of harmonized standards, plays a role in the substantive quality of the norms.[39] In fact, Mak argues that standardization in areas such as consumer law, despite being embedded in public governance gives expression to norms, albeit those developed by private actors'.[40]

Another factor pointing at standardization as a norm-making activity relates to the establishment of procedural safeguards. Standardization bodies or the public regulators often establish procedural safeguards for specific types of standards. Safeguards may concern the quality of standards, the procedural legitimacy and the representation of interests, or other issues. Returning to the previous example of toy safety standards, the Toy Safety Directive establishes a right granted to the Member States and the European Commission to formally object to a standard published on the basis of the Directive.[41] As Joerges and others describe from a political science viewpoint 'standardization is –public and private—"governance; it can neither be reduced to the application of legal rules and principles nor to a purely technocratic exercise but requires political decisions over normative issues and economic interests; and it is for exactly this reason that standardization needs legitimacy.'[42]

Beyond the issue of whether and when standards and standardization in general channel normativity, it is necessary to explore whether (and when) standardization qualifies as a normative *ordering*, which is discussed in the following section.

4.1.3 Types of Normative Orderings and Standardization

Different normative orderings do not possess the same distinctive characteristics. However, non-exhaustive groupings of normative orderings for the purpose of studying those systems and their interactions in-depth are possible. Tamanaha

[39] Mak, 'Pluralism in European Private Law' (n 4), 173.
[40] Mak, 'Pluralism in European Private Law' (n 4), 173.
[41] Directive 2009/48/EC art 14. The right to object in the case of toy safety is established when the standard does not entirely satisfy the requirements set out in the Directive. See also Chapter 7 in this book.
[42] Joerges C, Schepel H and Vos E, 'The law's problems with the involvement of non-governmental actors in Europe's legislative processes: the case of standardisation under the 'new approach', Working Paper, EUI LAW, 1999/09 (1999).

proposed a framework of systems of normative ordering, which helps identify underlying rationales of standardization as a normative ordering.[43] Among Tamanaha's groupings, there are three categories relevant for this analysis.[44]

The first is the official or positive legal system. The positive legal system is linked to institutions and enforcement mechanisms, and gives rise to powers, rights, agreements and sanctions. The second grouping is the market imperative normative systems. Those systems (or orderings) range from informal norms that govern business communities to private law-making such as codes of conduct, transnational commercial norms, and arbitration institutions.[45] The third category is the functional normative systems, which are organized for the pursuit of a particular function, purpose or activity that goes beyond purely commercial pursuits.[46] The functional normative systems possess a degree of autonomy, self-governance and internal ordering mechanisms, according to Tamanaha, and they interact with the official legal systems that belong to the first category. While functional normative systems may also have commercial aspects, economic goals are not decisive to shape their nature and characteristics, as opposed to the market imperative normative systems.[47]

Standardization is connected to the market rationale in the Union, and may also at times be characterized as a functional normative system, when pursuing goals such as environmental protection or data protection. As per the market rationale, multiple policy initiatives alongside the Union legal framework on standardization broadly appeal to the use of standards as a means of achieving the goals of the Single Market. In a global setting, standardization facilitates trade,[48] and has been studied as affecting economic growth and innovation.[49] Thus, the connection of

[43] Tamanaha explains that the use of the term 'social arena' signifies a given area of study. Tamanaha, 'Understanding legal pluralism') (n 13), 397 fn 79.

[44] Other categories identified were the customary, indigenous, and religious normative systems, as well as the community and cultural systems. Tamanaha, 'Understanding legal pluralism') (n 13), 397.

[45] Tamanaha names this category as economic/capitalist normative systems. I choose the moderate term market imperative (also used by Tamanaha for the same category), to disentangle any political connotations accompanying the term 'capitalist' system, which are out of the scope of this book Tamanaha, 'Understanding legal pluralism' (n 13), 398.

[46] Twining, discussing normative pluralism, similarly identifies different groupings (although admittedly less elaborate categories). Twining distinguishes between the institutionalized normative orders (such as the WTO) and other constellations of discrete sets of norms (such as a constitution) or looser aggregations. Twining, 'Normative and legal pluralism' (n 27), 478. It should be noted here that by the term *norms* Twining means rules that are 'normative', in the sense that they can be expressed as mandatory (ought to), permissive (may) or power conferring (can). In turn, the term rule signifies 'empirical generalisations, practices and customs and logical types of general prescription'.

[47] Tamanaha, 'Understanding legal pluralism') (n 13), 399. Tamanaha describes universities and the Internet as a network as examples of functionally oriented normative systems.

[48] Büthe T and Mattli W, 'Standards for Global Markets: Domestic and International Institutions' in Enderlein H, Wälti S, Zürn Michael (eds) *Handbook on Multi-level Governance* (Edward Elgar Publishing 2010), 455.

[49] For an overview of relevant studies on the economic goals and impacts of standardization, see Blind K, 'The impact of standardization and standards on innovation: compendium of evidence on the effectiveness of innovation policy intervention' Nesta Working Paper No. 13/15, Manchester Institute of Innovation Research, Manchester, UK (2013).

standardization to the market imperative normative systems is straightforward. Standardization may also work as a functional normative system, thus serving goals beyond commercial pursuits.

An example is the goal of European (harmonized) standards to harmonize technical rules across Member States. Harmonization is seen by the European regulator as an essential goal of standardization, which is one of the reasons that the Standardization Regulation is based on art 114 TFEU on approximation of laws.[50] Another example is the public safety goals pursued with the development of specific technical standards in the Union and elsewhere along with the collaboration of private standardization organizations and the regulator.[51]

Other goals or functions cannot be *prima facie* excluded, as would be the case by accepting only a market imperative goal of standardization, which is one of the hypotheses to be explored in this book. What one should keep from the discussion on standardization in relation to Tamanaha's framework is that private or semi-public rule-making in the Union in the form of standards fit in one or more categories/ groupings of normative orderings identified in the legal pluralism discourse. This both confirms to some extent the argument that standardization can be approached as a normative ordering, but also provides information on the underlying rationales and roles of standards as norms.

4.1.4 Normativity and Autonomy in the Development of Standards

Pluralists identify the element of *autonomy* or *semi-autonomy* as a qualifying characteristic of a normative ordering. Autonomy in this context implies that an ordering or sphere is capable of generating rules and customs internally, but also vulnerable to rules of other orderings, such as, state law. Arguably, standardization enjoys at least a degree of semi-autonomy in the sense of being capable of self-governing without relying on the state (operational autonomy).[52] International standardization bodies are subject to the local rules of the jurisdiction of their establishment, but other than that they are self-governed, generally bound by internal rules of operation and conduct.[53] The ISO and the IEC are self-regulated

[50] Regulation 1025/2012 (Standardization Regulation). See Chapter 3 section 3.3 in this book.

[51] Those standards are developed in a broad range of topics such as critical infrastructures, crisis management, and health. See European Commission, The 2024 annual Union work programme for European standardization, Commission notice, C/2024/1364, OJ 15.2.2024.

[52] See in the same vein Schiek who uses autonomy not as a term referring to individuals sustaining themselves in isolation, 'but rather denotes that persons are not governed externally'. Schiek, Dagmar, 'Private rule-making and European governance-issues of legitimacy' European Law Review 32, no 4 (2007), 443.

[53] Scholarship relates the self-imposed principles and procedures aiming at increasing accountability of international standardization bodies to Global Administrative Law (GAL). Read Lindahl H, *Authority and the Globalisation of Inclusion and Exclusion* (CUP, 2018), 377. Read further on GAL: Kingsbury B, Krisch N, and Stewart R B, 'The emergence of global administrative law.' (2005) 68 Law and contemporary problems, 15.

by their ISO/IEC Directives, which set out rules for the organizational structure, responsibilities for the technical work, and development of international standards.[54] The ISO/IEC Directives also establish appeals procedures against the decisions of Technical Committees developing ISO/IEC standards and decisions of the technical management board.[55] Other international standardization bodies, such as the ITU have similar *modus operandi*, with self-imposed sets of rules and structures, including provision for internal and external audits, rules of procedure for its organs dealing with issues of organization, responsibilities, documentation, voting and others, as well as staff regulations.[56] The ITU in particular, as a specialized agency of the United Nations, is additionally subject to rules imposed by the internal regulations of the UN.[57]

The ESOs enjoy a (lesser) degree of autonomy, when it comes to their activity, stakeholders, and procedures. One should more accurately speak of semi-autonomy, rather than autonomy, as there is an established Union legal framework in line with which the European Standardization Organizations operate in relation to European standards supporting Union policies and legislation.[58] The European legislation on standardization frames and formalizes the interaction of standardization as a normative ordering within the legal order of the European Union. The element of semi-autonomy is manifested in several provisions of the Regulation itself that acknowledge the freedom of the standardization bodies to accept or reject a request from the European Commission to develop standards,[59] to decide on the topics of future standards[60] with the simultaneous obligation however to establish a work programme identifying the topics of future standards and make it publicly available,[61] the obligation to only encourage and facilitate stakeholder participation instead of imposing stricter representation requirements.[62]

Studying the International Organization for Standardization, Lindahl goes beyond the element of autonomy, and identifies normative *authority* in (international) standardization bodies. He argues that organizations such as the ISO

[54] ISO/IEC Directives Pt 1 and Consolidated ISO Supplement, v01/2024, 2024, ISO/IEC Directives Pt 2, 9th ed, 2021.

[55] ibid v01/2024 s 4. Other rules regarding the structure and work of ISO are established in the ISO Code of Ethics and Conduct and a number of Annexes in the ISO/IEC Directives. International Organization for Standardization, ISO Code of Ethics and Conduct for the technical work, 2023.

[56] See ITU website https://www.itu.int/en/council/Pages/documents.aspx [accessed 15 April 2024).

[57] Although the ITU was founded before the UN, it entered in an agreement with the UN in 1949 to operate under the umbrella of the UN, as a specialized agency. Specialized agencies of the UN are autonomous organizations, but their work is coordinated by the Chief Executives Board for Coordination (CEB).

[58] See Chapter 3 in this book on Standardization Regulation.

[59] Standardization Regulation art 10(2).

[60] Standardization Regulation art 10(2).

[61] Standardization Regulation art 3(3).

[62] Standardization Regulation art 5.

prove to be emergent normative orders, that 'refuse accommodation on either side of the divide between state and international law'.[63] Lindahl explains:

> [...] *The emergence of normative orders that are diversely qualified as 'trans-national', 'post-national', or 'denationalised', can no longer be described in terms of the canonical features of the state – namely, the exercise of exclusive power over the population within a bounded territory. These orders pose a challenge to the assumption that for there to be a legal order, at least in the full-fledged sense of the term, each of the traditional elements that is associated with statehood must be present: power that is both normative and enforceable [...]. As to the first element, the notion of soft law calls into question the assumption that the enforceability of normative power is a constitutive feature of legal orders. As to the second element, we are witness to the 'unbundling' of the normative power, such that emergent orders may claim to regulating domains of behaviour that had previously been under the aegis of state power.*[64] [emphasis added]

Despite therefore not fitting in the traditional perception of legal or normative ordering as conceived in relation to state law, in the sense of the power to enforce the norms it produces,[65] standardization bodies such as the ISO derive their power from other elements.[66] Lindahl argues that for example the authority of international standards depends on mechanisms that ensure a rich normative discussion about the purposes of standardization in the framework of ISO, especially since ISO claims to posit standards on behalf of the international community.[67]

Other types of normative authority—and to some extent regulatory power—have been attributed to standardization bodies by Lerner and Tirole, who identify, for example, three main functions of standard-setting bodies; the discovery function, which relates to learning about, and certifying the value of, various combinations of functionalities;[68] the standardization function, which relates to steering

[63] Lindahl H, 'ISO standards and Authoritative Collective Action,' in Delimatsis P (ed), *The Law, Economics and Politics of International Standardisation* (CUP, 2015), 43 (hereafter Lindahl, 'ISO standards').

[64] ibid.

[65] Standardization organizations do not have enforcement powers vis-à-vis the standards they produce, but they have the power to enforce their internal rules to their members.

[66] An interesting point made by Hans Lindahl is that the activity international standardization bodies is often interpreted as 'technical' (in fact the author claims there is a bias in favour of a technical interpretation of standardization), while substantive normative and political issues are also dealt within the diverse organs and committees of ISO. The technical element is emphasized by the standardization bodies themselves, as for example their statutes name the ISO organs as 'Technical Board', 'technical committee' and so on, even though their actual work might be decision-making on affected interests by the development of an international standard. See Lindahl, 'ISO standards' (n 63), 52.

[67] Lindahl, 'ISO standards' (n 63). 52. Lindahl also brings the example of how international standards are forming the basis for internal regulation of Members States in the context of the World Trade Organization's Agreement on Technical Barriers to Trade to demonstrate his argument on the normative authority of ISO. WTO Agreement on Technical Barriers to Trade art 2.4.

[68] Lerner J and Tirole J, 'Standard-Essential Patents' (2015) 123 Journal of Political Economy, 547.

market expectations towards a specific technology, and third, the regulation function. The regulation function is exercised in order to diffuse the benefits of standardization function[69] to different actors. When for example standard-setting organizations require patent-owners covered by the standard to grant licences on fair, reasonable, and non-discriminatory terms are exercising such a regulatory function. Cafaggi suggested that private standards aim at changing the *status quo*, by improving conditions for their regulatees in areas such as safety and environment.[70] The regulatory power and normative authority of standardization bodies is primarily directed and impacts organizations (and individuals) that participate in the development process and conform to standards. In parallel, the authority of standardization bodies indirectly impacts third parties, that are confronted with applied standards.[71] Therefore, regarding standardization as a semi-autonomous normative ordering demands re-exploring the relationship of standardization with other normative orderings that co-exist in the same regulatory space, and the state law in particular.[72]

The relationship of state law and non-state normative orderings might manifest in different ways, varying from uncoordinated to overlapping.[73] Swenson identified four archetypes of the state law—non-state norms interaction, namely combative (or conflicting), competitive, cooperative, and complementary.[74] While those archetypes are neither exhaustive nor absolute, they represent well the discussion in the literature on the relationship of state and non-state systems, help conceptualize the core features of the relationship and offer the first steps for developing an analytical framework for the discussion in this book. Similar distinctions are found in Transnational Private Regulation scholarship, such as the one proposed by Cafaggi on competive, coordination, collaborative, and hybridization.[75] Those conceptualizations offer insights into the exploration of the interaction of standardization and the Union vis-à-vis a regulated field, the field of data protection.

Combative relationships exist when non-state actors reject the state's ideological foundations, while *competitive* relationships imply collusion or tensions, but the

[69] Delimatsis P, 'Introduction: Continuity and change in international standardisation' in Delimatsis P (ed), *The Law, Economics and Politics of International Standardisation* (CUP 2015).

[70] Cafaggi F, 'The Many Features of Transnational Private Rule-Making: Unexplored Relationships between Custom, Jura Mercatorum and Gloval Private Regulation' (2015) 36 U. Pa. J. Int'l L., 875 (hereafter Cafaggi 'The Many Features of Transnational Private Rule-Making').

[71] ibid 932; Winn illustrates the regulatory effect of ICT standards over human behaviour Winn JK, 'Technical Standards as Data Protection Regulation' in Gutwirth S and others (eds), *Reinventing Data Protection?* (Springer 2009) (hereafter Winn, 'Technical Standards as Data Protection Regulation').

[72] In this section, Union law is also more broadly referred to as 'state law' in line with the legal pluralism literature.

[73] Tamanaha, 'Understanding legal pluralism' (n 13), 375.

[74] Swenson G, 'Legal Pluralism in Theory and Practice' (2018) 20 International Studies Review, 438 (hereafter Swenson, 'Legal Pluralism').

[75] Cafaggi F, 'New foundations of transnational private regulation.' (2011) 38 Journal of law and society, 20.

clashes do not endanger the state's authority.[76] The other two categories concern situations where the state law and non-state ordering have accepted each other's normative legitimacy.[77] In the case of *cooperative* relationships, the non-state normative system and the state legal system cooperate for shared goals, and any clashes concern the goals, and not each other's existence.[78] *Complementary* relationships take cooperation one step further, by illustrating how from a regulation perspective the state has 'outsourced' decision-making or procedures to non-state normative systems.[79] In this case, the non-state normative system is subordinated and structured by the state system.[80] An example is private arbitration and mediation that often constitute a *sine qua non* requirement to access state courts for civil law disputes.[81] The form of the interaction depends on a number of variables, such as the nature of the pluralistic systems (industrialized, globalized or other) and individual conditions such as the maturity of the legal system.

In mature legal orders, as the European Union, a collaborative or complementary relationship is more likely to develop between the Union's law and other normative orderings.[82] However, in line with the ordered legal pluralism approach adopted in this book, if standards are to play a role supporting EU data protection law, the normativity and the authority of the non-state ordering needs to be afforded by the formal legal order, that is the Union law. In other words, for the collaboration or complementarity to work, the non-state normative system would need to be *recognized* by the 'state' legal order. Such (external) recognition often comes in the form of law.[83] In the case of standardization, the Standardization Regulation functions as a general recognition rule for standardization. While being a Union law, the Regulation acknowledges the existence and significance of standardization, and establishes rules for cooperation among the standardization organizations, and the establishment of European standards and others. The scope of the Regulation is focused on the technical standards that can support Union legislation and policies,[84] concerning thus not only European standards,

[76] Swenson, 'Legal Pluralism' (n 74), 445.

[77] Swenson, 'Legal Pluralism' (n 74), 444.

[78] Swenson, 'Legal Pluralism' (n 74), 444.

[79] In Transnational Private Regulation scholarship, Caffaggi has named this type *vertical* complementarity. Cafaggi F,. 'A comparative analysis of transnational private regulation: legitimacy, quality, effectiveness and enforcement' *Quality, Effectiveness and Enforcement* (2014), 75.

[80] Swenson, 'Legal Pluralism' (n 74), 445.

[81] Swenson, 'Legal Pluralism' (n 74), 445f.

[82] Cafaggi 'The Many Features of Transnational Private Rule-Making' (n 70), 881 and 892.

[83] Read: Scott C, Cafaggi F and Senden L, 'The Conceptual and Constitutional Challenge of Transnational Private Regulation' (2011) 38 Journal of Law and Society, 1

[84] Regulation 1025/2012 art 1 provides: 'This Regulation establishes rules with regard to the cooperation between European standardization organizations, national standardization bodies, Member States and the Commission, the establishment of European standards and European standardization deliverables for products and for services in support of Union legislation and policies, the identification of ICT technical specifications eligible for referencing, the financing of European standardization and stakeholder participation in European standardization.'

but also international standards[85] developed outside the Union from private non-state actors.[86] Therefore, Union law not only recognizes standards, but also regulates them.

4.1.5 Functions of Standardization in Relation to Law

4.1.5.1 Post-law, pre-law, and para-law functions of standardization

Standardization may have a regulatory function in relation to legislation, when engaged to fulfil goals with societal impact.[87] The existence of a law and the stage of the law's maturity can be useful variables to distinguish among the different functions of standards in relation to legislation.

In 2017, in a case concerning the judicial review of a Commission Recommendation, AG Bobek found:

> [...] on the general level, in view of the changing legislative landscape of (not only) EU law, which is marked by a proliferation of various soft law instruments, access to the EU courts should be adapted in order to respond to those developments. In this sense, and as far as the theoretical pun permits, the approach should indeed become somewhat more Dworkinian, recognising the fact that *there are norms generating significant legal effects that find themselves beyond the binary logic of binding/non-binding legal rules.*[88] [emphasis added]

[85] For example, there are references to international standards (art 2) and to ICT technical specifications (arts 13, 14, Annex II) Regulation 1025/2012.

[86] The Standardization Regulation is not the only example of recognition of norms developed by non-state actors. The Unfair Contract Commercial Practices Directive (UCCP) provides such a recognition rule for deontological codes of conduct. The Directive, which is adopted without prejudice to 'the deontological codes of conduct or other specific rules governing regulated professions', provides that private actors ie deontological code owners, may conduct controls to identify unfair commercial practices. The Directive therefore acknowledges the role of deontological codes of conduct in governing the profession of traders, without intervening in establishing rules for those codes of conduct. In this manner, the legislator links the non-law mechanism of codes of conduct with the enforcement system based on the legal rules Both the Standardization Regulation and the UCCP Directive offer two examples of recognition of rules of non-law norms that co-exist with the formal legal system, the Union law. Article 10 reads, 'This Directive does not exclude the control, which Member States may encourage, of unfair commercial practices by code owners and recourse to such bodies by the persons or organizations referred to in Article 11 if proceedings before such bodies are in addition to the court or administrative proceedings referred to in that Article. Recourse to such control bodies shall never be deemed the equivalent of foregoing a means of judicial or administrative recourse as provided for in Article 11.' Directive 2005/29/EC.

[87] Private regulation instruments are often studied as fulfilling objectives of public nature e.g. to protect consumers. See, among many, Cafaggi F and Watt HM (eds), *The Regulatory Function of European Private Law* (Edward Elgar Publishing 2009)

[88] Opinion of Advocate General Bobek 12 December 2017 Case C-16/16 P, *Kingdom of Belgium* v *European Commission*, EU:C:2017:959, para 4.

In the same Opinion, AG Bobek characterized 'soft law instruments' as a type of imperfect norm, on the one hand sharing a '*normative ambition of inducing compliance on the part of their addressees. On the other hand, no instruments of direct coercion are attached to them. Usually adopted in the wake of a process of consultation with the different stakeholders (a bottom-up approach), they may contain "mild obligations" or "robust exhortations"*'.[89]

Standards are often referred to as private regulation instruments with soft law effects or self-regulation with effects that are not enforceable by ordinary legal mechanisms. Indeed, standards in principle do not have binding force, but they do have practical effects. As with soft law, standards may have legal effects, when they have a *de facto* binding nature, as seen in Chapter 3.

One prominent distinction, that will be used for organizing possible functions of standards in this book, is the pre-law, post-law, and para-law functions. The distinction, proposed by Senden and others, using the existence of law as distinctive criterion to categorize the functions in relation to law is useful,[90] in that it offers an analytical tool to further explore the potential functions of standards in relation to data protection law and their different roles within those functions. The functions of standardization on a given application field should be distinguished between where there is absence of state law and where state law on a regulatory field exists.[91] In the case of absence of state law, standardization has a *para-law* function.[92] It provides rules exactly because state law is absent in a field where some sort of regulation is deemed necessary by actors active in that field. Instead of a *regulatory* vacuum, non-law approaches are adopted by the actors and parties affected.[93] In other words, to refer to the normative pluralism discussion, a normative ordering may set rules, since there is no rule-making in the regulatory space by the legal order.[94] This *legal* vacuum, covered by self-regulation instruments, may be unintentional or intentional. Unintentional would be due to, for example, vast technological developments, such as in the field of quantum computing, where the legislator assesses the need for specific policy or legislation, while standardization

[89] ibid, paragraph 86.

[90] One of the recommendations of Senden was that soft law instruments should be linked to one particular function and not perform multiple functions (Senden L, *Soft Law in European Community Law* (Hart Publishing 2004), 499.

[91] For the simplicity of the argument and due to the scope of the book, I refer only to standardization and Union or state law. There might be other normative orders that influence the regulation of a topic/issue/behaviour in a given regulatory space.

[92] Thürer D, 'The Role of Soft Law in the Actual Process of European Integration' in Jacot Guillarmod O (ed), *L'avenir du libre-échange en Europe: vers un Espace économique européen* (Sculthess Zürich 1990), 133, Senden L, *Soft Law in European Community Law* (Hart Publishing 2004) (hereafter Senden, 'Soft law'), 119.

[93] Creutz K, 'Law versus Codes of Conduct: between convergence and conflict' in Klabbers J and Piiparinen T (eds), *Normative Pluralism and International Law* (Cambridge University Press 2013).

[94] A relevant discussion is the case that the legal order intentionally leaves space for self-regulation to regulate an issue. Read further: Braithwaite J, 'Enforced Self-Regulation: A New Strategy for Corporate Crime Control' (1982) 80 Michigan Law Review, 1466.

bodies are ahead in setting rules in the area.[95] Intentional would be encountered in jurisdictions that traditionally favour self-regulation within boundaries permitted by a legal framework, such as common law countries, or when the legislator deems instruments alternative to legislation as more effective.

Standards may pre-empt state law in a field, by advancing existing policies or orienting the agenda for the legislation to be adopted. Standards then perform a *pre-law* function, afforded by the normative nature of standardization and its ability to articulate norms before the actual legislative process takes place.[96] Senden identifies both a procedural and a substantive aspect in the pre-law function.[97] The procedural aspect refers to the adoption of a non-legal instrument with a view to the preparation of future Union legislation and policy. This function in the case of standardization is admittedly not common in the Union; legislative initiatives formally emerge from the European Commission,[98] and in any case the formal institutions of the Union[99] and do not include the intentional engagement of standardization for the purpose of preparing legislation and policy. However, the substantive aspect of the pre-law function is more relevant for standardization.

The substantive aspect refers to the indirect preparation of the conditions for the acceptance of a future policy or law. The development and use of technical standards in a field where there is no specific legislation at Union level invokes, gradually, an increased basis of support for rule-making in the field,[100] and often, the specific rules included in those technical standards. The pre-emptive function here lies with shaping the range of conceivable and acceptable solutions for the future.[101] As AG Bobek vividly described it 'in this way, the soft law of today becomes the hard law of tomorrow'.[102] In this vein, Hustinx, a former European Data Protection Supervisor, has explained that self-regulation such as codes of conduct, can be used as a means 'to experiment and to prepare for legislation in a flexible

[95] See for example the new ISO/IEC committee, ISO/IEC JTC 3, Quantum technologies, https://www.iso.org/news/new-joint-committee-quantum-technologies [accessed 20 August 2024].

[96] Opinion of Advocate General Bobek, Case C-16/16 P, *Kingdom of Belgium v European Commission*, EU:C:2017:959, para 95. The Opinion refers to soft law instruments in general, not standardization as such.

[97] Senden, 'Soft law' (n 92), 119.

[98] TFEU art 17(2) provides, 'Union legislative acts may only be adopted on the basis of a Commission proposal, except where the Treaties provide otherwise. Other acts shall be adopted on the basis of a Commission proposal where the Treaties so provide.'

[99] TFEU art 225, 'The European Parliament may, acting by a majority of its component Members, request the Commission to submit any appropriate proposal on matters on which it considers that a Union act is required for the purpose of implementing the Treaties. If the Commission does not submit a proposal, it shall inform the European Parliament of the reasons'.

[100] Mifsud Bonnici provides the example of access to content on the Internet, which was regulated by a standardized 'notice and take down' system, devised by the Internet Service Providers, before the EU e-Commerce Directive was put in place. Bonnici JPM, *Self-Regulation in Cyberspace* (TMC Asser Press 2008). (hereafter Mifsud Bonnici, 'Self-regulation in cyberspace'), 51.

[101] Opinion of Advocate General Bobek, Case C-16/16 P, *Kingdom of Belgium* v *European Commission*, EU:C:2017:959, para 95.

[102] ibid, para 95.

way'.[103] One such–admittedly rare–example in EU data protection legislation is an ICT specification on Internet tracking, which has influenced the EU legislator on how to formulate a legal obligation for the design of software.[104]

If there is interaction between the normative ordering and the legal order—thus, the relationship is collaborative or complementary—standardization may have a *post-law* function. Eijlander has explained that in the Union, co-regulation entails that the rules are laid down in the law and the co-regulation's function is to provide mechanisms of the general legal rules.[105] A post-law function is in general fulfilled when non-legal instruments, such as private regulation, are used to supplement or support Union law,[106] by facilitating, for example, the correct interpretation,[107] and its uniform application,[108] effecting the further implementation of the legislation,[109] or assisting with the enforcement of the Union law.[110] Standardization has indeed been used in the Union in several ways. The New Approach model belongs to this category, since the essential requirements of the legislation are substantiated via voluntary European standards.[111] Another post-law function of standardization is the determination of the state-of-the-art in technological and technical spheres.[112] Standards are used to calibrate what is considered as satisfactory in terms of technical or technological sophistication, that cannot be pre-determined in a legislative act. A prominent example is provided by the field of information security and cybersecurity.[113] Another example at national level is the state of scientific and technical knowledge in the framework of civil liability legislation.[114]

The post-law function of standardization can therefore appear in a range of forms. Post-law includes the possibility of standardization providing rules independently of the state law. This would be the case for example with international standardization bodies that do not seek to influence regional legislation, or interact with it in any manner. This could lead to a combative or competitive relationship between standardization as a normative ordering and the legal order.

[103] Hustinx P 'The role of self-regulation in the scheme of data protection' 13th Conference of Data Protection Commissioners, Strasbourg 1991, http://www.alfred-buellesbach.de/PDF/27_Hustinx.pdf [accessed 20 September 2023].

[104] See Chapter 8 section 8.4 in this book.

[105] Eijlander P., 'Possibilities and constraints in the use of self-regulation and co-regulation in legislative policy: Experiences in the Netherlands-Lessons to be learned for the EU?' European Journal of Comparative Law 9, 1 (2005), 7.

[106] Senden, 'Soft law' (n 92), 120.

[107] Senden, 'Soft law' (n 92), 120.

[108] Senden, 'Soft law' (n 92), 120.

[109] Senden, 'Soft law' (n 92), 120.

[110] Bonnici JPM, 'Self-regulation in cyberspace' (n 100), 52.

[111] Schepel H, and Falke J, 'Legal Aspects of Standardisation in the Member States of the EC and EFTA' (2000) vol 1, Office for official publications of the European communities (hereafter Schepel and Falke, 'Legal aspects of Standardization'), 200

[112] ibid, 200.

[113] NIS2 on standardization art 25.

[114] Schepel and Falke, 'Legal aspects of Standardization' (n 111), 203ff.

The focus of the book is primarily on post-law functions of standardization in the field of personal data protection in the Union, due to the challenges in the application of data protection law. Besides, given the existence of the data protection legal framework, a para-law function is not applicable in the Union vis-à-vis data protection in the EU.

4.1.5.2 Functions of private regulation: the case of personal data protection

The functions of standards identified in data protection related literature can be grouped in three broad categories: First is clarity and interpretation of the law, second is implementation and compliance, and third is technology-triggered functions and uses. Next to the three post-law functions, a pre-law function is also identified in the literature.

First, as regards clarity and interpretation, Dumortier and Goemans[115] explain that general data protection standards may be used to define basic principles, such as consent and accountability. In the same vein, Kosta and Stuurman argue that concepts used but not defined in the data protection law may be clarified by the use of standards. Hirsch, goes one step further, suggesting that private regulation instruments in data protection invite a dialogue between industry and courts or other public authorities, and thus shape knowledge about the underlying data protection law.[116]

Second, with regard to implementation and compliance, Papakonstantinou suggests that private regulation instruments help with the efficient application of the data protection law and enforcement, providing a benchmark for authorities.[117] An auditing function of standards in support of data protection law has been flagged also by Kosta and Stuurman.[118] Most recently, from the perspective of the regulatees and the supervisory authorities, Lachaud identifies mainly two roles of the private regulation instrument of certification. One, as an enforcement tool of principles of the data protection law, but without real teeth, due to its voluntary character.[119] Second, the author explored certification as a consistency tool

[115] Dumortier J, Goemans C, 'Data Privacy and Standardization. Discussion paper prepared for the CEN/ISSS Open Seminar on Data Protection', (2000) (hereafter Dumortier and Goemans, 'Data privacy and standardization').

[116] Hirsch D, 'Going Dutch: Collaborative Dutch Privacy Regulation and the Lessons It Holds for US Privacy Law' (2013) Mich. St. L. Review 83.

[117] Papakonstantinou researched codes of conduct and privacy professionals. Despite pinpointing at several critical weaknesses of the studied instruments especially under the previous data protection regime and national data protection laws, the author identified several functions. Papakonstantinou V,. *Self-regulation and the Protection of Privacy* (Nomos-Verlag-Ges. 2002) (hereafter Papakonstantinou, 'Self-regulation').

[118] Kosta E and Stuurman K, 'Technical Standards and the Draft General Data Protection Regulation,' in Delimatsis P (ed), *The Law, Economics and Politics of International Standardisation* (CUP 2015) (hereafter Kosta and Stuurman, 'Technical standards and the draft general data protection regulation').

[119] Lachaud EMT, *What could be the contribution of certification to data protection regulation?* (Doctoral dissertation, Tilburg University, 2019) 27.

by assessing the case of certification of data protection officers (DPO) and the integration of competences thereof in DPO certifications.[120] In relation to standards for data protection certification, Lachaud argues that those play an auxiliary role by providing auditable requirements.[121]

In fact, the role of standards in compliance and accountability is a recurring theme. Some authors have written about the role of private regulation instruments in accountability of organizations that voluntarily follow them, going beyond the expected minimum legal standard of compliance.[122] This is a point also made by Hustinx, who argues that private regulation instruments can 'provide solutions beyond the scope of existing legislation'.[123] Goemans and Dumortier explain standards may provide operational guidelines to those who seek compliance with EU data protection law and help them assess the organizational impact of compliance with data protection law.[124] Christofi and others view standards as a source of guidance that may help 'operationalise vague concepts' and 'bridge the gap between principles and their application'.[125] Another function relates to standardized tools to support 'specific data protection tasks', such as the communication of privacy practices by organizations to individuals.

In terms of responsibility and liability, Koops and others identify an opportunity for establishment of liability of entities using private regulation instruments, since those publicly claim that individuals may rely depend on 'a certain level of privacy or consumer protection.'[126] A similar proposal is made by Papakonstantinou, who finds an evidentiary value of private regulation instruments, however without autonomous legal force.[127]

Goemans and Dumortier also argue that sector specific standards such as in healthcare or electronic commerce, may be designed to deal with sector specific challenges in applying data protection principles. In fact, the GDPR, and its predecessor the Data Protection Directive, have been characterized as *omnibus regimes*, in that they apply to both public and private actors, are sector neutral, and enforced by specialized independent regulatory entities.[128] Focusing on sector

[120] ibid, 27

[121] ibid, 40.

[122] Centre for Information Policy Leadership, Organizational Accountability—Past, Present and Future, White paper (30 October 2019).

[123] Hustinx P, 'Co-regulation or self-regulation by public and private bodies – the case of data protection' [2002] Freundesgabe Büllesbach, 283 (hereafter Hustinx, 'Co-regulation'). https://autoriteitpersoonsgegevens.nl/sites/default/files/downloads/artikelen/art_phu_2002_coregulation.pdf [accessed 20 September 2023].

[124] Dumortier and Goemans, 'Data privacy and standardization' (n 115).

[125] Christofi A and others, 'Erosion by Standardisation: Is ISO/IEC 29134: 2017 on Privacy Impact Assessment Up to (GDPR) Standard?' in Gupta M (ed), *Advances in Information Security, Privacy, and Ethics* (IGI Global 2020), 140ff.

[126] Koops B-J, Lips M, Nouwt S, Prins C, and Schellekens M, 'Should self-regulation be the starting point? Starting points for ICT regulation: Deconstructing prevalent policy one-liners' in Koops B-J, Lips M, Prins C, and Schellekens M (eds), *Starting Points for ICT Regulation* (T.M.C. Asser Press 2006).

[127] Papakonstantinou, 'Self-regulation' (n 117).

[128] Lynskey O, *The Foundations of EU Data Protection Law* (OUP 2015), 15ff.

neutrality, the GDPR rules are not specified vertically, that is by sector.[129] Koops has criticized the omnibus nature of Union data protection law, in that both the Data Protection Directive and the GDPR are difficult to apply in practice since they necessitate *inter alia* to be 'translated' into 'workable, sector-specific, and context-specific rules and practices'.[130] Koops argued that the regulatory disconnection between data protection law and data processing in practice should not be 'more-of-the-same law'.[131] The GDPR connects its *omnibus* nature and private regulation instruments for sector and application with specific answers. For example, codes of conduct are suggested to 'contribute to the proper application' of the GDPR, 'taking account of the specific features of the various processing sectors and the specific needs of micro, small and medium-sized enterprise'.[132] Besides, private regulation offers a platform for consensus building,[133] in parallel with specifying the application of rules to sectors.[134]

Those considerations on possible regulatory disconnection and the need for specification of rules are more evident, when considering, for example, the implications of applying the sector-neutral rules of the GDPR to consumer-oriented IoT. The WP29 had flagged that the multitude of entities processing personal data in a smart home with personal assistants, for example, raise issues on how the distribution of responsibility should take place and the duties be complied with.[135] Issues concern the quality of consent, the application of the data processing principles, the non-obtrusive nature of IoT devices,[136] the exercise of data subjects' rights and others. While sector-specific legislation is an option for the regulator, the slow pace of the legislative procedures, as manifested with the ePrivacy legislation reform, in combination with fast paced technology, points often at soft law measures, not as an alternative to sector-specific laws, but for as long as those do not exist.

Supervisory authorities are often issuing guidance to cover the need for particularization. However, other means for guidance on the application of rules in sectors or certain situations, which can be more specific and developed bottom up with high expertise are private regulation measures. Codes of conduct in the GDPR are a prominent example. The law encourages the drafting of codes of

[129] A relevant exception– for this book—to the sector-neutral character of the data protection rules is introduced with the ePrivacy legislation, which applies in the telecommunications sector. This was also highlighted by Simitis. Simitis S, 'Reconsidering the premises of labour law: Prolegomena to an EU regulation on the protection of employees' personal data.' (1999) 5 European Law Journal, 53.

[130] Koops B-J, 'The Trouble with European Data Protection Law' (2014) 4 International Data Privacy Law, 256ff. (hereafter Koops, 'The trouble with European data protection law').

[131] ibid, 256.

[132] GDPR art 40.

[133] Koops, 'The trouble with European data protection law' (n 130), 259.

[134] Edwards Land Veale M, 'Slave to the algorithm: Why a right to an explanation is probably not the remedy you are looking for' Duke L. & Tech. Rev. 16 (2017): 18.

[135] Article 29 Data Protection Working Party 'Opinion 8/2014 on Recent Developments on the Internet of Things' (2014).

[136] ibid.

conduct, which take into account 'specific characteristics of the processing carried out in certain sectors'.[137] While private regulation instruments cannot and should not replace data protection legislation, the absence of sector-specific rules creates some regulatory room for such instruments.[138]

Third, technology-triggered functions imply that the technology relevance of a provision is a strong component. One example is standardized 'privacy-enabling technologies' for providing anonymity.[139] In a similar vein, Tamó-Larrieux has, for example, identified security, anonymity, autonomy, and transparency as technical areas where technical tools, including standards, are necessary to protect 'privacy'.[140] One of such areas, as proposed by Jakobi and others is the provision of information to online users about processing and the design of software agents to facilitate the provision of valid consent.[141] In relation to privacy enhancing technologies, it was proposed that the standardization of such technologies made them accessible to a broader range of companies.[142] Hustinx has also suggested that private regulation instruments offer solutions in relation to various technological challenges that put pressure on the scope and boundaries of the law and its capacity to regulate them.[143]

Lastly, some authors, including Papakonstantinou, acknowledged that due to their flexibility and intense negotiations among stakeholders, private regulation instruments may create conditions of acceptance for data protection laws (thus a pre-law function).[144] Also, private regulation instruments may serve to standardize processing of personal information in fields in which regulatory intervention is not suitable. In that case, private regulation instruments provide a set of minimum legal standards for a sector or a field. A meta-function has to do with the use of standards supporting data protection in public procurement and, thereby promotes compliance with legal requirements.[145]

To sum up, the reviewed literature points at mainly post-law functions of private regulation instruments and standards in particular, as shown in Table 4.1. Those functions relate to efforts to tame the (often intentional) vagueness of data protection law and specify its application in relation to different sectors and technologies

[137] Recital 98 GDPR.

[138] This is also evident from the sectorial nature of the majority of codes of conduct, which have been approved by supervisory authorities under the GDPR. See the EDPB repository: https://www.edpb.europa.eu/our-work-tools/accountability-tools/register-codes-conduct-amendments-and-extensions-art-4011_en [accessed 10 August 2024].

[139] Dumortier and Goemans, 'Data privacy and standardization' (n 115).

[140] Tamò-Larrieux A, *Designing for Privacy and Its Legal Framework: Data Protection by Design and Default for the Internet of Things* (Springer 2018).

[141] Jakobi T and others, 'Web Tracking Under the New Data Protection Law: Design Potentials at the Intersection of Jurisprudence and HCI' (2020) 19 i-com, 31.

[142] Winn, 'Technical Standards as Data Protection Regulation' (n 71).

[143] Hustinx, 'Co-regulation' (n 123).

[144] Papakonstantinou, 'Self-regulation' (n 117).

[145] Kosta and Stuurman, 'Technical standards and the draft general data protection regulation' (n 118).

Table 4.1 Overview of functions of standards in data protection law based on literature review

Clarity & interpretation	Implementation and compliance	Technology-triggered
Definition of concepts	Uniform application across companies, Member States, sectors	Translation of legal requirements to technical auditable requirements and controls
Interpretation of principles and provisions	Assisting enforcement, providing a benchmark for supervisory authorities	Technical measures for compliance, state of the art
	Accountability for those with a duty to comply	Enforcement by means of technology

or leverage the technical character of standards to help regulatees comply with their legal obligations. Accountability and operationalization of the data protection rules seem to be prominent reasons for resorting to standardization. Two additional functions were identified, the use of standards for interpretation of legal concepts and the use of standards as benchmarks for supervisory authority audits. As regards pre-law functions, private regulation instruments, including standards, may be treated as a forum of consensus building.

4.2 Development Modes: Processes, Actors, and the Role of Public Regulators

Standards, as defined by the Standardization Regulation, are developed by recognized standardization organizations as discussed in the previous Chapter.[146] Formal standardization organization bodies demonstrate a mimetic isomorphism,[147] in that their organizational structure and process for development of standards usually follows similar stages such as inception, drafting, consultation, publication, review. However, the agenda, goals and governance issues such as participation of civil society are influenced, and in some cases shaped by the involvement of the public regulator. This is the case mainly for regional

[146] Chapter 3 section 3.4 in this book.

[147] Werle Eand Iversen EJ, 'Promoting legitimacy in technical standardization' (2006) 2 Science, Technology & Innovation Studies, 19; DiMaggio PJ and Powell W, 'The Iron Cage Revisited: Institutional Isomorphism and Collective Rationality in Organizational Fields' in Powell, W and DiMaggio PJ (eds), *The New Institutionalism in Organizational Analysis* (Chicago: The University of Chicago Press, 1991), 63ff.

standards such as the European harmonized standards, and less so for international standards.[148]

The degree of involvement of the public regulator in the process of standards development differs significantly depending on the type of organization and –specifically in the EU–the topic, whether, for example, there is Union harmonization law in that regulatory area. In some cases, the involvement of the public regulator is such that it essentially amounts to co-development,[149] while in others there is passive involvement (such as being informed on the progress of the development of a standard) or no involvement, in which case the SDO develop standards autonomously. The degree and form of involvement may be formalized, as with the European harmonized standards, or non-formalized, as in the US where it is incidental or occasional. Further, the public regulator may be involved after the standard is published, for example by publicly endorsing or acknowledging the usefulness of a specific technical standard. In that case, the influence the regulator exercises in the private regulation activity—in terms of development–concerns its take-up, that is how companies and other regulatees are nudged to conform to the said standard.

The array of varying involvement, intensity and, modes is discussed in the next part of this Chapter. Two main development modes of technical standards are distinguished: the autonomous mode and the co-development mode.

As an example of autonomous standards development one may consider the development of standards performed in recognized standardization bodies such as CEN and ISO, by the Technical Committees of those bodies, without any decisive capacity by public regulators, (committee-based standards development). In addition, autonomous mode is the development of technical standards by non-recognized SDO, such as fora and consortia (market-based standards development). The co-development of standards, where the public regulator has a formal role in the development process, is mainly encountered in the EU in the case of European harmonized standards, developed to support Union harmonization policy or law. The Union formalizes the cooperation between the ESOs and the Commission.[150] The co-development is grounded in the Standardization Regulation, and essentially starts with a standardization request by the

[148] See however the case of the ISO/IEC 27701 standard on Privacy Management Information Systems, in the development of which the European supervisory authorities (the EDPB in particular) engaged and provided comments on the draft standard. Read further on the standard in Chapter 8 section 8.3 in this book.

[149] Co-development is associated with the principle of co-regulation as provided in the Better Regulation Toolbox and defined as 'a mechanism whereby the Union Legislator entrusts the attainment of specific policy objectives set out in legislation or other policy documents to parties which are recognised in the field (such as economic operators, social partners, nongovernmental organizations, standardization bodies or associations'. European Commission 'Better Regulation Toolbox' (2017), 109.

[150] The term 'co-development' implies a prominent role for both the European Commission and the ESO, but not an equally distributed and certainly not the same role.

Commission to the ESOs to develop harmonized standards on the basis of Union law or policy.

The following two sections explain the co-development and autonomous development of technical standards.

4.2.1 Co-development of Technical Standards in the EU: Commission Standardization Requests

Cooperation is in general a recurring concept in the Standardization Regulation.[151] In fact, the subject matter of the Standardization Regulation precisely refers *inter alia* to the cooperation between European standardization organizations, national standardization bodies, Member States and the Commission.[152] The embodiment of this cooperation is found in the development of harmonized technical standards. The Commission has the power to request the ESOs to develop a standard or other standardization deliverable, for example a technical report, setting out the objectives and scope of the standard, as well as other details such as a deadline. The standardization requests, which have the form of a Commission Implementing Decision[153] are issued on the basis of Union policy or law. The role of the standardization request is to provide the working framework for the ESOs.[154] The European Commission, in its 2015 Vademecum,[155] stressed that there must be a 'well-defined need for standards'.[156] The Vademecum interpreted the criterion of 'well-defined need' as being met, for example by an 'established' Union policy in the case that non-legislative documents, such as Commission Communications, which state that European standardization 'could promote defined policy objectives'.[157] A standardization request may be based on Union legislation and non-legislative documents. European standards developed on the basis of standardization requests need to be developed as both 'market-driven' and taking into account the public interest.[158]

[151] In Recital 27 Standardization Regulation the legislator stresses the urgency of the collaboration of the Commission and the standardization bodies by referring to conditions of viability of the relationship.

[152] Standardization Regulation art 1.

[153] See however critical comments by Cuccuru who describes how standardization requests, despite formally Commission Implementing Decisions, have an 'aftertaste' of contractual relationship. Cuccuru P, 'Regulating by Request: On the Role and Status of the Standardisation Mandate under the New Approach.' In Eliantonio M., Cauffman Caroline (eds), *The Legitimacy of Standardisation as a Regulatory Technique* (Edward Elgar Publishing 2020) (hereafter Cuccuru, 'Regulating by request'), 57.

[154] European Commission, Commission Staff Working Document, Vademecum on European standardization in support of Union legislation and policies, PART II, Preparation and adoption of the Commission's standardization requests to the European standardization organizations, SWD (2015) 205 final, 14 (hereafter EC Vademecum).

[155] Ibid, 14.

[156] Art. 10(1) and (2) Standardization Regulation.

[157] EC Vademecum (n 154), 14.

[158] Standardization Regulation art 10(1).

The co-development process breaks down into several steps where decision-making is either at the hands of the Commission or the ESOs, under the observation of the Commission. The Commission Implementing decision requesting the standards is subject to prior consultation with the ESOs.[159] The most significant expression of the ESOs decisional competence is the right to accept or reject the request, which relates to the private ordering nature of standardization.[160] The ESOs in that respect enjoy quite some flexibility, as they may also choose the content of the standards, how and to what extent they cover legal requirements and whether standards also cover subject matter not supporting the application of Union legislation.[161] With the latest amendment of the Standardization Regulation,[162] only those ESOs that fulfill certain requirements may be requested to develop European harmonized standards. Namely the ESOs that *inter alia* ensure that decision-making about the acceptance or refusal of standardization requests and decisions on the adoption, revision and withdrawal of European standards.[163]

Throughout the process of the drafting of the European standard, the Commission has the right to be informed about the development of the standard,[164] and it is a usual practice that a Commission project officer attends meetings of the Technical Committee as an observer. Finally, after the requested standard or other deliverables are drafted, the Commission together with the ESO assesses their compliance with the standardization request.[165]

There is a strong link between New Approach and personal data protection, established in a New Approach Directive and not in a Union data protection law. The New Approach Directive which concerns the regulation of radio equipment, which provides for data protection requirements, is the Radio Equipment Directive (RED).[166] The RED sets the conditions for placing radio equipment in the market. The Directive's broad material scope, as determined by *inter alia* the definition of radio equipment[167] captures a range of wireless devices including

[159] Also the European stakeholder organizations of Annex III such as ANEC, ECOS, and others.

[160] This involvement of the ESO in the preparation of the request has been criticised as influencing the content and creating a sort of function creep, since the ESO are consulted for an EU binding act which they are later called upon to carry out. Cuccuru, 'Regulating by request' (n 153).

[161] See, however, *James Elliot* case in Chapter 3 section 3.3 in this book; EC Vademecum (n 154), 16.

[162] Regulation 2022/2480 art 1.

[163] See art 1 ('provided that the European Standardization Organization concerned complies with paragraph 2a' and the new Art. 2a in the Standardization Regulation).

[164] Standardization Regulation art 10(5).

[165] Standardization Regulation art 10(5).

[166] Directive 2014/53/EU of the European Parliament and of the Council of 16 April 2014 on the harmonization of the laws of the Member States relating to the making available on the market of radio equipment and repealing Directive 1999/5/EC,[2014] OJ L153/62.

[167] Radio equipment is defined as '*an electrical or electronic product, which intentionally emits and/or receives radio waves for the purpose of radio communication and/or radiodetermination, or an electrical or electronic product which must be completed with an accessory, such as antenna, so as to intentionally emit and/or receive radio waves for the purpose of radio communication and/or radiodetermination.* RED art 2(1)(1).

Internet of Things devices, some of which process sensitive information and information about children.[168] The RED provides a set of essential requirements to be met by any radio equipment under its scope, before its placement on the market.

Protection of personal data and privacy are an *essential requirement* in the RED. The data protection essential requirement was firstly introduced with the revision of the RED, that took place in 2014, coinciding with the data protection law reform process. This was an important development for data protection standardization because personal data protection and privacy as an essential requirement established a legal basis for the adoption of European harmonized data protection standards. Article 3(3)(e) RED provides:

> Radio equipment within certain categories or classes shall be so constructed that it complies with the following essential requirements [...]
>
> [e] radio equipment incorporates safeguards to ensure that the personal data and privacy of the user and of the subscriber are protected

After specifying in a Delegated Regulation, the types of equipment to which the RED provision on privacy and data protection applies,[169] the Commission decided in 2022 to exercise its power to request to CEN and CENELEC to develop technical standards on the basis of the RED.[170] The requested standards to be developed must include detailed technical specifications and test methods to verify compliance of the radio equipment to the essential requirement of RED.

The harmonized standards on data protection and privacy that will be developed based on the RED, will bring about two significant consequences. One is that radio equipment conforming to those harmonized standards will be presumed to comply with the data protection requirement in RED. Second, the notification obligation of Member States will be triggered; Member States will have to identify radio-connected products presenting a serious risk to personal data and privacy and notify this to other states through the Rapid Alert System for dangerous

[168] Examples are pacemakers or radio-connected smart toys and baby monitors, smart watches and others, or recording the daily habits and preferences of users such as home automation systems or RFID tags.

[169] European Commission, Commission Delegated Regulation (EU) 2022/30 of 29 October 2021 supplementing Directive 2014/53/EU of the European Parliament and of the Council with regard to the application of the essential requirements referred to in Article 3(3), points (d), (e) and (f), of that Directive, [2022] OJ L7/6.

[170] Commission Implementing Decision of 5.8.2022 on a standardization request to the European Committee for Standardization and the European Committee for Electrotechnical Standardization as regards radio equipment in support of Directive 2014/53/EU of the European Parliament and of the Council and Commission Delegated Regulation (EU) 2022/30, C (2022) 5637 final, as amended by Commission Implementing Decision of 23.8.2023 amending Implementing Decision C (2022) 5637 on a standardization request to the European Committee for Standardization and the European Committee for Electrotechnical Standardization as regards radio equipment in support of Directive 2014/53/EU of the European Parliament and of the Council and Commission Delegated Regulation (EU) 2022/30, C (2023) 5624 final.

products (RAPEX). While the free movement of those devices would not be banned, being part of the RAPEX would mean that the notified products are blacklisted as presenting serious risks.

4.2.2 Committee and Market-Based Standardization (Autonomous Development)

Standardization activity that takes place without the involvement of any public regulator is quite common. At ISO and IEC level, such activity represents the majority of the standards being developed, since ISO and IEC are operating without ties to national or regional legal orders.[171] At the ESOs, the ratio is different, since some of the 'homegrown' European standards are developed with some form of interaction with the Union. In committee-based standardization, that is in recognized standardization bodies, the initiative for the development of a new standard lies with market actors, which is facilitated via national standardization bodies—members of ISO.[172] At CEN, proposals for new standards without the regulator's involvement may originate from a CEN member—that is national standardization bodies–, a CEN Technical Committee, an international organization, or a European trade, professional, technical or scientific organization.[173]

At ISO, the new work item proposal is subject to voting by the relevant Technical Committee members, which may lead to adoption of the proposal or 'pre-adoption', a status before adoption in which questions of feasibility of the proposed work and the market needs for such a standard must be resolved. If the proposal is approved, a working group of experts is usually set up to prepare a working draft. This is the main preparation phase of the process. There may be several versions of Working Drafts until the working group is satisfied with the result.[174] Next, the Working Draft is submitted to the parent committee of the drafting working group and the draft is distributed to the Technical Committee participating members. The draft at this stage is called Committee Draft and is submitted for comment and vote to

[171] It is true however that ISO welcomes the use of their standards for public policy purposes. ISO states that they 'wish to make their portfolio of International Standards more visible to public policy makers and ensure that their standards address the needs and concerns of public policy makers'. ISO and IEC 'Using and referencing ISO and IEC standards to support public policy' (no date) https://www.iso.org/files/live/sites/isoorg/files/store/en/PUB100358.pdf [accessed 20 September 2023].

[172] Sometimes, the initiative comes from a committee within ISO, such as COPOLCO, which is an ISO Committee on Consumer Policy, the members of which are national standardization bodies members of ISO. An example of such a standard is the ISO 31700-1:2023 Consumer protection—Privacy by design for consumer goods and services.

[173] CEN CENELEC website https://boss.cen.eu/reference%20material/Guidancedoc/Pages/TCNewWI.aspx [accessed 20 September 2023].

[174] ISO/IEC Directives Part 1 and Consolidated ISO Supplement, Procedures specific to ISO, V01/2024, 2024. (hereafter ISO/IEC Directives Part 1) Clause 2.4, https://www.iso.org/sites/directives/current/consolidated/index.html [accessed 10 August 2024].

the participating members of the Technical Committee.[175] The goal of this stage is to reach consensus on the content by the participating members of the Technical Committee, which may require several revisions of the Committee Draft. If consensus is achieved on the Committee Draft,[176] the *enquiry stage* follows, for which the text (called at this stage Draft International Standard) is submitted to the ISO Central Secretariat for circulation to all the national standardization bodies which are member of ISO in general (not only the Technical Committee).

After a voting period of twelve weeks the draft is approved if a two thirds majority of the votes by the participant members of the Technical Committee is in favour and not more than one quarter of the total number of votes (so, also non-participant members) are negative.[177] When those conditions are met and there are no requests for technical changes, ISO proceeds to publication of the standard (*publication stage*). If the conditions are not met a revised draft may be circulated for comments, in an attempt to resolve the negative votes. If these conditions are met, but there are technical comments, then the draft moves to a final draft International Standard and the so called '*approval stage*'.[178] It is relevant to note that the ISO Directives oblige the Technical Committees to respond to all the received comments.[179]

At the approval stage, there is yet another voting round, in which the national standardization bodies, members of ISO have the right to submit votes. If the draft is approved, it proceeds to the publication stage. If not, the Technical Committee may modify the draft and resubmit it for voting, publish a Technical Specification or cancel the project. Every decision of a subcommittee, committee, and the technical management board is subject to appeal by national standardization bodies that are members of ISO. Moreover, participating members in a Technical Committee may appeal against 'any action, or inaction' on a number of grounds including 'public factors such as safety, health, or environment'.[180]

In the same category of autonomous development, 'market-based standardization' refers to market initiatives, including fora and consortia, which either intentionally or *de facto* develop 'standards'.[181] The initiative, process and conditions for participation vary in each forum, since this is purely market-based activity, not

[175] ISO/IEC Directives Part 1 (n 163), cl 2.5. See also https://www.iso.org/sites/ConsumersStandards/voting_iso.html [accessed 20 September 2023].

[176] In case not all technical comments are resolved and agreed upon within 'appropriate time limits' the TC may decide to publish the text as Technical Specification. ISO/IEC Directives Part 1 (n 174) cl 2.5.10.

[177] ISO/IEC Directives Pt 1 (n 174). The options for voting are 'positive', 'negative', 'abstention'.

[178] ISO/IEC Directives Pt 1 (n 174), cl 2.7.

[179] ISO/IEC Directives Pt 1 (n 174), cl 2.6.5(d).

[180] ISO/IEC Directives Pt 1 (n 174), cl 5.1.2.

[181] The distinction on market-based v committee-based standards is made among others in Werle E and Iversen EJ, 'Promoting legitimacy in technical standardization' (2006) 2 Science, Technology & Innovation Studies, 19.

formally legislated with public law or centrally regulated by a SDO. An example is 'standardization' activity from market actors such as Amazon or Apple, which impose their own specifications on their collaborating partners, or simply a spontaneous adoption. Another example is organizations such as the Alliance for Internet of Things Innovation, which has a permanent structure and its own internal statutes (AIOTI Code of Conduct).[182] Certain consortia and fora have a significant role in developing specification on various aspects of data protection, and a few of those have attracted endorsement by data protection authorities.[183]

4.3 Integration of Technical Standards in a Legal Order

Standards are extra-legal, the outcome of a private normative ordering, and for them to be assigned a role to support Union law, integration of standards in the EU legal order needs to take place. Integration works as *recognition* of standards by the Union legal order.[184] The need for recognition is expressed also in the requirement of standardization bodies to be 'recognized' in order to develop *standards* under the Standardization Regulation.[185]

4.3.1 Incorporation by Reproduction and by Reference

Standards may be integrated in the EU legal order by *reproduction* in the text of the EU act or by *reference*. Integration by reproduction means verbatim reproduction of the wording of existing standards.[186] Reproduction in EU binding or non-binding acts usually occurs for market-based standardization, developed by consortia and fora.[187] Due to the copyrighted nature of technical standards, which often prevents the reproduction in legislation, more common is the integration by reference. This mechanism is common in the US, where standards are

[182] AIOTI Code of Conduct (WG03).

[183] See Chapter 8 section 8.4 in this book.

[184] Recognition of a standard by the public regulator should not be confused with the acceptance by the market.

[185] See Chapter 3 section 3.3.3 in this book.

[186] Volpato A and Eliantonio M, 'The Contradictory Approach of the CJEU to the Judicial Review of Standards: A Love–Hate Relationship?' in Eliantonio M and Cauffman C (eds), *The Legitimacy of Standardisation as a Regulatory Technique* (Edward Elgar Publishing 2020) (hereafter Volpato and Eliantonio, 'The Contradictory Approach of the CJEU'). Schepel and Falke, 'Legal aspects of Standardization' (n 111) 184; Schepel Hand Falke J (eds), *Legal Aspects of Standardization in the Member States of the EC and EFTA.* vol 2. Country reports. Office for official publications of the European communities, 2000. This section refers to public legal order. In private law, standards are incorporated in contracts for example, see Chapter 7, section 7.4 in this book for implications in terms of judicial review and liability.

[187] Volpato and Eliantonio, 'The Contradictory Approach of the CJEU' (n 186), 95.

incorporated in federal regulations.[188] A reference in a binding or non-binding act may manifest itself in a variety of forms. Falke and Schepel distinguish a typology of references depending on the exclusive or indicative character of the reference, the precision, ie, a reference to a body of standards or a specific standard, and direct or indirect.[189] In *direct* references a specific standard is directly quoted within a legally binding act.[190] The direct reference to a specific standard is the most immediate manner to link standards and a legal act in terms of consequences. First, it is often the case that when a standard is directly referenced in the law, it is made *de facto* mandatory. This is the case for the ISO/IEC 17065 standard referred to in the GDPR.[191] Furthermore, a reference to a specific standard signals the legislator's approval of the content of the standard. In turn, for a standard to be referenced in a law, it should be deemed necessary that the standard aligns with—or at least it does not contradict—the aims and provisions of the law in which it is referenced, but also its terminology.

Direct references are further classified as *dated* and *non-dated*. A dated reference, eg ISO/IEC 17065:2012, entails that the law refers to the specific version of the standard published in year 2012. Standards are often revised and updated, so that they represent the latest best practices and state of the art. A dated reference however is tied to the version specified in the law. When a standard is updated, the reference does not automatically refer to the new version of the standard. This is a way for the legislator to maintain some control over the reference, since a non-dated reference would mean that the latest version of the standard would form part of the referring law, without the legislator being aware of the new version's content.

Indirect references to standards are made where the legislator aims at promoting or allowing the voluntary use of standards.[192] Those can take place by either referring to 'standards' ('specific'), or to linked concepts such as the 'state of the art' or 'acknowledged rules of technology'[193] ('abstract'). The distinction between indirect references referring specifically to the concept of standards or in an abstract manner to relevant concepts is important for the data protection law, which mostly includes indirect references. While in abstract indirect references, standards are one of the relevant regulation instruments to play a supplementary role to the relevant provision, in the case of specific indirect references to 'standards' or 'specifications', the legislature expresses a preference for standardization. Thus, the use of

[188] Read further on the regulatory technique of Incorporation By Reference (IBR) in Sheffner DJ, 'Integrating Technical Standards into Federal Regulations: Incorporation by Reference' in Contreras JL (ed), *The Cambridge Handbook of Technical Standardization Law: Volume 2: Further Intersections of Public and Private Law* (CUP 2019).

[189] Schepel and Falke, 'Legal aspects of Standardization' (n 111), 185ff.

[190] European Commission 'Methods of referencing standards in legislation with an emphasis on European legislation', Entreprise Publications (2002). (hereafter EC 'Methods of referencing standards').

[191] GDPR art 43(1)(b).

[192] EC 'Methods of referencing standards' (n 190), 10.

[193] ibid, 13.

the term 'standards' or 'specifications' does not leave room for interpretation in the preferred instrument.

4.3.2 The Role of the Involvement of the Public Regulator

The engagement or involvement of the public regulator in the development of standards plays a role for their integration in the EU legal order. Harmonized standards are destined to be incorporated in the EU legal order by terms of reference in the Official Journal of the Union, unless the Commission finds these do not align with the standardization request and thus do not fulfill their purposes.[194]

The main aim of committee-based standards on the other hand is not *per se* to influence or have any impact on state legislation. However, those may gain importance or become relevant to Union law or policy after their development, because of their widespread adoption in the market, or their technical relevance or other reasons. Thus, the European Commission may decide to make use of those committee-based standards that were not developed under its auspices. In fact, this post-development recognition of committee-based standards is possible not only via reference in the law or another act, but also via the adoption of existing committee-based international standards in response of a Commission standardization request. After accepting a standardization request, it is possible that the ESOs decide not to develop a new standard, but adopt an existing international standard as a European harmonized one, and submit that standard as response to the standardization request.[195]

According to the Commission, referencing national, international, or European standards in European legislation can offer those standards 'legal quality', since they 'become part of the requirements of a specific legislative act or of the system'.[196] Indeed, the case law of the CJEU especially in cases such as *Fra.bo, James Elliot,* and *Public.Resource.Org.* confirmed that the use of standardization in support of European legislation has consequences for the private nature of standards.[197] While one may argue that from a trade perspective, the practice of adopting existing international standards as European harmonized ones favours international standards that enjoy market acceptance wider than the EU Single Market, from a legitimacy perspective might be problematic, since the public regulator loses sight of the standards' actual development.[198]

[194] Volpato Aand Eliantonio M, 'The Butterfly Effect of Publishing References to Harmonised Standards in the L series,' European Law Blog (7 March 2019).
[195] EC Vademecum (n 154), 16.
[196] EC 'Methods of referencing standards' (n 190), 3.
[197] See Chapter 3 in this book.
[198] Judgment of the Court of 5 March 2024, Case C-588/21 P, *Public.Resource.Org Inc.*, EU:C:2024:201.

Further, market-based specifications may gain some formal recognition in the Union as well, mainly by means of reference in public procurement, on the condition they meet the criteria of Annex II of the Standardization Regulation. This is an essential step aiming to counterbalance the lack of guarantees for minimum legitimacy safeguards during their development process, since their development is not subject to the procedural guarantees of the Standardization Regulation.[199] In terms of integration in the EU legal order, while this has been rather limited, there have been several developments that indicate the intention of the EU legislators to make use of technical specifications for EU law and policy. An example can be found in the recent Cyber Resilience Act (CRA),[200] which is the Regulation providing essential requirements for products with digital elements. The CRA stipulates that in case a standardization request has not been accepted, the standards based on the request are not delivered in time or the standards do not comply with the standardization request, the European Commission has the power to 'adopt implementing acts establishing common specifications covering technical requirements'.[201] Those common specifications could either be developed by the Commission, but given the complexity and need for expert technical knowledge, would most likely be market-based specifications. In the area of personal data protection, certain technical specifications, such as the W3C Do Not Track specification, play a significant role.[202]

4.4 Synthesis: Four Streams of Standards' Integration in the EU Legal Order

Standardization when understood as a normative ordering, enjoys an authority to develop norms that are accepted from a target audience broader than the standard-setting actors. This Chapter has analysed through the lens of legal pluralism the roots of this 'authority' of standardization organizations to develop norms and rules, the (semi-)autonomy of standardization, and its interaction with the Union legal order. As regards the content of the complementary interaction of standards with Union (data protection) law, and specifically how standards may complement Union (data protection) law, this Chapter outlined a framework of functions and clarified the focus of the book mainly in post-law functions, namely

[199] Standardization Regulation on Identification of ICT technical specifications eligible for referencing and Annex II Regulation 1025/2012 art 13.

[200] Regulation (EU) 2024/2847 of the European Parliament and of the Council of 23 October 2024 on horizontal cybersecurity requirements for products with digital elements and amending Regulations (EU) No 168/2013 and (EU) 2019/1020 and Directive (EU) 2020/1828 (Cyber Resilience Act) OJ L/1 ('CRA').

[201] CRA art 27.

[202] Chapter 5 section 5.1.3 and Chapter 8 section 8.4 in this book.

Table 4.2 Streams: Development modes and types of standards

Name	Development	Type of standards	Stream
Co-development	Co-development	European standards	Stream 1a
		European harmonized standards under New Approach	Stream 1b
Committee-based	Autonomous	International standards	Stream 2a
		European standards	Stream 2b
		National standards	Stream 2c
Market-based	Autonomous	International technical specifications	Stream 3a
		European technical specifications	Stream 3b
		National technical specifications	Stream 3c
Combined	Autonomous	International to European harmonized standards	Stream 4a

functions of standards with a view in supporting the EU data protection law. The literature review on functions of standards in data protection law showed three key themes: clarity and interpretation, implementation and compliance, and technology related uses.

The cooperative and complementary interaction of standardization and the Union public regulator is expressed in different modes of development and recognition by integration of standards in Union binding and non-binding acts. Co-development is taking place with the standardization requests by the Union which initiate development of standards. As regards autonomous development, international standards have been developed outside the Union's auspices may be recognized *ex post facto* by the Union public regulator. Thus, one may speak of four main streams of standards developed and integrated in the Union public order: co-development (Stream 1), committee-based (Stream 2), market-based (Stream 3), and combined (Stream 4). In the latter, committee or market-based standards and specifications are adopted as European standards and provided in response to a Commission standardization request.

Those different development and recognition channels are all relevant to standardization in the field of personal data protection. Depending on their subject matter and legal basis, data protection standards may be developed as international committee-based standards, European standards, or harmonized European standards following the New Approach and the NLF model. The development and recognition of standards carries consequences for their legitimacy, legal regulations to which they are subject, alignment with Union legislation and policy, and others, which are analysed in the following Chapters.

5
EU Data Protection Law as a Basis for Standardization

5.1 An Overview of the EU Data Protection Law: The General Data Protection Regulation and the ePrivacy Directive

5.1.1 Protection of a Fundamental Right in the EU

Data protection, although a relatively new autonomous[1] fundamental right established in art 8 CFREU, traces its roots to the period when most of the human rights and values were formally recognized. Data protection did not enjoy from the beginning a status of protection on its own merits in the significant instruments and treaties, but it was treated as an aspect of the protection of private life.[2] Data protection slowly gained the recognition of being worth its own protection, with the ultimate act of recognition being the incorporation in the CFREU, and the binding effect of the Charter with the Lisbon Treaty,[3] a process that led to its so called 'constitutionalization'.[4] Simitis had suggested that computerization led to the compilation of activities and behaviours of the individual, which is detrimental to the individual's autonomy, as those compilations are designed to facilitate 'better adjustment, not to improve the individual's capacity to act and decide'.[5] The threat of adverse effects and, the need for fairness on how information about individuals is treated contributed to the right to personal data protection gaining an autonomous

[1] Autonomous in this context means a right that is 'applicable irrespective of another right's applicability' González Fuster G, *The Emergence of Personal Data Protection As a Fundamental Right of the EU* vol 16 (Springer 2014), 270ff.

[2] Bygrave LA, 'Privacy and Data Protection in an International Perspective' (2010) 56 Scandinavian Studies in Law, 156; Read also: Bygrave LA, *Data Protection Law* (Wolters Kluwer Law & Business 2002); Rodotà S, 'Data Protection as a Fundamental Right,' in Gutwirth S and others (eds), *Reinventing Data Protection?* (Springer 2009).

[3] Treaty of Lisbon amending the Treaty on European Union and the Treaty establishing the European Community, signed at Lisbon, Official Journal of the European Union [2007] C 306/1.

[4] De Hert P and Gutwirth S, 'Data Protection in the Case Law of Strasbourg and Luxemburg: Constitutionalisation in Action,' in Gutwirth S and others (eds), *Reinventing Data Protection?* (Springer Netherlands 2009).

[5] 'Whatever the original incentive for computerisation may have been, processing increasingly appears as the ideal means to adapt an individual to a predetermined, standardized behaviour that aims at the highest possible degree of compliance with the model patient, consumer, taxpayer, employee, or citizen' Simitis S, 'Reviewing Privacy in An Information Society' (1987) University of Pennsylvania Law Review, 733ff.

Standardizing Personal Data Protection. Irene Kamara, Oxford University Press. © Irene Kamara 2025.
DOI: 10.1093/9780191997037.003.0005

standing on its own merits. The right to data protection is established in art 16 TFEU under the provisions with general application.[6] Thus, alongside the recognition of the right to protection of personal data as an autonomous right in art 8 CFREU, this significant development has signaled the emancipation of the right to protection of personal data from the right to privacy.[7]

5.1.2 Secondary EU Data Protection Law: The General Data Protection Regulation

The importance of data, the evolution of technologies, and problems in the application of the data protection law, led to several reforms in the secondary EU data protection law.[8] In its 2010 Communication, the Commission outlined its vision for a comprehensive approach to data protection.[9] The key objectives of the long overdue reform of a legal framework essentially established before the Internet era[10] reinforced the control rationale of data protection, but also emphasize the importance of movement of data within the Union—in terms of the Internal Market– and outside its borders in terms of data transfers to non-EU Member States. The Commission referred to effective control over one's own data, and the challenge of exercise of an individual data subject's rights in an online environment.[11] In 2012, the Commission published the Proposal for a Regulation, which was adopted with the ordinary legislative process in 2016, and started to apply two years later. The GDPR is a full harmonization instrument, in that it aims at 'consistent and high level of protection of natural persons' by ensuring a level of protection that is equivalent in all Member States.[12] As regards its material scope,

[6] For a comprehensive study on Art. 16 TFEU read: Hijmans H, *The European Union as Guardian of Internet Privacy: The Story of Art 16 TFEU* (Springer 2016).

[7] De Hert P 'The Right to Protection of Personal Data. Incapable of Autonomous Standing in the Basic EU Constituting Documents?' (2015) 31 Utrecht Journal of International and European Law, 1; See also González Fuster G, 'Fighting for Your Right to What Exactly-The Convoluted Case Law of the EU Court of Justice on Privacy and/Or Personal Data Protection.' (2014) 2 Birkbeck L Rev, 263; Kokott J and Sobotta C, 'The Distinction between Privacy and Data Protection in the Jurisprudence of the CJEU and the ECtHR' (2013) 3 International Data Privacy Law, 222; Brkan M, 'The Essence of the Fundamental Rights to Privacy and Data Protection: Finding the Way Through the Maze of the CJEU's Constitutional Reasoning' (2019) 20 German Law Journal, 864; Lenaerts K, 'Limits on Limitations: The Essence of Fundamental Rights in the EU' (2019) 20 German Law Journal, 779; Porcedda MG, 'On Boundaries – Finding the Essence of the Right to the Protection of Personal Data,' in in Leenes R, Van Brakel R, De Hert P, and Gutwirth S (eds), *Data Protection and Privacy* (Hart Publishing 2019).

[8] This Chapter focuses on the General Data Protection Regulation, the ePrivacy Directive, and Proposal for an e-Privacy Regulation.

[9] Commission, Communication from the Commission to the European Parliament, the Council, the Economic and Social Committee, and the Committee of the Regions. A comprehensive approach on personal data protection in the European Union, COM (2010) 609 final (hereafter 'COM (2010) 609').

[10] Simitis S 'Privacy—An Endless Debate?' (2010) California Law Review, 1989.

[11] COM (2010) 609 (n 9), 10.

[12] Recital 10 GDPR. The Recital further provides 'Consistent and homogenous application of the rules for the protection of the fundamental rights and freedoms of natural persons with regard to the processing of personal data should be ensured throughout the Union.' Doubts have been expressed

it applies to processing of personal data that is conducted by automated means, wholly or partly, and to the processing which forms or is intended to form as part of a filing system.[13]

The GDPR is a mixture of principles-based and rule-based regulation, in that the Regulation provides a set of overarching general principles, together with the more defined rules on rights, duties, and powers of the several actors. GDPR art 5 establishes the principles relating to processing, formerly known as 'data quality' principles under the Data Protection Directive.[14] The principles both provide general imperatives (eg data should be kept up-to-date) and constitute legal standards for the interpretation of the remainder of the GDPR rules. Article 5(1) provides for six principles,[15] namely lawfulness, fairness,[16] transparency, purpose limitation,[17] data minimization, accuracy and storage limitation (formerly retention under the Directive), integrity and confidentiality.[18] The principle of accountability is introduced in art 5(2) GDPR.[19]

Controllers are bound by a series of legal obligations, which put into effect the principles relating to the processing of personal data and prescribe requirements for positive (both proactive and reactive/redress) action for protection of the individuals, but also establish grounds for liability. Controllers bear a general responsibility to take organizational and technical measures to ensure the Regulation is not violated.[20] The general responsibility is not exhausted by taking measures, but requires controllers to be able to demonstrate that processing is performed in accordance with the GDPR.[21] In *Google Spain,* the CJEU adopted a broad understanding of the concept of responsibilities of data controllers, on the basis of the Data Protection Directive, given that the data protection law 'seeks to ensure a high level of protection of the fundamental rights and freedoms of natural persons'.[22]

however on the impact of the several opening clauses of the GDPR, which allow discretion for Member States, on the harmonization effect. Miscenic E and Hoffmann A-L, 'The Role of Opening Clauses in Harmonization of EU Law: Example of the EU's General Data Protection Regulation (GDPR)', (2020) 4 EU and Comparative Law Issues and Challenges Series, 44.

[13] GDPR art 2(1). For the definition of personal data, see Bygrave LA and Luca T, 'Article 4(1) Personal Data' in Kuner C, Bygrave LA, and Docksey C (eds), The EU General Data Protection Regulation (GDPR): A Commentary (OUP 2020).

[14] Data Protection Directive art 6.

[15] For an analysis of the principles of GDPR art 5 read De Terwagne C, 'Article 16. Right to Rectification' in Kuner C, Bygrave LA, and Docksey C (eds), The EU General Data Protection Regulation (GDPR): A Commentary (OUP 2020), 309ff.

[16] Read further on fairness: Clifford D and Ausloos J, 'Data Protection and the Role of Fairness' (2018) 37 Yearbook of European Law, 130.

[17] Read further on the purpose limitation principle: Article 29 Data Protection Working Party 'Opinion 03/2013 on purpose limitation', WP203 (2013).

[18] See discussion in Kamara I, 'Misaligned Union laws? A comparative analysis of certification in the Cybersecurity Act and the General Data Protection Regulation.' in Hallinan D, Leenes R, and De Hert P, *Privacy and Data Protection: Artificial Intelligence* (Hart 2021)

[19] See also Judgment of 11 November 2020, Case C-61/19 *Orange România SA*, EU:C:2020:901.

[20] GDPR art 24.

[21] GDPR art 5(2).

[22] Judgment of 13 May 2014, Case C-131/12, *Google Spain v AEPD*, EU:C:2014:317, para 66.

In extension to the general responsibility under art 24 GDPR, data controllers have a range of varying duties that aim either at ensuring the processing in accordance to the Regulation such as the duty of data protection by design and by default (art 25), and security of processing (art 32), and duties such as record keeping of processing activities (art 30) conduct data protection impact assessments (art 35)[23] and others. Controllers also bear some communication duties such as the obligation to notify security breaches to authorities and data subjects (arts 33 and 34), but also to cooperate with supervisory authorities (art 35). Next to those duties, data controllers must facilitate the exercise of data subjects' rights, such as the right to data portability (art 20).

5.1.3 Secondary EU Law: The ePrivacy Directive and Its Reform

The ePrivacy Directive was adopted as part of the EU package for the electronic communications sector,[24] which made the Directive part of two worlds, data protection and electronic communications, and inherited the complexity of both. Following the reform of the data protection legislation, the adoption of the GDPR, and the need for re-evaluation of the relevance of the ePrivacy Directive,[25] the Commission published in 2017 the Proposal for ePrivacy Regulation.[26] The transposition of the ePrivacy Directive in Member State national legal orders had been far from ideal. One of the reasons was the transposition of the Directive's rules in a range of national legal frameworks, such as data protection, electronic communications, or consumer protection, which has resulted in inconsistencies.[27]

The ePrivacy Regulation Proposal supports both fundamental rights protection and the Internal Market, as it is based on art16 TFEU on the right to personal data protection, and art 114 TFEU on the approximation of laws for the establishment

[23] See conditions in GDPR art 35. Read also: Article 29 Data Protection Working Party 'Guidelines on Data Protection Impact Assessment (DPIA) and determining whether processing is "likely to result in a high risk" for the purposes of Regulation 2016/679' (adopted 4 April 2017, rev 4 October 2017WP 248 rev.01., endorsed by the EDPB).

[24] Dumortier J and Kosta E, 'ePrivacy Directive: assessment of transposition, effectiveness and compatibility with proposed Data Protection Regulation' (2015) European Publications Office, 18ff (hereafter Dumortier and Kosta, 'ePrivacy Directive'). Read also: Kosta E, *Consent in European Data Protection Law* (Brill 2013), 217ff.

[25] GDPR art 98 on review of other Union legal acts on data protection, but also GDPR art 95 which clarifies that the GDPR 'does not impose additional obligations in relation to processing in connection with the provision of publicly available electronic communications services in public communication networks' which are subject to the ePrivacy Directive.

[26] Proposal for a Regulation of the European Parliament and of the Council concerning the respect for private life and the protection of personal data in electronic communications and repealing Directive 2002/58/EC, COM(2017) 10 final ('Proposal for ePrivacy Regulation'). See González EG, De Hert P, and Papakonstantinou V, 'The Proposed ePrivacy Regulation: The Commission's and The Parliament's Drafts At A Crossroads?' In Hallinan D, Leenes R, Gutwirth S, and De Hert P (eds) *Data Protection and Privacy. Data Protection and Democracy* (Hart Publishing 2020).

[27] Read further on the scope of the transposition of the 2002 Directive in Dumortier and Kosta, 'ePrivacy Directive' (n 24) 30.

of the Internal Market. Furthermore, the Proposal recalls arts 7 and 8 CFREU on the protection of private life and communications and personal data respectively[28] The ePrivacy Regulation Proposal is put forward as *lex specialis* in the relation to the GDPR.[29]

As regards the material scope, the ePrivacy Directive applies to the 'processing of personal data in connection with the provision of publicly available electronic communications services in public communications networks in the Community'.[30] The Directive therefore aims at applying to personal data in electronic communication services. On the other hand, the material scope of the ePrivacy Regulation, according to the Commission Proposal, has been broadened to include not only publicly available electronic communications services in public communications networks, but also services such as Voice over IP and instant messaging,[31] which are regarded as functionally equivalent to traditional communication means.[32] In practice, this would mean that IoT providers and Machine to Machine interactions might be captured by the scope of the proposed Regulation.[33] The Regulation would regulate 'electronic communications data', which are defined as 'electronic communications content and electronic communications metadata'.[34] Content data are the 'content exchanged by means of electronic communications services', namely 'text, voice, videos, images, and sound', such as the content of an email message.[35] Further, the definition of electronic communications metadata is formulated in a broad inclusive manner.[36] As metadata may reveal sensitive information about individuals, such as political affiliations or health issues, a broad definition is

[28] Treaty establishing the European Community Official Journal [1997] C 340/0213,—Consolidated version (valid at the time of adoption of the Directive 2002/58/EC) art 95; Recital 2 Directive 2002/58/EC.

[29] Recital (5) EC proposal for ePrivacy Regulation. See also Recital (173) GDPR provides that the GDPR 'should apply to all matters concerning the protection of fundamental rights and freedoms vis-à-vis the processing of personal data which are not subject to specific obligations with the same objective set out in Directive 2002/58/EC of the European Parliament and of the Council (18), including the obligations on the controller and the rights of natural persons.' In *Tele2Sverige*, the Advocate General confirmed that the ePrivacy Directive is *lex specialis* in relation to the Data Protection Directive. See opinion of AG Saugmandsgaard Øe of 19 July 2016, *Tele2 Sverige*, Joined Cases C-203/15 and C-698/15, EU:C:2016:572.

[30] ePrivacy Directive art 3, amended 2009.

[31] Explanatory memorandum of Proposal for ePrivacy Regulation para 1.3.

[32] González EG, De Hert P, and Papakonstantinou V, 'The Proposed ePrivacy Regulation: The Commission's and The Parliament's Drafts At A Crossroads?' in Hallinan D, Leenes R, Gutwirth S, and De Hert P (eds) *Data Protection and Privacy. Data Protection and Democracy* (Hart Publishing 2020), 267.

[33] WP29 'Opinion 01/2017 on the Proposed Regulation for the ePrivacy Regulation (2002/58/EC)' WP247 (adopted 4 April 2017).

[34] EC Proposal for ePrivacy Regulation art 4(3)(a).

[35] EC Proposal for ePrivacy Regulation art 4(3)(b).

[36] EC Proposal for ePrivacy Regulation art 4(3)(c) reads, 'data processed in an electronic communications network for the purposes of transmitting, distributing or exchanging electronic communications content; including data used to trace and identify the source and destination of a communication, data on the location of the device generated in the context of providing electronic communications services, and the date, time, duration and the type of communication.'

justified.[37] Metadata may include telephone numbers, 'websites visited, geographical location, the time, date and duration when an individual made a call'.[38] In *Rīgas satiksme*, the Advocate General stressed the risks stemming from of *inter alia* the assembling and harvesting of metadata.[39]

In terms of rules, the ePrivacy Directive includes a mix of provisions, which are drafted with the sector of electronic communications as a focal point, rather than a behaviour (eg processing of data). This focal point has led to a combination of provisions that offer a broad variety of obligations, ranging from security of processing, to confidentiality of communications, and to directories of subscribers. Security of processing requires that providers of publicly available electronic communications services take technical and organizational measures to ensure *inter alia* personal data against unauthorized access, accidental or unlawful destruction, loss or alteration, storage, access or disclosure, and maintain security policies.[40] Data breaches need to be notified to competent national authorities, an obligation introduced several years later also in the GDPR. Confidentiality of communications and traffic data,[41] which is one of the aims of the Directive, is protected independently of the lawfulness of a business practice.[42] Member States are obliged to ensure confidentiality, in particular by prohibiting 'listening, tapping, storage or other kinds of interception or surveillance'.[43] Traffic and location data are also regulated in the ePrivacy Directive.[44] Traffic data must be erased or made anonymous when no longer necessary for the transmission of a communication.[45] Location data (other than traffic data) may be processed either

[37] Article 29 Data Protection Working Party, 'Opinion 04/2014 on Surveillance of Electronic Communications for Intelligence and National Security Purposes' WP 215 (2014) 4ff. See also European Court of Human Rights ruling (1985) 7 EHRR 14, [1984] ECHR 10, 7 EHRR 14 'The comprehensive metering of telephone communications (origin, destination, duration), when effected for a purpose other than its sole accounting purpose, albeit in the absence of any interception as such, constitutes an interference in private life. On the basis of the data thereby obtained, the authorities are enabled to deduce information that is not properly meant to be within their knowledge. It is known that, as far as data banks are concerned, the processing of "neutral" data may be as revealing as the processing of sensitive data.' http://www.bailii.org/eu/cases/ECHR/1984/10.html [accessed 20 August 2024]. The ECtHR confirmed this view in the case *Bărbulescu v Romania* (App no 61496/08), (5 September 2017) http://hudoc.echr.coe.int/eng?i=001-159906 [accessed 20 August 2024].

[38] Recital (2) Proposal for ePrivacy Regulation.

[39] Opinion of Advocate General Bobek of 26 January 2017, *Rīgas satiksme*, C-13/16, EU:C:2017:43, parah 95. Read also: Mitrou L, 'Communications Data Retention: A Pandora's Box for Rights and Liberties' in Acquisti A and others (eds), *Digital Privacy: Theory, Technologies, and Practices* (CRC Press 2008). Article 29 Data Protection Working Party, 'Opinion 03/2016 on the Evaluation and Review of the ePrivacy Directive (2002/58/EC)' (2016) 10.

[40] ePrivacy Directive art 4(1)(a).

[41] Traffic data are defined in art 2(b) ePrivacy Directive as 'traffic data' means any data processed for the purpose of the conveyance of a communication on an electronic communications network or for the billing thereof'.

[42] ePrivacy Directive Recital 23.

[43] ePrivacy Directive art 5(1).

[44] ePrivacy Directive respectively arts 7 and 9.

[45] ePrivacy Directive art 7(1).

on the condition they are anonymized or with the consent of the users or subscribers.[46] The distinction between traffic and location data has been criticized as leaving room for discretion to Member States as regards their interpretation and applicability.[47]

Several of these rules have been proposed to be updated and modernized in the Proposal for ePrivacy Regulation, which provides mainly two groupings with substantial rules. The first regulates the protection of electronic communications of natural and legal persons, and of information stored in their terminal equipment. This includes provisions on confidentiality of electronic communications data and the grounds for processing, together with detailed provisions on the storage and erasure of data and, protection of information stored and related to end-users' terminal equipment.[48] The second group of rules concerns the rights of individuals and legal persons to exercise control of electronic communications.[49] These rights maintain the rationale and relevance to electronic communications (eg art 14 'incoming call blocking'), often some of these rights function as a bridge with the rights of data subjects in the GDPR.

5.2 Standards for Data Protection Law: An Analytical Framework

5.2.1 The Rationales of the General Data Protection Regulation: Accountability, Individual Control, and Supervision

The GDPR is a secondary law designed to give expression to the fundamental right to protection of personal data, alongside other rights and freedoms. As such, it defines the content, scope of application and modes of protection of the fundamental right of art 8 CFREU.[50] It provides a procedural dimension to the fundamental right, by implying a power to develop tools for exercising individual rights and enforcing the protections of the fundamental right.[51] Thus, the legal basis of

[46] ePrivacy Directive art 9(1).

[47] Article 29 Data Protection Working Party 'Opinion 03/2016 on the evaluation and review of the ePrivacy Directive (2002/58/EC)' WP240 (adopted 19 July 2016), 5ff.

[48] Proposal for ePrivacy Regulation arts 5–11.

[49] Proposal for ePrivacy Regulation arts 12–17.

[50] Muir E, 'The Fundamental Rights Implications of EU Legislation: Some Constitutional Challenges' (2014) 51 Common Market Law Review, 225ff.

[51] ibid. See also para 21 *Kücükdeveci* Judgment of 19 January 2010, *Seda Kücükdeveci v Swedex GmbH & Co. KG*, Case C-555/07, EU:C:2010:21, the Court provided that the Directive 2000/78 gives specific expression to the principle of non-discrimination. Similarily, in Case 43/75 *Defrenne* (para 54) the Court provided that the Directive 75/117 'provides further details regarding certain aspects of the material scope of Article 119 and also adopts various provisions whose essential purpose is to improve the legal protection of workers who may be wronged by failure to apply the principle of equal pay laid down by Article 119.' Judgment of 8 April 1976, Defrenne v Société anonyme belge de navigation aérienne Sabena, Case 43/75, EU:C:1976:56.

art 114 TFEU is remarkably absent,[52] since the GDPR is based on art 16(2) TFEU and art 8 CFREU.[53]

As regards the rationales of art 8 CFREU as mirrored and operationalized in the GDPR, one notes the strong emphasis on the objective to pursue fundamental rights and freedoms protection, and the protection of the right to personal data protection in particular. The principles for lawful processing,[54] present in the Data Protection Directive as well, and underlying art 8(2) and (3) are re-introduced, extended, and reinforced with the principle of accountability, according to which data controllers are responsible to comply, and demonstrate their compliance with the principles for lawful processing.

Hustinx, the former EDPS, identified four perspectives in the GDPR, which cement the message that the GDPR reflects the plurality of rationales of the right of art 8 CFREU.[55] The first perspective is the enhancement of control of data subjects over their personal information. Hustinx identifies control as an important objective of data protection law, even though he rightly acknowledges a distinction between control being an underlying goal of the law, and the law formally endorsing a right to informational self-determination.[56] Alongside control however, the data protection law introduces a system of safeguards, checks and balances aimed at protecting the individual from information and power asymmetries.[57] This is

[52] However, some scholars still view the Internal Market as a central motivation behind the instrument, mainly due to references to economic considerations and growth in the Recitals of the GDPR. See Kosta V, *Fundamental Rights in EU Internal Market Legislation* (Bloomsbury Publishing 2015), 140ff.

[53] There are still some references to free flow or movement of personal data art 51(1) GDPR, Recitals 6, 53, 123, 170, and most importantly art 1(3) which reads: 'The free movement of personal data within the Union shall be neither restricted nor prohibited for reasons connected with the protection of natural persons with regard to the processing of personal data.' Those references, which are not supported by a legal basis on art 114, as the GDPR is based on art 16 TFEU, and should be read in light of the four fundamental freedoms of the Union, translating essentially into that data protection should not serve as 'the basis for restrictions or prohibitions on the free flow of personal data between the Member States'(See Hijmans H 'Article 1). Subject matter and scope' in Kuner C, Bygrave LA, and Docksey C (eds), The EU General Data Protection Regulation (GDPR): A Commentary (OUP 2020), 51ff. Fuster has noted that the notion of 'free flow' is explicitly enshrined in the Treaties, which are informing the interpretation of the Charter, including art 8 CFREU. González Fuster G, 'The Emergence of Personal Data Protection as a Fundamental Right of the EU'. vol 16 (Springer 2014), 267.

[54] GDPR art 5.

[55] Hustinx P, 'EU Data Protection Law: The Review of Directive 95/46/EC and the General Data Protection Regulation' (2014) https://www.statewatch.org/media/documents/news/2014/sep/eu-2014-09-edps-data-protection-article.pdf [accessed 20 August 2024].

[56] Similarly, Kranenborg explains that the notion of informational self-determination, as conceptualized by German jurisprudence, places in its heart the notion of consent, while in the EU data protection law, consent is important, but only one of the grounds for lawful processing, which means that the EU data protection law creates a 'system of checks and balances which ensures lawful processing without asking consent of the person involved'. Kranenborg H, 'Article 8 – Protection of Personal Data,' in Peers, Stephen and others (eds), *The EU Charter of Fundamental Rights* (Nomos 2014), 229.

[57] Lynskey O, 'Deconstructing data protection: the 'added-value' of a right to data protection in the EU legal order.' (2014) 63 International & Comparative Law Quarterly, 569. Koops has also been sceptical in placing control in the centre of the data protection law by overlying on consent as a ground for lawful processing, one of the reasons being 'people's limited understanding of the consequences' of their choice to consent to the processing of their personal data. Koops B-J, 'The Trouble with European Data Protection Law' (2014) 4 International Data Privacy Law, 250.

demonstrated, according to Lynskey, by prohibiting consent[58] as a ground for lawful processing where such asymmetry exists.[59] In the same vein with Lynskey, Ausloos views control as an 'architecture of control design in functions of individuals', protecting those individuals from power asymmetries, 'ensuring a minimum level of individual control over personal data[60]'. Control is, according to Ausloos, the essence of the right to protection of personal data and thus sees the GDPR as laying down a 'legal framework to regulate legitimate interferences with fundamental rights and freedoms'.[61]

Second, another additional perspective as put forward by Hustinx is accountability. The aim of this perspective in the GDPR is to emphasize that controllers are endowed with proactive obligations to develop 'adequate data management in practice'.[62] In other words, controllers have to comply with the principles and facilitate the exercise of rights, but also take all the appropriate measures to comply and be in the position to demonstrate that these measures exist and continue to be effective. The principle of accountability, according to Hustinx, should lead to better data management in practice. This dimension of how the law is applied 'on the ground' was also shared by the Article 29 Data Protection Working Party, which viewed the accountability principle as moving data protection from 'theory to practice' by strengthening the role and responsibility of data controllers.[63]

Third, enforcement and independent supervision, are important pillars of the GDPR, and also present in arts 8 CFREU and 16 TFEU. Lastly, the GDPR offers an international dimension to data protection, via its extraterritorial effect and the special data transfers regime, which practically entail that the law may apply beyond the Union borders. While this aspect is not directly part of art 8, one could say that is reflected in the scope of application of the right to protection of personal data to 'any person', thus not only European Union citizens.[64]

[58] Kosta has criticized the reliance on consent to legitimize situations that would otherwise infringe the right. Kosta E, *Consent in European Data Protection Law* (Brill 2013), 313.

[59] Lynskey O, 'Deconstructing Data Protection: The "Added-Value" of a Right to Data Protection in the EU Legal Order' (2014) 63 International & Comparative Law Quarterly, 569.

[60] Ausloos J, *The Right to Erasure in EU Data Protection Law* (OUP 2020).

[61] ibid.

[62] For example, phrases such as 'all appropriate measures to ensure compliance' and 'demonstrating' are manifestations of this perspective.

[63] Article 29 Data Protection Working Party 'Opinion 3/2010 on the principle of accountability' WP173, 13 July 2010, 19. Read further on the accountability principle in data protection law: Alhadeff J, Van Alsenoy B, and Dumortier J, 'The Accountability Principle in Data Protection Regulation: Origin, Development and Future Directions,' in Guagnin, D and others (eds), *Managing Privacy through Accountability* (Palgrave Macmillan 2012).

[64] CFREU art 8(1).

5.2.2 Standards in the Legislative History of the General Data Protection Regulation

Having seen the rationales of the EU data protection law, it is interesting to study the legislative history of the GDPR to identify specific areas where the legislator had identified a link between standardization, as a form of private regulation, and data protection matters. While not all identified links in the 2012 Commission Proposal survived the legislative process and trialogue negotiations, and thus did not make it to the final text, studying the legislative history first shows potential standardization areas, and second it uncovers political debates surrounding the use of standards to support the EU data protection law. It should be noted that independently of any references in the GDPR—or any other legal instrument—standardization may be initiated bottom up, from the industry, regulatees, or technical committees and consortia, as discussed in Chapter 4.[65]

The Union data protection law overall regards standardization as an extra-legal private ordering. Concretely, this means that—with a few exceptions—references to standards and specifications in the several data protection laws, legislative proposals and policy documents are mainly indirect.

In 2012, the Proposal for a General Data Protection Regulation ('Commission GDPR proposal') reflected an overall positive stance towards developing and using standardization for data protection purposes. References to standards, in the meaning of a standard as prescribed in the Standardization Regulation,[66]are made mainly in relation to provisions with a prominent technical component[67] such as the right to data portability, data protection by design and by default. Those standards aim at harmonizing the implementation of the law. The extensive implementing powers of the Commission, put forward in the 2012 Commission Proposal, were met with criticism by the WP29, which opined that the international standardization bodies and the EDPB should be consulted by the Commission when drawing up standards.[68] The Commission would identify on a need-to basis the relevant standards and publish those in the form of an implementing act. This is a common practice in other areas of law, such as electronic identification and trust services, where a list of relevant international and European standards is typically provided in an implementing act.[69] The rationale

[65] See Chapter 4 section 4.2 in this book.

[66] Recital 66 GDPR Proposal.

[67] See respectively arts 18, 23, and 39 GDPR Proposal.

[68] Article 29 Data Protection Working Party 'Opinion 01/2012 on the data protection reform proposals' WP 191 (2012) 11 (hereafter WP 191 (2012):11).

[69] Commission Implementing Decision (EU) 2016/650 of 25 April 2016 laying down standards for the security assessment of qualified signature and seal creation devices pursuant to Articles 30(3) and 39(2) of Regulation (EU) No 910/2014 of the European Parliament and of the Council on electronic identification and trust services for electronic transactions in the internal market, [2016] OJ L109/40.

is that the public regulator intervenes with an act aiming to harmonize the implementation of the law, only after having observed how the law works in practice.[70] Overall, the WP29 found that implementing powers are reasonable when it comes to *technical conditions* for the implementation of the Regulation such as standardized forms and procedures.[71]

In 2014, substantial amendments to the Commission's proposal were put forward by the European Parliament in its First Reading ('Parliament First Reading'), including the references to standardization. The references to 'standards' were reduced significantly. The wording predominantly changed to 'standardized forms' and 'standardized formats', or 'technical measures' and similar terms. A reason could be that standards were mostly referred to in relation to Commission implementing powers. Since references to Commission powers were significantly reduced in the Parliament First Reading, references to standards were subsequently also reduced. The WP29's input on the proposed implementing acts gives a signal on how the implementing acts were received overall by supervisory authorities. For example, the WP29 proposed that the power of the Commission to adopt implementing acts for specifying technical standards for data portability (art 18(3) Commission GDPR Proposal), should be replaced by a delegated act without referenced standards. The delegated act work 'with minimum requirements instead of complete technical instructions', as in technical standards.[72] The WP29 thus recommended the use of a stronger binding regulatory instrument– the one of delegated acts–which formally complements the text of the Regulation. The WP29 considered technical standards more prescriptive and less flexible than a delegated act, which is admittedly an unusual argument, since non-binding standards are a more flexible regulation instrument, than an EU binding act. The Parliament aligned with the position of the WP29 with regard to both the instrument of implementing acts and the subsequent fewer direct references to technical standards. Overall, the Parliament in its First Reading reduced substantially the role of standardization, and the proposed amendments in the remaining standards-related provisions signaled an intention for meta-control by the supervisory authorities.

The Council General Approach almost eliminated the references to standardization of the Commission Proposal.[73] Standards had a role to play according to

[70] ibid.

[71] WP29 'Opinion 08/2012 providing further input on the data protection reform discussions' WP199 (2012) 9.

[72] WP29 'Working Document 01/2013. Input on the proposed implementing acts' (adopted 22 January 2013) WP200.

[73] There were references to standardized formats in some provisions such as art 54(a)(5) Council General Approach, which dealt with the communication means of the supervisory authorities with one another and the EDPB. 'Technical protection measures' are mentioned in Recital 69, as in the GDPR Proposal.

the Council, in certification. The Council General Approach maintained a provision on the power of the Commission to adopt implementing acts laying down technical standards for data protection certification mechanisms, seals and marks. The Council introduced a reference to an international ISO standard to be used as a benchmark by National Accreditation Bodies.[74]

While the Parliament also deleted several standardization references in its First Reading, especially those linked with Commission implementing powers, it had also introduced new references to standards in the text, such as in relation to the right to object.[75] The Council General Approach however did not follow the same approach with the Parliament. In fact, provisions such as data protection by design and by default and the right to data portability, which the Commission GDPR Proposal linked expressly to standards, were later instead associated with data protection certification mechanisms of arts 39 and 39a of the Council's General Approach. We cannot speak of one-to-one replacement of references to standardization to references to certification, since those are two quite different instruments in essence and in practice. However, looking at the bigger picture, the Council's introduction of certification references in the same provisions where standards were referenced in the Commission GDPR Proposal is not circumstantial; it first signals the technical nature of those legal rules and their 'availability' or suitability to be supplemented with a private regulation instrument, but also a general hesitation assigning such a role to standardization.

What this overview demonstrates is that back in 2012 standardization in the area of data protection, essentially in support of a law safeguarding a fundamental right, was a matter for debate. Several references of the initial proposal to 'standards' or 'specifications' were eliminated from the final text. Yet, despite the mainly indirect references, standards were implicitly correlated to specific roles in all versions of the preparatory works of the EU institutions. Indirect abstract references to standards (referring to 'state of the art' or components of the definition of standards, according to the Standardization Regulation)[76] remained part of the GDPR. Those eliminated references and the remaining indirect references offer guidance on the areas potentially suitable for standardization.

Standards have thus played a pre-law function of informing the legislative reform, but also several post-law functions in the GDPR, the ePrivacy Directive, and the ePrivacy Regulation Proposal.[77]

[74] Council General Approach art 39a.
[75] Parliament First Reading art 19(2)(b).
[76] European Commission 'Methods of referencing standards in legislation with an emphasis on European legislation', Entreprise Publications (2002), 10.
[77] See Chapter 4, section 4.1.5 in this book.

5.2.3 An Analytical Framework for Technical Standardization in Personal Data Protection Law

In regulatory spaces where private regulation, an expression of which is technical standardization, and legislation interact, there are different levels of architecture that may be identified, from a macro- and micro-governance perspective: single organizations, single regimes, and multiple regimes.[78] Within the same single regime, in this case the EU personal data protection law, different regulatory relationships are formed. Those relationships include regulatees (eg data controllers and data processors) and beneficiaries (eg data subjects), regulators and beneficiaries, (public) regulators eg supervisory authorities and regulatees; but also, private regulators (eg standardization organizations) and regulatees/data controllers, private regulators and supervisory authorities. Viewed with a juristic pluralistic lens,[79] those relationships are to a large extent based on the regulatory design of each legal instrument. The right of a data subject to lodge a complaint with the supervisory authorities in the GDPR for example is an aspect of the relationship between (public) regulators and beneficiaries. The right to not be subject to automated decision making in art 22 GDPR is an aspect of the relationship between the data subjects and the data controllers. The obligation to implement data security measures in art 32 GDPR is an aspect of the relationship of data controllers and data subjects, since it concerns the personal data of the data subject, but also the one of data controllers and supervisory authorities, in case there is a violation of the legal obligation.

Within the regime of the data protection law, the rules in the examined legal instruments concern regulatees, beneficiaries, and also regulators. The rules provide principles to interpret the specific legal requirements (eg art 5 GDPR), or stipulate obligations (eg art 24 GDPR) and rights, be it substantive rights (eg art 20 GDPR on the right to data portability) or procedural rights (eg art 82 GDPR on the right to compensation). There are some other rules that concern the functioning of the law itself and its implementation. Those latter provisions specify aspects of the legal rules in terms of how they will be implemented in practice or further specified, where there is a need (eg sector specific) or a mandate (eg a power of the Commission to adopt implementing acts). Often such provisions involve some form of self- or co-regulation.

Standardization and in general private regulation are often viewed as maintaining a role in decreasing fragmentation and enhancing coordination among different regimes or rules.[80] Standards in the case of the Union data

[78] Cafaggi F, 'The architecture of transnational private regulation.' [2011] EUI Department of Law Working Papers 2011/12.

[79] See Chapter 1, section 1.5.2 in this book.

[80] Cafaggi F 'Transnational Private Regulation: Regulating Global Private Regulators' in Cassese S (ed), *Research Handbook on Global Administrative Law* (Edward Elgar Publishing 2016).

protection legislation may work as meta-rules, in that they may ensure homogeneity on how some data protection rules are applied. This is particularly the case for aspects of data protection law that require a degree of flexibility, yet uniformity in their application. Further, standardization may work as a tool for compliance through operationalizing legal duties, as also seen in Chapter 4.[81] Standards may be utilized to specify requirements already existing in the data protection law either due to open legal standards and the necessary contextualization regarding sectors and types of processing (eg distribution of actor responsibility in different cloud computing models).[82] And finally, standards may operationalize legal rules and offer standardized technical means to data subjects to convey their wishes as regards the processing of their personal data, or exercise rights.

For analytical purposes in this Chapter,[83]therefore, standards in relation to EU data protection law are organized in three groups:

(i) standards that provide guidance for the implementation of the regulation (standards as meta-rules)
(ii) standards that aim at assisting regulatees, namely data controllers and/or processors, with compliance to their legal obligations and other legal requirements (standards for legal compliance)
(iii) standards assisting with data subjects' rights (standards for beneficiaries)

These last two groups correspond also to two of the rationales of EU data protection law: accountability and control over one's own personal data, as seen earlier in this Chapter. The groups are not mutually exclusive, a topic or legal provision may be relevant for standardization for different groups in parallel.

Within the identified groupings, the role of standards may further encompass a *facilitating* nature or *enabling* nature, depending on the necessity of standardization for the materialization of the goal of the relevant legal provision. Standards, as *facilitators*, are a useful, but not a *sine qua non* condition to achieve a goal laid down in data protection law. The usefulness of standards stems from the expert knowledge they embody, as they are developed in a multi-stakeholder environment with high expertise.[84] The *enabling* nature, which is more rarely encountered, usually concerns aspects of duties or compliance measures with a strong

[81] See functions in Chapter 4 section 4.1.4.2 in this book.
[82] Read further: De Hert P, Papakonstantinou V and Kamara I, 'The Cloud Computing Standard ISO/IEC 27018 through the Lens of the EU Legislation on Data Protection' (2016) 32 Computer Law & Security Review, 16.
[83] See Cafaggi F 'The Many Features of Transnational Private Rule-Making: Unexplored Relationships between Custom, Jura Mercatorum and Gloval Private Regulation' (2015) 36 U Pa J Int'l L, 875.
[84] Cafaggi F, 'New Foundations of Transnational Private Regulation' (2011) 38 Journal of law and society, 20; Kamara I, 'European Cybersecurity Standardisation: A Tale of Two Solitudes in View of Europe's Cyber Resilience' [2024] Innovation: The European Journal of Social Science Research.

technical component, such as pseudonymization and encryption of personal data.[85]

In the following sections, the different groupings of standards in relation to data protection law are further analysed and juxtaposed against the relevant standardization activity.

5.3 Technical Standards for Regulatees Facilitating Legal Compliance

5.3.1 Standards, Accountability, Scalability, and the Risk-Based Approach

Standardization playing the role of calibrating and specifying technical and organizational measures, would aim at ensuring that measures are appropriate to the risks likely to occur from data processing operations, as well as the conditions of processing. This aspect of standardization in data protection law is closely linked to accountability and the risk-based approach, introduced with the GDPR. As regards accountability and the risk-based approach, the GDPR maintains a core set of principles, but also includes prescriptive rules for its regulatees. Some of those rules despite being prescriptive include an open-ended component, in that their implementation requires an additional *assessment* to determine what is an appropriate measure to be taken by data controllers. It has been argued that the word 'appropriate' means that the measures are scalable, 'enabling the determination of concrete measures to be applied depending on the processing being carried out [...].'[86] In fact, the WP29 had argued that the application of the principles of art 5 GDPR is *inherently* scalable, because of their wording ie 'adequate', 'appropriate', 'reasonable', 'necessary' which requires taking to account the context, scope, purposes, and nature of processing.[87]

The scalability depends on a number of factors provided for in the relevant provisions, such as the scope and purpose of processing, the nature of the personal data.[88] This additional assessment to determine what is an 'appropriate' measure for a given processing operation has been linked to the so called 'risk based approach',[89] highlighting a need for considering the specific risks posed to the rights

[85] See art 32 GDPR.

[86] Docskey C, 'Article 24. Responsibility of the controller' in Kuner C, Bygrave LA, and Docksey C (eds), The EU General Data Protection Regulation (GDPR): A Commentary (OUP 2020), 562.

[87] WP29 'Statement on the role of a risk-based approach in data protection legal frameworks' WP218 (adopted 30 May 2014).

[88] See for example arts 25 and 32 GDPR.

[89] See for a comprehensive overview of the concept of risk-based approach in data protection: Gellert R, *The Risk-Based Approach to Data Protection* (OU P 2020); See also: Demetzou K, 'Data Protection Impact Assessment: A Tool for Accountability and the Unclarified Concept of 'High Risk' in the General Data Protection Regulation' (2019) 35 Computer Law & Security Review 105342.

and freedoms of individuals by specific processing operations. The notion of risk is a reference point in light of which data controllers can assess whether the organizational and technical measures taken offer a sufficient level of protection.[90] The WP29 had stressed that the risk-based approach has been introduced as a core element of the accountability principle itself.[91] The risk-based approach has been criticized for the decisional competence it affords to controllers.[92] An example is the assessment of whether their processing presents a high risk and are thus obliged to conduct a data protection impact assessment.[93]

Linked to the general responsibility for implementing technical and organizational measures that are appropriate, Recital 74 refers to measures that are *effective*. The effectiveness of the measures needs to be demonstrable, as is the case with the appropriateness of measures. The emphasis on the effectiveness of the measures taken by the regulatees, and the effectiveness of the protection of personal data and the individual through the data protection rules,[94] relates to the ongoing debate of data protection working on the ground and, avoiding the label of a formalistic process-oriented legislation, without delivering actual protection to individuals. Making data protection rules work on the ground—as opposed to a mere box-ticking compliance exercise for controllers and processors—was one of the challenges for the legislative reform of the Data Protection Directive. The elusive concept of 'effective protection' has been regularly used as a legal standard by the CJEU and Advocate General Opinions in data protection related case law, admittedly with some inconsistency as to the target of the effective protection being at times the (personal) data, the individuals or the rights and freedoms of the individuals.[95] What has been consistent throughout the CJEU data protection case law is

[90] Quelle C, 'Enhancing Compliance under the General Data Protection Regulation: The Risky Upshot of the Accountability-and Risk-Based Approach' (2018) 9 European Journal of Risk Regulation, 502 (hereafter Quelle,'Enhancing Compliance').

[91] WP29 'Statement on the role of a risk-based approach in data protection legal frameworks' WP218 (adopted 30 May 2014).

[92] Quelle,'Enhancing compliance' (n 90); Leiser, M R 'Private Jurisprudence' and the Right to Be Forgotten Balancing Test' (2020) 39 Computer Law & Security Review, 105458.

[93] GDPR art 35.

[94] GDPR Recital 11.

[95] For example: in *Google Spain*, the CJEU referred to 'effective and complete protection of data subjects' Judgment of 13 May 2014, *Google Spain and Google*, Case C 131/12, EU:C:2014:317 para 38; in the 2015 *Schrems I* in para 39 it refers to 'effective and complete protection of the fundamental rights and freedoms of natural persons'(see Judgment of 6 October 2015, *Schrems I*, Case C-362/14, EU:C:2015:650); in *Tele2Sverige* the CJEU in para 122 referred to 'appropriate technical and organizational measures to ensure the effective protection of retained data' (in relation to the ePrivacy Directive) (see Judgment of 21 December 2016, *Tele2 Sverige*, Joined Cases C-203/15 and C-698/15, EU:C:2016:970); in the 2020 *Schrems II* case in para 126 it referred to 'effective protection of personal data transferred' (see Judgment of 16 July 2020, *Schrems*, Case C-311/18, EU:C:2020:559); in Case C-507/17 in para 70 the Court referred to 'the effective protection of the data subject's fundamental rights' (see Judgment of 24 September 2019, Google v CNIL, Case C-507/17, EU:C:2019:772). Read further on effective and complete protection: Mahieu R, Van Hoboken J, and Asghari H, 'Responsibility for Data Protection in a Networked World: On the Question of the Controller, Effective and Complete Protection and Its Application to Data Access Rights in Europe' (2019) 10 JIPITEC, 84.

the use of the concept of effective protection to signal that compliance of processing operations and any measures taken by the regulatees should be assessed in light of the actual, dynamic circumstances of each processing activity. This interpretation was made clear in the *Schrems II* case, in which the Court did not only take into account the law of the US as third country, but also the *practice* in that country.[96]

Private regulation instruments such as standards and certifications are generally often associated with the principle of accountability and the risk-based approach.[97] Private regulation instruments are often grouped in data protection scholarship and policy documents as 'accountability-based mechanisms', making a connection between these instruments and the principle of art 5(2) GDPR, as well as the general responsibility of controllers under art 24(1) GDPR. Besides, the use of private regulation for the purpose of calibration of obligations in view of the intended result is supported by the wording of the GDPR. For example, Recital 98 provides that 'codes of conduct could *calibrate* the obligations of controllers and processors taking into account the risks likely to result from the processing for the rights and freedoms of natural persons'.[98] Further, art 42(1) provides that data protection certifications, as regulated in the GDPR, should take into account the 'specific needs of micro, small and medium enterprises'.[99] Thus, the GDPR connects in this manner private regulation to the obligations that require an additional assessment and include qualifying notions.

Data protection standards for legal compliance should be a) horizontal,[100] such as on privacy management, quality or guidance standards or b) vertical (sectorial)

[96] In relation to Standard Contractual Clauses as a legal ground for transfers the Court found that an EU data controller and the recipient of the data in the third country 'are required to verify, prior to any transfer, whether the level of protection required by EU law is respected in the third country concerned.' Judgment of 16 July 2020, Case C-311/18 *Schrems II*, EU:C:2020:559, para 142. Also in para 126 the Court found '*Therefore, although there are situations in which, depending on the law and practices in force in the third country concerned, the recipient of such a transfer is in a position to guarantee the necessary protection of the data solely on the basis of standard data protection clauses, there are others in which the content of those standard clauses might not constitute a sufficient means of ensuring, in practice, the effective protection of personal data transferred to the third country concerned. That is the case, in particular, where the law of that third country allows its public authorities to interfere with the rights of the data subjects to which that data relates*' [emphasis added].

[97] EDPB 'Guidelines 1/2019 on Codes of Conduct and Monitoring Bodies under Regulation 2016/679' (v. 2.0, adopted 4 June 2019) p.7; EDPB 'Guidelines 1/2018 on certification and identifying certification criteria in accordance with Articles 42 and 43 of the Regulation' (v.3.0 adopted 4 June 2019) 6; Centre for Information Policy Leadership 'What Good and Effective Data Privacy Accountability Looks Like: Mapping Organizations' Practices to the CIPL Accountability Framework' May 2020, 19; Article 29 Data Protection Working Party 'Opinion 3/2010 on the principle of accountability' WP173 (adopted 13 July 2010); Article 29 Data Protection Working Party 'The Future of Privacy. Joint contribution to the Consultation of the European Commission on the legal framework for the fundamental right to protection of personal data' WP168 (adopted 1 December 2009); Read further: Kamara, I 'Art. 42 Certification' in Spiecker gen. Döhmann I, Papakonstantinou E, Hornung G, and De Hert P (eds), *General Data Protection Regulation* (Nomos Verlagsgesellschaft mbH & Co KG 2023).

[98] GDPR Recital 98.

[99] GDPR art 42(1).

[100] Horizontal standards are those that can be applied across all sectors. See Chapter 2 section 2.3 in this book.

standards that provide controls and elucidate requirements and policies necessary for organizations seeking to achieve certain goals and by extension comply with legal duties.

5.3.2 The Example of the GDPR Security of Processing Obligation

Security of processing is one of the obligations of controllers and the processors. Art. 32 GDPR on security of processing is an example of a basis for standardization. The significance of security of processing shows not only in the GDPR which has elevated integrity and confidentiality of personal data to a protection principle,[101] but also the CJEU case law which connects data security to the core of the right to protection of personal data.[102]

Information security standards specifying the state of the art, appropriate security measures in a given sector, or data security techniques such as pseudonymization and encryption are types of standards that help data controllers comply with their security of data processing obligations. The EU legislature adopts a pragmatic approach on security technical and organizational measures[103] and establishes scalable obligations requiring additional assessment.[104] The controller must evaluate the risks and implement mitigating measures, which ensure an appropriate level of security, including confidentiality, integrity and availability.[105] The reference to appropriateness has been characterized as an expression of the proportionality principle, whereby the means used to achieve an aim are necessary for its achievement and correspond to the importance of the aim.[106] Recital 74 explicitly requires the controller to be able to demonstrate the compliance to the GDPR, including the effectiveness of the measures.[107] Thus, the

[101] GDPR art 5(1)(f). On top of constituting a duty in itself, and linked to a principle, security of processing is interconnected to other duties of the controller. A characteristic example is the Data Protection Impact Assessment, which among other elements needs to include 'the measures envisaged to address the risks, including safeguards, security measures and mechanisms to ensure protection of personal data' and to demonstrate compliance', art 35(7)(d) GDPR. See analysis on this issue in Kosta E and Stuurman K, 'Technical Standards and the Draft General Data Protection Regulation,' in Delimatsis P (ed), *The Law, Economics and Politics of International Standardisation* (Cambridge University Press 2015).

[102] Judgment of 8 April 2014, *Digital Rights Ireland*, Joined Cases C 293/12 and C 594/12, EU:C:2014:238, para 40.

[103] Wolters PTJ, 'The Security of Personal Data under the GDPR: A Harmonized Duty or a Shared Responsibility?' (2017) 7 International Data Privacy Law, 165.

[104] GDPR art 32(1) and (2).

[105] Recital 83 and art 5(1)(f) GDPR.

[106] Burton C, 'Article 32 Security of Processing' in Kuner C, Bygrave LA, and Docksey C (eds), *The EU General Data Protection Regulation (GDPR)* (OUP 2020). Read on the proportionality principle in EU data protection law: Dalla Corte L, 'On proportionality in The Data Protection Jurisprudence of the CJEU' (2022) 12 International Data Privacy Law 12, 259ff.

[107] Recital 74 GDPR.

measures should amount to a level of security appropriate to the risks posed to rights and freedoms of data subjects.

Security of processing is closely linked to the use of standards, as also acknowledged by the data protection public regulator, both the Commission[108] and the supervisory authorities.[109] This close link of security of processing and standardization is also evident by the activity of ISO and IEC, which develop a variety of data protection related standards under the umbrella of IT security, but also standardization bodies such as the US National Institute for Standards and Technology (NIST) focusing on specific security techniques.[110]

Article 32 includes indirect references to standards. First, it refers to the concept of state of the art,[111] and second to specific security measures, goals and means to achieve them. Examples of security measures include encryption and pseudonymization; security goals are confidentiality, integrity, availability, resilience, of processing systems and services, access to personal data in the event of an incident, and means to achieve those goals are testing, assessing, and evaluating the effectiveness of the technical and organizational measures.[112]

The EU legislature and policymakers often point at standards as providing the state of the art for technical and organizational measures in other areas of law.[113] As Joerges and others have suggested, references to 'the state of the art' should be regarded as a rule of incorporation of technological reason in legislation by means of private standard-setting.[114] The ESOs are in fact obliged by their internal

[108] Recital 66 2012 GDPR Proposal referred to 'technical standards and organisational measures to ensure security of processing'.

[109] The WP29 for example has acknowledged that 'encryption must remain standardised, strong and efficient [...]' WP29 'Statement of the WP29 on encryption and their impact on the protection of individuals with regard to the processing of their personal data in the EU' (April 2018) 3. See also European Data Protection Supervisor reference to standardization of Personal Information Management Systems, EDPS 'Opinion on Personal Information Management Systems. Towards more user empowerment in managing and processing personal data' Opinion 9/2016 (2016) 10.

[110] See for example the work of NIST on cryptography https://www.nist.gov/cryptography [accessed 20 August 2024].

[111] The term 'state of the art' should be distinguished from other 'states of technology': the generally accepted rules of technology, which are proven in practice and enjoy general recognition, and the existing scientific knowledge and research which stands for innovative and highly dynamic measures. The state of the art can be defined as 'procedures, equipment or operating methods available in the trade in goods and services for which the application thereof is most effective in achieving the respective legal protection objectives'. IT Security Association Teletrust. 'IT Security Act (Germany) and the EU General Data Protection Regulation: Guideline "State of the art". Technical and organizational measures' 2020, 11–12.

[112] GDPR art 32(1)(b)–(d).

[113] One example is found in the regulation of medical devices. The Commission standardization request points at standards as a means to provide the state of the art. Commission Implementing Decision of 15.5.2020 on a standardisation request to the European Committee for Standardization and the European Committee for Electrotechnical Standardization as regards medical devices in support of Regulation (EU) 2017/745 of the European Parliament and of the Council and in vitro diagnostic medical devices in support of Regulation (EU) 2017/746 of the European Parliament and of the Council, M/565, C(2020) 2532 final, 16.

[114] Joerges C, Schepel H, and Vos E 'The law's problems with the involvement of non-governmental actors in Europe's legislative processes: the case of standardisation under the "new approach"' Working Paper, EUI LAW, 1999/09 (1999), 30.

regulations to take into account the state of the art when developing standards.[115] In principle therefore, standards reflect the state of the art in relation to their field and scope. However, by conforming to (information) security standards controllers do not necessarily ensure that they take into account the state of the art, as prescribed by art 32 GDPR. The scope of the standard(s) needs to correspond to the security needs and level of security appropriated to the specific risks of processing of controllers or processors conforming to those security standards. It is possible that a standard covers only some aspects of the state of the art eg with regard to encryption techniques, but not all, or only technical and no organizational measures.[116] In addition, standards are revised in principle every five years. Thus, updates and newer measures may not be reflected in the standard, but the revision will eventually reflect the evolution of the state of the art. Furthermore, the reliability of the content of standards as providing the state of the art is not undisputed.[117]

In other areas of law, such as the New Approach legislation, the legislature accepts standards as *providing a good indication of the state of the art* at the time the standards were adopted.[118] In cases of harmonized standards based on a standardization request of art 10 Standardization Regulation outside the New Approach, those 'may provide useful indicators' of the state of the art.[119] Therefore, consideration of state of the art may rely on standards, but individual assessment for each processing operation is required to determine whether measures are suitable and necessary.[120] In relation to security of processing overall, standards are informing

[115] The Internal Regulations of CEN and CENELEC (Pt 2) provide that Technical specification serves as a normative document in areas where the actual state of the art is not yet sufficiently stable for a European standard. Furthermore, once a Technical Committee of CEN or CENELEC (that is the two of the three European Standards Organisations) is to be established, the so called Business Management Plan needs to explain the state of the art in the field addressed by the scope of the CEN Technical Committee, recent or expected technological changes/major innovations, and how the Technical Committee is expected to respond to these.

[116] Another possibility is that the controls in a standard are broadly framed so that they remain up-to-date and adaptable to developments and advancements. For example, see the mapping of art 32 technical and organizational security measures proposed by ENISA to the ISO/IEC 27001:2013 controls ENISA. 'Handbook on Security of Personal Data Processing' (December 2017), Annex A.

[117] In *Dyson*, the applicant made an argument that 'Cenelec's task was to ensure that all published standards were consistent, clear and accurate and took full account of the state of the art', but the General Court found that there were doubts as to whether a test described in a CENELEC standard was reproducible. Judgment of the Court 11 May 2017, Case C-44/16 P *Dyson*, EU:C:2017:357, paras 40 and 41. See also the ruling on appeal (which however did not rule on the CENELEC standard claim). Judgment of the Court 8 November 2018, Case T-544/13 Dyson, RENV EU: T:2018:761.

[118] European Commission 'Guide to application of the Machinery Directive 2006/42/EC' edn 2.2 (October 2019): 75. In the New Approach legislation, where the essential requirements are provided for in the legislation, standards need to fulfil the essential health and safety requirements and employ the most effective technical means that are available for a cost which takes into account the seriousness of the potential harm. European Commission 'Guide to application of the Machinery Directive 2006/42/EC' edn 2.2 (October 2019): 155.

[119] European Commission 'Guide to application of the Machinery Directive 2006/42/EC' edn 2.2 (October 2019): 157.

[120] 'IT Security Act (Germany) and the EU General Data Protection Regulation: Guideline "State of the Art". Technical and organizational measures' (2020), 64.

and providing guidance to controllers and processors aiming to comply with their legal duties.

5.3.3 The Example of Obtaining Consent in ePrivacy Law

The ePrivacy Regulation Proposal introduces a centralized approach to obtaining consent, via the technical settings of software programs. The software programs could be Internet browsers, as explained by the Commission in the Explanatory Memorandum for the 2017 Proposal, or apps and software interfaces for Internet of Things-connected devices.[121] While this sort of centralized approach was not included in the original 2002 ePrivacy Directive,[122] it was already hinted in the 2009 Directive that revised it:

> Where it is technically possible and effective, in accordance with the relevant provisions of Directive 95/46/EC, the user's consent to processing may be expressed by using the appropriate settings of a browser or other application. The enforcement of these requirements should be made more effective by way of enhanced powers granted to the relevant national authorities.[123]

The WP29 showed scepticism about providing consent in this manner and had supported the view that provision of valid consent via browser settings would happen in 'very limited circumstances', because of the various conditions that should be cumulatively met.[124] First, the browser should not accept by default the collection and processing of the user's information and any inaction of a user by not setting the browser to refuse tracking technologies (such as cookies) does not provide a clear and unambiguous indication of the user's wishes.[125] Second, it should not be possible to bypass the settings as configured by the user. Third, consent needed to be specific, so bulk consent to receive cookies for future processing could not be valid. Browsers would need to convey clear and visible information to users, including about the purposes of cookies and further processing. The WP29 had stressed the importance of default privacy protective settings to ensure that data subjects effectively give their consent.[126]

[121] WP29, Opinion 01/2017 on the Proposed Regulation for the ePrivacy Regulation (2002/58/EC), wp247.

[122] See Recital 17 of Directive 2002/58/EC which provided that consent maybe given 'by any appropriate method enabling a freely given specific and informed indication of the user's wishes.'

[123] Recital 66 Directive 2009/136/EC of the European Parliament and of the Council of 25 November 2009.

[124] WP29, Opinion 2/2010 on online behavioural advertising, WP171 (22 June 2010) 13.

[125] ibid 14.

[126] The proposal of the WP29 was in favour of a status of 'non-acceptance and non-transmission of third party cookies setting'. Read further: Kosta E, 'Peeking into the Cookie Jar: The European

The ePrivacy Regulation Proposal does not specifically address the concerns voiced by the WP29. Article 9(2) provides that 'where technically possible and feasible [...] consent may be expressed by using the appropriate technical settings of a software application enabling access to the internet.'[127] Recital 24 provides further conditions for the implementation of this provision. The web browsers should require a clear and affirmative action from the end-user to signify a freely given, specific, informed, and unambiguous agreement to the storage and access of third-party tracking cookies both incoming and outcoming from the terminal equipment.[128]

To qualify as affirmative action and fulfil the relevant condition for valid consent,[129] the end users should be required to actively select 'accept third party cookies' after they are given the necessary information.[130] Thus the Commission seems to support the default setting being neither 'accept cookies', nor 'reject cookies', but rather a neutral status. The browser should inform the end users about the privacy settings different possibilities and 'ask them to make a choice' at the moment of its installation.[131] Since users are not likely to be familiar with the significance of their choice and its consequences, the information should be presented in an objective manner, not dissuading them from selecting privacy settings, and should provide the risks related to browsing histories records and their use for targeted advertising.[132] In addition, the Commission encourages –but does not oblige–providers of web browsers to offer user-friendly solutions to users for changing their initial chosen settings, and to allow them to make exceptions and whitelist certain sites.

Despite the considerable improvement of moving the technical settings provision from a Recital in the previous regime to the main text of the Proposal, the wording did not change much. Instead, all the valuable clarifications and the conditions are in Recital 24 of the Proposal, instead of art 9(2). The EDPS highlighted

Approach towards the Regulation of Cookies' (2013) 21 International Journal of Law and Information Technology, 398ff.

[127] EC Proposal for ePrivacy Regulation art 9(2).

[128] In the REFIT exercise, the Commission had considered three technical options to obtaining consent. Those were 1) the browser solution, which entailed that all communication would be centralized via the browsers, 2) the tracking company solution, where the party placing the cookie would be responsible to obtain consent, and 3) publishers solution where individual websites would be responsible for obtaining consent. Deloitte 'Evaluation and review of Directive 2002/58 on privacy and the electronic communication sector' Final Report (2017), 331f.

[129] For conditions of valid consent read among many: EDPB Guidelines 05/2020 on consent under Regulation 2016/679, vol 1.1. (May 2020); Kosta E 'Article 7' in Kuner C, Bygrave LA, and Docksey C *The Oxford Handbook of Empirical Legal Research*(eds), The EU General Data Protection Regulation (GDPR): A Commentary (OUP 2020); and Judgment of the Court, Case C-673/17 *Planet49 GmbH*, EU:C:2019:801.

[130] Recital 24 Proposal for ePrivacy Regulation.

[131] ibid.

[132] ibid.

that the scope of art 8 should include current and future tracking techniques such as active and passive tracking, and in different environments, where information is not necessarily stored in the terminal equipment, but can be nonetheless obtained from the device.[133] Besides, a known problem with obtaining consent via technical settings, which is not addressed with the proposed provision of art 9(2), is that websites tend to ignore any signal objecting to the accessing and storing information to the user's terminal equipment.[134] The Parliament Report took note of the shortcomings of the EC Proposal and proposed substantial amendments in the text of art 9(2):

> Without prejudice to paragraph 1, where technically possible and feasible, for the purposes of point (b) of Article 8(1), consent may be expressed or withdrawn by using technical specifications for electronic communications services or information society services which allow for specific consent for specific purposes and with regard to specific service providers actively selected by the user in each case, pursuant to paragraph 1. When such technical specifications are used by the user's terminal equipment or the software running on it, they may signal the user's choice based on previous active selections by him or her. These signals shall be binding on, and enforceable against, any other party.[135]

The Parliament therefore addresses the scope and framework under which those technical settings would work and clarifies that art 9(2) concerns both providing and withdrawing consent. It explicitly refers to technical specifications instead of software applications, and most importantly, the binding nature and enforceability of the received signals.

The relation of expressing or withdrawing consent with standardization is straightforward. The absence of standardization would lead to diverse signals with different scopes and meanings lost in between non-interoperable systems, as the past has shown. The 'no tracking' signals were interpreted by websites in great variety–by disabling targeted advertising but continue tracking for other purposes, disable tracking by third party websites but continue tracking and offer targeted content for their website, or other.[136]

[133] European Data Protection Supervisor 'EDPS Opinion on the Proposal for a Regulation on Privacy and Electronic Communications (ePrivacy Regulation)' Opinion 6/2017, 28.

[134] Kamara I and Kosta E, 'Do Not Track Initiatives: Regaining The Lost User Control' (2016) 6 *International Data Privacy Law*, 276 (hereafter Kamara and Kosta 'Do Not Track Initiatives').

[135] Amendment 103, art 9(2) European Parliament, ***I REPORT on the proposal for a regulation of the European Parliament and of the Council concerning the respect for private life and the protection of personal data in electronic communications and repealing Directive 2002/58/EC (Regulation on Privacy and Electronic Communications) (COM (2017)0010 – C8-0009/2017 – 2017/0003(COD)) Committee on Civil Liberties, Justice and Home Affairs, 20.10.2017.

[136] Hofman, Chris 'Why Enabling Do Not Track does not help you from being tracked' (16 October 2020) https://www.howtogeek.com/126705/why-enabling-do-not-track-doesnt-stop-you-from-being-tracked/ [accessed 20 August 2024].

5.3.4 The Flip Side of the Coin: Standards as a Benchmark for Supervisory Authorities

Standards in this category may in parallel facilitate the work of supervisory authorities. Standards may, under the condition of development with the Union data protection law in mind, offer benchmarks for supervisory authority audits. In a case of an administrative fine imposed to a hospital for weak data security measures in violation of art 32 GDPR, the Dutch data protection authority used as a benchmark information security national standards published by NEN, the Dutch Standardization Institute.[137] Those national standards were frequently referred to in the relevant legislation as good practices for security, and were eventually made open access by NEN.[138] Similarly, the French DPA CNIL has announced that the international standard ISO/IEC 27701 represents the state of the art in (personal) data security,[139] not excluding taking it into account during its supervisory tasks.

There are two eminent issues for the utility of data protection standards for compliance and benchmarks for investigation. One is the risk of 'creative compliance' which practically entails that companies will follow rules to the letter but 'find ways to evade their spirit and thus undermine the objectives of the regime'.[140] Thus conforming to the prescriptive rules of standards might lead to a box-ticking exercise, instead of meaningful compliance aiming at responsible and fair processing of personal data. Such a risk would lead, for example, to superficial compliance, having a privacy policy or doing a risk analysis because the standard requires it, but of disputable quality. The risk is mitigated by embedding compliance-assisting standards in the broader context of the relevant data protection law, and even the foundations in the primary Union law, which reminds one that conforming to standards, and specific provisions on which those relate, is not an end in itself but

[137] NEN 7510 is a standard specifying the requirements of the ISO/IEC 27001 information security standard in the healthcare sector and NEN7513 which relates to logging and recording of actions in electronic patients' files. See the Dutch DPA decision (in Dutch): https://autoriteitpersoonsgegevens.nl/sites/default/files/atoms/files/besluit_haga_-_ter_openbaarmaking.pdf [accessed 20 August 2024].

[138] See Louis Jonker 'NEN standards for data protection in health care now freely available' VanDoorne blog (2015) https://www.vandoorne.com/en/knowledge-sharing/news/nen-standards-for-data-protection-in-health-care-now-freely-available/ and relevant case *Knooble* case NL:GHSGR:2010:BO4175 https://uitspraken.rechtspraak.nl/inziendocument?id = ECLI:NL:GHSGR:2010:BO4175 [accessed 20 August 2024], and relevant: Stuurman K, 'Annotatie bij Rechtbank Den Haag 31 december 2008 (Knooble/Staat en NNI)' AMI/Tijdschrift voor auteurs-, media en informatierecht, 2009:2.

[139] CNIL 'ISO 27701, an international standard addressing personal data protection' (April 2020) https://www.cnil.fr/en/iso-27701-international-standard-addressing-personal-data-protection [accessed 20 August 2024]. Read further on the ISO/IEC 27701 standard Lachaud E, 'ISO/IEC 27701 Standard: Threats and Opportunities for GDPR Certification' (2020) 6 European Data Protection Law Review, 194.

[140] Scott C, 'Standard-Setting in Regulatory Regimes' in Baldwin R, Cave M and Lodge M (eds), *The Oxford Handbook of Regulation* (OUP2010), 104.

rather the means to achieve compliance. The second risk has to do with legal (un) certainty by the existence of a multitude of sorts of 'relevant' standards, which are nonetheless not referenced in the law or formally endorsed by the legislature in other means. This is problematic because the controller/processor does not know on which to base the suitable standard to its processing and what will assist with its compliance to their legal obligations.[141]

5.4 Technical Standards for Beneficiaries Facilitating the Exercise of Data Subject's Rights

Individual control over personal data is pivotal in data protection law, both as a concept instrumentalizing the essence of the fundamental right to personal data protection, and as an organizing notion of the legal obligations and substantive rights in the secondary law.[142] The GDPR shields data subjects with provisions such as data protection by design and by default, the implementation burden of which lies with the controller or processor, and substantive rights, such as the right to object to processing, the exercise of which lies with the individual whose data are processed. Thus, two types of roles are identified here. One is standards that provide the (technical) means to data subjects to have their wishes and preferences heard, and thus in principle help data subjects balance out the power asymmetry between controllers/processors and data subjects. Examples of such a role is demonstrated with the right to object.[143] The second type of role concerns framing the duties of the controllers to accommodate the preferences and wishes of the data subjects. For instance, standardized means of electronic transmission so that a data subject can effectively port data from one provider is an example of such a role. Another example is using products or services that are designed to consider the right to data protection and enable controllers to fulfil their obligations, in general, including towards the data subject. This is particularly the case for the European standard on data protection by design and by default, which provides both process and product/service requirements and guidance on liability issues of manufacturers and service providers.[144]

[141] Gleeson NC and Walden I, 'It's a Jungle Out There?: Cloud Computing, Standards and the Law' (2014) 5 European Journal of Law and Technology, 2.

[142] Read further: Hustinx P, 'EU Data Protection Law: The Review of Directive 95/46/EC and the General Data Protection Regulation' (2014) https://www.statewatch.org/media/documents/news/2014/sep/eu-2014-09-edps-data-protection-article.pdf [accessed 20 August 2024]; Lynskey O, 'Deconstructing data protection: the 'added-value' of a right to data protection in the EU legal order' (2014) 63 International & Comparative Law Quarterly, 569; Kranenborg H, 'Article 8 – Protection of Personal Data,' in Peers, Stephen and others (eds), *The EU Charter of Fundamental Rights* (Nomos 2014).

[143] GDPR art 21.

[144] See Chapter 8 Case Study 1 in this book.

5.4.1 The Example of the Right to Data Portability in the GDPR

The right to data portability is strongly connected with the data subject empowerment.[145] Article 20 GDPR provides *inter alia* the right of data subjects to receive their personal data in a 'in a structured, commonly used and machine-readable and interoperable format'[146] and 'where technically feasible' to have the data transmitted directly from one controller to another.[147] Recital 68 encourages controllers to develop formats that are interoperable.[148] Scholars argue that standardization is necessary to make portability meaningful.[149]

As the ISO/IEC 19941 standard provides,[150] data portability from a standardization point of view concerns the ability to *easily* transfer data from one system to the other. Portability implies some previously specified knowledge of the system of the controllers[151] then may benefit from adequate interoperability[152] to transfer the requested data. There has been extensive committee-based and market-based standardization activity, in particular concerning cloud computing.[153] W3C has been developing a 'Data Privacy Vocabulary' and the International Society for Automation (ISA) the 'Core Vocabularies' aiming at eliminating ambiguous definitions and in turn enable interoperability of semantics.[154] In sum, standardization has the potential for a significant, *enabling* role in relation to portability, and specifying requirements for sectorial application of the right of art 20 GDPR.

[145] Recital 68 GDPR provides 'to further strengthen the control over his or her own data [*The Oxford Handbook of Empirical Legal Research*] the data subject should also be allowed to receive personal data [...]'.

[146] See analysis in Ursic H, 'Unfolding the New-Born Right to Data Portability: Four Gateways to Data Subject Control' (2018) 15 SCRIPT-ed, 42.

[147] GDPR art 20(1) and (2).

[148] Recital 68 GDPR.

[149] Graef I, Husovec M, and Purtova N, 'Data Portability and Data Control: Lessons for an Emerging Concept in EU Law' (2018) 19 German Law Journal, 1359. Graef and others also pinpoint other problems such as transferring value added services ie product comparison services to competitors, which however relate to the existence of a right to data portability and not its standardization.

[150] ISO/IEC 19941:2017 Information technology - Cloud computing - Interoperability and portability.

[151] Markoska E, Chorbev I, Ristov S, and Gusev M, ('Cloud portability standardization overview' in 2015 38th *International Convention on Information and Communication Technology, Electronics and Microelectronics* (MIPRO), IEEE, 286.

[152] Interoperability is defined as the 'ability of a service customer to interact with a service and exchange information according to a prescribed method and obtain predictable results' while portability is the 'ability of service customers to move their data or their applications between multiple service providers at low cost and with minimal disruption'. See ISO/IEC 17788:2014 and Rec. ITU-T Y.3500 (08/2014).

[153] An example of market-based standardization is the OASIS specification on Lipton P, Lauwers C, and Tamburri D, 'Oasis topology and orchestration specification for cloud applications (tosca) tc.' March 2017 (2017). See further ETSI Cloud Standards Coordination Phase 2; Interoperability and Security in Cloud Computing ETSI SR 003 391 (2016)

[154] See an overview of the state of the art: Pandit HJ and others, 'Standardisation, Data Interoperability, and GDPR' in Jacobs K (ed), *Advances in Standardization Research* (IGI Global 2020).

5.4.2 The Example of the Right to Object in the GDPR

The right to object to processing concerns lawful processing based on the performance of a task for public interest or the legitimate interest of the controller.[155] In cases of direct marketing and profiling, the right to object to processing is unconditional. In the context of the use of Information Society services,[156] data subjects may exercise their right to object by automated means using technical specifications.[157] Article 21(5) GDPR thus introduces by means of an indirect reference a legal basis for the exercise of data subject's right using standards.

The exercise by automated means implies that the data subjects have expressed their wish or intention to exercise the right and those are automatically communicated to the controller once specific conditions pre-determined by the data subjects are met. For example, a data subject objects to processing for third party analytics, which takes place with the placement of cookies in the terminal device of the data subject. When this processing is based on the legitimate interest per art 6(1)(f) GDPR of the controller or the third parties placing the cookies, the data subject may object to such processing.

Since the right to object per art 21(1) applies only to limited grounds for processing, when implementing such a technical specification the controller would need first to automatically communicate to the data subject the ground for processing, and the indication of the objection would then be sent only in case of the allowed grounds. Alternatively, the data subjects would indicate their conditional objection, which would be respected only on the condition the controller is relying on legitimate interest or a task carried out in the public interest ground.[158] In the latter case, there are risks related to a false perception of the data subjects thinking they have effectively exercised a right to object, while this would not be the case. For that reason, additional transparency mechanisms should need to be in place, such as a message made visible to the data subject (not only readable by the device) that the exercise of the right was not respected,

[155] Recital 69 GDPR provides 'where personal data might lawfully be processed [...]'

[156] Information Society service is 'any service normally provided for remuneration, at a distance, by electronic means and at the individual request of a recipient of services', whereby 'at a distance' means that the service is provided without the parties being simultaneously present'; 'by electronic means' means that the service is sent initially and received at its destination by means of electronic equipment for the processing (including digital compression) and storage of data, and entirely transmitted, conveyed and received by wire, by radio, by optical means or by other electromagnetic means; 'at the individual request of a recipient of services' means that the service is provided through the transmission of data on individual request.' Directive 2015/1535 of the Parliament and of the Council of 9 September 2015 laying down a procedure for the provision of information in the field of technical regulations and of rules on Information Society services (codification), OJ L 241/1, art 1(1)(b).

[157] GDPR art 21(5).

[158] Kamara, Kosta 'Do Not Track Initiatives' (n 134).

so that the data subject can make use of other rights or the legal remedies provided in the GDPR against the controller or processor. The conditions for art 21(2) and direct marketing, including profiling, are less burdensome in the sense that the exercise of the right is not conditioned on the ground for lawful processing.

The use of specifications or standards for the exercise of the right to object relies on the technical character of standards, and especially the possibility of their implementation by technical (automated) means. This role of a technical specification, which approaches the notion technoregulation, attaches significance not only on the content of the standard, but also its implementation or enforcement of 'standards' by means of technology.[159] An example of such implementation is ICT specifications incorporated in the manufacturing of a product or a system, from which the user cannot (easily) opt-out, except for choosing another product or system. In data protection in the online environment such specifications often take the form of a protocol such as the Platform for Privacy Preferences (P3P)[160] or a recent effort for a web browser specification.[161] The implementation of standards by means of technology however needs to ensure that the voluntary character of standards is not compromised by the automation of application involved. Last, there is a close link of the provision of art 21(5) with the ePrivacy legislation. Both aspects need to be assessed in light of the art 21 requirements for a specification to qualify as (effective) exercise of the right to object in the meaning of art 21(5) GDPR.

[159] 'Technoregulation' is a much broader topic exceeding the scope and limits of this book. The focus here is on the aspect of enforcement and compliance to standards by means of technology. On technoregulation, see in general, among many, Reidenberg JR, 'Lex Informatica: The Formulation of Information Policy Rules Through Technology' (1997) 56 Tex L Rev, 553; Lessig L, *Code: and Other Laws of Cyberspace*, 2.0 (Basic Book 2006); Brownsword R, 'What The World Needs Now: Techno-regulation, Human Rights and Human Dignity' in *Global Governance and The Quest for Justice* (Hart Publishing 2004), 203; Yeung K, 'Towards An Understanding of Regulation by Design' in Brownsword R and Yeung K, *Regulating Technologies: Legal Futures, Regulatory Frames and Technological Fixes* (Bloomsbury Publishing 2008); Leenes R, 'Framing Techno-Regulation: An Exploration of State and Non-State Regulation by Technology' (2011) 5 Legisprudence, 143; Gutwirth S, De Hert P, and De Sutter L, 'The Trouble with Technology Regulation: Why Lessig's 'Optimal Mix' Will Not Work,' in Brownsword R and Yeung K (eds), *Regulating Technologies: Legal Futures, Regulatory Frames and Technological Fixes* (Hart Publishing 2008), 193; Nissenbaum H. 'From Preemption to Circumvention: If Technology Regulates, Why Do We Need Regulation (and Vice Versa)' (2011) 26 Berkeley Tech LJ, 1367; De Vries K and van Dijk N, 'A Bump in the Road. Ruling Out Law from Technology,' Ius Gentium: Comparative Perspectives on Law and Justice (Springer 2013), 89; Leenes R and Lucivero F, 'Laws on Robots, Laws by Robots, Laws in Robots: Regulating Robot Behaviour by Design' (2014) 6 Law, Innovation and Technology, 193; Black J and Murray AD, 'Regulating AI and Machine Learning: Setting the Regulatory Agenda' (2019) 10 European Journal of Law and Technology, 3.

[160] Read more on the project on the W3C website: https://www.w3.org/P3P/ [accessed 20 August 2024]. The project however was suspended due to lack of support.

[161] Global Privacy Control (GPC) https://globalprivacycontrol.github.io/gpc-spec/ [accessed 20 August 2024].

Table 5.1 Overview of standardization areas in GDPR & ePrivacy (Regulatees & Beneficiaries)

Provision	Topic	Integration mechanism	Type of function	Nature of function
Recital 32, art 7(1), 8 GDPR	Consent	Indirect abstract reference	For beneficiaries	facilitating
art 8(2) GDPR	Age verification – consent of child	Indirect abstract reference	Compliance	enabling
art 12	Information on data processing via icons	Indirect specific reference	For beneficiaries	facilitating
art 20 GDPR	Data portability	Indirect abstract reference	For beneficiaries & Compliance	enabling
art 21(1) GDPR	Right to object	Indirect specific reference	For beneficiaries	enabling
art 25(1) GDPR	Data Protection by design	Indirect abstract reference	Compliance	facilitating
art 32 GDPR	Security of processing	Indirect abstract reference	Compliance	facilitating
art 14 ePrivacy Directive	Design of terminal equipment	Indirect specific reference	For beneficiaries	enabling
art 9(1) COM Proposal ePR	Consent	Indirect specific reference	For beneficiaries	enabling
at 10 COM Proposal ePR/ EP 1st Reading	Software architecture design	Indirect specific reference	For beneficiaries	enabling
art 8(4) COM Proposal ePR	Information on data processing via icons	Indirect specific reference	For beneficiaries	facilitating

5.5 Technical Standards as Meta-rules

The use of standards for implementing data protection certification mechanisms in the GDPR provided the main example in this category. In general, seals and marks that are not easily recognizable for data subjects defeat their transparency purpose. Thus, a degree of uniformity is important for the effectiveness of the data protection certification mechanisms, which explains art 43(9) GDPR providing the power to the Commission to adopt implementing acts specifying standards for data protection certification mechanisms. Those standards are intended to prescribe to both private regulators (ie certification bodies) and public regulators (supervisory authorities and Member States) common requirements and implementation rules.

Another example is the provision of art 43(2), and the international standard providing requirements for accreditation of certification bodies.[162] The standard, as mentioned, is mandatory for National Accreditation Bodies (NAB) conducting assessments for the suitability and competence of certification bodies. In addition to the generic requirements of art 43(1) and (2), the NAB must follow the requirements of the ISO/IEC 17065:2012, and in turn, all certification bodies aiming at providing certification services per arts 42 and 43 GDPR, are subject to the requirements of this standard, when their assessment is conducted by a NAB. Complementarity thus in this context means the provision of additional binding rules to what is provided in the law. An instrument formally complementing a Union law would normally be a Commission delegated act, which would be subject to several safeguards such as that a delegated act is not permitted to change essential elements of the law and may be revoked by the Parliament and the Council.[163] This is not however the case with the ISO/IEC 17065 standard, the reference to which is inserted directly in the text. This is admittedly, unusual for a Union data protection law, and probably this is why GDPR art 43(1)(b) is the single example of a direct reference to a standard.

The question of why the legislator resorted to standardization while the instrument of a regulation has exactly this purpose of achieving a high degree of harmonization is a valid one.[164] Looking back at the example of GDPR art 43(9) and the implementing acts laying down standards for recognition of certifications across Member States, there could be a number of reasons justifying the choice of not directly including the measures in the GDPR, such as postponing setting the rules on this matter for after data protection certification mechanisms have been approved by the DPA and the market has developed and matured, or because such detailed requirements for non-essential elements do not belong in a regulation.

When standards functioning as meta-rules are not imposed as binding rules –as seen in the example of art 43(2)–or imposed in a binding Union act, their meta-rule function is dependent on a broad (voluntary) use and market acceptance. Such a potential function is then dependent on factors such as the added value and clarity, so that the Commission or supervisory authorities decide to endorse or refer to those standards in their acts. However, standardization bodies are intensifying their standardization activities developing a wide range, sometimes (partially) overlapping, standards or standardization on a topic viewed

[162] ISO/IEC 17065:2012.

[163] TFEU art 290.

[164] In the Explanatory Memorandum for the GDPR Proposal, the Commission explained that the adoption of a Regulation as a chosen instrument would 'reduce legal fragmentation [..] by introducing a harmonised set of core rules' European Commission 'Proposal for a Regulation of The European Parliament and of the Council on the protection of individuals with regard to the processing of personal data and on the free movement of such data (General Data Protection Regulation) COM/2012/011 final' Section 3.

Table 5.2 Overview of standardization related issues in GDPR & ePrivacy legislation (Meta-rules)

Provision	Topic	Integration mechanism	Type of function	Nature of function
art 43(2) GDPR	Accreditation assessment	Direct dated reference	Meta-rule	enabling
art 43(9) GDPR	Implementing act for uniform implementation of certifications	Indirect specific reference	Meta-rule	facilitating
art 43(8) GDPR	Implementing act for certification criteria	Indirect specific reference	Meta-rule	facilitating

from a different perspective ie consumer policy or organizational management.[165] Multiple standards covering more or less the same aspects bear the risk of undermining the harmonization function of standards for data protection law. In those cases, supervisory authorities or the Commission, if it has the power to adopt an act on the topic, should specify which standard is relevant for what purpose, after having thoroughly assessed its alignment with the data protection law.

In general, the function of standards as meta-rules in data protection seems to be more limited than the other roles for compliance and data subject's rights, also due to the limited examples in the examined EU data protection law.

5.6 Legal Effects of References to Standards in the GDPR and the ePrivacy Legislation and Limitations

In the field of data protection, the GDPR is not New Approach type of legislation:[166] it is not drafted following the 1985 Council Resolution establishing the New Approach and the New Legislative Framework (NLF) on conformity assessment, its main goal is to protect fundamental rights as shown by its legal basis. Its regulatory target is neither products nor services, it does not provide *essential requirements*, but detailed duties and rights, alongside its principles and operative rules. Most importantly, the GDPR does not include any reference to presumption of conformity with its provisions offered by compliance with standards. However,

[165] See for example the internatonal standard under development ISO/AWI 31700 Consumer protection—Privacy by design for consumer goods and services.

[166] Its *lex specialis*, the ePrivacy Directive, is not a New Approach type of law either for the same reasons, except for the legal basis, which is art 95 Treaty establishing the European Community ('Approximation of laws').

the GDPR and its *lex specialis*, the ePrivacy Directive, can serve as the legal basis for the development of standards under the General co-development mode, but also the committee and market-based mode. Conforming to standards in the GDPR and ePrivacy legislation is voluntary with the exception of the EN ISO/IEC 17065: 2012 in relation to art 43(5) GDPR, which has become *de facto* mandatory. However, personal data protection becomes an essential requirement for radio equipment subject to the Radio Equipment Directive (RED). Harmonized European standards based on the RED will offer a presumption of conformity to the RED, and in particular art 3(3)(e) on privacy and personal data protection. Similarly, aspects of personal data protection such as record keeping, processing of special categories of personal data and others, will be assessed in the framework of harmonized standards based on art 10 of the AI Act, which is also based on the New Approach and NLF.

The different roles standards may assume to complement the law are subject to several limitations. One such limitation stems from the difference in the legal basis for the adoption of the Union data protection law and the Standardization Regulation, which reveals different aims of the laws and reasonably the underlying measures and instruments regulated therein. The GDPR aims primarily at protecting fundamental rights, since it is based on art 8 CFREU and art 16 TFEU. The Standardization Regulation is based on art 114 TFEU, hence striving to approximate rules in the Union in order to achieve the Internal Market. As a consequence, the legal bases are a notable difference hinting that standardization, as regulated in Regulation 1025/2012 is an Internal Market instrument and is introduced in the Union legal order as such, while the data protection legislation aims at protecting (universal) fundamental values, rooted in human rights.[167] This difference should be kept in mind, but should not be seen to be an irreparable gap. The selection of legal bases of legal instruments may reflect a formalism, an institutional choice.[168] The history of data protection law reveals that the GDPR predecessor was based on the approximation of laws legal basis, *inter alia,* due to the lack of a vertical legal basis on data protection, as the one of art 16 TFEU later established with the Lisbon Treaty. Besides, the ePrivacy Regulation is proposed to be based on both art 114 TFEU and art16 TFEU.[169] Further, while the basis of the

[167] The rights and freedoms enshrined in the Charter do not depend on Union Member States nationality criteria, but are granted to 'everyone'.

[168] TFEU art 114 has been characterized as an 'almost unlimited "one-fits-it-all" power to harmonise laws in the internal market', Engel A, *The Choice of Legal Basis for Acts of the European Union* (Springer International Publishing 2018), 138.

[169] The Explanatory Memorandum provides a rather awkward explanation though for the selection of the art 114 TFEU basis next to art. 16 TFEU, 'Since the initiative pursues a twofold purpose and that the component concerning the protection of communications of legal persons and the aim of achieving the internal market for those electronic communications and ensure its functioning in this regard cannot be considered merely incidental, the initiative should, therefore, also be based on Article 114 of the TFEU.' Commission, Explanatory Memorandum to a Regulation of the European Parliament and of the Council concerning the respect for private life and the protection of personal

Standardization Regulation undoubtedly sets the tone for the orientation of standardization towards harmonization of conditions to enable the functioning of the Internal Market, the standards in the scope of the Standardization Regulation are one fragment of the available standards and specifications in the field of data protection.[170] Thus, one cannot exclude in advance that some technical specification developed for example by a committed group of privacy engineers will be developed to respond to motivations for adopting value-sensitive design, instead of (or next to) market needs.

Further, standards, as defined in the Standardization Regulation, are essentially technical specifications, which prescribe requirements to be fulfilled by a product, process, or service. Thus, one can already identify a different regulatory target between data protection law and standards: while the Union data protection law[171] refers to 'processing' of personal data, standards are regulating products, processes, or systems. Processing is a broad concept meaning 'any operation or set of operations which is performed on personal data or on sets of personal data'.[172] The difference in the scope and regulatory target of standards and data protection, as those are framed by the definitions of their constitutive elements (product, system, etc) essentially means that, from a data protection point of view, standards may regulate peripheral components of a processing operation. In the case of an IoT personal assistant, the voice of the user and the query for information, which are the user's personal data, are being collected and analysed—thus processed–by several elements peripheral to the processing components such as a terminal device, an automated speech recognition software, a multi-task processing module and in general components of the different application program interfaces,[173] which make the collection, analysis, storage etc of the voice and requested information possible.

Another limitation relates to the voluntary character of technical standards, which is a significant constraint for standards to assume a substantive role in enabling data subjects' rights. This is shown in the example of the voluntary Do Not Track specification, or the earlier P3P specification, which while designed for communicating privacy and data protection preferences of data subjects, were largely

data in electronic communications and repealing Directive 2002/58/EC (Regulation on Privacy and Electronic Communications) COM/2017/010 final. The dual legal basis is maintained in the Parliament Report. See the adopted text without changes European Parliament, ***I REPORT on the proposal for a regulation of the European Parliament and of the Council concerning the respect for private life and the protection of personal data in electronic communications and repealing Directive 2002/58/EC (Regulation on Privacy and Electronic Communications) (COM (2017)0010 – C8-0009/2017 – 2017/0003(COD)) Committee on Civil Liberties, Justice and Home Affairs, 20.10.2017.

[170] See scope of the Standardization Regulation in Chapter 3 section 3.2 in this book.

[171] GDPR art 2(1) and ePrivacy Directive art 1(1).

[172] GDPR art 4(1).

[173] ITU-T 'Requirements and architecture for indoor conversational robot systems' Recommendation ITU-T F.746.9 (May 2019).

unnoticed by website providers. Both efforts eventually faded and were quitted due to the low motivation of controllers to conform to those specifications. In the case of standards facilitating legal compliance, the motivation of controllers and processors to conform to standards is linked to the motivation to comply with the law. The voluntary character of standards therefore is somewhat hindering the role of standards in this function. It should be noted that the efforts of a controller or processor to conform to a standard might need to be externally audited by another party, to ensure conformity to the standard. Such an audit may be second party (from another controller or processor in business to business relations) or a third party, namely a certification body.

5.7 Synthesis

This Chapter provided an analytical framework to identify roles for standards complementing the Union data protection law. Standards for controllers and processors may assist with compliance with legal duties, while standards relating to the exercise of data subjects' rights have the potential to empower data subjects to be in control and make decisions about their data. A third—more limited—function concerns standards working as meta-rules for the implementation and application of data protection law. Those roles are subject to limitations as regards to what is regulated with technical standards and to what extent, but also their effectiveness due to their largely voluntary character.

As a direct basis for standardization, the GDPR is limited, since the majority of the Commission powers to adopt standards were abolished from the final text. However, the GDPR provides several areas for standardization in terms of subject matter, as pointed to by the indirect references. Those may also lead to the adoption of standards in support of the GDPR through mainly committee-based standardization (stream 2) or market-based (stream 3). With the exception of clarity and interpretation, the identified areas of standardization generally correspond to the post-law functions of private regulation instruments discussed in Chapter 4, such as uniform application, technical measures for compliance, and others.[174]

Technology-triggered duties and rights such as data portability, data protection by design and by default play a prominent role. In addition, compliance with data protection rules and calibration of obligations, is another area for standardization. Standards as a benchmark for the state of the art or guidelines for organizational measures are such examples. Next, another aspect has to do with facilitating certification, which is a means to demonstrate the organizational and technical measures taken to comply with the GDPR. The role of standards is providing the basis

[174] Chapter 4 section 4.1.5.2 in this book.

Table 5.3 Legal and informative bases, types of data protection standards and corresponding integration mechanisms

Basis	Type of act	Relevant streams of standards	Types of (possible) references
General Data Protection Regulation	Binding act, art 288 TFEU	Stream 2: committee-based Stream 3: market-based	Direct dated Indirect (specific) Indirect (abstract)
Directive on Privacy in Electronic Communications (and reform: Commission Proposal for ePrivacy Regulation)	Binding act, art 288 TFEU	Stream 2: committee-based Stream 3: market-based	Indirect (specific) Indirect (abstract)
Radio Equipment Directive (New Approach)	Binding act, art 288 TFEU	Stream 1: European harmonised Stream 4: mixed	Indirect (specific)
Standardization Regulation art 10	Binding act, acceptance of standardisation request	Stream 1: European harmonised Stream 4: mixed	Indirect (specific)
Delegated act on the basis of 1. art 3 Radio Equipment Directive or art 12(8) and art 43(8) GDPR	Binding act, art 290 TFEU, art 44 RED art 92 GDPR	Stream 1: European harmonised Stream 2: committee-based Stream 3: market-based	Direct dated Direct non-dated Indirect (specific) Indirect (abstract) Incorporation
Implementing act art 43(9) GDPR or Standardization request	Binding act, art 291 TFEU	Stream 1: European harmonised Stream 2: committee-based Stream 3: market-based	Direct dated Direct non-dated Indirect (specific) Indirect (abstract) Incorporation
Commission Communication	Non-binding act, art 292 TFEU	Stream 2: committee-based Stream 3: market-based	Direct dated Direct non-dated Indirect (specific) Indirect (abstract) Incorporation
Data protection supervisory authority Opinion	Non-binding, art 58(3)(b) GDPR	Stream 2: committee-based Stream 3: market-based	Direct dated Direct non-dated Indirect (specific) Indirect (abstract) Incorporation

for criteria and requirements for the data protection certification mechanisms and the accreditation requirements for assessing *inter alia* the independence and expertise of certification bodies. In the case of certification, standards also have a harmonizing function, ensuring a common threshold for data protection certification mechanisms, seals, and marks (art 43(9) GDPR). With regard to data subjects' rights, standards and specifications may, in principle, offer a mechanism for exercising the right to object to processing of personal data.[175]

The 2017 Commission ePrivacy Regulation Proposal re-introduced the idea of using specifications to express the consent of the user to the processing of personal data. An important amendment was put forward by the Parliament, according to which the signals sent from the user's technical equipment would be binding and enforceable. In relation to the GDPR, the 2017 Commission Proposal for ePrivacy Regulation includes fewer references to standardization, but with a more focused target. While the GDPR, provides a range of roles for standards, mainly by means of indirect (specific) references, such as facilitating compliance, user control, and the implementation of the GDPR's rules, standardization related issues in ePrivacy concern the protection of the user.

The indirect references show an intention of the data protection legislature to leverage benefits of standardization, without however stepping in to regulate the standardization activity for the data protection context as such. The hesitation of the EU legislature to refer to formal standards[176] originates from the complexity of the standardization system in the EU and concerns over its suitability to support the protection of fundamental rights, such as privacy and data protection. Integrating standards in the law brings along legal consequences according to the Standardization Regulation, which are beyond the supervisory control of data protection authorities or data protection legislatures. Similarly, in the case of technical specifications and informal standards, the standardization activity is detached from the public regulator, relying mainly on own rules and procedures.

[175] See however Chapter 8 case study 3 on the limitations for such a role.

[176] There is an exception to this. GDPR art 43(2) explicitly makes a dated reference to an international standard.

6

Lessons from the US

Standardization, CCPA, and COPPA

6.1 Introduction

The United States has enacted a range of regional and sectoral privacy laws. Despite efforts for a federal privacy and personal data protection law,[1] there has–to this date– no such a law with a wide scope and effect similar to the GDPR has yet been adopted. Nevertheless, the US offers useful lessons in terms of incorporating standardization in privacy laws. One example is the California Consumer Privacy Act (CCPA), which is part of the Civil Code.[2] The 2018 CCPA is considered a pioneering law as it is a general privacy state law that establishes obligations for businesses and individual rights for consumers, such as the right to be informed about the personal information that a business processes.[3] The CCPA, *inter alia,* provides for a right to opt out of the sale or sharing of personal information. Businesses subject to the CCPA must provide methods for a global opt-out, which may take the form of an 'opt-out preference signal [...] based on technical specifications.'[4] The second example is a federal law on children's online privacy, the Children's Online Privacy Protection Rule ('COPPA').[5] The 1998 COPPA provides rules for operators of websites and online services regarding the collection, use, and disclosure of children's data on the Internet. A central point for any child-related regulation is age verification, namely the verification of whether an Internet user is a child or has reached the age of digital consent.[6] Due to its complex nature, age verification, and

[1] See Moira Warburton, 'US lawmakers push for federal data privacy law; tech industry and critics are wary' (Reuters, 2024): https://www.reuters.com/world/us/federal-data-privacy-laws-gain-support-us-congress-critics-remain-2024-06-26/ [accessed 10 August 2024]; Wilson, CS and US Commissioner, 'A defining moment for privacy: The time is ripe for Federal Privacy Legislation.' in a speech at Future of Privacy Forum by Commissioner of US Federal Trade Commission (FTC), vol. 6. 2020.

[2] CCPA §§ 1798.100–199 (2018).

[3] For a comparative analysis of CCPA and the GDPR read: Chander A, Kaminski ME and McGeveran W, 'Catalyzing Privacy Law' (2021) 105 Minn L Rev, 1733 (hereafter Chander and others 'Catalyzing Privacy Law').

[4] CCPA §1798.135(b).

[5] Code of Federal Regulations 16, Part 312 Children's Online Privacy Protection Act of 1998, 15 U.S.C.§§ 6501–6505, Children's Privacy; 1.

[6] See van der Hof S and Ouburg S, 'We Take Your Word For It—A Review of Methods of Age Verification and Parental Consent in Digital Services' (2022) 8 European Data Protection Law Review 61, 11.

Standardizing Personal Data Protection. Irene Kamara, Oxford University Press. © Irene Kamara 2025.
DOI: 10.1093/9780191997037.003.0006

more generally age assurance, has given rise to technical work at standardization bodies. Although there are only indirect references to standardization in COPPA, as will be discussed in this Chapter, several mechanisms have been developed and standardized for age verification. Those mechanisms have been developed both by industry fora and the National Standards Institute (NIST).[7]

Against this backdrop, this Chapter generates lessons from the US paradigm of the different roles and functions that sectoral and regional privacy laws may assign to technical standards, and specifications more broadly.

6.2 The California Consumer Privacy Act

6.2.1 The CCPA in a Nutshell and the Right to Opt Out From Sale/Sharing of Personal Information

The CCPA is the first general privacy law in the US, which aims to offer consumers control over their personal information. It applies to personal information of Californian consumers, independently of the location of the establishments collecting and using the personal information. The CCPA therefore establishes an extraterritorial effect, which renders its protections holistic. Businesses collecting personal information of consumers have—*inter alia*—information duties about for example the type of personal information they intend to collect and the purposes for their collection or use,[8] are obliged to implement security measures,[9] to enter into contractual agreements with third party service providers,[10] and are subject to the principle of data minimization.[11] Alongside obligations for businesses, the CCPA provides a number of individual rights to consumers, strengthening their control over the personal information, such as the right to erasure.[12] A 2020 amendment to the CCPA provided additional rights, such as the right to correct inaccurate personal information.[13]

Among those individual rights, consumers are granted the right to 'opt out of sale or sharing of personal information'.[14] The consumer is specifically granted

[7] NIST Special Publication 800-63A, Digital Identity Guidelines, Enrollment and Identity Proofing Requirements, June 2017 (updated in 2020), https://doi.org/10.6028/NIST.SP.800-63a [accessed 10 August 2024].

[8] See CCPA § 1798.100(a) on 'General Duties of Businesses that Collect Personal Information.'

[9] CCPA §1798.100(e).

[10] CCPA §1798.100(d).

[11] CCPA §1798.100(c).

[12] CCPA §1798.105.

[13] CCPA § 1798.106. In 2020, the CCPA was amended by the California Privacy Rights Act. At the time of writing the book the CCPA is undergoing a new amendment. See Stauss David and others, 'California Privacy and AI Legislation Update: August 19, 2024' Byte Back: https://www.bytebacklaw.com/2024/08/california-privacy-and-ai-legislation-update-august-19-2024/ [accessed 20 August 2024].

[14] CCPA § 1798.120.

the right to 'direct a business that sells or shares personal information about the consumer to third parties not to sell or share the consumer's personal information.'[15] The right may be exercised at any time, which implies before or even after the sharing[16] or selling of information has started. Thus, businesses subject to the CCPA may sell or share personal information of Californian consumers, unless directed otherwise by the consumers themselves. To facilitate the exercise of the right to opt out of sale or sharing, the CCPA also establishes an obligation for businesses to provide a notice to consumers about the possibility of their personal information being shared or sold and of their right to opt out.[17] Following the exercise of the right by a consumer, it is prohibited for the business that received the direction (otherwise preference) of the consumers to sell or share their personal information. Such an action of selling or sharing the personal information with third parties is possible only if the consumers eventually provide their consent.[18]

Overall, while the effectiveness of the CCPA is under scrutiny and subsequent improvements by the legislators are due,[19] several provisions have been adopted by other states. For example, the CCPA opt-out right has been followed by several other state privacy laws, such as the Colorado Privacy Act and the Connecticut Data Privacy Act.[20] The CCPA thus sets a model for other laws to follow.[21]

6.2.2 Standardization and the CCPA: The Right to Opt Out of Sale or Sharing

The right to opt out gives rise to questions of practical implementation, eg how the consumers may communicate their preferences without having to repeat manually the process to every single online service provider. In anticipation of such questions, the CCPA authorized the Attorney General to adopt regulations further defining requirements for the signal with which the consumers may opt out.[22] Indeed,

[15] ibid. There are different conditions as regards children. See CCPA § 1798.120(c).

[16] 'Sharing' is defined as ' sharing, renting, releasing, disclosing, disseminating, making available, transferring, or otherwise communicating orally, in writing, or by electronic or other means, a consumer's personal information by the business to a third party for cross-context behavioral advertising, whether or not for monetary or other valuable consideration, including transactions between a business and a third party for cross-context behavioral advertising for the benefit of a business in which no money is exchanged.' CCPA § 1798.140(ah).

[17] CCPA § 1798.120(b).

[18] CCPA § 1798.120(d).

[19] See, among several, O'Connor S and others, '(Un)Clear and (In)Conspicuous,' Proceedings of the 20th Workshop on Privacy in the Electronic Society (ACM 2021), 59ff; Van Nortwick M and Wilson C, 'Setting the Bar Low: Are Websites Complying with the Minimum Requirements of the CCPA?' (2021) 2022 Proceedings on Privacy Enhancing Technologies, 608.

[20] Part 13—Colorado Privacy Act § 6-1-1301 and Connecticut Data Privacy Act: Senate Bill 6: An Act Concerning Personal Data Privacy and Online Monitoring.

[21] Chander and others 'Catalyzing Privacy Law (n 3) 1764.

[22] CCPA § 1798.185, 19(A)

to communicate this 'direction' of the consumer, the CCPA Regulations adopted by the Attorney General, specify business practices for handling consumer requests.[23] Section 7025 of the CCPA Regulations specifically concerns opt-out preference signals, which are a method with which the consumers can automatically exercise the right to opt out of sale and sharing with the businesses with which they interact online.[24] For businesses, receiving or detecting such a signal entail a 'valid request to opt-out of sale/sharing [...] for the browser or device and any consumer profile' connected to that browser or device.[25] The CCPA Regulation requires that the signal is transmitted in commonly used form (e.g. HTTP header) and that the mechanism sending the preference signal 'makes it clear to the consumer [...]'whether it has the 'effect of opting the consumer out of the sale and sharing of their personal information.'[26]

The possibility to automate the exercise of the right to opt out and the indirect references was viewed as an area suitable for standardization by several organizations. Standardizing the opt-out signal aims at simplifying compliance with the opt-out provision of the CCPA, but also more generally making privacy protection easier on the Internet.[27] Standardization would play a technology-triggered role, where processes mandated by law and the exercise of individual's rights are automated.[28]

Shortly after, the W3C initiated the works of a new technical specification, taking into account the CCPA. This post-law activity complementing the CCPA, aims at facilitating a uniform application of the law and supporting consumers in exercising their right. The resulting work from this activity was the General Privacy Control (GPC), which is a draft technical specification designed to convey the preference of individuals to have their personal information not shared or sold with third parties.[29] The GPC is communicated by the user-agent to the website and the preference is cached 'on each top-level navigation'.[30] The GPC explicitly refers to the link with legislation, the standard '*is intended to work with existing*

[23] See CCPA Regulations § 7025. Opt-out Preference Signals. 11 CA ADC § 7025 Barclays Official California Code of Regulations, Division 6. California Privacy Protection Agency, chapter 1. California Consumer Privacy Act Regulations, art 3. Business Practices for Handling Consumer Requests (hereafter CCPA Regulations or CCR). https://govt.westlaw.com/calregs/Document/IFA415050D45011EDA6283814282AA05E?viewType=FullText&originationContext=documenttoc&transitionType=CategoryPageItem&contextData=(sc.Default) [accessed 20 August 2024].

[24] ibid11 CCR § 7025(a).

[25] ibid11 CCR § 7025(c)(1).

[26] CCR § 7025(b)(2).

[27] Zimmeck S and Alicki K, 'Standardizing and Implementing Do Not Sell,' Proceedings of the 19th Workshop on Privacy in the Electronic Society (ACM 2020), 15.

[28] See chapter 4, section 4.1.5.2 in this book.

[29] Global Privacy Control (GPC) Proposal 22 March 2024, https://privacycg.github.io/gpc-spec/ [last accessed 20 August 2024].

[30] Read further: Human S and others, 'Data Protection and Consenting Communication Mechanisms: Current Open Proposals and Challenges' 2022 IEEE European Symposium on Security and Privacy Workshops (IEEE 2022) (hereafter Human and others, 'Data Protection and Consenting Communication Mechanisms').

and upcoming legal frameworks that render such requests enforceable' and specifically the CCPA: '*Under the CCPA, the GPC signal will be intended to communicate a Do Not Sell request from a global privacy control, as per §999.315 for that browser or device, or, if known, the consumer.*'[31] Further, according to the Attorney General of California, the right to opt out may be exercised via a 'user-enabled global privacy control, like the GPC'.[32] Despite being a draft technical specification, the GPC is already available as a browser extension or incorporated in browsers such as Mozilla Firefox.[33] To the extent businesses are transparent about whether they respect the signal–and that is an important point of criticism–studies show that the GPC signal is respected by businesses,[34] but not always.[35] Another criticism is the involvement of consent management companies conveying the consent preferences from the publishers ie the businesses with which consumers interact, to third parties.[36]

6.2.3 Lessons Learned

The CCPA opt-out from selling and sharing is an individual right, which has attracted the attention of standardization fora such as the W3C. In terms of legislation, the CCPA provision establishing the opt-out right does not explicitly refer to standardization but to technical means to exercise the right ('opt-out preference signal').[37] The CCPA regulations specify aspects of the CCPA that provide technical and legal requirements for the opt-out preference signal as a means to exercise the right to opt out from selling and sharing. Thus, through an indirect reference to standardization, the legislator instigated standardization activity. Quite important seems to be the endorsement of the GPC specification by the Attorney General of California, who also clarifies the legal effects for businesses of receiving a GPC opt-out signal. This formality casts any doubt about the validity of the GPC signal and therefore creates a strong motivation for compliance. Nevertheless, the specification remains voluntary. If consumers do not use it to communicate their wishes

[31] GPC para 5.1.
[32] See Q&A B(3): https://oag.ca.gov/privacy/ccpa#sectionb [accessed 20 August 2024].
[33] Human and others, 'Data Protection and Consenting Communication Mechanisms' (n 30).
[34] Zimmeck S and others, 'Usability and Enforceability of Global Privacy Control' (2023) 2023 Proceedings on Privacy Enhancing Technologies, 265.
[35] Charatan J and Birrell E, 'Two Steps Forward and One Step Back: The Right to Opt-out of Sale under CPRA' (2024) 2024 Proceedings on Privacy Enhancing Technologies, 91.
[36] Aziz MAB and Wilson C, 'Johnny Still Can't Opt-out: Assessing the IAB CCPA Compliance Framework' (2024) 2024 Proceedings on Privacy Enhancing Technologies, 349. Read further on the GPC in relation to the CCPA and the GDPR in Crepax T, 'Global Privacy Control and Portability of Privacy Preferences Through Browser Settings: A Comparative Study of Techno-Legal Challenges Under the Ccpa/Cpra and the Gdpr' Available at SSRN: https://ssrn.com/abstract=4710372 [accessed 20 August 2024].
[37] CCPA § 1798.135(b)(1).

and exercise their right to opt out, the GPC is of little use for the purposes of the CCPA. In that sense, the possibility to technically implement a feature by standardizing it does not always imply that this feature is also technically enforceable. In general, a common issue encountered in such control-based solutions, is the requirement for affirmative action from the consumer, as Solove has pointed out about the design of the CCPA.[38] Another challenge in the implementation of such technical specifications is their adaptability to different environments, such as IoT and smartphones.[39]

6.3 The Children's Online Privacy Protection Act

6.3.1 The COPPA in a Nutshell

The Children's Online Privacy Protection Act (COPPA) is a federal law, which establishes a range of measures and obligations aiming at protecting digital privacy of children under thirteen years old.[40] Children, when using the Internet are likely to have a false sense of intimacy, often sharing information with their social interactions, but also providers of online services, such as social media.[41] Next to risks of personal data sharing and privacy concerns, exploitation and abuse risks of children online are prominent.[42] The COPPA was adopted in 1998 at the early stages of the Internet, establishing prohibitions of unfair and deceptive practices as regards the collection, use, and disclosure of personal information regarding children.[43]

COPPA has three main pillars: a) the obligation for operators of websites or providers of online services (hereafter 'operators') to provide notices on their website or online service and directly to the parents,[44] b) the requirement of the operator to obtain 'verifiable parental consent' prior to any information collection, use, or disclosure,[45] and c) safe harbour programmes, which are self-regulation

[38] Solove has argued that 'Rights can help put people in a cockpit with a lot of buttons, levers, settings, toggles, and choices, but if people don't know how to fly the plane, these controls are meaningless.' Solove, D, 'The Limitations of Privacy Rights' (2023) 98 Notre Dame L Rev, 975ff.

[39] Human and others, 'Data Protection and Consenting Communication Mechanisms' (n 30), 8.

[40] 15 U.S.C Chapter 91—CHILDREN'S ONLINE PRIVACY PROTECTION (COPPA).

[41] See, among many, Livingstone S, Stoilova M, and Nandagiri R, 'Children's data and privacy online: growing up in a digital age: an evidence review.' (2019), London: London School of Economics and Political Science, available: https://eprints.lse.ac.uk/101283/1/Livingstone_childrens_data_and_privacy_online_evidence_review_published.pdf (last accessed 20 August 2024).

[42] See, among many, Gezinski LB and Gonzalez-Pons KM, 'Sex Trafficking and Technology: A Systematic Review of Recruitment and Exploitation' (2022) 10 Journal of Human Trafficking, 497; UNICEF, Ending Online Child Sexual Exploitation and Abuse, Lessons learned and promising practices in low- and middle- income countries, 2021, https://www.unicef.org/media/113731/file/Ending%20Online%20Sexual%20Exploitation%20and%20Abuse.pdf [accessed 20 August 2024].

[43] 16 CFR § 312.1 Scope of regulations COPPA.

[44] 16 CFR § 312.4 COPPA.

[45] 16 CFR § 312.5 COPPA.

programs to which operators may adhere and be presumed to comply with their obligations under COPPA.[46] COPPA does not establish a right to compensation for individuals. Its provisions however may be enforced and sanctioned by public enforcement agencies. In fact, there have been several cases, where the Federal Trade Commission brought action against operators, for example of game platforms.[47] After COPPA started applying, operators sought to find mechanisms for implementing several of the provisions of the COPPA, such as mechanisms automating obtaining valid parental consent. There are several consent mechanisms available in the market, however only a handful are approved as valid parental consent methods under the Federal Trade Commission.[48] Other mechanisms relevant to COPPA's implementation are age verification mechanisms, which are discussed in the following section.

In general, COPPA has been an important milestone in protecting children online at a federal level. As with every legal instrument regulating aspects of online behaviour that has been introduced more than twenty years ago, there have been criticisms on the effectiveness and needs for revisions.[49]

6.3.2 Standardization and the COPPA: Age Verification Mechanisms

Age verification is essential as it determines the applicability of COPPA, and subsequently the need for parental consent in case of children.[50] Even though the text of the law does not in itself refer to standardization,[51] the market needs for age verification mechanisms instigated some activity in the field. One prominent example

[46] 16 CFR §312.11 COPPA.

[47] Read in detail: Olivia Levinson, 'Embedded Deception: How the FTC's Recent Interpretation of the Children's Online Privacy Protection Act Missed the Mark' (2020) 105 Minn L Rev 2007, 2015 and 2038.

[48] See Federal Trade Commission (FTC), Verifiable Parental Consent and the Children's Online Privacy Rule, (no date) https://www.ftc.gov/business-guidance/privacy-security/verifiable-parental-consent-childrens-online-privacy-rule, [accessed 20 August 2024].

[49] At the time of writing a proposed amendment for COPPA, which, among other things, would raise the age of children from 13 to 16 years old was recently adopted. See 'Representatives Walberg and Castor Announce Companion Bill to COPPA 2.0' Hunton Andrews Kurth Law Blog (April 2024), https://www.huntonak.com/privacy-and-information-security-law/representatives-walberg-and-castor-announce-companion-bill-to-coppa-2-0 [accessed 20 June 2024] and US Senate Committee on Commerce, Science, & Transportation 'Kids Online Privacy Protections – Finally – Set to Pass Senate' Press Release (July 2024), https://www.commerce.senate.gov/2024/7/kids-online-privacy-protections-finally-set-to-pass-senate [accessed 20 August 2024].

[50] Read about the legal standard of knowledge in the COPPA in Altieri C, 'Now, On the Internet, Will Everyone Know if You're a Child?' Future of Privacy Forum.

[51] COPPA refers to 'performance standards', which should not be confused with technical standards or specifications. Performance standards in this context means the level of performance required to meet the legal obligations. See for example 16 CFR 312.11 (b).

is the work of NIST, which has developed a voluntary specification for identity proofing.

The NIST 800-63A[52] provides requirements for identity proofing, where 'an applicant provides evidence to a credential service provider (CSP) reliably identifying themselves, thereby allowing the CSP to assert that identification at a useful identity assurance level.'[53] This specification allows for the identification of a user without however disclosing their full identity. While the specification is not limited to be used only in the context of age verification for COPPA, it is applicable for that purpose and it in fact it provides considerations for minors under COPPA. For example, that parents or legal guardians should also be involved.[54] Examples of standardized age verification mechanisms or relevant guidance may be found also at the ISO and CEN CENELEC.[55] Those standards or standardization deliverables however are not tailored and do not explicitly take into account the legal requirements of COPPA, and as a result their alignment to the US legal framework is not guaranteed.

6.3.3 Lessons Learned

COPPA has been a law ahead of its time, aimed at protecting one of the most vulnerable groups online, children. An essential element for the core obligations of the COPPA for operators of websites and service providers to apply is the age verification of the user. Since the burden of identifying whether a user is a child lies with the regulatees, those created a market need for relevant age verification mechanisms. The market need for automation of age verification in technical specifications and standards shows that standardization is often corresponding to market needs, created by regulatory change. In this Chapter, a voluntary NIST specification was examined. Such specifications often take into account the legal frameworks such as the COPPA and incorporate several technical requiremements. In the case of the NIST 800-63A, it explicitly refers to the COPPA and additional points of attention that any entity implementing the specification should address.

[52] NIST Special Publication 800-63A Digital Identity Guidelines 'Enrollment and Identity Proofing Requirements' (2017), https://pages.nist.gov/800-63-3/sp800-63a.html [accessed 20 August 2024]. (hereafter NIST 800-63A).

[53] ibid.

[54] NIST 800-63A s 5.3.4.

[55] See, for example, CWA 18016, 'Age appropriate digital services framework', September 2023. Read further: European Commission: Directorate-General for Communications Networks, Content and Technology, Raiz Shaffique, M. and van der Hof, S, *Mapping age assurance typologies and requirements—Research report*, Publications Office of the European Union, 2024, https://data.europa.eu/doi/10.2759/455338 [accessed 20 August 2024].

6.4 Synthesis

The review of two prominent laws in the area of privacy, one state specific and one federal sector specific, shows that privacy laws might offer opportunities for standardization, either with indirect references, or because they create a relevant market need for standardized mechanisms assisting regulatees with compliance. Those specifications mainly perform post-law functions, in terms of compliance or helping individuals exercise their rights, such as the CCPA right to opt out. The endorsement of the GPC by the Attorney General of California has the effect of being an authoritative source of approval and is certainly a strong motivation for companies to adopt the standard, while it is not in itself prescribed in the law. In terms of implementation, the voluntary nature of conformity to the specifications and the scarce sources of supervisory authorities, has led companies not always conforming to specifications, despite their claims. This is a lesson both in terms of output legitimacy of standardization, especially its acceptability, and the trustworthiness of standardization as an instrument complementing privacy and data protection law, and supporting public policy goals in general.

7

Procedural Legitimacy in Data Protection Standardization

7.1 Framing the Debate: The Importance of 'Who' and 'How' of Standard-Setting

Standardization has been called a 'public law in private disguise'[1] and 'extra-constitutional rule-making'.[2] Such conceptualizations of standardization largely aim at stressing its normative nature and its often law-resembling effects (eg *de facto* binding)[3], while not being subject to the democratic legitimacy guarantees that legislation provides. Van Gestel and Micklitz relate legitimacy requirements to the use of standards to interpret or fill in norms in law, thereby gaining a quasi-legal status.[4] In *James Elliot* the AG asserted that harmonized standards are not 'a case of purely private technical standardization, carried out on the initiative of the CEN and unconnected to EU law',[5] since the Commission exercises significant control over the procedure for the drafting of harmonized standards. In the same case, and the most recent *Publicresource.org,* the Court found that a harmonized standard, published in the Official Journal, is part of EU law.[6] In another case however, the CJEU found that a certain technical standard was a purely private activity, developed by a private standards organization, unconnected to EU legislation, and for that reason the contested clause was explicitly excluded from the scope of the reference in the Official Journal.[7]

[1] Van Gestel R and Micklitz H-W, 'European Integration through Standardization: How Judicial Review Is Breaking down the Club House of Private Standardization Bodies' (2013) 50 Common Market Law Review, 150.

[2] Schepel H, 'Rules of Recognition: A Legal Constructivist Approach to Transnational Private Regulation,' in Ys PJ, Kjaer PF and Yatsunami R, *Regulatory Hybridization in the Transnational Sphere* (Martinus Nijhoff Publishers 2013), 192.

[3] See Chapter 3 section 3.3 in this book.

[4] Van Gestel and Micklitz 'European integration through standardization' (n 1).

[5] Opinion of AG Campos Sanchez-Bordona, Case C-613/14 *James Elliot,* EU:C:2016:63, para 46.

[6] Judgment, Case C-613/14, *James Elliot,* EU:C:2016:821, para 40; Judgment, Case C-588/21 P *Public.Resource.Org Inc and Right to Know CLG,* , ECLI:EU:C:2024:201, para 89.

[7] Judgment, Case C-185/08, *Latchways plc,* EU:C:2010:619, paras 32–33. The case concerned a standard which had been drafted on the basis of a Commission standardization request, based on a New Approach Directive, and published in the OJ, but the claim in this case was about one type of device (Class A 1 anchor devices) which was explicitly excluded from the scope of the reference in the OJ and therefore did not offer a presumption of conformity to the harmonized legislation for that type of device.

Standardizing Personal Data Protection. Irene Kamara, Oxford University Press. © Irene Kamara 2025.
DOI: 10.1093/9780191997037.003.0007

While there is no case law explicitly adjudicating on the direction of standards development amounting to public law-making, the above assertions about the nature of standards and their relation to law-making have their merits, and bring to the foreground questions regarding the development of rules and principles of standardization. The rules and procedures under which standards are drafted, adopted, and published are significant for ensuring that the data protection standards live up to an aspirational role to support the protection of a fundamental right. In other words, as flagged by Senden, the public dimension of standards and in support of public policy goals and the possibility of *de facto* binding standards invites further investigation of such issues.[8] The answers to 'who' develops standards and 'how' are also important for building trust in the quality and reliability of data protection standards endorsed by data protection legislatures and policy makers, so that controllers or processors (or manufacturers) *voluntarily* conform to them.

In its 2011 Communication, preparing for the reform of the standardization legal framework, the Commission stressed that standards affect several groups in society, not only businesses but also individual citizens.[9] Therefore a 'sufficiently wide range of participants' is deemed necessary for standardization to be inclusive and committed to core values such as openness, transparency and scientific solidity.[10] However, an open and all-encompassing process of standard-setting should not be taken for granted. Participation in Technical Committees is most often subject to a number of conditions, sometimes including fees, which hinder the participation of consumer groups, academia, or other associations representing societal interests.[11] At the same time, the interests represented in a Technical Committee might be aligned in promoting the interests of the participants in the standard-setting process, even in cases where those are against societal interests or public goals.[12]

[8] Senden L, 'Towards a More Holistic Legitimacy Approach to Technical Standardisation in the EU,' in Eliantonio M and Cauffman C (eds), *The Legitimacy of Standardisation as a Regulatory Technique* (Edward Elgar Publishing 2020).

[9] Commission Communication, A Strategic Vision for European Standards: Moving Forward to Enhance and Accelerate the Sustainable Growth of the European Economy by 2020, COM 2011/311 final.

[10] COM (2011) 311 (n 9).

[11] van Eecke P, and Truyens M, 'Standardization in the European Information and Technology Sector: Official Procedures on the Verge of Being Overhauled.' (2009) 5 Washington Journal of Law, Technology & Arts, no. 3, 7. A 2006 study on the lack of links between standardization and academia had found as prominent reasons the lack of funding for researchers and the mutual lack of knowledge from both academia and standardizers about each other's activities. See Jakobs K and Blind K, 'ICT Standardisation Policy in Europe - Recent Past, Presence, and Future(?),' 2011 7th International Conference on Standardization and Innovation in Information Technology (SIIT) (IEEE 2011), 6.

[12] A study conducted by anti-tobacco supporters concerning which organizations were involved in the development of tobacco related standards showed that the tobacco industry dominated the process of setting standards for tobacco and tobacco products. This was reported as meaning that the tobacco industry influenced the determination method of measuring tar and nicotine in cigarettes and the manner those were displayed to consumers in package labelling. Those ISO standards however, did not claim to be health related standards. Bialous SA and Yach D, 'Whose Standard Is It, Anyway? How the Tobacco Industry Determines the International Organization for Standardization (ISO) Standards for Tobacco and Tobacco Products' (2001) 10 Tobacco Control, 96.

Intentional or not, the participants in standard-setting processes are vulnerable to capture by particular interests, such as industries that take advantage of information asymmetries existing among participants to promote their own interests.[13] Informational asymmetries exist even among the SDOs. For example, national standardization bodies themselves do not always have access to the full documentation regarding a draft standard, unless they participate in the drafting process or express an interest to follow the development of a specific standard.[14]

Furthermore, the decision-making process is largely unknown to those who are not part of a Technical Committee. Standards are adopted based on consensus, which however does not mean unanimity.[15] This practically means that not every voting member needs to agree to the adoption of a standard, but instead that there are not serious objections by some voting members. While public consultation for formal standards is usually established to enable interested parties of the general public to provide feedback on the text of a draft standard, this is infrequently communicated properly, which raises questions about how meaningful the consultation is.[16]

Werle and Iversen draw attention to four aspects of the standard-setting process, namely; a) the setting in which the process takes place that is recognized organizations or fora, b) the rationale that triggered the process eg support of a public policy goal or establishment of interoperability, c) the mechanisms for involvement and active participation of stakeholders eg membership conditions, and d) voting rights, and characteristics of the outcome, the standard.[17] These four aspects, according to Werle and Iversen, influence the legitimacy 'requirements' and expectations for different standards. For example, regulatory standards that serve a public goal such as environmental protection require different degrees of legitimacy, and safeguards embedded either in the statutes of the SSO or in a legal framework. Other scholars have used the maturity stage of standard development as a criterion to determine where more stringent safeguards are necessary. Beisheim and Dingwerth have argued that procedural safeguards might not be very important at the beginning of a standardization process, eg. when a new standardization item is proposed, as much as later towards the finalization of

[13] Delimatsis P, 'Into the abyss of standard-setting: an analysis of procedural and substantive guarantees within the International Organization for Standardization (ISO)' EUI RSCAS, 2015/35, Global Governance Programme-170, Global Economics (2015), 10.

[14] Delimatsis 2015 (n 13), 10.

[15] See ISO Directives https://www.iso.org/developing-standards.html [accessed 20 September 2023]

[16] For example, the British Standards association posts a call for expert contributions to the public consultation for international standards on their website via a press release: https://www.bsigroup.com/en-GB/about-bsi/media-centre/press-releases/2019/january/public-consultation-process-launched-for-new-international-privacy-information-management-standard/ [accessed 20 September 2023].

[17] Werle E, and Iversen EJ, 'Promoting legitimacy in technical standardization.' (2006) 2 Science, Technology & Innovation Studies, 19.

process, when the technical standard is close to adoption and consensus making efforts take place.[18]

Independently of the criteria used in scholarship to identify legitimacy thresholds, many of the issues may be well summarized in the following statement from Schepel: 'the central problem with standardization … is not the privatization of public law making but the political instrumentalization of private rulemaking'.[19] Yet, the fact remains that even when standards are sometimes treated in scholarship as a legal transplant, a foreign body to fields such as safety, health, and environment, they formally continue being used for public policy goals and in support of the legislation. So, acknowledging—instead of or in parallel to contesting—this reality,[20] allows one to further explore how to shield standardization procedures and their outcomes from side effects such as capture and (mis)use, and yield benefits from private regulation instruments.

This Chapter explores the legitimacy of data protection standardization from a procedural perspective, looking at the safeguards, with which standardization is equipped to prevent commonly reported issues in relation to private regulation instruments such as lack of transparency. It analyses the types of requirements the Union data protection law provides for other private regulation instruments and assesses whether those are adequately addressed by the internal rules and regulations, as well as the Standardization Regulation, to which technical standards are subject. The Chapter thus explores the guarantees, as well as the principles of standardization, as applied in the field of data protection. The hypothesis is that due process requirements[21] such as transparency and stakeholder participation, and other safeguards, provide, in theory, guarantees for standardization in support of the data protection legislation. The procedural perspective is a first good indicator of what should be considered as legitimate standard-setting in data protection. While the existence of such guarantees has

[18] Beisheim, M, and Dingwerth K, 'Procedural Legitimacy and Private Transnational Governance: Are the Good Ones Doing Better?' Berlin DFG-Sonderforschungsbereich 700, Governance in Räumen begrenzter Staatlichkeit 2008, 26ff.

[19] Schepel H, *The Constitution of Private Governance: Product Standards in the Regulation of Integrating Markets* (Hart Publishing 2005), 237 (hereafter Schepel 'The Constitution of Private Governance').

[20] Schepel 'The Constitution of Private Governance' (n 19) does not argue that standardization is incompatible with serving public policy, but he proposes that the normative answer to that problem is not the reinvigoration of the public, but, rather, to recreate self-regulation in a manner that accounts for public and societal interests ('public-regardingness').

[21] Colin and others conclude that it is necessary for Transnational Private Regulation instruments such as standards to 'find alternative sources of legitimacy based in procedural and other mechanisms'. Scott C, Cafaggi F and Senden L, 'The Conceptual and Constitutional Challenge of Transnational Private Regulation' (2011) 38 Journal of Law and Society, 1. Kanevskaia argued that in order to prevent standards being driven by the interests of small groups the standards development organizations should follow due process principles. Kanevskaia Whitaker O, *The Law and Practice of Global ICT Standardization* (Cambridge University Press 2023)

an important result that the use of standards in the field of data protection is not *ab initio* prohibitive, careful consideration to legitimacy issues have to be given on a case-by-case basis.

7.2 Safeguards for Private Regulation Instruments in Data Protection Law

The issues discussed in the previous section do not leave the use of standardization in data protection untouched. Constraints and safeguards applicable and specific to data protection need to be further explored. How is the Union data protection legislation considering and tackling those issues? The General Data Protection Regulation (GDPR), the main instrument regulating data protection in the Union, establishes safeguards for the private regulation instruments, which it explicitly regulates. The focus of this section lies in how three specific private regulation instruments are introduced by the data protection legislature in the GDPR.[22] The GDPR explicitly regulates codes of conduct, certification, and Binding Corporate Rules (BCR) in their own dedicated frameworks of rules. These rules lay down the objectives, actors, checks and balances, and thus provide a threshold of safeguards for those private regulation instruments according to the data protection legislation.[23] Considering the absence of a dedicated framework vis-à-vis standardization in the data protection law –despite the references to standards therein–[24] the procedural safeguards for other private regulation instruments provide insights on what the EU secondary data protection legislator expects from private regulation instruments at large.[25] This section therefore takes a closer look at those embedded safeguards as a yardstick for standards in data protection in terms of procedural legitimacy.

[22] The ePrivacy Directive does not include any such specific framework of rules for private regulation instruments.

[23] GDPR arts 40 and 41 on codes of conduct, GDPR arts 42 and 43 on certification, and GDPR art. 47 on Binding Corporate Rules. Other GDPR instruments are also interesting to explore. For example, DPIAs can be considered a private regulation instrument due to their role in regulating how controllers of high-risk processing operations assess and evaluate those risks, without the proactive intervention from or any prior notification to the supervisory authority. Quelle C, 'Enhancing Compliance under the General Data Protection Regulation: The Risky Upshot of the Accountability- and Risk-Based Approach' (2018) 9 European Journal of Risk Regulation, 502. In fact, this is why DPIAs have also been characterized as a meta-regulation tool, in the sense of 'legal meta-regulation of internal corporate self- regulation'. Binns argues that DPIAs by formally being introduced in the GDPR and regulated have been transformed by a self-regulation to a meta-regulation tool. Binns R, 'Data Protection Impact Assessments: A Meta-Regulatory Approach' (2017) 7 International Data Privacy Law, 22.

[24] See Chapter 5 section 5.2 in this book.

[25] The differences among the private regulation instruments are highlighted where necessary throughout the analysis. See also Chapter 3, section 3.5 in this book.

7.2.1 Codes of Conduct

Codes of conduct are part of the reformed general data protection Union law.[26] Their aim is the proper application of the GDPR, especially with regard to sectorial needs and conditions for the application of the GDPR rules, and the processing needs of small and medium enterprises (SMEs). Thus, codes of conduct seem to be of use mainly for specifying the application of the GDPR for groups of controllers or processors in sectors which present particularities for example because of the intensiveness of processing, such as the advertising sector, or the nature and inherent risks of the type personal data such as in the health sector.[27] While codes of conduct were formally also part of the Data Protection Directive,[28] their re-introduction in the reformed law is more prescriptive and in a sense, restrictive.

7.2.1.1 Requirements for private law bodies drafting and operating Codes of Conduct

A first set of requirements concerns the *actors* involved in drafting a code of conduct per arts 40 and 41 GDPR. The GDPR allows only associations and 'other bodies representing categories of controllers and processors' to prepare, amend, or extend a code of conduct.[29] Only bodies which represent controllers and processors are qualified to take on such a role. These bodies are usually motivated by the increased visibility and number of members the code will generate for them or for the actual added value of such a code into streamlining the specification of requirements across the sector. While the GDPR does not offer qualitative or quantitative criteria to limit the entry qualification of relevant representative bodies,[30]it makes explicit that those bodies should represent controllers or processors, ie the persons that are expected to voluntarily conform to those codes.

Since the data subjects are nowhere to be found in those bodies, the GDPR urges drafters of codes to *consult* relevant stakeholders, including data subjects.[31] Accordingly, the governance of the codes is conducted by a body that has an appropriate level of expertise in the subject matter and has received accreditation.[32] Thus, bodies other than those that drafted the codes may take over the governance, but under the condition of *competence on the subject matter*, which has been verified—in the form of an '*accreditation*' process by the competent supervisory

[26] GDPR arts 40 and 41.

[27] Recital 98 GDPR. The codes are required to provide rules within the limits of the GDPR, thus not going 'above and beyond' type of accountability imposed.

[28] Directive 95/46/EC art 27.

[29] GDPR art 40(2).

[30] Kamara I, 'Article 40 Commentary' in Kuner C, Bygrave LA and Christopher D (eds), *The EU General Data Protection Regulation (GDPR): A Commentary* (OUP 2020), 721ff. (hereafter Kamara 'Article 40')

[31] Recital 99 GDPR.

[32] GDPR art 41(1).

data protection authority. In addition to the competence condition, further procedural requirements need to be fulfilled.[33] The monitoring body needs to be *independent*. Independence concerns the ability to carry out an assessment on whether a controller or processor conforms to a code of conduct.[34] Furthermore, the monitoring body needs to have demonstrated to the supervisory authority that its tasks and duties will not result in a *conflict of interest*.[35]

A due process requirement is that the monitoring body needs to establish procedures to *monitor compliance with the code* of those controllers and processors who have adhered to it, periodically review the operation of the code and have *complaint mechanisms* in place.[36] These procedures and structures need to be *transparent* to the data subjects and the public. To ensure that the monitoring of compliance with the code is not just an empty threat, monitoring bodies are vested with powers (and the obligation) to *take action in case of infringement of clauses* of the code of conduct. These actions are taken independently of any action taken by the supervisory authorities concerning the violation of the GDPR, and might include a *suspension or exclusion* of the infringing controller or processor.[37] Monitoring bodies are also tasked to *periodically review* the operation of the codes.

7.2.1.2 Checks and balances by supervisory authorities

In addition to the statutory requirements for the private law bodies participating in the drafting and monitoring of the codes of conduct, the GDPR establishes *checks and balances* by the supervisory authorities before and after the codes become operational. In fact, the very decision on whether a code will become operational lies with the data protection authority in case of a code with validity in one Member State or the European Commission, when the code of conduct concerns all Member States and is intended to have general validity in the Union.[38] The rigorous assessment and 'tortuous process' of approval of codes of conduct under the Directive,[39] is now streamlined with a two-step assessment process in the GDPR.[40]

[33] GDPR art 41(2).

[34] The auditing standard ISO/IEC 17065 for certification bodies relates independence to impatiality and other concepts such as freedom from conflicts of interest, freedom from bias, freedom from prejudice, neutrality, fairness, open-mindedness, even-handedness, detachment and balance. ISO/IEC 17065:2012 Conformity assessment—Requirements for bodies certifying products, processes and services. The GDPR however adds independence and absence of interest as two different requirements, provided in art 41(2)(a) and 41(2)(d) GDPR respectively.

[35] GDPR art 41(2)(d). Kamara 'Article 40' (n 31), 728.

[36] GDPR art 41(2)(c).

[37] GDPR Art. 41(4).

[38] GDPR art. 40(8).

[39] Korff Douwe, 'EC Study on the Implementation of Data Protection Directive 95/46/EC' Study for the European Commission (2002) 198.

[40] See the EDPB registry of approved Codes of Conduct: https://www.edpb.europa.eu/our-work-tools/accountability-tools/register-codes-conduct-amendments-and-extensions-art-4011_en [accessed 10 August 2024].

For a code to be operational, an *opinion* from the competent supervisory authority is necessary, which may be followed by an *approval* from the same authority. The decision on approval is an administrative act, and may be appealed against via the national administrative law rules against the competent authority that issued the act. The two-step process seems to uphold the legitimacy gates for codes of conduct. The EDPB has provided guidance towards the supervisory authorities regarding the elements to assess before approving a code of conduct. First, the supervisory authorities need to assess the admissibility of a draft code, which essentially entails a number of procedural steps such as competence of the authority, supporting documents, the element of *representation*, material and territorial scope, oversight mechanisms and monitoring body, information on the extent of consultation carried out per Recital 99 GDPR, and conformity with national legislation. Further, the *cumulative* substantial criteria for approving codes relate mostly to the 'added value' of the code in relation to the legal rules. According to the EDPB, the codes should:[41]

- meet a particular need of a sector or processing activity,
- facilitate the application of the GDPR,
- specify the application of the GDPR, and provide sufficient *added value*, meaning providing 'sufficiently clear and effective solutions',[42]
- provide sufficient safeguards, calibrating expected measures to risks of processing or sector, **and**
- provide effective mechanisms for monitoring compliance with the code.

Finally, there is a number of general *transparency and publicity* measures, such as the maintenance by the EDPB of a public register with all approved 'Codes of conduct, amendments, and extensions'.[43]

7.2.1.3 Scope of Codes of Conduct

As per the content and subject matter of the codes of conduct, the GDPR provides a non-exhaustive list of topics of varying types related to the principles of art 5 GDPR, the grounds for lawful processing, but also technical provisions such as pseudonymization, or legal technical dispute resolution procedures pursuant to

[41] EDPB Guidelines 1/2019 vol 2.0 s 6, 14.

[42] EDPB 1/2019 (n 41) para 35, 15. An example from the application of this criterion comes from the Dutch supervisory authority's assessment of the Dutch Code of Conduct for SME's in the ICT sector. The Code provides that applicant controllers and processors need to fill in a statement about their processing, handling of rights of those affected by data leaks, evaluation and adjustment of security measures. The Data Pro Statement should be included in the data processing agreements between controllers and processors or processors and sub-processors, and in this manner inform in a standardized manner the contracting party. Autoriteit Persoonsgegevens 'Besluitinzake de verklaring omtrent Gedragscode Data Pro Code van Nederland ICT1; z2018-11482', 9.

[43] GDPR art 40(11).

arts 77 and 79 GDPR.[44] Although this is an indicative list, it is difficult to imagine codes going beyond this list. In practice, it may well be the case that drafters of a candidate code select more than one topic from the list, aiming for a bigger target group with a broader scope.

7.2.2 Data Protection Certification Mechanisms

Data protection certification mechanisms are another private regulation instrument regulated in the GDPR, aiming similarly to the codes of conduct to enhance the accountability toolbox of data controllers and processors.[45] Despite the non-aligned views of the regulators on the exact role and framework for certification in the GDPR during the law-making procedure,[46] the approach in the final text allowed a moderate introduction of certification in the data protection law. Articles 42 and 43, together with the provisions on the powers and competences of the supervisory authorities offer a set of safeguards to ensure that the instrument will be used as intended.

7.2.2.1 Requirements for private law bodies drafting and operating certification

Data protection certifications are operated by certification bodies, which are private law organizations.[47] Unlike codes of conduct, there are no requirements for the actors drafting data protection certifications. Thus, there are no requirements for representation or consultation with stakeholders, although these are advisable, according to the EDPB guidance, for data processing with non-mitigated or residual risks.[48] As with codes of conduct, certification bodies need to be *accredited* for their competences, which include granting and revoking certifications. The authority granting accreditation to certification bodies may be either the supervisory authority, or the National Accreditation Body (NAB), or both.[49]

[44] GDPR art 40(2)(a)–(k).

[45] Kamara I and De Hert P, 'Data Protection Certification in the EU: Possibilities, Actors and Building Blocks in a Reformed Landscape,' in Rodrigues R and Papakonstantinou E (eds), *Privacy and data protection seals* (TMC Asser Press 2018), 7. Lachaud, E, 'Quelle peut être la contribution de la certification a la protection des données personnelles?' (2017) 20 Trinity CL Rev, 212.

[46] Read ibid Kamara and De Hert (n 45).

[47] While the GDPR does not define the term 'certification body' or 'certification', the EDPB commonly refers to the ISO/IEC 17000:2004 standard for definitions. See ISO/IEC 17000:2004 Vocabulary and general principles.

[48] See EDPB guided supervisory authorities to investigate whether the criteria, require 'prior consultation concerning the remaining risks that could not be mitigated, based on the results of the Data Protection Impact Assessment (DPIA)'. EDPB, Guidelines 1/2018 on certification and identifying certification criteria in accordance with Articles 42 and 43 of the Regulation—version adopted after public consultation, vol 3.0 (2019) (hereafter EDPB 1/2018). Annex 2, 27.

[49] Kamara I, 'Article 43 Certification bodies' in Spiecker gen. Döhmann I, Papakonstantinou E, Hornung G and De Hert P (eds), *General Data Protection Regulation* (Nomos Verlagsgesellschaft mbH & Co KG 2023) (hereafter Kamara 'Article 43').

The legislation aimed at leveraging the practical experience of NABs established under Regulation 765/2008,[50] did not exclude the supervisory authorities, and found therefore a middle ground by introducing optional models in art 43 and left Member States to decide which accreditation option to follow in their own jurisdiction. Accreditation, when conducted by the NAB follows the requirements of the conformity assessment ISO/IEC 17065, which is referenced directly in art 43(2). Certification bodies are required to demonstrate *independence* and *expertise* in relation to the subject matter of the certification,[51] having established *procedures for issuing, reviewing periodically, and withdrawing certifications* (and seals or marks),[52] transparent *complaint handling* procedures[53] and lack of *conflict of interest*.[54] In addition, the certification body needs to undertake to respect the approved certification criteria.[55] Accreditation is granted for a maximum period of five years and may be revoked at any time by the granting authority, which forces the certification body to be alert and up to date in the performance of its tasks.

7.2.2.2 Checks and balances by supervisory authorities

Supervisory authorities play a pivotal role in gatekeeping the legitimacy of certification in the GDPR. Alongside the requirements for certification bodies, and their powers to review and withdraw certifications, data protection authorities (DPA) are granted powers to maintain an overview of and intervene, when necessary, in relation to both the certification and accreditation processes. Especially, when it comes to certification, it is possible that supervisory authorities provide certification instead or in parallel with certification bodies in their jurisdiction.[56]

To be able to maintain oversight, the DPA enjoys an essential power to receive *information* from certification bodies, prior to their issuing,[57] renewing,[58] and withdrawing[59] certifications. As with the codes of conduct, there is an *approval act* by the supervisory authority. In certification, the approval concerns the certification criteria, namely the content requirements (as opposed to procedural requirements such as documentation). The EDPB has provided criteria guiding the assessment procedure of the DPA, or the EDPB itself in case of a common European Data

[50] Regulation (EC) No 765/2008 of the European Parliament and of the Council of 9 July 2008 setting out the requirements for accreditation and market surveillance relating to the marketing of products and repealing Regulation (EEC) No 339/93, OJ L 218/30.
[51] GDPR art 43(2)(a).
[52] GDPR art 43(2)(c).
[53] GDPR art 43(2)(d).
[54] GDPR art 43(2)(e).
[55] GDPR art 43(2)(b) and 42(5).
[56] However, such parallel action would invoke competition between the DPAs and certification bodies and raise questions of function creep. Kamara I, Burnik J, 'Recommendations on European Data Protection Certification' Report for ENISA (2017), 25.
[57] GDPR art 43(1).
[58] GDPR art 43(1).
[59] GDPR art 43(5).

Protection Seal.[60] The criteria should aim: a) to properly reflect the requirements and principles of the GDPR, and b) to contribute to the consistent application of the GDPR. Further, the certification criteria should focus on verifiability, significance, and suitability to demonstrate compliance with the GDPR,[61] be relevant to a target group, flexible and scalable for application to different types and sizes of organizations.[62] Remarkably, the EDPB guidance on the certification criteria advises entities drafting certification criteria to take into account and be compatible with other standards, such as national or international (ISO) standards.[63] In handling the applications, the supervisory authorities should operate in a fair and non-discriminatory way, according to a publicly available procedure.[64]

When it comes to ensuring the certification is not a snapshot of how a controller or processor processes data only in a given moment (during the assessment) but for as long as the certification is valid there are certain safeguards for the period after the granting of certification. Supervisory authorities bear the task to *periodically review* issued certifications,[65] a task which would also be carried out by an accredited certification body. Most importantly, supervisory authorities are competent to *withdraw* a certification or order a certification body to do so, or to order the certification body not to issue a certification, when it comes to the DPA's attention that requirements are not (longer) met.[66] These *corrective powers* of the supervisory authorities are subject to judicial review.[67]

7.2.2.3 Scope of certifications

The subject matter of certification is not pre-determined in the GDPR and unlike the relevant provisions of codes of conduct, there is no indicative list of potential subject matters in the certification provisions. In that sense, the content might be determined by interested parties to draft a certification and submit it for approval to the competent authority.[68] The GDPR does provide limitations regarding what can be certified under the data protection certification mechanisms. The GDPR requires that only processing operations are certified under the data protection certification mechanisms, not persons, products, systems, or other.[69]

[60] EDPB 1/2018 (n 48), 12 and Annex II.
[61] EDPB 1/2018 (n 48), 15.
[62] EDPB 1/2018 (n 48), 20.
[63] EDPB 1/2018 (n 48), 21.
[64] EDPB 1/2018 (n 48), 12.
[65] GDPR art 57(1)(o).
[66] GDPR art 58(2)(h).
[67] See GDPR art 78. Georgieva L and Schmidl M, 'Article 58. Powers' in Kuner C, Bygrave LA, and Christopher D (eds), *The EU General Data Protection Regulation (GDPR): A Commentary* (OUP 2020), 947.
[68] There are however some pointers in several other provisions, showing where certification could be useful, without however limiting the scope to only those topics. See Kamara I, and others 'GDPR Certification Study', European Publications Office, (2019) Chapter 3.
[69] Leenes R, 'Commentary Article 42 GDPR' in Kuner C, Bygrave LA, and Christopher D (eds), *The EU General Data Protection Regulation (GDPR): A Commentary* (OUP 2020), 15ff.

Within the scope of limitations, it is safeguarded that absurd situations will be avoided in which a controller would aim for example to demonstrate compliance with a provision by virtue of a certified data protection-friendly information management system. In reality, components such as the Personal Information Management System (PIMS) or even measures relating to the training of the personnel will in all likelihood be part of an assessment, but not the object of a data protection certification as such. Last but not least, for reasons of transparency and reliability the EDPB is obliged to maintain a *public register* of granted certifications.[70]

7.2.3 Binding Corporate Rules

Binding Corporate Rules (BCR) are an instrument providing a legal basis to EU controllers and processors to transfer personal data to a controller or processor established in a third country outside the Union or an international organization.[71] Due to the lack of competence of the EU supervisory authorities over processing that takes place in the third country,[72] the legislator shielded this private regulation instrument with a broad range of safeguards. It should also be noted that the safeguards for BCR[73] are also serving a somewhat different objective than private regulation instruments destined for demonstrating compliance: that is to ensure that when data are transferred outside the Union, the high level of protection of the EU is not undermined by the transfer.[74]

Binding Corporate Rules are essentially data protection policies to which an EU controller or processor established in an EU country adheres (data exporter). The aim is to transfer data to non-EU controllers or processors (data importers) which

[70] See https://www.edpb.europa.eu/our-work-tools/accountability-tools/certification-mechanisms-seals-and-marks_en [accessed 10 August 2024].

[71] GDPR arts. 46(2)(b) and 47. See in general about BCR Moerel L, *Binding Corporate Rules: Corporate Self-Regulation of Global Data Transfers* (OUP 2012)

[72] Judgment of 6 October 2015, Schrems, Case C-362/14, EU:C:2015:650 (Schrems I) para 44. See however para 45 of the same judgment, the EU supervisory authorities are competent for the transfer, which constitutes data processing.

[73] The same is valid for codes of conduct art 40(1) GDPR, and the data protection certification mechanisms of art 42(1), as opposed to the codes of conduct of art 40(3) and art 42(2) certification mechanisms suited for international transfers and controllers and processors not subject to the GDPR. See also art 46 GPDR.

[74] GDPR art 44. The CJEU both in the *Schrems I* 2015 and in *Schrems II* 2020 cases used the legal standard of 'essential equivalence' of the level of protection offered by the transfer mechanism when data are transferred outside the Union with the level of protection the data (and the data subject) enjoy in the Union. Judgment of 16 July 2020, Schrems, Case C-311/18, EU:C:2020:559 (Schrems II), para 105. Read further: Kuner. C, , 'Reality and illusion in EU data transfer regulation post Schrems.' German Law Journal 18, no 4 (2017): 881, 900ff; Drechsler L, 'What Is Equivalent? A Probe into GDPR Adequacy Based on EU Fundamental Rights.' (February 21, 2019), Jusletter IT 21; Drechsler L and Kamara I, 'Essential Equivalence as a Benchmark for International Data Transfers after Schrems II,' in Kosta E and Leenes (eds), *Research Handbook on EU Data Protection Law* (Edward Elgar Publishing 2022), 314.

belong to the same group of undertakings or enterprises with a joint economic activity[75] and are established in a non-EU and non-adequate country.[76] BCR belong to the category of transfers subject to appropriate safeguards, when there is no adequacy decision from the European Commission on the level of protection offered by the third country or international organization.[77]

7.2.3.1 Checks and balances by supervisory authorities and the Commission

The data exporter that relies on the ground of art 47 GDPR to transfer data by means of appropriate safeguards does not require prior authorization for the specific transfer or set of transfers. Thus, to ensure that the BCR provide appropriate safeguards, both on paper but also in terms of practice and effectiveness, the GDPR regulates extensively the instrument of BCR. As with the codes of conduct and the data protection certification mechanisms under the GDPR, an approval from the competent supervisory authority is necessary *prior* to the instrument being valid and operational. The BCR approval is conditional on three criteria:

a. That the BCR are legally binding and apply to and are enforced by every member of the group of undertakings or enterprises with joint economic activity.[78]
b. That the BCR are expressly conferring enforceable rights on data subjects when it comes to processing of their personal data.[79]
c. That they fulfil a number of substantial and procedural conditions, laid down in art 47(2) GDPR.[80]

Furthermore, the consistency mechanism of art 63 is triggered for BCR, according to which if the competent supervisory authority aims at approving the BCR, the EDPB needs to provide an opinion, which while not mandatory,[81] will most likely be adopted by the competent supervisory authority.[82]

[75] This is meant to include business partners with some stable collaboration, who nonetheless do not qualify as an undertaking. Tosoni L, 'Article 4(20)' in Kuner C, Bygrave LA, and Docksey C (eds), *The EU General Data Protection Regulation (GDPR): A Commentary* (OUP 2020), 262.
[76] See art 4(20) GDPR for definition.
[77] GDPR art 46.
[78] GDPR art 47(1)(a).
[79] GDPR art 47(1)(b).
[80] GDPR art 47(1)(c). See following section under 'Scope'.
[81] GDPR art 64(7) provides that the competent supervisory authority shall 'take utmost account of the opinion of the Board' and communicate to the EDPB whether it will maintain or amend its draft decision.
[82] See an example of an EDPB Opinion: EDPB Opinion 16/2019 on the draft decision of the Belgian Supervisory Authority regarding the Binding Corporate Rules of ExxonMobil Corporation (November 2019) and the Belgian DPA decision: Decision of the General Secretariat n° 03/2019 of 4 December 2019, https://www.edpb.europa.eu/system/files/2021-10/be_sa_final_decision_bcr-c_exxonmobil_20191204.pdf [accessed 10 August 2024].

7.2.3.2 Scope of Binding Corporate Rules

The conditions of art 47 GDPR refer to the principles, duties, and in general data protection rules to which data importers need to adhere.[83] The BCR must at least specify[84] the application of the data protection principles of art 5 GDPR, and in particular purpose limitation, data minimization, limited retention period, data quality, and additionally data protection by design and by default, the legal basis for processing, the processing of special categories of personal data, data security measures, and requirements vis-à-vis onward transfers.[85]

When it comes to procedural guarantees, these can be grouped into ones adding to transparency such as how data subjects are informed about the processing,[86] and others ensuring compliance, oversight, and redress. Among the conditions of art 47(2), there are several procedural guarantees aiming to strengthen the position of the data subject. The BCR need to state *inter alia* the means to exercise the data subject's rights, the right to lodge a complaint with the competent supervisory authority and the courts, and the means to obtain redress, including for a violation of the BCR.[87] In addition, data exporters need to provide complaint procedures,[88] internal mechanisms for ensuring compliance, including audits and corrective actions,[89] mechanisms for reporting and recording changes,[90] and data protection training of personnel.[91] Further, an obligation for cooperation with the supervisory authorities is established, for the period after the BCR approval by the competent supervisory authority, and the obligation to report any contradicting national or regional legislation,[92] to which a data importer is subject, and might have an adverse effect on the guarantees provided by the BCR.[93] In terms of liability, the GDPR required from the EU data controller or processor the acceptance of strict liability for any breach of the BCR by any member concerned not established in the Union.[94]

[83] Recital 110 GDPR and art 47(2)(d).
[84] GDPR art 47(2).
[85] Onward transfers are any further transfers of personal data from the non-EU controller or processor to a non-EU controller or processor in another third country.
[86] GDPR art 47(2)(g).
[87] GDPR art 47(2)(e).
[88] GDPR art 47(2)(i).
[89] GDPR art 47(2)(j).
[90] GDPR art 47(2)(k).
[91] GDPR art 47(2)(n).
[92] GDPR art 47(2)(l). This obligation is particularly important in light of governmental access to the transferred data and surveillance by governmental authorities of third countries. See Case C-311/18, *Schrems II* 2020, Judgment Case paras 63ff, the findings of the Irish High Court about surveillance programs and activities by US governmental agencies; Case C-362/14 *Schrems I* 2015, Judgment Case, para 85; See further WP29 guidelines flagging this issue, WP29 'Working Document 01/2016 on the justification of interferences with the fundamental rights to privacy and data protection through surveillance measures when transferring personal data (European Essential Guarantees)' WP237 (2016).
[93] GDPR art 47(2)(m).
[94] GDPR art 47(2)(f). There is an exemption established in case the controller or the processor that proves that that member is not responsible for the event giving rise to the damage.

As with the other two instruments examined, the EDPB is obliged to maintain a public registry with the approved BCR.[95]

7.2.4 Administrative Fines and Civil Liability in Data Protection Law

The GDPR establishes a system of remedies offering both administrative law and civil law remedies.[96] On top of guarantees specific to the private regulation instruments, as described in the previous sections, the GDPR equips data subjects with procedural rights that are applicable for damage suffered as a result of violation of the GDPR.[97] These can be imposed for violation of the provisions of codes of conduct, data protection certification mechanisms, and BCR and the other private regulation instruments in the GDPR. The administrative remedies channel entails that data subjects lodge a complaint with a supervisory authority.[98] Supervisory authorities, in the framework of their supervision and enforcement duties, as prescribed in art 57(1)(a) GDPR, may impose fines for violations of the GDPR, independently of a data subject complaint.[99]

Infringements of the obligations of a certification body or a monitoring body of codes of conduct may bring administrative fines by the supervisory authorities according to art 83(4)(b) and (c). In addition, violation of obligations of controllers and processors vis-à-vis certification also may be punished with high fines.[100] Further, the infringement of the provisions of BCR establishes a claim for the highest fine possible under the GDPR.[101] The WP29 has adopted an interesting interpretation of art 83 which provides mitigating and aggravating factors for the DPA's decision of whether to impose a fine and the determination of the fine; according to WP29, non-compliance with self-regulatory measures is potentially indicative of the controller's or processor's negligence or intentional behaviour of non-compliance.[102]

[95] See EDPB website: https://edpb.europa.eu/our-work-tools/accountability-tools/bcr_nl [accessed 20 September 2023].

[96] This is laid down in chapter VIII of the GDPR on remedies, liability, and penalties.

[97] The remedies analysed in this section do not include any additional or alternative remedies available from bilateral contractual relationships and breach of contract, for example between the certification body and the controller or processor who has been granted certification.

[98] GDPR art 77.

[99] GDPR art 58(2)(i) equips supervisory authorities with the corrective power to impose an administrative fine in line with GDPR art 83.

[100] GDPR art 83(4)(a). Oddly, this is not the same for controllers and processors vis-à-vis their obligations stemming from arts 40 and 41 (thus, codes of conduct).

[101] GDPR art 83(5)(c).

[102] WP29 'Guidelines on the application and setting of administrative fines for the purposes of the Regulation 2016/679' WP 253 (2017) 16. The Guidelines are endorsed by the WP29 successor, the EDPB.

Independently of the administrative fines, data subjects have the right to an effective judicial remedy against a controller or processor.[103] The right is triggered by an (alleged) infringement of data subject's rights following the processing of personal data in a manner non-compliant with the GDPR.[104] Further, not only the right to an effective remedy is established, but also the right to receive compensation about incurred material and non-material damages.[105]

The GDPR does not specify nor limit the provisions that may lead to damage in the case of controllers.[106] Any breach of the duties, rights, or other provisions, may cause damage, and lead to compensation of the data subject, or any person[107] who has suffered damage from the infringing behaviour.[108] In the case of processors, those are liable for the damage caused by processing which did not comply with an obligation directly imposed on them by the GDPR, or where they acted outside the instructions of the controller. The controller or processor may be exempt only when they prove they were not responsible in the event that gave rise to the damage.[109] This reversal of the burden of proof is beneficial and to some extent necessary, since the person who suffered damage could not possibly have an overview of the exact processing activities and measures taken by the controller, or even more the processor, to adduce proof of the liability of the controller/processor.

> Any violation of the Binding Corporate Rules for example which causes damage to a data subject, such as the violation of requirements for onward

[103] GDPR art 79. Read further on civil liability in data protection law: Van Alsenoy B, 'Liability under EU Data Protection Law: From Directive 95/46 to the General Data Protection Regulation' 7 (2016) JIPITEC, 271, para 1; Van Alsenoy, *Data Protection Law in the EU: Roles, Responsibilities and Liability* (Intersentia 2019).

[104] It should be noted that while GDPR art79 refers to data subjects only, art 82 refers to the much broader term 'any person', including legal and natural persons, of which data subjects and non-data subjects.

[105] GDPR art 82. One of the landmark cases to first establish the possibility of data subjects able to bring claims for non-pecuniary damages suffered by the misuse of personal data was the (pre-GDPR) UK case *Vidal Hall v. Google*. Court of Appeal, Google Inc v Vidall-Hall & Ors [2015] EWCA Civ 311, Read further: https://www.fieldfisher.com/en/services/privacy-security-and-information/privacy-security-and-information-law-blog/vidal-hall-v-google-a-new-dawn-for-data-protection-claims [accessed 20 September 2023].

[106] Damage as a concept is mentioned also in Recital 146 GDPR. Examples of material damage include increase in costs of a service that was the result of unlawful transmission of data, non-execution of an employment contract, while immaterial damage includes anxiety and distress, unwelcome public exposure, discrimination. Cordeiro AM, 'Civil Liability for Processing of Personal Data in the GDPR' (2019) 5 European Data Protection Law Review, 492 (hereafter Cordeiro 'Civil liability'). Read further: Zanfir-Fortuna G, 'Article 82 GDPR' in Kuner C, Bygrave LA, and Christopher D (eds), *The EU General Data Protection Regulation (GDPR): A Commentary* (OUP 2020) (hereafter Zanfir-Fortuna 'Article 82').

[107] See, in the same vein, Cordeiro 'Civil liability' (n 106) 492 and the debate in German scholarship as reported by Cordeiro between a more restrictive interpretation (data subjects only) or a literal interpretation meaning indeed any natural or legal person that suffered damage from non-compliance with the GDPR.

[108] GDPR art 82(2). Read: Trakman L, Walters R and Zeller B, 'Tort and Data Protection Law' (2019) 5 European Data Protection Law Review, 505ff.

[109] GDPR art 82(3).

transfers,[110] gives rise to damage claims for compensation. Another example in the case of certification for the business-to-business cases, not involving thus data subjects, would be the violation of the obligation of a processor (that applies for certification) to provide the certification body with all the relevant information and access to its processing activities.[111] So such a processor not providing the required information on some processing activities (for example because they are not complying with the GDPR), could (mis-)lead a certification body to grant the certification.[112]

Finally, the GDPR establishes joint and several liability for controllers and/or processors;[113] each controller and/or processor is deemed liable for the entire damage, if those are involved in the same processing and are responsible for any damage that was caused by that processing.[114] Practically, from the perspective of the data subject, this means that the person that suffered the damage, may choose one entity to sue for the entire damage, or sue all the entities jointly.[115]

7.3 *Ex Ante* Safeguards in Standard-Setting

Having analysed that the safeguards the GDPR provide for the three private law instruments of codes of conduct, certifications, and BCR, this section explores what standardization offers in terms of *ex ante* safeguards,[116] thus the standardization process, before the standard is available in the market. *Ex ante* safeguards mostly relate to input and throughput legitimacy,[117] ensuring that guarantees are in place with regard to the development and adoption of standards. The need for *ex-ante* safeguards is created by the private nature of standardization, and the imperative to bridge the legitimacy mismatch between private and public authority.[118]

110 GDPR art 47(2).
111 GDPR art 42(6).
112 A (counter)argument here could be that in any case the certification body is responsible for the proper assessment leading to the certification, per art 43(4) GDPR.
113 Zanfir-Fortuna 'Article 82' (n 106), 1176.
114 GDPR art 82(4). The controllers and processors that paid full compensation for the damage, are entitled to claim back from the others that are also liable, the amount of compensation that corresponds to their part of responsibility, according to art 82(5) GDPR.
115 The provision of art 82(4) GDPR protects only data subjects.
116 I have borrowed the division between *ex ante* and *ex post* control mechanisms in standardization from Eliantonio M, 'Judicial Control of the EU Harmonized Standards: Entering a Black Hole?' (2017) 44 Legal Issues of Economic Integration, 395.
117 See Schmidt V and Wood M, 'Conceptualizing Throughput Legitimacy: Procedural Mechanisms of Accountability, Transparency, Inclusiveness and Openness in EU Governance' (2019) 97 Public Administration,727.
118 See Chapter 4 section 4.1 in this book. Read also: Partiti E, Bijlmakers S, and Delimatsis P, 'Evolutionary dynamics of transnational private regulation' (2022) 13 Transnational Legal Theory, 437ff.

Table 7.1 *Ex ante* procedural safeguards and relavant standardization streams

Source of safeguards	Applicable to standardization stream
Standardization Regulation – participation, transparency, accessibility	Stream 1a: general harmonized standards Stream 1b: New Approach harmonized standards
Standardization Regulation – Compliance assessment	Stream 1b: New Approach harmonized standards Stream 4: mixed (if committee-based put forward for a New Approach standardization request)
Standardization Regulation requirements for ICT specifications	Stream 3: market-based specifications (only ICT)
Internal Regulations and Codes of Practice	Stream 1: harmonized standards Stream 2: committee-based standards Stream 4: mixed (committee-based to harmonized standards) Stream 3 (depending on the nature of the organization/forum)
External Agreements and Memoranda of Understanding	Stream 1: harmonized standards Stream 2: committee-based standards Stream 4: mixed (committee-based to harmonized standards) Stream 3 (depending on the nature of the organization/forum)

The *ex-ante* safeguards in recognized standardization bodies are mainly provided for by their internal regulations and codes of practice, bilateral or multilateral inter-institutional agreements and Memoranda of Understanding, and legislation. In terms of legislation, the Union Standardization Regulation is analysed,[119], as the main instrument regulating formal standards in the Union, and providing safeguards for standard-setting.[120] The following Table offers an overview of the sources of safeguards discussed in this Chapter and the correlated standardization streams, based on the categorization as provided in Chapter 4.[121]

[119] For other legal frameworks such as Global administrative law (GAL) read: Kingsbury B, Krisch N and Stewart R B, 'The emergence of global administrative law.' (2005) 68 Law and contemporary problems, 15; Büthe T and Mattli W, *The New Global Rulers: The Privatization of Regulation in the World Economy* (Princeton University Press 2011); Scott C, Cafaggi F and Senden L, 'The Conceptual and Constitutional Challenge of Transnational Private Regulation' (2011) 38 Journal of Law and Society, 1; Esty DC, 'Good Governance at the Supranational Scale: Globalizing Administrative Law' (2006) 115 The Yale Law Journal, 1490; Kanevskaia Whitaker O, 'Technology Standard-Setting Under the Lens of Global Administrative Law: Accountability, Participation and Transparency of Standard-Setting Organizations' TILEC Working Paper (2016); Murphy CN and Yates J, *The International Organization for Standardization (ISO): Global Governance Through Voluntary Consensus* (Routledge 2009); Company B, 'A Public Law Approach to Internet Standard Setting.' Goettingen J. Int'l L. 7 (2016): 49.

[120] See Chapter 3 section 3.3 in this book.

[121] See Chapter 4 section 4.4 in this book.

7.3.1 Legislation: Safeguards in the Standardization Regulation (Stream 1)

The Standardization Regulation introduces two significant due process principles, namely transparency[122] and participation.[123] The Standardization Regulation refers to transparency and participation, in the framework of the so called 'founding principles' of standardization, together with coherence, openness, consensus, voluntary application, and independence from special interests and efficiency.[124] These principles are inspired by the WTO principles for standardization and eventually become the threshold[125] for providing procedural guarantees in private regulation, in general, and standardization, in specific.

Transparency and participation, as introduced in the Standardization Regulation are multi-faceted concepts, that admittedly also cover some of the aspects of the other founding principles, such as consensus and openness, as explained in the following sections. It has been argued that compliance with procedural safeguards contributes to both democratic legitimacy[126] and substantive accuracy of standards.[127] Yet, one cannot assume that transparency and participation related safeguards can make up for the lack–in this general Standardization Regulation on standards–of assessment and compatibility of standards with their supporting Union policies and laws. Some safeguards of this kind are offered in harmonized standards.

7.3.1.1 Stakeholder participation

Participation in the Technical Committees of recognized standardization organizations is usually via membership, which is awarded to entities such as companies. At ETSI, there is direct participation of the ETSI members to Technical Committees.[128] At CEN, CENELEC, ISO and IEC the *national delegation principle*

[122] Medzmariashvili M, 'Regulating European Standardisation through Law: The Interplay between Harmonised European Standards and EU Law.', Doctoral dissertation, Lund University, 2019, 204. TEU art 11 vis-à-vis participation and Prechal S, and de Leeuw ME, 'Transparency: A general principle of EU Law.' in*General principles of EC Law in a process of development* (2008): 201–242.

[123] Regulation 1025/2012 ch II.

[124] Regulation 1025/2012 Recital 2.

[125] Kanevskaia O, 2023 (n 21), 242.

[126] Kallestrup M, 'Stakeholder Participation in European Standardization: A Mapping and an Assessment of Three Categories of Regulation' (2017) 44 Legal Issues of Economic Integration 381.

[127] Glinski C and Rott P, 'Deficient Standards by European Standardisation Organisations: Between State Liability and Tort Liability,' in Eliantonio M and Cauffman C (eds), *The Legitimacy of Standardisation as a Regulatory Technique* (Edward Elgar Publishing 2020), 137.

[128] Specifically for harmonized European standards, ETSI will be subject to the newly introduced requirement in the Regulation 1025/2012, as amended by Regulation (EU) 2022/2480, in art 10(2) '2(a) ...*each European standardization organization shall ensure that the following decisions concerning European standards and European standardization deliverables referred to in paragraph 1* ***are taken exclusively by representatives of the national standardization bodies within the competent decision-making body of that organization:*** *(a) decisions on the acceptance and refusal of standardization requests; (b) decisions on the acceptance of new work items that are needed for the fulfilment of the*

is followed, the members participate in national standardization bodies, which in turn are members of the international or European standardization organizations ('national delegations'). ETSI is an exception to the national delegation principle, as it allows for direct participation of companies and other stakeholders such as SMEs and academia in its Technical Committees.[129] Participating experts in the Technical Committees are delegates of those entities. Although according to the internal rules of recognized standardization bodies, experts commit to promote the interests of the international community, over those of their organization—usually their employer—it is reasonable to question to what extent this holds in practice for every member of those committees.[130] The concern is heightened by the fact that the experts are non-remunerated by the SSO, but participation in a Technical Committee is likely to be reflected in their employment relationship with their organization.[131]

In addition to the issue of the interests represented by technical experts, another issue is the balance of interests and representation of societal interests in Technical Committees.[132] Despite the fact that the national delegation principle strives for fair participation opportunities for national delegations, it might come short in guaranteeing which type of organizations actually forms part of an ESO or ISO/IEC/ITU Technical Committee or a working group, since this is a matter of composition of the national mirror committees[133] and is to be decided by the national standardization bodies. CEN and CENELEC may grant the status of *observer* to organizations 'having an interest for cooperation at overall corporate and technical level', as long as they are non-for-profit, European or international, and represent a specific expertise, sector, or societal interest.[134] There is a question of

standardization request; and (c) decisions on the adoption, revision and withdrawal of European standards or European standardization deliverables.' [emphasis added]

[129] 'ETSI creates standards by consensus Members participate directly in the standards-making process rather than via a national delegation or a National Standards Organization (NSO)' https://www.etsi.org/newsroom/news/16-membership [accessed 20 September 2023].

[130] See for example p 29 ISO 'My ISO job. What delegates and experts need to know' 2018 edition,https://www.iso.org/files/live/sites/isoorg/files/archive/pdf/en/my_iso_job.pdf[accessed 20 September 2023] and ISO 'ISO Code of Conduct for the technical work' (2020 edition) and the commitment in p 5 to 'Work for the net benefit of the international community'.

[131] See claims made by the applicant in EMC Development in the General Court. While the claims were not proven in this case, the mere existence of those claims gives the impression that such issues are not only part of academic debates. Judgment of the General Court of 12 May 2010, Case T-432/05, *EMC Development AB*, , EU:T:2010:189, para 40.

[132] See discussion Volpato A and Eliantonio M, 'The Participation of Civil Society in ETSI from the Perspective of Throughput Legitimacy' [2024] Innovation: The European Journal of Social Science Research 1.

[133] A mirror committee is a Technical Committee of a national standardization body which is 'responsible for following and contributing to the development of standards at European and/or international level'. CEN website https://www.cen.eu/you/participate/Pages/default.aspx [accessed 20 September 2023].

[134] CEN CENELEC Internal Regulations pt 2 (2018) and CEN-CENELEC 'Guide 25 – The Concept of Partnership with European Organizations and other Stakeholders' (2017). Read on interest representation: Cuccuru P, 'Interest Representation in European Standardisation: The Case of CEN and CENELEC' Amsterdam Law School Research Paper 2019-52 (2019).

interest representation in development of standards with some role beyond the merely private rule-setting, thus in Union public policy or law, especially in cases where fundamental rights are at stake, such as the right to protection of personal data, which are of heightened importance.

The Standardization Regulation has introduced an obligation for the European standardization organizations to encourage and facilitate 'appropriate representation' and 'effective participation' of 'relevant stakeholders'.[135] Representation in that context refers to societal interests and participation of societal stakeholders not only of organizations representing employees' rights, but mainly interests of 'greater societal relevance' such as the environment and consumer protection.[136] The EU supports financially the participation to standards making of non-for-profit organizations that represent societal interests, provided they fulfil several conditions about their legal nature and their statutory objectives.[137]

Participation however for societal stakeholders in that sense essentially provides a right to access the documentation, participate in the technical discussions, submit comments on the draft standards, and the opportunity to be heard, but no stronger forms of participation which may influence directly the outcome of the development process,[138] such as voting rights or a *veto*.[139] As opposed to this situation at CEN and CENELEC, ETSI provides voting rights, but due to a weighted voting system based on the membership fee the Annex III societal stakeholders have small direct impact on the outcome of the voting.[140] It should be noted nonetheless, that the national delegation system at CEN and CENELEC offers the right to such stakeholders to participate and vote at a national level. This might lead to some impact on the voting or consultation result. Further, CEN and CENELEC provide societal organizations with a partnership status giving the right to appeal before the CEN-CENELEC Director General in relation to matters associated with work carried out by CEN and/or CENELEC Technical Bodies to which the partner organization has contributed.[141] As regards decision-making, the

[135] Regulation 1025/2012 art 5.

[136] Recital 17 Regulation 1025/2012.

[137] Regulation 1025/2012 art 16. Annex III of the Regulation 1025/2012 identifies four thematic areas: representation of Small Medium Enterprises (SME), consumers, environment, and social interests. The Commission may update the list with an Implementing Decision.

[138] The Final Report on Independent Review of the European Standardization System found that inclusiveness was a key strength of the European Standardization system, but that ' stakeholders impacted by standardization do not all have the same ability to take part in the standard development, as the cost for participating in standardization are relatively high, as compared to the resources available and the benefits expected". EY 'Independent Review of the European Standardization System Final Report' (March 2015) 113.

[139] Recital 23 Regulation 1025/2012.

[140] The weights are calculated according to the membership fee paid by each organization-member of ETSI, which inevitably creates an advantage for member organizations that pay more than others. The consumer association of Annex III, ANEC, reported a few years ago that it had a single vote as opposed to forty five votes of a larger company with higher fee contribution. See ANEC https://anec.eu/about-anec/the-standardization-regulation[accessed 20 September 2023].

[141] CEN CENELEC Internal Regulations 2018 (n 134).

Standardization Regulation requires decisions at ESOs developing standards and standardization deliverables based on standardization requests[142] to be made by *consensus*.[143] Further, the Standardization Regulation provides an obligation for Member States to encourage participation of public authorities in national standardization activities aimed at the development of standards at the request of the European Commission.[144]

In comparison with the safeguards for the GDPR private regulation instruments examined in the first part of this Chapter, the Standardization Regulation admittedly provides more extensive safeguards in relation to participation in the development and the decision-making at large, than the GDPR. As discussed, the GDPR does not impose participation rights for societal stakeholders such as civil rights organizations, but mere consultation by exception, only for codes of conduct. The GDPR private regulation instruments do get scrutinized by supervisory authorities, which are independent. It is not certain whether the approval from a supervisory authority, which is mandatory for all three examined private regulation instruments, outweighs the lack of participation or proper consultation of interested or affected parties in their development.[145] Such a requirement for consulting stakeholders or the public on the draft codes of conduct, certification, or BCR, is not imposed for supervisory authorities reviewing the private regulation instruments. In that regard, while it is true that societal stakeholders (organizations of Annex III) do not have an equal standing as industry participants in the standard development process, they are granted more participation rights than the private regulation instruments regulated in the GDPR with a dedicated framework.

7.3.1.2 Transparency and access

Safeguards to ensure transparency in the Standardization Regulation are embodied in two obligations. First, the obligation concerning the publication of a work programme by every ESO and national standardization body.[146] Secondly, and more importantly, transparency in relation to standards.[147] With regard to the latter, it is noteworthy that the obligation relates mainly[148] to inter-institutional transparency with regard to the development of national or European standards,

[142] Standardization Regulation art 10(1).
[143] Consensus is defined as 'a general agreement, characterised by the absence of sustained opposition to substantial issues by any important part of the concerned interests and by a process that involves seeking to take into account the views of all parties concerned and to reconcile any conflicting arguments. Consensus does not imply unanimity'. See Annex II Regulation 1025/2012
[144] Standardization Regulation art 7.
[145] As mentioned earlier, consultation is not mandatory for any of the three GDPR private regulation instruments analysed in this Chapter. It is only mentioned in a Recital in relation to codes of conduct. The EDPB 'highly recommended' consultation of the members of the association of controllers or processors drafting the relevant code by the EDPB 1/2018 (n 48) 13.
[146] Standardization Regulation art 3(1).
[147] Standardization Regulation art 4.
[148] Standardization Regulation art 4(1)–(3) and 4(4)(b).

rather than transparency measures for interested parties, be it societal stakeholder organizations or individuals, for example data subjects. Inter-institutional transparency with regard to standards aims mainly at preventing an overlap and competition among standards, eg national and European ones. This is different from transparency of standards for any interested party.[149] This issue is not remedied by the provision of art 4(4)(a) Standardization Regulation, which obliges national standardization bodies to ensure access to draft national standards to *all relevant parties* and provide them with the opportunity to submit comments.[150] First, there is much leeway for standardization bodies to decide who is a *relevant* party, and secondly, this provision relates only to standards under preparation, and not the final published result, or the standard-setting process.

An exception to the main focus on inter-institutional transparency is established with regard to the accessibility of SMEs to standards.[151] The Standardization Regulation obliges national standardization bodies *inter alia* to give access to SMEs to the standardization activities, to provide free access to draft standards, and to provide free access or special rates to participate in standardization activities.[152]

The European standardization system lacks, in that sense, some safeguards introduced in the GDPR for the examined private regulation instruments. There is no public registry for all the available instruments, maintained by a trusted independent party (in the GDPR, this is the EDPB), neither a common registry with all companies that have been found or claim to conform to those standards. In addition, there is no explicit obligation of transparency of the certification of the process as in the GDPR.[153] Most importantly, the GDPR requires the publication of the content of certification criteria and codes of conduct, in the EDPB registry, while there is obviously no such obligation with regard to standards, which are publicly available, but for a fee.

7.3.1.3 Compliance assessment (Streams 1 and 4)

In a case study of the ISO 26000 standard on social corporate responsibility, Bijlmakers and Van Calster found that despite an intensive and participatory standard-setting procedure, discussions may turn political, and thus threaten the credibility of the end result, the standard to be published.[154] Examples like this

[149] For example, art 43 GDPR refers to an international conformity assessment standard, also adopted as European. The standard is publicly available, but for a fee. The WP29 flagged this issue and requested the publication of the ISO/IEC 17065 standard free of charge. See WP29 'Request to publish free of charge the ISO 17065 standard' Letter to the President of ISO (2018). https://ec.europa.eu/newsroom/article29/item-detail.cfm?item_id = 625011 [accessed 20 September 2023].

[150] Standardization Regulation art 4(4)(a).

[151] Standardization Regulation art 6.

[152] Standardization Regulation art 6(1)(a)–(f).

[153] GDPR art 42(5).

[154] Bijlmakers S and van Calster G, 'You'd Be Surprised How Much It Costs to Look This Cheap! A Case Study of ISO 26000 on Social Responsibility,' in Delimatsis, P, (ed), *The Law, Economics and Politics of International Standardisation* (Cambridge University Press 2015), 275.

one show that safeguards pertaining to participation and transparency are not panacea. Thus, additional safeguards relating to the *ex ante* reviewability of the standard and its fit-for-purpose check might be necessary.

These kind of additional safeguard are in place under art 10(6) Standardization Regulation. Harmonized standards are developed on the basis of a standardization request by the European Commission, and the relevant harmonization legislation. Standards developed at the request of the European Commission are usually published in the Official Journal.[155] Publication in the Official Journal is conditional on the positive assessment of compliance of the harmonized standards with the relevant harmonization law, on which those standards are based, and the standardization request.[156]

To perform the assessment the Commission relies on three criteria: a) whether the standard covers the actual legal requirements of the legislation on which it is based, b) whether the standard covers the specific requirements of the standardization request, and c) whether it takes into account the state of the art. This task is assigned to expert consultants, called Harmonized Standards (HAS) Consultants.[157] The HAS Consultants are independent experts which conduct an assessment of the standard at different stages of its development process, and definitely after its publication, with the aim to make recommendations to the Commission.[158] Further, in the aftermath of *James Elliot*,[159] the Commission assesses harmonized standards not only in terms of the applicable legislation and standardization request ('technical aspects'), but also 'other elements of the Standardization Regulation, such as whether their development process has been inclusive'.[160]

[155] Standardization Regulation art 10(6).

[156] After the CJEU *James Elliot* case, the Commission published the assessment criteria for the publication of the standard in the Official Journal. European Commission, Verification of conditions for the publication of references of harmonised standards in the Official Journal, 16 November 2016.

[157] Until 2018, those expert consultants were called New Approach Consultants and were operating under a different framework. See Commission, 'Communication from the Commission to the European Parliament, the Council and the European Economic and Social Committee harmonised standards: Enhancing transparency and legal certainty for a fully functioning Single Market' COM (2018) 764 final (hereafter COM (2018) 764). See *contra* the argument made in this section: Dingermann and Kottman who argued that the Commission 'does not have jurisdiction to conduct a comprehensive and detailed technical assessment of the harmonised standards'. Dingermann K and Kottmann M 'Legal Opinion on the European System of Harmonised Standards' Commissioned by the German Federal Ministry for Economic Affairs and Energy (BMWi) 2020, 38.

[158] The outcome of the assessment can be; 1) Compliant, which entails that the HAS consultant recommends the publication of the standard in the Official Journal. . 2) Partially compliant, which entails that publication of the standard in the Official Journal is possible, with a notice regarding the non-compliant aspects. 3) Non-compliant (or lack of compliance) which entails that the publication of the standard in the Official Journal is not recommended before the document is revised. See CEN-CENELEC BTWG 12 'Harmonised standards and the European regulatory framework. HAS system for BOSS', draft proposal for the new process HAS contractor/consultants system interaction with the CEN-CENELEC process, published on the website of CEN-CENELC.

[159] See Chapter 3 section 3.3 in this book.

[160] Commission (2018) 764 final (n 157), 3.

This 'compliance check' of harmonized standards[161] with the requirements of the relevant legislation is an important difference from other standards under committee-based and market-based standardization. It could be argued that harmonized standards require this additional scrutiny of their content because of their visibility through the publication in the Official Journal, and the presumption of conformity for the New Approach harmonized standards. Yet, committee-based standards that do not offer a presumption of conformity are not free from other effects.[162] In any case, companies are often urged to conform to standards endorsed by the Commission or public authorities or simply mentioned as an authoritative source in policy or other documents[163]. Besides it is often reported, that technicians consider standards to be equivalent to 'laws'.[164]

It is true that the European Commission and the data protection authorities are carefully endorsing standards, in that they do it with a disclaimer about the use of standards not entailing compliance with the data protection law. However, it is doubtful whether the disclaimer suffices to properly inform controllers, processors, but also data subjects about the lack of any prior proper compliance check of the endorsed standard with the data protection law. In any case, a quality or alignment check prior to the endorsement of any standard should take place by a public regulator, independently of the disclaimer and how it is perceived by the audience

[161] 'Mandated standards' and 'standards developed at the request of the Commission' are used interchangeably in this Chapter.

[162] See Chapter 3 section 3.3 in this book.

[163] Some examples: the WP29 for example mentions the ISO 31000:2009 standard for the definition of risk and the ISO/IEC 29134:2017 which provides guidance on Privacy Impact Assessment, WP29 'Guidelines on Data Protection Impact Assessment (DPIA) and determining whether processing is "likely to result in a high risk" for the purposes of Regulation 2016/679' WP 248 rev.1; the EDPB Guidelines on certification (vol 3 2019) refer to the ISO/IEC 17000 standard for the definition of 'certification;' the French Data Protection Authority CNIL referred to the ISO/IEC 27701 standard on management systems and security requirements for the processing of personal data. CNIL stated that while the standard is not GDPR specific, it did take into account the GDPR, and that the standard's proximity with the GDPR is materialized in an Annex, that it represents the state of the art in terms of privacy protection. https://www.cnil.fr/en/iso-27701-international-standard-addressing-personal-data-protection [accessed 20 September 2023]; the State Commissioner for Data Protection and Freedom of Information Baden-Württemberg in its Guidance on Video surveillance by non-public bodies, advised controllers and processors to consult two international standards with regard to art 32 GDPR and security measures, namely the ISO/IEC 27001 on ISMS and the IEC TS 62045 Multimedia security—Guideline for privacy protection of equipment and systems, Der Landesbeauftragte für den Datenschutz und die Informationsfreiheit Baden-Württemberg Orientierungshilfe Videoüberwachung durch nichtöffentliche Stellen, (17 July 2020) https://datenschutz.hessen.de/sites/datenschutz.hessen.de/files/Video%c3%bcberwachung%20durch%20nicht_%c3%b6ffentliche%20Stellen_0.pdf [accessed 20 September 2023].the International Working Group on Data Protection in Telecommunications refers to an international standard for the definition of the term 'biometrics' (ISO/IEC 2382:2015) and to the activity of standardization technical committees, International Working Group on Data Protection in Telecommunications 'Working Paper on Biometrics in Online Authentication' (22-23 November 2016)https://www.datenschutz-berlin.de/fileadmin/user_upload/pdf/publikationen/working-paper/2016/23112016_en.pdf [accessed 20 September 2023].

[164] Spindler G, 'Market Processes, Standardisation, and Tort Law' (1998) 4 European Law Journal, 331ff.

of the guidance. Compared with the GDPR private regulation instruments discussed in this Chapter do go through such a compliance check in the framework of their approval by the supervisory authorities. The check could be performed by experts such as the HAS Consultants and with a standardized transparent methodology or directly by a public regulator such as the supervisory authorities. In all, the compliance check applies to harmonized standards only,[165] and not all the other standards stemming from other streams such as committee-based standards.

7.3.2 Requirements for ICT Technical Specifications (Stream 3)

Market-based 'standardization' refers to market initiatives, which either intentionally or *de facto* develop 'standards'.[166] Specifications of this kind may be used for public procurement processes in the Union and Member States, only after they meet the criteria of Annex II of the Standardization Regulation. This is an essential step aiming to counterbalance any lack of minimum safeguards, during their development process.

The requirements of Annex II of the Standardization Regulation include the WTO principles and extend to matters of quality and coherence, but also market acceptance.[167] In particular, the technical specifications should be developed by non-for-profit organizations, via open, consensus-based and transparent processes. The ICT specifications need to be publicly available for implementation and use,[168] relevant in the sense that they respond to market needs and regulatory requirements, provide for maintenance mechanisms so that they remain up to date, and have intellectual property rights assigned on a fair, reasonable, and non-discriminatory basis. Two additional requirements are essential for providing necessary safeguards. First, the ICT specifications should be *neutral* and *stable*, namely to be based on advanced scientific and technological developments, not distort the market, and if possible, performance-oriented.[169] Secondly, the Standardization Regulation requires that the quality of the ICT specifications is such that allows for different implementations of products and services that are interoperable.

[165] Standardization Regulation art 10(5)–(6).

[166] The distinction on market-based v committee-based standards is made among others in Werle, E, and Iversen EJ 'Promoting legitimacy in technical standardization' (2006) 2 Science, Technology & Innovation Studies, 19. See analysis in Chapter 4 section 4.2.2.

[167] The Annex of Regulation 1025/2012 provides that market acceptance may be proved by 'operational examples of compliant implementations from different vendors'.

[168] This does not mean free of charge.

[169] As opposed to performance oriented specifications, design based specifications with descriptions of characteristics do not allow for flexibility. See CEN CENELEC Internal Regulations pt 3, Principles and rules for the structure and drafting of CEN and CENELEC documents, July 2022, 18 https://boss.cen.eu/media/BOSS%20CEN/ref/ir3_e.pdf [accessed 20 September 2023].

7.3.3 Internal Regulations and Codes of Practice (Streams 1–4)

The principles provided in the Standardization Regulation are reflected in the internal regulations and statutes of the recognized standardization bodies.[170] All the recognized standardization bodies operate on the basis of internal regulations which regulate governance structures, decision-making, financing, intellectual property rights, and include setting rules on the work of the Technical Committees, participation and accessibility aspects. Additionally, standardization bodies may issue internal guidelines on specific matters. CEN and CENELEC for example have published a short common internal guide on how to account for consumer interests in the preparation of European standards.[171]

Next to the internal regulations and specific guides, standardization bodies often establish codes of conduct or practice for their members. These are inspired by corporate good governance principles proposed *inter alia* by the OECD.[172] ISO has established its internal Code of Ethics for each standardization organization member of ISO.[173] The Code of Ethics is a mix of corporate social responsibility type of measures and image management of ISO.[174] Furthermore, recognized standardization bodies have established internal codes of conduct.[175] As opposed to the brief Code of Ethics, the ISO Code of Conduct is more comprehensive. The ISO Code is mandatory for experts participating in Technical Committees, as well as other ISO actors, such as national standardization bodies, committee chairs and the ISO secretariat. The ISO Code includes commitments on work ethics, active participation and the upholding of the key principles of international standardization (consensus, transparency, openness, impartiality, effectiveness, relevance,

[170] From the list of recognized standardization bodies of Regulation 1025/2012, this and the following sections looked into the ESO, ISO, IEC and ITU, and did not look into national standardization bodies.

[171] CEN CENELEC Guide 2 'Consumer interests and the preparation of European Standards; (edn 1, 2001).

[172] OECD, G20/OECD Principles of Corporate Governance, OECD Publishing, Paris (2015). According to the OECD, companies are motivated to adhere to such frameworks of good governance principles with the aim to reassure their shareholders and other stakeholders that their rights are protected and increase trust. For standardization bodies, such frameworks may also be viewed as their ticket to be recognized by the public regulator and have their standards endorsed or used in support of public regulation and policies.

[173] ISO Code of Ethics (2004) https://www.iso.org/files/live/sites/isoorg/files/archive/pdf/en/code ethics_2004-en.pdf [accessed 20 September 2023].

[174] For example, the ISO code of ethics (n 173) provides: 'ISO parties shall contribute to ISO/s actions to help its members from developing countries improve their capacity and their participation in international organization.' 3.

[175] See CEN/CENELEC 'Code of conduct for delegates, experts and observers participating in the technical work of CEN/CENELEC' (October 2018) [accessed 20 September 2023]; ETSI focuses on Intellectual Property Rights, Antitrust issues, and description of procedures and drafting Rules in its ETSI Directives Rulesbook (v. 41 February 2020), with a brief reference to ETSI values in its latest version. See ETSI Directives Rulebook (v.47 30 June 2023) (hereafter ETSI Directives v.47) https://portal.etsi.org/directives/47_directives_june_2023.pdf [accessed 10 August 2024].

coherence, and development).[176] ITU has a dedicated Ethics Office, a code of ethics and several guidance documents and policies on whistleblowing, declaration of interests, and fraud and corruption.[177]

7.3.4 External Agreements and Memoranda of Understanding (Streams 1–4)

The recognized standardization bodies have concluded agreements and Memoranda of Understanding and collaboration with each other. As mentioned in another Chapter,[178] ISO and CEN have signed the Vienna Agreement,[179] and have agreed on common guidelines for the implementation of the agreement.[180] ETSI has signed bilateral agreements with ITU[181] and CEN and CENELEC.[182] Although the main objective of those agreements is to set out the terms of bilateral collaboration, they confirm a shared understanding of the parties regarding the principles of standardization, such as transparency, openness, coherence, impartiality and relevance.[183]

Among the agreements concluded by standardization bodies, the European Standardization Organizations (ESOs) additionally conclude framework partnership agreements with the European Commission.[184] These agreements are based on art 17(5) of the Standardization Regulation, and set the cooperation objectives of the collaboration between the ESOs and the Commission, and provide a common understanding of the goals and values of standards and standard setting-processes. Other significant administrative and financial arrangements also form part of those agreements.[185] However, the majority of the framework agreements

[176] ISO 'ISO Code of Conduct for the technical work' (2022 edition), https://sfs.fi/wp-content/uploads/2022/09/ISO-Code-of-Conduct-for-the-Technical-Work.pdf [accessed 10 August 2024].

[177] See ITU website https://www.itu.int/en/ethics/pages/default.aspx [accessed 20 September 2023].

[178] See Chapter 3.

[179] IEC and CENELEC have signed the Frankfurt Agreement, which replaced the Dresden Agreement.

[180] General Guidelines for the co-operation between CEN, CENELEC and ETSI and the European Commission (EC) and the European Free Trade Association (EFTA). 28 March 2003 OJ C 91, 16.4.2003, 7–11.

[181] See Memorandum of Understanding between ETSI and ITU (2012), https://www.itu.int/dms_pub/itu-r/oth/0a/0e/R0A0E0000920001PDFE.pdf [accessed 10 August 2024]. Interestingly, ETSI has only liaison agreements with ISO at the level of technical committees.

[182] Basic Co-operation Agreement between CEN (European Committee for Standardization), CENELEC (European Committee for Electrotechnical Standardization) and ETSI EC/EFTA.

[183] See for example Vienna Agreement, cl 3 para 3 ('basic principles') 2. ISO CEN, Agreement on Technical Co-operation between ISO and CEN (Vienna Agreement), 2001, codified

[184] Those have followed the General Guidelines for the Co-operation between CEN, CENELEC, ETSI and the European Commission. The Framework Agreements are bilaterally concluded between the European Commission and each of the ESOs. See https://www.efta.int/eea/policy-areas/goods/standardization-mra-technical-cooperation/standardization [accessed 20 September 2023].

[185] Tovo argues that those framework agreements constrain the functional autonomy of the ESOs, since their income relies on more than a third on those agreements. Tovo C, 'Judicial Review of Harmonized Standards: Changing the Paradigms of Legality and Legitimacy of Private Rulemaking under EU Law' (2018) 55 Common Market Law Review 1187.

are not made public,[186] which is contradictory to a transparent European standardization system.[187] Information about these agreements can be derived from the internal documentation of the ESOs, the majority of which is accessible to the public.[188]

Finally, CEN and CENELEC conclude agreements with parties that do not qualify to become members of CEN and CENELEC. These collaboration agreements are concluded with national standardization bodies of non-EU countries or European research projects for example, and offer those some benefits such as access to European standards and the possibility to adopt European standards. There are three types of such agreements at CEN and CENELEC; a) the partnership[189], b) the affiliation,[190] and c) the companion agreements.[191] The partnership agreements offer six categories of partners, including partner organization, liaison, and associated body. The partnership entails that the partner organizations participate as observer at the governing bodies without voting rights, but with the right to appeal in a limited number of matters. In terms of actual technical work, the partnership status allows access to documentation, participation at the technical bodies, submission of technical contributions and preparatory work to support ongoing standardization activity. Partner organizations do not have voting rights at the level of Technical Committees either. The benefits of the partnership are subject to conditions, which are at the discretionary power of the Technical Board to decide upon them. For example, the Technical Board may withdraw the participation

[186] This is the case for the 2009 Framework Agreement. C (2011)9569/1 ENTR (Enterprise and Industry) 15/12/2011 Commission Decision Décision de la Commission relative à la révision des conventions-cadres de partenariat FPA/CEN/ENTR/2009/C(2008)8758, FPA/CENELEC/ENTR/2009/C(2008)8758 et FPA/ETSI/ENTR/2009/C(2008)8758 entre la Commission et les organismes européens de normalisation (CEN, CENELEC et ETSI).

[187] A digital copy of the text of the 2011 Agreement C (2011)9569/1 is not publicly accessible, but was electronically sent to the author, after exercising an access to documents request on the basis of Regulation 1049/2001 (Response letter to the access request: Reference Ares (2020)5556820 dated 15/10/2020, in file with the author).

[188] In general, the agreements signed with external partners are often also adopted as internal guidelines by the ESOs. CEN-CENELEC GUIDE 4 'General Guidelines for the Cooperation between CEN, CENELEC and ETSI and the European Commission and the European Free Trade Association' 2003 (edn 2). The 2003 CEN CENELEC agreement with the European Commission and EFTA provides that standardizers 'remain fully accountable to all interested parties in Europe' in that they take into account 'the broadest possible range of views in drawing up standards' and their procedures during development, inquiry and voting are open and transparent.Due to the broad responsibility of the 'European standardization system' to all interests, it should not act 'on the basis of vested interests'. Some information can be derived from CEN-CENELEC 'Guide 18 concerning the execution of Specific Agreements issued to CEN and CENELEC in accordance with the EC and EFTA Framework Partnership Agreements 2009 (FPA 2009) covering the tasks to be assigned to CEN and CENELEC relating to European standardization' 2010.

[189] CEN-CENELEC 'The concept of Partnership with European Organizations and other stakeholders' Guide 25, vol 3 (2021) (hereafter CEN CENELEC Guide 25) updated version in January 2024. Also see in Annex I of the same document the list of fees.

[190] CEN-CENELEC 'The concept of affiliation with CEN and CENELEC' Guide 12, ed.4 (2016).

[191] CEN-CENELEC 'The concept of Companion Standardization Body with CEN and CENELEC' Guide 13, edn 4 (2016).

of a partner organization from a technical body for the reason that the partner organization does not contribute to the corresponding work.[192] ETSI also concludes partnership agreements of three types; a) letter of intent, b) Memorandum of Understanding and c) Co-operation Agreement,[193] the latter being the strongest form of collaboration. Furthermore, many national standardization bodies, members of ISO[194] and CEN, have signed the WTO Code Good Practice for the Preparation, Adoption and Application of Standards.[195]

7.4 *Ex Post* Safeguards for Standards

7.4.1 Standards as Part of EU Law and Judicial Reviewability

Ex post safeguards relate to the outputs of the standard-setting process, after their adoption by the standard-setting body. *Ex post* safeguards, such as judicial review, may compensate for some limitations of *ex ante* control of standards.[196] While this may not be the case for all *ex ante* safeguards such as societal representatives participation, it is true that judicial reviewability has a remedying function.[197] Besides, the data protection law provides both *ex ante* (eg the approval of codes of conduct by the supervisory authority) and *ex post* safeguards (eg revocation of accreditation, GDPR redress mechanisms) for the private regulation instruments it regulates with a dedicated framework. This section therefore explores whether and under which conditions standards may be subject to judicial review. This question offers insights as to what extent standards are subject to scrutiny from independent fora, rather than any internal dispute resolution and other mechanisms of the standard-setting organizations. Judicial reviewability is a significant *ex post* procedural legitimacy safeguard that has the potential to not only rule on the merits of the disputed standard, but also shape practices and procedures of standard setting in general.

[192] CEN-CENELEC Guide 25 (n 189) 7.

[193] ETSI Directives, version 41, February 2020, 116f.

[194] See list of ISO members: https://tbtcode.iso.org/sites/wto-tbt/list-of-standardizing-bodies.html [accessed 20 September 2023].

[195] TBT Agreement, Annex 3 https://www.wto.org/english/docs_e/legal_e/17-tbt_e.htm#annexIII [accessed 20 September 2023].

[196] Eliantonio M, 'Judicial Control of the EU Harmonized Standards: Entering a Black Hole?' (2017) 44 Legal Issues of Economic Integration, 395 (hereafter Eliantonio 'Judicial Control'). Read also: Colombo C and Eliantonio M, 'Harmonized Technical Standards as Part of EU Law: Juridification with a Number of Unresolved Legitimacy Concerns?' (2017) 24 Maastricht Journal of European and Comparative Law, 323

[197] Volpato argues that the availability of judicial review of harmonized standards amounts to judicial accountability. Volpato A, 'Controlling the Invisible: Accountability Issues in the Exercise of Implementing Powers by EU Agencies and in Harmonised Standardization' (2019) Review of European Administrative Law 12, no 1, 75–96. On the concept of judicial accountability, see Busuioc M, *European Agencies: Law and Practices of Accountability* (OUP Oxford 2013), 56.

Standards being subject to judicial review entails first that the courts are competent to verify the compatibility of (harmonized) standards with the legislation. However, judicial review by national administrative courts or the CJEU is not a given for standardization, due to its private nature. One may argue that judicial review, especially in the case of harmonized standards, is justified by the EU law principle of effective judicial protection enshrined in art 47 CFREU.[198] In particular, because standards affect health, the environment and other matters, which are protected values by the EU, Eliantonio argued that the CJEU should be able to review standards to effect the principle.[199] Alternatively, it has been argued CJEU competence may be based on the delegation of discretionary powers by the Commission to standard setting organizations and those should be subject to judicial control mechanisms.[200] The CJEU has had several occasions to rule over its competence, showing it's not unwilling to shift the scale away from the public law 'immunity' of standards as a purely private law activity.[201] However, the relationship[202] of the CJEU and standards, cannot be assumed to be steadily progressing towards establishing a general competence for judicial review. While harmonized standards form part of the EU law and are subject to interpretation by the CJEU,[203] there is no straightforward answer when it comes to an annulment procedure of art 263 TFEU. Typically, harmonized standards are part of Commission Implementing Decisions, which are in turn published in the Official Journal. Non-harmonized standards may be referenced in a regulatory act as well. For example, the Commission has the power to adopt implementing acts specifying technical standards for data protection certification mechanisms.[204] As regards whether the conditions of art 263 TFEU are met, Tovo explains that harmonized standards would not meet the admissibility conditions of art 263(1) TFEU, for the reason that standards are 'incapable of autonomously –that is, without being referenced in the OJ–producing legal effects vis-à-vis third parties.'[205] Van Waeyenberge and others argue that annulment would be possible

[198] Eliantonio, 'Judicial Control' (n 196).
[199] ibid.
[200] ibid.
[201] In *James Elliot* the CJEU ruled on its competence to review harmonized standards as part of EU law in preliminary rulings.
[202] Volpato A, and Eliantonio M, 'The Contradictory Approach of the CJEU to the Judicial Review of Standards: A Love–Hate Relationship?.' in Eliantonio M, and Cauffman C (eds.) *The Legitimacy of Standardization as a Regulatory Technique* (Edward Elgar Publishing 2020), (hereafter Volpato and Eliantonio, 'The Contradictory Approach').
[203] Judgment of the Court of 27 October 2016 Case C-613/14, *James Elliot*, EU:C:2016:821, para 40; and Judgment of the Court of 5 March 2024, Case C-588/21 P, *Public.Resource.Org Inc*, EU:C:2024:201, para 80.
[204] GDPR art 43(9).
[205] Tovo C, 'Judicial Review of Harmonized Standards: Changing the Paradigms of Legality and Legitimacy of Private Rulemaking under EU Law' (2018) 55 Common Market Law Review, 1202.

against the Commission's Implementing Decision, which is a regulatory act of general application, 'which produces legal effects without any further intervention required'.[206] In fact, Volpato and Eliantonio explain that the change in the practice of the Commission to publish the reference to harmonizsed standards in the L, instead of C series of the Official Journal does not put into question anymore the reviewability of the nature of the Commission decision to publish the reference, which 'opens up a clearer avenue for reviewing harmonised standards'.[207] Indeed, the General Court in *GGP Italy*, found that the 'decisions relating to the publication of harmonised standards are legal acts against which an action for annulment may be brought'.[208]

Finally, uncertainty surrounds the judicial review of non-harmonized standards that are incorporated in EU law. This is particularly relevant for this book, given the direct reference of an international conformity assessment standard in Union data protection law.[209] Volpato and Eliantonio argue that an international standard incorporated in EU law becomes part of EU law through the reference in the Official Journal.[210] However, in *Lietuvos Respublikos*, the Court did not accept its jurisdiction to interpret an international specification despite being incorporated by reproduction in a Commission Decision.[211]

7.4.2 Civil Litigation: Breach of Contract and Extra-contractual Liability of SSOs

The increase in the use of technical standards for public goals by EU policy makers and legislature entails more opportunities for the Court to rule over framing the conditions for judicial reviewability of standards. Beyond this not yet crystallized framing however, there is an additional channel for judicial review, civil liability. Several legal bases have been explored in scholarship for establishing civil

[206] Van Waeyenberge A, and Restrepo Amariles A, 'James Elliott Construction: A New (ish) Approach to Judicial Review of Standardisation' (2017) 6 European law review, 892ff.

[207] Volpato A, Eliantonio M, 'The Butterfly Effect of Publishing References to Harmonised Standards in the L series' European Law Blog, (7 March 2019) https://europeanlawblog.eu/2019/03/07/the-butterfly-effect-of-publishing-references-to-harmonised-standards-in-the-l-series/ [accessed 20 September 2023].

Volpato and Eliantonio, 'The Contradictory Approach'(n 202).

[208] Judgment of 26 January 2017, Case T:2017:36 *GGP Italy*, EU: T:2017:36, para 60.

[209] GDPR art 43(1)(b).

[210] Volpato and Eliantonio, 'The Contradictory Approach' (n 202), 101; similar view by Gamito discussing the *James Elliot* case. Cantero Gamito M, 'The Legitimacy of Standardisation as a Regulatory Technique in Telecommunications,' in Eliantonio M and Cauffman C (eds), *The Legitimacy of Standardisation as a Regulatory Technique* (Edward Elgar Publishing 2020), 238.

[211] Volpato and Eliantonio, 'The Contradictory Approach' (n 202), 104. Judgment of 15 June 2017, Case C-587/15 *Lietuvos Respublikos transporto priemonių draudikų biuras*, EU:C:2017:463.

liability.[212] One is breach of contract, either a contract that incorporates standards, or the contract between the SSO and the buyer of a standard.[213] In the first case of the business-to-business contract that incorporates standards, an example comes from cloud computing.

> Service Level Agreements for cloud computing contracts often include references to standards as a means to assist the customer assess the cloud service[214] and for providing well defined targets and common metrics.[215] In those cases, standards will likely be part of the assessment of whether there is a violation of the agreements between contractual parties. Standards will not be assessed however against relevant legislation. Any comments or assessments of the courts *obiter dictum* are possible, but not expected and circumstantial.

In the case of the general conditions of sales between a SSO and a buyer of a standard, these are usually shielded with clauses indemnifying SSOs for any civil liability towards third parties caused by the performance of the contract including violations of intellectual property rights and privacy laws, and in any case limiting any damages to their insurance coverage.[216] Besides, a general duty of care of ESOs towards entities relying on harmonized standards, given the societal relevance of the fields within which some standards are developed, while appealing as a concept, is not easily justified due to the non-binding nature of standards and the role ESOs as non-for-profit organizations.[217]

[212] Stuurman K, 'IT Standards Regulation' (1992) 8 Computer Law & Security Review, 2 (hereafter Stuurman, 'IT standards regulation'); Schepel H, and Falke J 'Legal Aspects of Standardisation in the Member States of the EC and EFTA' (2000) vol 1, Office for official publications of the European communities; Van Leeuwen B, *European Standardisation of Services and Its Impact on Private Law: Paradoxes of Convergence* (Bloomsbury Publishing 2017); Verbruggen P, 'Tort Liability for Standards Development in the United States and European Union,' in Contreras JL, *The Cambridge Handbook of Technical Standardization Law: Volume 2: Further Intersections of Public and Private Law* (Cambridge University Press 2019) (hereafter Verbruggen, 'Tort Liability for Standards Development'); Glinski C and Rott P, 'Deficient Standards by European Standardisation Organisations: Between State Liability and Tort Liability,' in Eliantonio M and Cauffman C (eds), *The Legitimacy of Standardisation as a Regulatory Technique* (Edward Elgar Publishing 2020) (hereafter Glinski and Rott, 'Deficient Standards').

[213] Read on voluntary nature of standards in relation to contract and tort law: Micklitz H-W, 'Soft law, technical standards and European private law.' in Eliantonio M, Korkea-aho E and Mörth U, *Research Handbook on Soft Law* (Edward Elgar Publishing 2023), 145.

[214] Cloud Select Industry Group (C-SIG) 'Cloud Service Level Agreement Standardization Guidelines' (2014), 28 https://ec.europa.eu/commission/presscorner/detail/en/IP_14_743[accessed 20 September 2023].

[215] Gleeson NC and Walden I, 'It's a Jungle Out There'?: Cloud Computing, Standards and the Law' (2014) 5 European Journal of Law and Technology, 6ff.

[216] Verbruggen, 'Tort Liability for Standards Development' (n 212), 60.

[217] A duty of care however cannot be excluded *ab initio*, see in Glinski and Rott, 'Deficient Standards' (n 212).

> The Court of Justice in *Schmitt*, which is connected to the PIP Scandal,[218] explored whether TÜV Rheinland as notified body[219] for CE marking[220] of medical devices, was liable for the harm caused to Mrs Schmitt by defective breast implants made of silicone.[221] The CJEU found that notified bodies under the Medical Devices Directive were under a 'general obligation to act with all due diligence when engaged in a procedure relating to the EC declaration of conformity'[222] and that the purpose of the procedure is to ensure protection for the health and safety of persons.[223] However the Court concluded that a culpable infringement of the obligations of a notified body does not render it liable vis-à-vis the end users of medical devices under the relevant Directive,[224] but such an option is possible under national law.[225]

Liability may be established by the breach of EU rules in some cases though, as shown in *Fra.bo.* In that CJEU case, rules of the internal market law were breached by an association, which, while private, had nonetheless *de facto* the power to restrict free movement of goods.[226] The national referring court, following the CJEU's preliminary ruling, held that the private association DVGW was liable for breach of contract with the plaintiff *Fra.bo.*[227]

Another basis explored is damages from defective products conforming to standards. However, the causal link between the development of the standard and the damage caused by a product is weak.[228] It is doubtful that a standardization

[218] Wallerman A, 'Pie in the Sky When You Die? Civil Liability of Notified Bodies under the Medical Devices Directive: Schmitt' (2018) 55 Common Market Law Review, 265; Glinski C and Rott P 'Regulating Certification Bodies in the Field of Medical Devices: The PIP Breast Implants Litigation and Beyond.' (2019) 27 European Review of Private Law; Verbruggen P, and Van Leeuwen B, 'The liability of notified bodies under the EU's new approach: The implications of the PIP breast implants case.' (2018) 43 European Law Review, 394.

[219] A 'notified body' is 'an organization designated by an EU country to assess the conformity of certain products before being placed on the market. These bodies carry out tasks related to conformity assessment procedures set out in the applicable legislation, when a third party is required.' Commission website: https://ec.europa.eu/growth/single-market/goods/building-blocks/notified-bodies_en [accessed 20 September 2023].

[220] CE marking is defined as 'marking by which the manufacturer indicates that the product is in conformity with the applicable requirements set out in Community harmonization legislation providing for its affixing' art 2(20) Regulation (EC) No 765/2008 of the European Parliament and of the Council of 9 July 2008 setting out the requirements for accreditation and market surveillance relating to the marketing of products and repealing Regulation (EEC) No 339/93, 2008 L 218/30/30.

[221] Judgment of 16 February 2017, Case C-219/15, *Elisabeth Schmitt v TÜV Rheinland*, EU:C:2017:128.

[222] CJEU Case C-219/15, para 46.

[223] CJEU Case C-219/15, para 53.

[224] CJEU Case C-219/15, para 62.

[225] CJEU Case C-219/15, para 59.

[226] Judgment of 12 July 2012, Case C-171/11, *Fra.bo SpA*, EU:C:2012:453; Schepel H, 'Case C-171/11 Fra.Bo SpA v Deutsche Vereinigung Des Gas- Und Wasserfaches' (2013) 9 European Review of Contract Law.

[227] Verbruggen, 'Tort Liability for Standards Development' (n 212).

[228] Stuurman, 'IT standards regulation' (n 212) 5.

body maintains control over organizations that conform to its standards.[229] In addition, there might be several other causes that relate to the actual defect of the product and the subsequent damage, and evidence-wise it is difficult to prove that a standard providing requirement is (mainly) to blame for a defective product. Especially, in the case of harmonized standards, the embedded (public law) safeguards would rather prevent extra-contractual liability of the ESOs, than support it.[230] Besides, the material scope of the Product Liability Directive[231] is limited to 'producers', thus standardization bodies are excluded from the scope of the Directive.[232]

Despite the difficulty of holding the standardization body or its Technical Committee liable for breach of contract, duty of care or damages from defective products conforming to standards, there are in general circumstances that influence whether standardization organizations are exposed to civil liability, as identified by Verbruggen.[233] Those include the legal or *de facto* control to direct compliance with (harmonized) standards, the intended purposes of developing specific standards, representations about expertise in the development of standards making SSOs vulnerable to extra-contractual liability when standards cause harms, commercial benefits, and good governance in the sense that inclusiveness and transparency standard-setting processes, as well as revision processes may show that the SSO showed care in the development of standards.

7.5 Synthesis

In this Chapter, procedural safeguards of standardization in recognized standardization bodies were analysed in the context of the general legal framework of the Standardization Regulation, inter-institutional agreements and internal commitments, in the form of guidelines and regulations, but also their judicial reviewability. The need for safeguards, same as the need for integration of standards in the EU legal order examined in Chapter 4, in general stems from the nature

[229] Verbruggen, 'Tort Liability for Standards Development' (n 212).

[230] Glinski and Rott explain that the attainment of procedural guarantees without 'manifestly and gravely' disregarding duties is a deterring factor for finding liability for breach of law in line with art 340(2) TEU. Besides, to trigger the application of art 340(2) TFEU on non-contractual liability of the European Union, would require that ESO qualify as Institutions of the European Union. Glinski and Rott, 'Deficient Standards' (n 212).

[231] Council Directive 85/374/EEC of 25 July 1985 on the approximation of the laws, regulations and administrative provisions of the Member States concerning liability for defective products OJ L 210,/29 7.8.1985, amended by Directive 1999/34/EC of the European Parliament and of the Council of 10 May 1999 L 141/20. In December 2023, the European Parliament and the Council agreed on a new Product Liability Directive, the text of which both institutions later approved. The publication in the OJ at the time of writing is pending.

[232] Verbruggen, 'Tort Liability for Standards Development' (n 212).

[233] Verbruggen, 'Tort Liability for Standards Development' (n 212).

of standardization as private normative ordering next to Union law and the role that standards assume in supporting policy and law in the Union. The need for safeguards is confirmed in the data protection legislation and the fact that the GDPR regulates with a dedicated framework of rules, checks and balances other private regulation instruments.

The analysis of the safeguards the GDPR introduces for the regulation of codes of conduct, data protection certification mechanisms and BCR, offered benchmarks for data protection standardization. The analysis showed that there is a range of safeguards embedded during the development process and after the private regulation instruments have been in operation. Requirements are imposed on private bodies, which draft and operate codes and schemes, but also on controllers that draft and are responsible for the BCR process. Private regulators maintain an overview and control of the operation of the instruments, and bear obligations to take action in case of violation of the terms for granting the code, certification, or BCR. Next, there are rules in the GDPR framing the subject matter of the examined private regulation instruments. These rules are however not setting any restricting or prohibitive boundaries and red lines. A code of conduct *may* address issues related to one or more of the grounds of art 40(2) GDPR, but not necessarily, since the list is indicative. In addition, with the exception of BCR that offer a presumption of appropriate safeguards, certifications and codes of conduct are not assigned any legal effect, such as a presumption of conformity with the law and any corresponding provisions. Surprisingly, public consultation of interested parties, including of data subjects, does not seem to be a requirement or a safeguard the GDPR expects from private regulation instruments, with the exception of codes of conduct. Further, the GDPR provides for publicity and transparency, in the form of registries, maintained by the supervisory authorities. In this manner, the interested and engaged audience has the opportunity to access and verify reliably the private actors offering the approved private regulation instrument, and the controllers and processors that conform to those instruments.

The cornerstone in safeguarding the legitimacy of private regulation instruments in the GDPR prior to their use is the task of the supervisory authorities to approve certification criteria, codes of conduct and BCR. The approval is an administrative act which essentially is gatekeeping data protection from being polluted with untrustworthy and non-legitimate private regulation instruments. Furthermore, the supervisory authorities maintain supervision, monitoring, and corrective powers towards controllers and processors that violate the conditions of the approved private regulation instruments to which they have voluntarily adhered, but also empowers sanctioning the private law actors such as monitoring bodies and certification bodies. This combination of corrective and sanctioning powers places the instruments under the indirect control of the authorities. In practice, the collaborative aspect will be more imminent than the sanction aspect of the relationship of private actors and the authorities, however with an omnipresent threat for sanctions.[234] Finally, the GDPR introduces a system of remedies against controllers and processors that violate the Regulation and cause material or immaterial damage to data subjects, and other persons that suffer such damage.

In terms of *ex ante* procedural safeguards, the general framework under which standardization operates in the EU introduces certain safeguards in terms of participation for societal stakeholders, and other interested parties. Those include the facilitation of participation, with for example financial support from the European Commission, access to draft documents, right to be heard by submitting comments, and others. Despite not creating a system of equality with other participants, due to the absence of voting rights at EU level or weighted votes based on payable fees, standardization offers some participation safeguards that are not present in the examined GDPR private regulation instruments. However, when it comes to transparency, despite the existence of some transparency requirements imposed in the Standardization Regulation, those do not live up to the measures of the public registries maintained by the EDPB in accordance with GDPR.

The only measure that resembles this approval action of the supervisory (data protection) authorities, can be found in harmonized standards only, which are not published in the Official Journal (but they are published by ESO and available for purchase) unless they are found to be compliant with the standardization request and the legislation, on the basis of which they are developed. While the approval of codes of conduct, data protection certifications, and BCR is an administrative act by an independent public authority, the HAS Consultant decision is a recommendation to the Commission of an individual expert.

AG Bobek has opined[235]

> [...] once an EU institution decides to incorporate an originally external legal act into EU law and to draw legal consequences from it by effectively enforcing it internally. If that happens, the same institution cannot later turn a blind eye and suggest that since that act was originally drafted by a third party, it is therefore not an act of that institution. Allowing for such 'black holes' of judicial review would be incompatible with the vision of a Union based on the rule of law.

Black holes of this kind or at least an element of uncertainty surrounding the judicial reviewability of standards seem to exist. Compared with the possibility for judicial review of the private law instruments regulated in the GDPR as discussed in

[234] This element however of a threat for sanctions by the supervisory authority due to the violation of the conditions of the private regulation instrument might inhibit the voluntary adherence to the instruments by controllers and processors.

[235] AG Opinion in the case C-587/15, EU:C:2017:234 para 82. The Court however reached a different conclusion regarding the question of competence to interpret the internal regulations of an insurers' organization, which was eventually appended in an Annex of a Commission Decision, and found no competence in that case. Judgment of 15 June 2017 Case C-587/15, *Lietuvos Respublikos transporto priemonių draudikų biuras* EU:C:2017:463.

this Chapter, there is much more ambiguity and uncertainty when it comes to technical standards. The established CJEU interpretative competence for harmonized standards certainly covers only one small part of the available or possible standards in the field, and most importantly, since there are currently no harmonized data protection standards under the New Approach, this judicial review channel is of limited practical value for data protection.[236] The examined GDPR private regulation instruments offer several options for judicial review, such as based on art 78 GDPR and the right to an effective judicial remedy against a supervisory authority that issued a legally binding decision for a natural or legal person (eg act of rejection of certification criteria), and art 79 GDPR on the right of data subjects to an effective judicial remedy against a controller or processor.

When it comes to standards, the GDPR judicial redress rights apply only to standards that are part of the data protection law, and only against the controllers or processors, and not the standardization bodies. Judicial review mechanisms of public law apply to standards that will be developed on the basis of a standardization request or be published in the Official Journal, which form part of EU law. For other data protection standards that are developed taking into account the data protection law, but without any formal link such as a reference or a standardization request, the option of civil liability of standardization bodies towards controllers and processors, but also data subjects can be further explored.

Another important aspect is that even if safeguards like the ones the GDPR provides for other instruments would hypothetically be embedded in the internal codes or even form part of a (standardization) law, there is still an important aspect that would need to be considered. This is that the GDPR codes of conduct, data protection certification mechanisms, and BCR are part of a data protection law, thus are subject to the principles, duties and rights of the GDPR, and meant to be interpreted in light of the legal basis of the GDPR, art 8 CFREU and art 16 TFEU. This is an important shortcoming of standards that are not incorporated in a legal instrument by means of reference or otherwise.

The question then arises: Should standards in the field of personal data protection be used for the support of data protection law and its underlying goals? Several arguments point in the direction that there is no 'incompatibility' as such and that standardization *may* be used to support the Union data protection law, but a cautious approach should be adopted, given the fundamental rights nature of the right to protection of personal data.

First, the analysis showed that standardization that supports EU law and policies is not void of regulation and its autonomous –or semi-autonomous nature–seems to be tamed to some extent, but not fully, with the introduction of *ex ante* and *ex post* safeguards both in public law, binding agreements with the Commission

[236] However, there is possibility for adoption of harmonized standards in data protection on the basis of the Radio Equipment Directive 2014/53/EC, art 3(3)(e). See Chapter 4 Section 4.2.1 in this book.

and inter-institutional agreements, which translate to internal commitments in internal regulations and codes of conduct.

Second, while it is indeed questionable whether those safeguards are comparable to those of the private regulation instruments extensively regulated in the GDPR, most of the questions would almost be eliminated if the Union data protection legislator would have decided to (more extensively) regulate technical standards in the text of the data protection law. Thus, it is not a matter of an inherently problematic or controversial nature of standards in comparison with the other private regulation instruments examined in this Chapter, but a matter of political and legislative choice that other private regulation instruments are enjoying the guarantees of detailed provisions in the text of the data protection law, and the system of principles and duties of the GDPR. In fact, if one looks for example at codes of conduct and data protection certifications bare of those guarantees, they are in their majority purely self-regulation instruments, lacking the network of safeguards present in standardization by recognized standardization bodies. Besides, standards may become part of the private regulation instruments, for example in certification, and thus indirectly be subjected to the safeguards the GDPR established for those private regulation instruments examined in this Chapter.

Lastly, in the hypothetical case that the safeguards embedded in the GDPR codes of conduct, certifications, and BCR would be met one to one by the standardization legal framework and rules, even those GDPR safeguards are yet to be (con)tested in court for their suitability and appropriateness, most probably on a case-by-case basis. In fact, it is not certain that GDPR safeguards for private regulation instruments such as the approval by the supervisory authority are suitable for example to address regulatory capture, which is a recurring issue in standardization.[237] Thus, standards may be in principle considered as an instrument for supplementing data protection law, as long as the principles, rationales, and rules of the data protection law and its underlying objective to protect the right of art. 8 CFREU are observed.

Ensuring that standardization bodies observe and follow these is not self-evident and should not be taken for granted. Standardization bodies are private bodies and are not directly bound by the CFREU. This is why the mode of development and integration in the EU law is important.

[237] To bring an example in the case of data protection certification mechanisms of art 42 GDPR, the supervisory authorities are required to approve the criteria according to art 42(5), which however does not require the authorities to examine how those criteria were developed and whether they reflect a balance of interests of different actors (controllers, data subjects, etc) or the approval is a matter of assessment of legality and alliance with the GDPR.

8
Case Studies
Data Protection by Design, International Data Transfers, and Online Tracking Protection

8.1 Introduction

The previous Chapters showed the diverse roles assigned to standards in the personal data legislation and which are the constraints and points of attention in using standards for supporting public goals. This Chapter assesses selected standards both in terms of substantive and procedural legitimacy. Every standard is assessed against legal requirements of the relevant applicable data protection law to gain a better understanding of the roles and limitations of the roles of those standards in practice. From a legal basis and alignment perspective, the analysis looks into how standards supplement the legal provisions at hand, but also their alignment with the data protection law. From a procedural legitimacy perspective, following the legal analysis of the different *ex ante* and *ex post* safeguards in Chapter 7, this Chapter examines the applicability of the analysed safeguards in the standards selected for in-depth analysis.

Three standards are analysed; first, the EN 17529:2022, a European standard on data protection by design and by default, developed by CEN and CENELEC at the request of the European Commission (Stream 1a), second, the ISO/IEC 27701, a committee based international standard on Privacy Information Management Systems, (Stream 2), and third, the Do Not Track, an ICT specification, developed by an international consortium developing specifications for the Internet, the World Wide Web Consortium ('W3C') (Stream 3). The European standard EN17529 is examined in relation to data protection by design and by default art 25 GDPR and the Commission standardization request from which it originated (M/530); the international standard ISO/IEC 27701 is examined in relation to data transfers; and the W3C Do Not Track specification is examined against the 2017 Commission Proposal for an ePrivacy Regulation.

Standardizing Personal Data Protection. Irene Kamara, Oxford University Press.
DOI: 10.1093/9780191997037.003.0008

8.2 Case Study 1: European Standardization and Data Protection by Design

8.2.1 Introduction

Data protection by design is introduced in the GDPR as a legal obligation in art 25 GDPR. The duty complements and operationalizes the general responsibility of the controller to ensure that processing is conducted in line with the Regulation.[1] The result to be achieved is the observance of the data protection principles of GDPR art 5, which are further detailed by legal duties, such as security of processing[2] and supported by accountability related provisions, such as documentation and record keeping.[3] The EDPS has explained that data protection by design incorporates a risk-based approach in that the controller needs to implement measures for effective protection of individuals.[4] Effectiveness according to the EDPB is assessed against three general benchmarks; that is ensuring and being able to demonstrate compliance with the GDPR, the implementation of data protection principles and the protection of the rights of data subjects.[5]

Data protection by design is one of those duties that requires an additional assessment in order to be implemented. The assessment components are provided for in the relevant provision and include the state of the art, cost of implementation, the nature, scope, context and purposes of processing, the risks and severity for rights and freedoms of individuals.[6]

Further, the 'by design' aspect of the obligation suggests that the controller has data protection 'designed into the processing of personal data' and this 'applies throughout the processing lifecycle',[7] from collection until erasure or anonymization. Data protection by default necessitates that by default only personal data that are necessary are processed. Necessary in this context means personal data for a specific purpose, in line with the law, and made transparent to the data subject. Data protection by default operationalizes the principle of purpose limitation, but its scope is broader addressing also the data limitation principle.[8]

In terms of standardization, an indirect abstract reference is made in art 25(1) GDPR in relation to the state of the art, which the controller needs to take into

[1] EDPS 'Preliminary Opinion on privacy by design' Preliminary Opinion 5/2018 (31 May 2018) (hereafter EDPS 5/2018), 5.

[2] GDPR art 32. EDPS 5/2018 (n 2), 6.

[3] GDPR art 30.

[4] EDPS 5/2018 (n 2), 6.

[5] EDPS 5/2018 (n 2), 6.

[6] GDPR art 25(1).

[7] European Data Protection Board 'Guidelines 4/2019 on Article 25 Data Protection by Design and by Default(version 2.0 adopted on 20 October 2020).

[8] Jasmontaite L, Kamara I, Zanfir-Fortuna G, and Leucci S, 'Data Protection by Design and by Default:' (2018) 4 European Data Protection Law Review, 168. (hereafter Jasmontaite and others, 'Data Protection by Design'), 186.

consideration in assessing how to comply with the obligation. Further, the measures provided as examples in art 25(1) GDPR have a strong technical character and are often associated with standards providing best practices.

While the 2012 Commission Proposal's reference to implementing acts laying down technical standards is not part of art 25 GDPR, and art 25(1) provides only for indirect abstract references to standards, standardization has a stronger role to play in facilitating data protection by design, but also data protection by default.[9] The very concept of by design protection—as opposed to mainly user control–[10] is based on the premise of technological design[11] implemented with standardized technological means.[12] A contribution of standardization in data protection by design is not only in translating abstract legal principles to technical measures, and implementing those by default, but also developing supportive organizational measures. Such a role of standardization has been highlighted also by the European Data Protection Supervisor.[13] To what extent and scale this is a feasible task has been debated in scholarship.[14] As it will be shown, in the analysis of the EN 17529:2022 standard on data protection by design and by default, there are certainly points of attention in developing standards to implement art 25 GDPR, but also significant added value.

In 2015, the European Commission published a standardization request in the form of a Commission Implementing Decision towards the European Standardization Organizations. The standardization request concerned deliverables for privacy and personal data protection management in support of the Union's security industrial policy. The standardization request aimed at supporting the right to protection of personal data on the basis of art 8 of the CFREU and art 16 TFEU and the Data Protection Directive, and the draft (at the time) GDPR.

[9] On the distinction between data protection by design and by default, see Jasmontaite et al., 'Data Protection by Design' (n 8), 186.

[10] Quelle C, 'Not Just User Control in the General Data Protection Regulation,' IFIP Advances in Information and Communication Technology (Springer 2016).

[11] Data protection by design is closely linked to the concept of value-sensitive design. See, among many, Friedman B (ed) *Human values and the design of computer technology*. v 72, (Center for the Study of Language and Inf 2004); Danezis, and others 'Privacy and data protection by design-from policy to engineering.' *arXiv preprint arXiv:1501.03726* (2015).

[12] By design protections are often criticized for following a paternalistic approach, removing autonomy and freedom of choice from the data subject. See however counter argument in the seminal work of Sunstein and Thaler. Sunstein CR and Thaler RH, 'Libertarian Paternalism Is Not an Oxymoron' (2003) 70 The University of Chicago Law Review, 1159.

[13] The EDPS referred specifically inter alia to the M/530 and the EN 17529:2022 (which was not yet numbered) and the work of NIST (the US standardization body) on privacy engineering. Brooks S, Garcia M, Lefkovitz N, Lightman S, and Nadeau E, 'NISTIR 8062. An Introduction to Privacy Engineering and Risk Management in Federal Systems.' *Information Technology Laboratory, National Institute of Standards and Technology* (2017). See EDPS 5/2018 (n 2).

[14] Koops B-J and Leenes R, 'Privacy Regulation Cannot Be Hardcoded. A Critical Comment on the 'Privacy by Design' Provision in Data-Protection Law' (2013) 28 International Review of Law, Computers & Technology, 159; Tamo-Larrieux, A, Mayer S, and Zihlmann Z, 'Not Hardcoding but Softcoding Privacy.' Workshop proceedings, (2020) https://www.alexandria.unisg.ch/262254/ [accessed 20 September 2023].

8.2.2 The EN 17529:2022 and a Role for Data Protection by Design and by Default

The EN 17529:2022 is based on the mandate addressed to CEN, CENELEC and ETSI, with a request for collaboration in order to carry out the mandated work. With regard to the expected deliverables, there is a request for two types of deliverables, namely European standards and other standardization deliverables that would guide manufacturers and service providers on implementing the European Standard(s). The requested standardization activities were the following:

1. One or more European standards on how to address and *manage* privacy and personal data protection issues during the design and development and the production and service provision processes of security technologies and services, allowing manufacturers and service providers to develop, implement, and execute a widely recognized 'Privacy by Design' (PbD) approach in their processes.
2. One or more related European standardization deliverable(s), addressed to the manufacturers of security products or systems and service providers when specifying the privacy and personal data protection management processes with an explanation how to realize them, including descriptions of the necessary roles, tasks, documentation, hardware and software requirements, and templates to be used when applying the requested standard(s).

The request was accepted by the ESOs, which established the Joint Working Group 8 (JWG8) with the aim to conduct the mandated work.

The standard provides developers with 'an early formalised process for identification of privacy objects and requirements, as well as the necessary guidance on associated assessments'.[15] While initially the scope of the standard was meant to be limited to the security sector as requested by the mandate, the final version provides broader requirements, formulated for cross-sector implementation. Together with the above standard, two Technical Reports were published on Video Surveillance and Biometric Control, aiming at specifying the application of the harmonized standard in relation to those technology application areas.[16] It should be noted, that while the EN 17529 and the Technical Reports are published in response to M/530 from the Joint Technical Committee of CEN and CENELEC,

[15] See CEN website: https://www.cen.eu/work/Sectors/Digital_society/Pages/Cybersecurity.aspx [accessed 20 September 2023].

[16] WI 002-Video surveillance (CEN/TR) and WI 003-Biometric for access control including face recognition (CEN/TR). See Miller, Mark and others, 'D4.4 EU Cybersecurity & Privacy Interim Roadmap', The European Watch on cybersecurity and Privacy Report (2019), 44. https://www.cyberwatching.eu/sites/default/files/D4.4_EU-Cybersecurity-%26-privacy-interim-roadmap_v.Final.pdf [accessed 20 September 2023].

ETSI has published its own standardization deliverables (Technical Reports and Technical Specifications) on the basis of the GDPR, taking a somewhat autonomous route from the other two European Standardization Organizations. While not all of those ETSI deliverables refer to M/530[17] they do explicitly refer to the GDPR, and often the 2002 ePrivacy Directive.[18]

8.2.3 Substantive Legitimacy: Legal Basis and Alignment with Legal Instruments

8.2.3.1 Scope of the EN 17529:2022

A standard with the scope of the EN 17529:2022 has the potential to facilitate the controllers fulfil their duty of data protection by design. Art. 25(1) GDPR concerns an obligation of controllers to implement data protection in the design of their processing, while the GDPR does not prescribe an obligation for manufacturers to design the actual products and systems in a way that supports data controllers to implement data protection by design. Recital 78 encourages producers of products, services and applications 'to take into account the right to data protection' in the development and design of their products, services and applications. However, this encouragement is by no means binding, and rather places the burden to controllers to use products, services, and applications for their processing which would facilitate data protection by design. While a relevant legal obligation for entities such as producers and services would be ideally best fit for purpose, even a softer private regulation instrument such as standardization could help with the implementation and compliance of the legal duties of Art. 25 GDPR. The reason is that not only a legal obligation for manufacturers is missing, but also practical guidance on how to design their products in line with Art. 25 GDPR.

The EN 17529:2022 is addressed to manufacturers and service providers, thus the target audience of Recital 78, who are not formally bound by Art. 25, since they are usually not data controllers, but largely capable of facilitating the compliance

[17] Those ETSI Deliverables however are listed on the ETSI website as associated to the M30 mandate, but not as 'harmonised standards'. See, for example, https://portal.etsi.org/webapp/WorkProgram/Report_WorkItem.asp?WKI_ID = 47653&curItemNr = 1&totalNrItems = 12&optDisplay = 12&titleType = all&qSORT = HIGHVERSION&qETSI_ALL=&SearchPage = TRUE&qINCLUDE_SUB_TB = True&qINCLUDE_MOVED_ON=&qSTOP_FLG = N&qKEYWORD_BOOLEAN = OR&qCLUSTER_BOOLEAN = OR&qFREQUENCIES_BOOLEAN = OR&qMandate_List=%27M%2F530%27&qSTOPPING_OUTDATED=&butExpertSearch = Search&includeNonActiveTB = FALSE&includeSubProjectCode = FALSE&qREPORT_TYPE = SUMMARY [accessed 20 September 2023].

[18] Some examples are the ETSI TR 103 370 V1.1.1 (2019-01) Personally Identifiable Information (PII) Protection in mobile and cloud services; ETSI TS 103 485 V1.1.1 (2020-08) Mechanisms for privacy assurance and verification. However, the ETSI TR 103 370 V1.1.1 (2019-01) Practical introductory guide to Technical Standards for Privacy explicitly states that it was prepared in response to the Commission M/530 request.

of the controllers with their duty. More specific, the EN 17529:2022 is addressed to those entities with the aim to implement 'Data protection and Privacy by Design and by Default [...] early in their development of their products and services, i.e. before (or independently of) any specific application integration, to make sure that they are as privacy ready as possible.'[19] Its primary target audience is system integrators and its secondary target audience is manufacturers of sub-components. Thus, a standard guiding those entities on how to design and build their products, systems, and services in line with the requirements of the GDPR is covering a gap, currently not addressed but identified in the GDPR, and has added value in that respect.[20]

Since conformity to this standard is voluntary, the actual contribution of the standard to the facilitation of compliance largely depends on the voluntary adherence to the standard by producers and service providers, and to the selection by controllers of the products and services that follow the EN 17529:2022.

8.2.3.2 Alignment with the standardization request and the GDPR

The EN 17529:2022 is a European standard, based on the M/530, the Union Security Policy and the Union data protection legislation. In *Anstar Oy* the CJEU interpreted a harmonized standard in light of the 'mandate' from which it originated. The Court clarified that the scope of a 'harmonised standard cannot be interpreted more broadly than that of the mandate on which it is based.'[21] Further, the harmonized standard is assessed in light of the legislation on which the standardization request is based, namely the GDPR.[22] The EN 17529:2022, as explained, provides a process for developers of components and subsystems to identify objectives and requirements on privacy and data protection, thus entities that are not as such subject to the GDPR.[23]

As regards scope and terminology, the EN 17529:2022 uses several terms from the GDPR, but also some others from international standards, such as the ISO/IEC 29134 on privacy impact assessments. The definition of a data protection impact assessment for example, adapted from the ISO/IEC 29134, refers to privacy impacts framed 'within an organization's broader risk management framework', which shows an orientation, if not prioritization to risks for the organization conforming to the EN 17529:2022, fragment of which forms the matter of risks to rights of individuals. This orientation is clear also from other parts of the standard where for example as regards a reasonable trade-off between market or

[19] Scope (1) EN17529.
[20] Recital 78 GDPR.
[21] Judgment of 14 December 2017, Case C-630/16, *Anstar Oy*, EU:C:2017:971, paras 35–36.
[22] The M/530 referred to the Data Protection Directive, and the proposal for a General Data Protection Regulation. Since however the GDPR was adopted in the meantime while the EN17529 was still being drafted, the EN17529 rightly refers to the GDPR.
[23] That is unless those entities also process personal data.

consumer needs and the data protection by design and by default requirements of the standard.[24] The standard drafters tried to make this approach transparent, by stressing the usefulness of the standard for Business to Business (B2B) relations instead of Business to Consumers relations. However, one should note that the choice of focusing on B2B relationships does not reduce the responsibilities on the shoulders of controllers towards the data subjects, and the fact that the risks to their rights and freedoms need to be assessed as prescribed by law and not based on arbitrary opaque trade-offs.

In response to the need for transparency, the standard provides a possibility to developers and service providers for a self-declaration of privacy aware design. The system of self-declaration, as described in the EN 17529:2022, allows for different levels of 'achievement' of requirements by suppliers of sub-components, and providers of services to system integrators. Those levels range from A, B (no trade-offs made) to C, D, E (considerations for a privacy aware design were made in general)[25] and Z (the application of requirements is underperforming).[26] While on the one hand it is indisputable that the GDPR does not foresee or is compatible with such calculation of percentages of fulfilment of legal requirements for the entities subject to its scope, on the other hand such an estimation from producers could offer some useful information to their potential customers (perspective controllers for example), as long as the self-declaration is further verified from independent auditors.

Further, the EN 17529:2022 provides a list of basic requirements on the design of products and services which include control objectives on data protection by design and by default. The applicability of the requirements to products is based on a categorization of product modules, and thereby module categories of which a product may consist.[27] An example of a requirement is data portability and the control objective for the relevant system is 'to enable record separation and export'.[28] The portability requirement aims at enabling the controller responding to data portability requests by data subjects per art 20 GDPR. These requirements of the EN 17529:2022 are process-oriented and strive to operationalize the components of art 20 GDPR, although admittedly not in great detail. The producer who would wish to follow the standard would probably need additional guidance on how those requirements may be applied in practice. Next to the design requirements, the EN 17529:2022 provides process requirements for development of products (and services), which are 'privacy aware'.[29]

[24] See cl 4.3 EN17529.
[25] The requirement fulfilment rate is $50\% \leq x < 80\%$.
[26] See cl 4.3 EN 17529:2022. The requirement fulfilment rate is lower than 50%.
[27] Those include component, device, operating system, system management and others. See EN 17529:2022 cl 5. A categorization is provided also for services.
[28] EN 17529:2022 cl 6.6.
[29] EN 17529:2022 cl 5.

The EN 17529:2022 offers some clarifications on the limitations of the standard, such as for example that the quality management approach followed by the standard is not sufficient to achieve data protection by design and by default, but conformity to specific requirements in the different layers of the product or service is necessary. Notably, the quality management approach in line with the ISO9001 was required by the Commission standardization request.[30]

A remarkable differentiation of the EN 17529:2022 from the Commission standardization request is its sector-neutral scope. The Commission request explicitly requested standards and other deliverables for the security sector and standards for security technologies and services.[31] The basis of the Commission Implementing Decision and the request itself is the Union's security industrial policy, together with the EU data protection legislation. Yet, the EN 17529:2022 is 'applicable to all business sectors, including the security industry',[32] which marks a deliberate choice for differentiation. This is a clear example of the semi-autonomous nature of standardization, even in instances of co-development of standards with the public regulator.

8.2.4 Procedural Legitimacy

8.2.4.1 EN 17529:2022: overview of applicable safeguards

The EN 17529:2022 is a European harmonized standard developed on the basis of the Commission standardization request in line with the Standardization Regulation. The main framework of procedural safeguards for the standard-setting activity is provided for by the Standardization Regulation, the standardization request, and the internal regulations of CEN and CENELEC. The standard is not based on New Approach legislation. In case the EN 17529:2022 is incorporated in one of the regulated private regulation instruments in the GDPR, mainly data protection certifications which are explicitly mentioned in art 25(3) GDPR, then the safeguards of arts 42, 43 GDPR and the supervisory authority powers, are indirectly applied to the EN 17529:2022 as part of that data protection certification mechanism.

[30] M/530 reads: 'The requested European standard(s) [...] shall be modelled to be compatible with EN ISO 9001 on quality management systems in order to allow integrate privacy and personal data protection management as an integral part of quality management.' Read further on principles of Quality Management according to ISO 'Quality Management Principles' (2015) https://www.iso.org/files/live/sites/isoorg/files/store/en/PUB100080.pdf [accessed 20 September 2023].

[31] See Standardization Request M/530, 6.

[32] Scope, EN 17529:2022 cl 1.

8.2.4.2 Procedural safeguards stemming from the Commission standardization request and the Standardization Regulation

The Commission determines the requirements as to 'the content to be met by the requested document and a deadline for its adoption'.[33] Indeed, the Annex to the Commission Implementing Decision M/530 sets the requirements for the standards and other deliverables to be developed by the ESOs. Once the request is accepted, all the terms and conditions in the standardization request are binding for the ESOs, which need to perform according to those commitments. While conditional acceptance is not permitted,[34] and the ESOs may not propose amendments or negotiate the content of the work to be undertaken, it is true that the ESOs are usually consulted during the drafting period of the standardization request. Further, the Annex of the Commission Implementing Decision provides requirements not only of substance but also of the standardization work, such as the preparation of a work plan by the ESOs with tasks, milestones, etc., a joint preliminary work programme with all the requested work items, technical bodies working on those. The ESOs were obliged to consult the WP29, and the work of the EDPS on privacy by design and by default, which is relevant to the topic of the standardization.[35] While the ESOs enjoy decisional discretion on how many standards and other deliverables are necessary to fulfil the standardization request, the Commission generally maintains oversight of the work. For example, the Commission needs to agree with the ESOs joint work programme, the ESOs have several reporting duties on the execution of the standardization request.[36] The standardization request also includes deadlines for publication of the deliverables, however those are flexible. As seen in the case of the EN 17529:2022, its development took more than double the originally calculated time of forty eight months.[37]

The Commission Implementing Decision was circulated for feedback with European institutions, including the EDPS, and once adopted it was published in the Official Journal. The ESOs formally accepted the standardization request of the Commission, as incorporated in the M/530. ANEC, the European Consumer Association for Standardization, formally participated in the meetings of the Joint Technical Committee of the ESOs working on developing European standards and standardization deliverables on the basis of the M/530, following art 5 of the Standardization Regulation.[38] ANEC, which is an Annex III EU funded

[33] Regulation 1025/2012 art 10(1).
[34] Annex of M/530 Commission Implementing Decision cl 2.
[35] Annex of M/530 Commission Implementing Decision cl 4.2.3.
[36] This is an annual reporting duty per cl 4.2.3, and a reporting duty on the joint annual report, and the final report per cl 5.5. Annex of M/530 Commission Implementing Decision.
[37] Appendix I of M/530 Commission Implementing Decision.
[38] See ANEC website: https://www.anec.eu/images/2019/Ed.8-2019/List-of-comments-2019.pdf [accessed 20 September 2023].

organization, has also issued relevant guidance towards national consumer associations participating in standardization activities on data protection and representing consumer interests.[39] There is little publicly available information however on other participants. The draft standard was open for public consultation and submission of comments by interested parties.[40]

8.2.4.3 Procedural safeguards stemming from the internal regulations of CEN and CENELEC

The standard was developed by CEN and CENELEC, which means that the Internal Regulations of both organizations, and their common regulations apply. Those Internal Regulations, address issues of procedural nature including regarding participation of national standardization bodies, drafting, voting, consensus and others.[41] While those rules are general, in that they do not apply to different types of standards and independently of the responsible Technical Committee, sometimes those include special rules for standardization activity based on a Commission Standardization request.[42]

8.2.4.4 GDPR safeguards for certifications

The last source of procedural safeguards examined in this Section concerns the ones stemming from the GDPR provisions on certification. While the other safeguards applied to the EN 17529:2022 as a self-standing private regulation instrument, the safeguards of Arts. 42 and 43 GDPR, and the GDPR in general, are applicable only if the EN 17529:2022 becomes part of a data protection certification mechanism per Art. 42 and 43 GDPR. In practice, this means that an entity drafting a data protection certification mechanism on data protection by design and by default[43] would use the EN 17529:2022 as basis for deriving the certification criteria of Art. 42(5) GDPR. Data protection certification mechanisms are provided in a defined framework in the GDPR, most importantly with oversight and intervention powers from the supervisory authorities in case of irregularities and other non-conformities.

[39] ANEC 'Pocket guide Consumer Representatives Guidance. Domestic Privacy and the privacy of digitally connected devices' May 2015. The guide explicitly mentions: 'For use when representing consumer interests on standards technical committees' http://www.anec.eu/images/Publications/position-papers/Digital/ANEC-ICT-2015-G-064.pdf [accessed 20 September 2023].

[40] See for example the website of the British Standards Institute (BSI), the EN 17529 was open for consultation from 18 June to 11 August 2020. See https://standardsdevelopment.bsigroup.com/projects/2020-00802#/section [accessed 20 September 2023]. Accessing the draft standard and submitting comments was possible upon free registration to the website of BSI.

[41] See Chapter 7 section 7.3.3 in this book.

[42] See for example: CEN/CENELEC Internal Regulations—Pt 2:2023, 25.

[43] GDPR art 25(3) provides 'An approved certification mechanism pursuant to Article 42 may be used as an element to demonstrate compliance with the requirements set out in paragraphs 1 and 2 of this Article.'

8.3 Case Study 2: International Standardization and International Data Transfers

8.3.1 Introduction

The GDPR establishes dedicated rules for the transfers of personal data from the EU to third countries and international organizations.[44] While flows of personal data are necessary for international trade, the transfer should not undermine the level of protection guaranteed in the Union.[45] For that reason, the GDPR requires personal data to be transferred outside the Union following certain requirements, without the observance of which, the transfers are prohibited. The GDPR introduces a multi-tiered framework for data transfers. The first tier of the regime has the concept of 'adequate level of protection' at its heart, according to which the Commission adopts decisions on the level of adequacy of protection of personal data in a third-non-EU- country.[46] The second tier provides the legal bases for data transfers subject to 'appropriate safeguards', whereby controllers and processors exporting personal data provide guarantees for the processing conducted by controllers or processors in the third countries.[47] Third, in some exceptional cases, derogations provided in art 49 GDPR offer grounds for lawful data transfers.[48] Controllers and processors are obliged to ground the transfer of personal data on one of the legal bases for data transfers provided in the GDPR.

8.3.2 An International Standard on Privacy Information Management Systems

In 2020 Cavoukian, the former Privacy Commissioner of Canada argued that standards offer best practices 'for businesses around the world interested in building privacy protection directly into their products and services'.[49] Following

[44] Recital 101 GDPR; art 44 GDPR. In general on data transfers: Kuner C, *Transborder Data Flows and Data Privacy Law* (OUP 2013); Weber RH, 'Transborder data transfers: concepts, regulatory approaches and new legislative initiatives.' (2013) 3 International Data Privacy Law, 117; Binns RD, Millard D and Harris L, 'Data Havens, or Privacy sans Frontières?,' Proceedings of the 2014 ACM conference on Web science (ACM 2014), 273; Fuster, González G, 'Un-mapping Personal Data Transfers.' *Eur. Data Prot. L. Rev.* 2 (2016): 160; Drechsler L and Kamara I, 'Essential Equivalence as a Benchmark for International Data Transfers after Schrems II,' in Kosta E and Leenes R (eds), *Research Handbook on EU Data Protection Law* (Edward Elgar Publishing 2022), 314.

[45] GDPR art 44.

[46] GDPR art 45.

[47] GDPR art 46.

[48] GDPR art 49.

[49] Cavoukian, A, 'Understanding How to Implement Privacy by Design, One Step at a Time.' IEEE Consumer Electronics Magazine 9, no 2 (2020), 78–82.

Schrems II in July 2020 and the annulment of the Commission Decision finding that the US provided a partially adequate level of protection, practitioners and scholars associated the ISO/IEC 27701 with data transfers.[50] Some have gone far in their analysis by claiming that certification against the ISO/IEC 27701 standard could sufficiently address even the issue of local surveillance laws in third countries.[51] The EDPB has also referred to ISO standards as supplementary measures to be taken for international transfers.[52] It is also relevant to note that the French Data Protection Authority participated in the development of the international standard, and the WP29 formally provided comments on a draft version of the standard.[53] Against this backdrop, the ISO/IEC 27701 is further analysed in this Section in relation to international data transfers.[54]

The analysis in this case study concerns therefore a committee-based international standard, which is not referenced in a binding EU act. The standard was adopted in 2021 as a European standard.[55] Its relevance stems from both how the standard positions itself in relation to the GDPR, and how it is perceived, or at least has been associated by supervisory authorities, practitioners and scholars. As regards the first reason, it is remarkable—and against common practice for international standards to make any reference to regional or national legislations or regulations—that the text of the ISO/IEC 27701 is providing a 'mapping' to the GDPR.[56] The Informative Annex D with the title 'Mapping to the General Data Protection Regulation' provides that the Annex 'shows how compliance to requirements and controls of this document can be relevant to fulfil obligations of the GDPR'. While the mapping is 'purely indicative', this is an invitation towards controllers and processors subject to GDPR to consider this international standard in their compliance efforts. Second, as mentioned, the ISO/IEC 27701 has gained attention from authorities, practitioners, and scholars as regards data transfers in particular.

[50] Lachaud, E, 'Third-Party Certification and Cross-Border Flows in the GDPR: Which Workable Option?' available at SSRN 3686132 (2020).

[51] Christie A and Mitchell A, Using ISO/IEC 27701 for cross-border data transfers post 'Schrems II', IAPP, https://iapp.org/news/a/using-iso-iec-27701-for-cross-border-data-transfers-post-schrems-ii/ [accessed 20 September 2023].

[52] EDPB Recommendations 01/2020 on measures that supplement transfer tools to ensure compliance with the EU level of protection of personal data (version for public consultation, adopted on 10 November 2020), Annex.

[53] See presentation of CNIL at an ENISA event (2017) https://www.enisa.europa.eu/events/enisa-cscg-2017/presentations/grall [accessed 20 September 2023]. Note: the ISO/IEC 27701 was initially developed with different numbering as 'ISO/IEC 27552'.

[54] ISO/IEC 27701:2019 Security techniques—Extension to ISO/IEC 27001 and ISO/IEC 27002 for privacy information management—Requirements and guidelines (hereafter ISO/IEC 27701).

[55] See EN ISO/IEC 27701:2021, https://standards.cencenelec.eu/dyn/www/f?p = 205:110:0::::FSP_PROJECT:70998&cs = 179946EE5F853FF7F63757556C6265C5E [accessed 10 August 2024].

[56] ISO/IEC 27701 (n 54), Annex D.

8.3.3 Substantive Legitimacy: Legal Basis and Alignment with Legal Instruments

8.3.3.1 Scope of the ISO/IEC 27701

Standards, as transnational private regulation instruments, are adopted from organizations independently of the location of their establishment. International standards especially are not bound to one jurisdiction. Motivation of a company located outside the Union to conform to a European standard can be rooted in either the law or be voluntary due to for example the intention to receive data from an EU controller or processor.[57] Conformity to standards of a different region as an act of accountability or due diligence is commonly demonstrated in B2B relationships. Cloud computing users for example often require that cloud service providers fulfil conditions on security, confidentiality, and the level of service in general, and that this is done in an auditable manner, via the conformity to one or more technical standards.[58]

The standard provides a catalogue of controls, based on the well accepted ISO/IEC 27001, on issues such as information security policy, asset management, human resource security, incident management, collection and processing of personal information.[59] Thus, the ISO/IEC 27701 could play a role in assisting data importers in terms of organizational measures. As the standard itself purports, by following the standard an organization 'will generate documentary evidence of how it handles the processing of PII'.[60] The EDPB has acknowledged the importance of a management system in integrating technical and organizational measures. Supervisory authorities, when assessing certification criteria in line with art 42(5) GDPR, do take into account whether there is a management system in place to 'demonstrate, inform, control and enforce data protection requirements'.[61] The French supervisory authority (CNIL) has explained that the ISO/IEC 27701 'represents the state of the art' and allows organizations to 'increase their maturity and demonstrate an active approach to personal data protection[62]'.

There are three constraints for the role of the ISO/IEC 27701 in supporting international data transfers. First, the usefulness of the ISO/IEC 27701 in light of

[57] An example is found in the New Approach: when manufacturers wish to circulate products in the Internal Market, they need to conform to European harmonized product standards See more on CE marking https://ec.europa.eu/growth/single-market/ce-marking_en [accessed 20 September 2023].

[58] Hon WK, Millard C and Walden I, 'Negotiating Cloud Contracts - Looking at Clouds from Both Sides Now' (2012) 16 Stanford Technology Law Review, 107.

[59] ISO/IEC 27701 (n 54)

[60] ISO/IEC 27701 (n 54), Introduction (0.1).

[61] EDPB, Guidelines 1/2018 on certification and identifying certification criteria in accordance with Articles 42 and 43 of the Regulation—version adopted after public consultation, v. 3.0 (2019) (hereafter EDPB Guidelines 1/2018), 27.

[62] CNIL 'ISO 27701, an international standard addressing personal data protection' (April 2020) https://www.cnil.fr/en/iso-27701-international-standard-addressing-personal-data-protection [accessed 20 September 2023].

data transfers could materialize *only* if embedded in one of the grounds for transfers, such as the data protection certification mechanisms.[63] Second, the standard is neither tailored to the EU data protection legislation, nor to facilitating data transfers, as further analysed in the following section. This practically means that its requirements need to be assessed by the entity drafting certification criteria of the data protection certification mechanism, and in any case the data importers and exporters on whether and how they contribute to their compliance with the requirements of data transfers.[64] Third, the ISO/IEC 27701 was developed as a committee-based standard, autonomously from any formal oversight from the public regulator. This is despite any feedback received from the WP29 and the EDPB,[65] which is by no means mandatory for the relevant ISO/IEC Technical Committee. It can therefore be safely assumed that its controls are *primarily* oriented towards safeguarding the interests of the organization that implements the standard, and not necessarily the ones of the individuals affected by the processing conducted by that organization.[66]

8.3.3.2 Alignment with the GDPR objectives and definition

The ISO/IEC 27701 standard 'specifies requirements and provides guidance' for Privacy Information Management Systems (PIMS).[67] The standard is designed to be applicable to all types and sizes of organizations, including public sector and non-for-profit organizations. Further, the standard provides requirements and guidance for controllers and processors of Personally Identifiable Information (PII). The standard is part of a broader set of standards, to which the ISO/IEC 27701 refers as 'normative references'.[68] The determination of its scope should therefore be assessed in light of those standards, where there is a relevant reference.

The focus on management systems instead on the processing of personal data taking place with the aid (or other engagement) of those management systems is not as such a mismatch with the scope of the GDPR transfers regime.[69] What is

[63] Certification pursuant to ISO/IEC 27701 cannot be regarded as such and go through the process of art 42, since the scope and object of the said standard does not match the requirements of art 42 GDPR.

[64] Arts 44 and 46 read jointly with art 42(2) GDPR. As mentioned, the standard maps GDPR requirements with the clauses of the standard. This overview does not sufficiently address the misalignments with the GDPR, as there is no explanation provided on how the 'matching' of the clauses of the standard with several GDPR provisions, including legal duties and principles, has been made.

[65] The WP29 and its successor the EDPB have a liaison status with the technical committee that developed the ISO/IEC 27701 standard.

[66] See also EDPB Guidelines 1/2018 (n 61), 21.

[67] PIMS is defined as 'information security management system which addresses the protection of privacy as potentially affected by the processing of PII' ISO/IEC 27701 clause 3.2.

[68] ISO/IEC 27701 (n 54) cl 2. The ISO/IEC 27701 is based on the ISO/IEC 27001:2013, Information technology—Security techniques—Information security management systems—Requirements and the ISO/IEC 27002:2013, Information technology—Security techniques—Code of practice for information security controls.

[69] EDPB Guidelines 1/2018 (n 61), 16.

assessed in the framework of data transfers mechanism of Art. 46 GDPR is whether the ground for transfer provides 'appropriate safeguards,' enforceable rights, and effective legal remedies.[70] Thus, in the case of the ISO/IEC 27701, it should provide safeguards in the framework of one of the mechanisms of Art. 46, most suitably certification.

As regards the terminology and scope, there are two aspects. One is there are terms in the said standard, which are also used in the GDPR but with a different meaning.[71] The second aspect concerns terms which are either used in the GDPR but are not defined, or not found in the GDPR, but commonly used in practice. For the latter case, definitions provided by the ISO/IEC 27701—and mainly its two key normative references EN ISO/IEC 29100 and the ISO/IEC 27001—are a useful navigation tool for regulatees, but also supervisory authorities. As regards the issue of deviating terminology however, this raises some concerns. The EN ISO/IEC 29100 standard and the ISO/IEC 27701 refer to *privacy* of individuals,[72] instead of protection of individuals with regard to the processing of personal data. The wording thus is closer to the GDPR's predecessor, the Data Protection Directive, which referred to the protection of the 'right to privacy with respect to the processing of personal data.'[73] The reference to privacy of individuals in the context of the processing of their personal information is nonetheless more limited than the material scope of the GDPR. The right to protection of private life is only one of the rights to be protected with the data protection law, thus this discrepancy results in a mismatch in the scope. Further, it is uncertain whether 'privacy' as mentioned in the ISO/IEC 27701 refers indeed to the right for respect to private life, or some other conceptualization of privacy eg a technical one. The normative references of the ISO/IEC 27701 do not provide clarifications, since the concept used is not defined. The EN ISO/IEC 29100 for example is called 'Privacy framework,' and uses the term regularly,[74] but does not explain the term. While the lack of a definition of 'privacy' or 'private life' may be justifiable for primary and even secondary law[75] in view of a need for adaptability and flexibility of the concept to new circumstances of interference, it is problematic for a standard such as the ISO/IEC 27701. Standards are by definition meant to be accurate, provide specific requirements and controls. If standards are to be vague,

[70] *Schrems II* Case C-311/18, para 103.

[71] Lachaud, E, 'ISO/IEC 27701 Standard: Threats and Opportunities for GDPR Certification.' European Data Protection Law Review 6, no 2 (2020): 194–210 (hereafter Lachaud, 'Threats and Opportunities').

[72] The ISO/IEC 29100:2011 is publicly available without fee: https://standards.iso.org/ittf/PubliclyAvailableStandards/index.html [accessed 20 September 2023].

[73] Data Protection Directive art 1(1).

[74] See 'privacy breach' cl 2.13, 'privacy controls' cl 2.14, 'privacy enhancing technology' cl 2.15, 'privacy policy' cl 2.16 and others ISO/IEC 29100:2011 Information technology - Security techniques - Privacy framework.

[75] The ePrivacy Directive does not define 'privacy' either, while referring to the term multiple times.

then their application invites and accommodates different approaches, leading to diverse implementations of the standard, which is against the very purpose of standardization. Given the fact that as opposed to public law, standards do not benefit from the interpretations of their concepts and clauses offered by courts, as they cannot be directly challenged as such, the need for accuracy and clarity of the terminology is heightened. Even more, in the case of a certifiable standard such as the ISO/IEC 27701, any lack of clarity of its scope and requirements due to the terminological issues would have an impact on the uniformity of the review by certification bodies.

Problematic in a similar sense might prove to be the use of the term 'Personally Identifiable Information' (PII) in ISO/IEC 27701. The description[76] of what constitutes PII reveals a more limited scope than personal data. The first part of the PII definition is information that can be used to identify the PII principal (thus the focus is only on the *use* of such information, not collection for example) and only information that relates to such PII principal. The second part of the clause admittedly opens the scope of the concept of PII, but not sufficiently to match the GDPR definition of personal data, as the PII definition refers to information that 'might be directly or indirectly linked to a PII principal.' Thus, for all the other information (not relating to the PII principal), the information should qualify as information that may be *linked* to the PII. It is however rather doubtful that this aligns with art 4(1) GDPR, as according to the WP29 linkability is one of the means/aspects/techniques of identifiability,[77] together with singling out and inferences.[78]

8.3.4 Procedural Legitimacy

8.3.4.1 Overview of applicable safeguards

The international standard was developed by the Joint Technical Committee of the recognized standardization bodies, ISO and IEC. The development, publication,

[76] ISO/IEC 29100:2011 Information technology—Security techniques—Privacy framework.

[77] WP29 'Opinion 4/2007 on the concept of personal data' WP136 (2007), 13–14. See also Recital 26 GDPR which provides 'to determine whether a natural person is identifiable, account should be taken of all means likely to be used, such as singling-out either by the controller or by another person to identify the natural person directly or indirectly.'

[78] WP29 has explained that linkability is 'the ability to link, at least, two records concerning the same data subject or a group of data subjects (either in the same database or in two different databases). If an attacker can establish (e.g. by means of correlation analysis) that two records are assigned to a same group of individuals but cannot single out individuals in this group, the technique provides resistance against "singling out" but not against linkability.' 'Singling-out' is defined as the 'possibility to isolate some or all records which identify an individual in the dataset,' and 'inference' is defined as 'the possibility to deduce, with significant probability, the value of an attribute from the values of a set of other attributes.' WP29 05/2014 on Anonymisation Techniques, WP216 (2014). While this is a technical discussion that is beyond the expertise of the author, the takeaway for this analysis is that there is uncertainty on whether linkability as provided in the ISO/IEC 29100 covers the same scope as the legal definition of 'personal data,' as interpreted by the WP29.

and maintenance of the ISO/IEC 27701 standard is subject to the internal regulations of those two international organizations. The European Standardization Regulation does not apply to this international standard setting activity. This standard is not developed on the basis of a New Approach Directive or any other Union policy. Despite references to the GDPR, those are made in an informative Annex, and without a request or any other sort of formal mandate in general for the development of such a standard. Further, the standard is not referenced by the Commission in a binding or non-binding Act. As such, it is not subject to judicial review by administrative courts or other review public scrutiny mechanism in the Union. Thus, except for the safeguards in the internal regulations of the standardization organizations that developed the standard, the standard exists in a (legal) vacuum in terms of safeguards; this is the case at least until it is incorporated in the Union legal order.[79]

8.3.4.2 Procedural safeguards stemming from the ISO and IEC internal regulations

The development process of ISO and IEC includes several voting rounds, as well as the opportunity to provide comments to the drafts. The comments may be submitted by experts in the Working Group drafting the standard, the members participating in the Technical Committee developing the standard, and finally all the members of ISO may comment on a mature draft. In the latter voting round, the draft International Standard becomes available on the website of each national standardization organization that is an ISO member and every interested party, may provide comments, usually upon the creation of a website account. The Internal Regulations of ISO and IEC, the so-called ISO/IEC Directives, further provide rules for the maintenance and review of the standard, which ensure that the standard is updated before it becomes irrelevant or obsolete.[80] Participation is open to all members of ISO and IEC, which are national standardization bodies. However, information about the development of each standardization project, including the ISO/IEC 27701, is not made available to the public by the standard-setting organizations or their members.

The lack of information to the wider public about the participants and the process that took place, and one may claim lack of transparency is precarious. On the one hand, this is an international standardization activity, that bears no formal link to the EU data protection law. However, data controllers and processors subject to the GDPR may adopt the standard with the aim to comply or demonstrate compliance with their legal duties pursuant the GDPR. This is even more likely due to the communication of the standard by various actors as relevant to the GDPR, also

[79] See Chapter 4 section 4.3 in this book.

[80] ISO/IEC Directives Pt 1 and Consolidated ISO Supplement, Procedures specific to ISO, V01/2024. (maintenance clause, s 2.9).

implicitly confirmed by the participation of the EU supervisory authorities in the standard-setting process.

The actual compliance of those controllers and processors would ultimately be assessed by the (data protection) supervisory authorities, should there be an investigation, and the courts, should there be a case of an alleged infringement of the GDPR. However, until such an investigation or court proceedings takes place, in which the merits of the GDPR mapping in the ISO/IEC 27701 will be incidentally assessed as part of the overall investigation of compliance or breach of the legal duties, personal data by all those companies will be processed in line with this international standard. The participation of the CNIL, a national data protection supervisory authority, in the development of the standard[81] and the involvement of the WP29/EDPB by providing comments to the draft, while offers information to the authorities about the workings of the Technical Committee and the development of the standard, it also bears some risks as regards the actual role of the supervisory authorities in reviewing and approving the content of the standard. In other words, while the participation of supervisory authorities might actually increase the output legitimacy of the standard (namely how it is perceived by its target audience), this will not be substantiated with an actual compliance assessment of its alignment with the GDPR by those national authorities or at least ensuring that any feedback and submitted comments by those authorities are indeed incorporated in the final published international standard.

8.3.4.3 Safeguards stemming from the GDPR

There are two occasions where safeguards stemming from the GDPR would be applicable to the ISO/IEC 27701 and similar international standards. One is if the standard is referenced in a Commission Implementing Act per art 43(9) GDPR for certification. The other occasion is if the drafters of a data protection certification mechanism might decide to use the ISO/IEC 27701 as one of the bases for the certification criteria of art 42(5) GDPR. In the first case, art 43(9) GDPR provides a legal basis for the Commission to adopt implementing acts 'laying down technical standards for certification mechanisms and data protection seals and marks[82]'. Thus, if the ISO/IEC27701 were to be considered in this framework of a Commission Implementing Act, some *ex post* safeguards would apply by virtue of the inclusion of the standard in the Commission Implementing Act. The draft implementing acts of the Commission are subject to an examination procedure

[81] See ISO Article referring to the active participation of the French data protection authority CNIL in the development of the standard and the statement of the CNIL representative: 'Despite the risks of not complying to these regulations, we know that many organizations are simply not ready and need guidance. With the number of complaints and fines related to privacy and data protection on the rise, the need for this standard is now obvious.' https://www.iso.org/news/ref2419.html [accessed 20 September 2023].

[82] GDPR art 43(9).

before a Committee, comprised of representatives of the Member States.[83] The Commission is not allowed to adopt the draft implementing act in case the Committee delivers a negative opinion.[84]

In the second case, the ISO/IEC 27701 could be incorporated in a data protection certification mechanism of art 42, subject to substantial and procedural safeguards. Safeguards concern in brief the approval of the certification criteria from the competent supervisory authority or the EDPB (in the case of a European Data Protection Seal),[85] accreditation of the bodies offering certification,[86] as well as requirements on the maintenance and revocation of certifications that do not fulfil the conditions under which they were granted. Next to those data protection certification-specific safeguards, persons that have suffered damages have compensation rights, and data subjects in particular are empowered with additional remedies. Should ISO/IEC 27701 be approved by supervisory authorities in the framework of a data protection certification mechanism, the above safeguards would apply.

An interesting question that arises is how to solve any conflicting requirements between those imposed by the internal regulations of international standardization bodies and GDPR requirements. One prominent example would be the requirement for publication of the certification criteria on a register by the competent supervisory authority.[87] International standards such as the ISO/IEC 27701 are traditionally made publicly available for a fee. It is questionable whether a DPA register with a link to the website of ISO, IEC, and their members, where the standard is offered for a fee, would meet the requirement for certification criteria being 'made public' by the DPA. Especially, considering that art 43(6) GDPR requires that those are made publicly available 'in an easily accessible form', which implies that interested parties would be able to consult the criteria and requirements in an unhindered manner.[88] Such conflicts might occur more often in the framework of using international standards for EU law purposes. While on a theoretical level and from a normative pluralism perspective, this is an issue which demands attention, this is not a real dilemma from a pragmatic (data protection law) perspective. If international standards such as the ISO/IEC 27701 are to be forming part of a data protection certification mechanism per art 42 GDPR, they should follow all the necessary requirements prescribed by the GDPR, and in the

[83] GDPR art 93(1)and (2) and Regulation 182/2011 art 3.

[84] Regulation 182/2011 art 5(3). However, see GDPR art 93(3) and Regulation 182/2011 art 8, which allow a derogation 'on duly justified imperative grounds of urgency'.

[85] GDPR art 42(5).

[86] GDPR art 43(1).

[87] GDPR art 43(6).

[88] See also Recital 100 GDPR which envisions data protection certification mechanisms as an instrument to enhance transparency, allowing data subjects to 'quickly assess the level of data protection of relevant products and services'.

above case be made available for free. If this does not happen, that standard would not be suitable for the data protection certification mechanism of art 42 GDPR.

8.4 Case Study 3: Technical Specifications and Data Subject's Consent

8.4.1 Do Not Track and Data Subject's Consent

The Do Not Track specification (DNT)[89] has gained attention in the discussions about the revision of the ePrivacy Directive, as a technical solution to obtaining consent of users or objecting to processing.[90] DNT is an ICT technical specification developed by W3C, an international organization. The rationale of DNT was that Internet users would be able to indicate via their browsers their preference on whether or not they would like to have their online activity traced by advertisers for the purpose of delivering advertisements matching their online interests.

Companies collect and use data to profile, evaluate, categorize individuals, with often have an adverse impact on the individual.[91] For the purpose of profiling[92] companies often deploy algorithms,[93] which are used extensively in several sectors.[94] In banking, algorithms are often used for credit scoring and the

[89] Formally called Tracking Preference Expression (DNT) https://www.w3.org/TR/tracking-dnt/ [accessed 20 September 2023].

[90] Marju Lauristin (EP Rapporteur). Explanatory Statement, 87 https://www.europarl.europa.eu/doceo/document/LIBE-PR-606011_EN.pdf [accessed 20 September 2023].

[91] Kamara I, 'Behavioural profiling in the post-constitutionalisation data protection regime.' in 'Human rights as a basis for reevaluating and reconstructing the law: Acts of the 4th ACCA Conference' Louvain-la-Neuve on 29 May 2015 (Bruylant 2016).

[92] See art 4(4) GDPR: 'profiling' means any form of automated processing of personal data consisting of the use of personal data to evaluate certain personal aspects relating to a natural person, in particular to analyse or predict aspects concerning that natural person's performance at work, economic situation, health, personal preferences, interests, reliability, behaviour, location or movements.

[93] Read among many on algorithmic profiling: Büchi M and others, 'The Chilling Effects of Algorithmic Profiling: Mapping the Issues' (2020) 36 Computer Law & Security Review, 105367; Mann M and Matzner T, 'Challenging Algorithmic Profiling: The Limits of Data Protection and Anti-Discrimination in Responding to Emergent Discrimination' (2019) 6 Big Data & Society 205395171989580; Van Otterlo, M, 'A machine learning view on profiling.' *Privacy, Due Process and the Computational Turn-Philosophers of Law Meet Philosophers of Technology* (Routledge 2013) 41–64; And on tracking: Al-Fannah NM, Li W, and. Mitchell CJ, 'Beyond Cookie Monster Amnesia: Real World Persistent Online Tracking' in *International Conference on Information Security*, 481–501; (Springer, Cham, 2018); Zuiderveen Borgesius F, 'Singling out People without Knowing Their Names – Behavioural Targeting, Pseudonymous Data, and the New Data Protection Regulation' (2016) 32 Computer Law & Security Review, 256; Evans DS, 'The Online Advertising Industry: Economics, Evolution, and Privacy' (2009) 23 Journal of Economic Perspectives, 37; Hildebrandt M and Gutwirth S, *Profiling the European citizen*, (Springer 2008). Tracking Preference Expression (DNT) W3C Working Group Note 17 January 2019.

[94] Read further on 'datafication' and consequences of dependence on algorithms: Prins and others, 'Vorebereiden op Digitale Ontwricthing' WRR, 2019 https://www.wrr.nl/publicaties/rapporten/2019/09/09/voorbereiden-op-digitale-ontwrichting [accessed 20 September 2023]

determination of whether an applicant is trustworthy for receiving a loan.[95] In education, algorithms are used to match prospective students with universities.[96] In law enforcement, predictive policing is used to analyse data and devise a likelihood for crimes occurring in neighbourhoods and create 'heat maps'.[97] All this processing is fuelled by data, including personal data processed and compiled in profiles, which form the basis for automated decision making. The potential of profiling and automated decision-making to encroach on the right to protection of personal data, by unlawfully processing personal data and discriminating between persons,[98] has led the European legislator to strengthen data subjects by providing them with substantial rights.

In its inception, DNT was a promising mechanism for the users to effectively communicate their preferences before the instalment of cookies or other identifiers,[99] and be heard, and in that manner, regain some control, while avoiding the consent fatigue caused by the multiple cookie windows or banners.[100] The standardization process at W3C has admittedly not been successful. Despite its promising force, the DNT has been characterized as a failure, as evidenced by the abrupt ending of the unfinished work of the drafting working group.

The development of the DNT specification was complicated. The proposal for the DNT specification was submitted in 2011 but made substantial progress only after 2015. The Tracking Protection Working Group with the participation of advertising associations, industry and civil society, started working in 2011 but disagreements on crucial matters did not allow the Working Group to reach an agreement. It is noteworthy, that after two years since its formation, the Working Group could not agree on the definition of 'tracking' and the scope of the draft specification. To solve this issue, or rather proceed with the process, the Working Group decided to draft two Recommendations, one concerning the expression of

[95] Read Report of Algorithmwatch for Sweden https://algorithmwatch.org/en/automating-society-sweden/ [accessed 20 September 2023] and NL https://algorithmwatch.org/en/automating-society-netherlands/ [accessed 20 September 2023].

[96] Read Report of Algorithmwatch for France: https://algorithmwatch.org/en/automating-society-france/ [accessed 20 September 2023].

[97] Read Report of Algorithmwatch for the Netherlands [accessed 20 September 2023]; Read further: van Schendel S, 'The Challenges of Risk Profiling Used by Law Enforcement: Examining the Cases of COMPAS and SyRI,' in Reins L (ed), *Regulating New Technologies in Uncertain Times* (TMC Asser Press 2019)

[98] Mendoza I and Bygrave LA, 'The Right Not to Be Subject to Automated Decisions Based on Profiling,' in Synodinou and others (eds) *Internet Law* (Springer International Publishing 2017). See further Kamara I and Kosta E, 'Do Not Track initiatives: regaining the lost user control.' (2016) 6 International Data Privacy Law, 276 (hereafter Kamara, Kosta, 'Do Not Track initiatives').

[99] The preference of the user would be sent via an HTTP header, which is sent by browsers before setting or sending cookies, and is read by all parties on a website. McDonald AM, 'Stakeholders and High Stakes,' in Sellinger E, Polonetsky J and Tene O, *The Cambridge Handbook of Consumer Privacy* (Cambridge University Press 2018) (hereafter McDonald, 'Stakeholders and high stakes'), 255.

[100] Read relevant research on legality of cookie banners: Santos C, Bielova N, and Matte C 'Are cookie banners indeed compliant with the law? deciphering EU legal requirements on consent and technical means to verify compliance of cookie banners' [2020] Technology and Regulation, 91.

the user regarding tracking[101] and one providing practices on how to comply with the user preference.[102] The Working Group formally ended the work on those specifications, admitting to the failure to publish them as Recommendations.[103] The result of the unfinished work of the Technical Committee was that the final version of the specification was published as an *informal note*, instead of a formal recommendation by W3C.[104]

8.4.2 Substantive Legitimacy: Legal Basis and Alignment with Legal Instrument: The Case of the EU ePrivacy Legislation

A DNT-style mechanism is valued by the public regulators, which have argued that adherence to a DNT-style mechanism should be binding,[105] and scholars, who have proposed that the standard should be user-friendly and backed by proper enforcement.[106] An ICT specification like DNT, originally conceived as one specification addressing both setting the preference of the user and its reception from the website provider could enable data subjects to communicate their wish to be tracked, with technical means, avoiding doubts and misinterpretations or meaningless box ticking exercises. As regards, internet-wide tracking, a standardized web browser signal may along those lines have added value in signalling in a uniform and automated manner the data subjects'/users' wishes regarding tracking.

Some limitations as regards the implementation, enforcement, but also expectation management of a DNT-style mechanism should be noted. Some of the limitations stem from the fact that DNT outsources the implementation of DNT signal by the website providers to another specification Tracking Scope and Compliance, which practically distinguishes the communication of the preferences from what the receivers do with this knowledge.[107]

[101] Tracking Preference Expression (DNT) W3C Working Group Note 17 January 2019.

[102] Tracking Compliance and Scope, W3C Working Group Note 22 January 2019.

[103] In the Tracking Preference Expression, the WG noted: 'Since its last publication as a Candidate Recommendation, there has not been sufficient deployment of these extensions (as defined) to justify further advancement, nor have there been indications of planned support among user agents, third parties, and the ecosystem at large. The working group has therefore decided to conclude its work and republish the final product as this Note, with any future addendums to be published separately.'

[104] See explanation under 'status of this document' section in Tracking Preference Expression W3C Working Group Note (17 January 2019) https://www.w3.org/TR/tracking-dnt/ [accessed 20 September 2023].

[105] EDPS 'Preliminary EDPS Opinion on the review of the ePrivacy Directive (2002/58/EC)' Opinion 5/2016, 16 argued that 'adherence to accepted technical and policy compliance standards by all parties concerned, including the operators of the website, should become obligatory'; WP29, wp247, (2017) 17.

[106] Zuiderveen Borgesius F, and others. 'An Assessment of the Commission's Proposal on Privacy and Electronic Communications.' Directorate-General for Internal Policies, Policy Department C: Citizen's Rights and Constitutional Affairs (2017) 23.

[107] See Tracking Scope and Compliance (2019) https://www.w3.org/TR/tracking-compliance/ [accessed 20 September 2023].

First, as explained in the Tracking Scope and Compliance specification, collection and use of data may still occur by first parties (website visited by the user) and third parties (other parties such as advertisers with which the user has not interacted).[108] The Tracking Scope and Compliance specification indicates a number of 'permitted uses' for which advertisers may collect and use data, but not personalize the advertisement, despite a no-tracking signal communicated by the user.[109] Second, the W3C DNT-style mechanism relates to internet-wide advertising, and does not address other tracking, and profiling not-internet related cases, nor types of other sophisticated cases of tracking,[110] which is highly relevant to an Internet of Things environment. Third, as with every voluntary mechanism, and especially one that distinguishes its technical component from scope and compliance in two different specifications as the W3C DNT, the lack of incentive, regulatory or otherwise, for industry to conform, is problematic and compromises the value of such a mechanism. Fourth, the mechanism's specific scope as opposed to what is implied by its all-encompassing name may lead to misconceptions and false expectations from users about no collection of their personal data. In turn, understanding the actual more limited scope of DNT may generate mistrust of such mechanisms in general.[111]

It is further doubtful whether the W3C DNT matched the scope of the ePrivacy Directive.[112] This is the case also with regard to the Commission Proposal for ePrivacy Regulation, despite several amendments in the final texts of the Do Not Track Specification and its Scope and Compliance specification. Discrepancies in the terminology, alignment of the concept of consent, and how users' preferences are treated[113] reveal significant limitations of the mechanism for direct implementation in the ePrivacy context.[114]

108 ibid.

109 An example of a 'permitted use' is the vaguely framed 'security' which means that 'Regardless of the tracking preference expressed, data MAY be collected and used to the extent reasonably necessary to detect security incidents, protect the service against malicious, deceptive, fraudulent, or illegal activity, and prosecute those responsible for such activity, provided that such data is not used for operational behavior beyond what is reasonably necessary to protect the service or institute a graduated response.' Tracking Compliance and Scope W3C Working Group Note 22 January 2019, 3.3.2.3.

110 An example is tracking through device batteries. See Harcourt A, Christou G and Simpson S, *Global Standard Setting in Internet Governance* (Oxford University Press 2020), 177ff (hereafter Harcourt and others 'Global Standard Setting').

111 Hoofnagle CJ 'Do Not Track Dilemma DNT – Do Not Advertise' Technology Academics Policy TAP (10 February 2011) (hereafter Hoofnagle, 'Do Not Track Dilemma').

112 Kamara, Kosta, 'Do Not Track initiatives' (n 98).

113 DNT(2019) s 7.2.8 concerns 'potential consent' and s 7.2.9 concerns 'conditions for disregarding consent', whereas the EU data protection legislation does not allow for such variations of consent. See GDPR art 6(1)(a), ePrivacy Directive art 593), Commission ePrivacy Regulation Proposal art 8.

114 DNT (2019) cl 2.3 defines tracking as 'collection of data regarding a particular user's activity across multiple distinct contexts and the retention, use, or sharing of data derived from that activity outside the context in which it occurred'.

8.4.3 Procedural Legitimacy

This ICT specification regarding online tracking was developed by an international consortium, thus by a non-recognized standardization organization. Thus, the applicable safeguards are solely a matter for the internal rules of W3C. The process at W3C however shows openness and transparency.

The W3C Do Not Track[115] was developed by the Tracking Protection Working Group, to which large corporations, but also SMEs, academia, civil rights organizations and government participated. McDonald, who led the standardization effort of Do Not Track at W3C for several years, reported that the process became an 'inter-disciplinary multistakeholder team by necessity' due to the increased interest that the Do Not Track specification attracted.[116] The increased interest by privacy advocates can be attributed to the potential of Do Not Track to become a user empowerment tool, where the wish of users to be tracked or not is communicated to advertisers. Advertising companies and industry joined, according to McDonald, because a Do Not Track was an alternative to blanket advertisement blocking; Do Not Track would still allow advertisers showing untargeted advertisements to users not interested in them to being tracked and receive targeted advertisements to their online browsing history and preferences, while advertisement blocking would not allow advertisers to show any advertisements. This was a 'weak' version of Do Not Track, as characterized by Hoofnagle, as it would allow tracking and collection of data.[117] Large corporations were motivated to join for several reasons such as the endorsement by the US Federal Trade Commission and a para-law function of the specification due to non-existing privacy legislation (otherwise: in place of 'risking' having privacy legislation in place).[118] Despite the increased participation from non-industry stakeholders, the outcomes were reported to be tilting towards industry's favour due to its stable commitment of resources to the process throughout the years.[119]

In a remarkably transparent process, the agenda, minutes and attendees list of all meetings are publicly available.[120] As regards decision making, in general, the W3C Recommendations are agreed in Working Groups, which include members,

[115] The Do Not Track specification was renamed to Tracking Preference Expression during its development process, but the original DNT is being used throughout the book for simplicity.

[116] McDonald, 'Stakeholders and high stakes' (n 99), 257.

[117] Hoofnagle, 'Do Not Track Dilemma' (n 111).

[118] McDonald, 'Stakeholders and high stakes' (n 99), 263.

[119] For example, McDonald explains from her own experience as chair of the Working Group, that some large companies could afford to send their staff to the meetings which took place in different locations. McDonald, 'Stakeholders and high stakes' (n 99), 262. The list of the face to face meetings of the Tracking Protection Working Group shows indeed that the meetings took place in different locations mainly in the EU and US. https://www.w3.org/Privacy/Historical.html [accessed 20 September 2023].

[120] See webpage of the Tracking Protection Working Group (which ceased its operations in 2019) https://www.w3.org/2011/tracking-protection/ [accessed 20 September 2023].

invited experts and personnel of the consortium.[121] The process includes several consultation rounds, but not formally with the general public. Each organization has one vote and decisions are made with consensus, which means that a 'significant number' of members support the Recommendation and there is no objection.[122] However, as argued by Doty and Mulligan, the consensus 'leaves participants in control of the boundaries of substantive compromise'.[123] In addition, objections are raised with the W3C Director, who is responsible for inviting experts and deciding on whether a proposal becomes a Recommendation.

Two further aspects stand out: one is that the Do Not Track specification, as with all W3C specifications, is publicly freely available. The second is a requirement for horizontal review of specifications.[124] The horizontal review entails that all W3C specifications are reviewed in terms of accessibility, internationalization, mobility, device independence, privacy, security, and technical architecture principles.[125] The review for privacy is performed internally by the Privacy Interest Group.[126]

8.5 Synthesis

The analysis of the harmonized standard on data protection by design and by default and the international Privacy Information Management Systems standard showed that in general such standards may have an added value in their supplementary functions in relation to the law. The gravitas of this value differs from case to case. In the case of data protection by design and by default, the scope of the analysed standard addresses a significant legal gap, as it is addressed to manufacturers of products that design products to take into account the requirements of art 25 GDPR. This is not the case however with the analysed international standard. As regards data transfers, the ISO/IEC 27701 provides requirements for a Privacy Information Management System, which is however one aspect of the components to be assessed by supervisory authorities, according to the EDPB guidance.[127] The analysis showed that the ISO/IEC 27701 has therefore added value to assisting data importers undertake and document organizational measures in preparation

[121] Harcourt and others, 'Global Standard Setting' (n 110), 50.
[122] Harcourt and others, 'Global Standard Setting' (n 110), 51ff.
[123] Doty N, and Mulligan D, 'Internet Multistakeholder Processes and Techno-Policy Standards: Initial Reflections on Privacy at the World Wide Web Consortium.' (2013) 11 J. on Telecomm. & High Tech. L 11, 135
[124] Doty N, 'Reviewing for privacy in Internet and Web standard-setting.' (2015) IEEE Security and Privacy Workshops, 185.
[125] W3C Guidebook 3.4 (Horizontal Review) https://www.w3.org/Guide/process/charter.html [accessed 20 September 2023].
[126] Harcourt and others, 'Global Standard Setting' (n 110), 52.
[127] EDPB Guidelines 1/2018 (n 61).

for a data protection certification mechanism, but it is by no means suitable to offer solutions to problems pertaining to data transfers, such as surveillance activities in third countries or a legal system without proper redress mechanisms. Finally, the assessment of both standards and the legal analysis confirmed the limitations of standards' function for clarity and interpretation of the concepts and principles of the GDPR.

The assessment of the ICT specification DNT, to which a pre-law function may be attributed in relation to ePrivacy, shows—and perhaps even justifies—the absence of a direct reference in the law; efforts on finalizing DNT by giving it the status of a W3C Recommendation have been abandoned by the organization developing the specification. Besides, the last published version of DNT, although improved in comparison to previous versions, is still not aligned with EU data protection law, in a manner that would allow a direct reference or even make the DNT mechanism mandatory for website providers.

As regards the procedural legitimacy aspects, the analysis of the examined standards in this Chapter, reveals a discrepancy between autonomous committee-based and co-development standardization. Co-development standardization based on standardization requests, as opposed to self-regulatory committee-based standardization, is subject to a richer network of safeguards, even though not without its limitations ie judicial reviewability and redress.

A final remark concerns the analysed process in an international standardization consortium, despite not subject to the EU safeguard 'machinery' of the Standardization Regulation, the GDPR or other, showed remarkable transparency, and some accessibility and the openness safeguards were also maintained. In addition, W3C has a horizontal review mechanism in place to ensure that significant matters *inter alia* privacy are properly taken into account by every specification. However, *ex post* safeguards as examined in this Chapter are not applicable in the case of the examined ICT specification, which is an important limitation.

9
Conclusion

9.1 Problem Statement: A Role for Standards in Data Protection?

The point of departure for the research was that Union secondary data protection law is undergoing pressure from its inherent characteristics and its application. These are the results of its broad material scope resulting in an immense amount of diverse entities with compliance duties, that is entities spread around the globe (due to the extraterritorial effect of the GDPR), and the unavoidable question of how rules apply to processing by new, data-intensive technologies and commercial companies willing to interfere with issues which were previously unimaginable. Those issues include examples of interference with national elections,[1] the spread of misinformation[2] blurring of facts and opinions,[3] the manipulation of emotions[4] in exchange for revenue, the scarce resources of (but admittedly strong willed) supervisory authorities, in combination with largely unaware, uninformed, uninterested or vulnerable data subjects, playing along, clicking 'accept all cookies' and 'liking' and 'sharing' often addictively their lives and lives of others online.

Such challenges create regulatory space for intensification of enforcement and awareness efforts, but also additional regulation instruments in data protection.

Among the several regulation instruments such as certification, codes of conduct, and data protection specific ones such as Binding Corporate Rules[5] and Data Protection Impact Assessments,[6] standardization stands out for many reasons: standardization is broader than Binding Corporate Rules and Data Protection Impact Assessments, and could encompass in principle those as well;

[1] Confessore, N 'Cambridge Analytica and Facebook: The Scandal and the Fallout So Far' New York Times, 4 April 2018. https://www.nytimes.com/2018/04/04/us/politics/cambridge-analytica-scandal-fallout.html [accessed 20 August 2024].

[2] Hameleers M, 'My Reality Is More Truthful Than Yours: Radical Right-Wing Politicians' and Citizens' Construction of "Fake" and "Truthfulness" on Social Media—Evidence From the United States and The Netherlands.' (2020) 14 International Journal of Communication, 18.

[3] As Latour has eloquently described it 'the former distinction between the circulation of facts and the dissemination of opinions has been erased in such a way that they are both graduating to the same type of visibility'. Latour B, 'Beware, your imagination leaves digital traces.' Times Higher Literary Supplement 6, no 4 (2007), 129–131.

[4] Goel V,. 'Facebook tinkers with users' emotions in news feed experiment, stirring outcry.' The New York Times 29 (2014). Read comprehensive study on this matter: Clifford D, *Data Protection Law and Emotion* (OUP 2024).

[5] GDPR art 47.

[6] GDPR art 35.

Standardizing Personal Data Protection. Irene Kamara, Oxford University Press.
DOI: 10.1093/9780191997037.003.0009

the normative[7] element of standards providing substantial rules more than just the rule of procedure is missing from certification and other conformity assessment tools; standardization bodies such as ISO and CEN constitute a unique network of stakeholders, one that is more structured and stable than certifications (and in any case certifications in data protection) and other private regulation instruments.

From a policy perspective, the European Commission already acknowledged in 2015 some added value of standards in support of data protection law by using its power to request the European Standardization Organizations to develop standards for data protection by design and by default. In parallel, standardization organizations, both international and European, have given data protection a prominent place in their agenda, as shown by rapidly growing activity in this field. Standards are often described as flexible, bottom-up, technology specific regulation instruments, attractive for areas, such as data protection, that are hampered by negative externalities of technological developments.

Returning to data protection laws' challenges, the question emerges: Can standards play a role in addressing the challenges the secondary data protection law is facing? And what are the boundaries of this complementing role, as determined for example by the regulatory target and the primary and secondary law implemented to protect it, and the nature and legal framework of standardization as private regulation instrument?

Thus, one aspect of the research topic, *explorative* in nature, concerned the supplementary role of standardization in the regulation of data protection. Another aspect, a *normative* one, was about whether standards *should* take on any role, even one supplementary to the data protection law, in light of their private regulation nature, which entails procedures for development, publication, review of norms different to public law making and its democratic legitimacy.

To answer these questions, the scope of the book mainly focused on standards adopted by recognized standardization bodies or standards more generally that may be integrated in the Union legal order, following the options offered in the Union; that is European standards drafted at the request of the Commission or international (mainly) standards recognized *ex post facto*. If those standards that are put forward by the EU legislator could be found to *not* have any role, then the same would go for all the other standards, which are not recognized in the Union legal order. However, if those recognized standards, could prove to have a potential role to play, then further future research could consider non-recognized standards as well to determine any potential role and boundaries.

The following sections summarize the Chapters and their main findings, and provide an answer to the main research question of the book, and provide an outlook for further research.

[7] By normative here is meant capable of generating substantial rules (as opposed to merely technical ones).

9.2 Data Protection and the Position of Standards

To understand what constitutes interference with the right to protection of personal data, and ultimately its core, Brkan has compared the process with peeling an onion, where the outer layer is the fundamental right as a whole, the next layer a justified interference, then a serious interference, and at the heart is the essence.[8] I am loosely borrowing this comparison to illustrate the argument of this book and make a point about the role of standardization in regulating the right to protection of personal data. Indeed, protecting individuals with regard to the processing of their personal data, as this protection is provided in the law, resembles a series of concentric circles, where the core constitutes both the ultimate aim and the reference point, the centre for all the other circles. Dignity, autonomy, liberty, and identity lie at the core and constitute the essence of the right to protection of personal data. An outer circle is comprised of its rationales, such as informational self-determination, development of personality, fairness, and integrity of information. Moving from the core towards the outer concentric circles, one moves from elements enshrined in primary law to elements and components of secondary law. Each outer layer adds elements and components, aiming to ultimately protect its inner layers, and being informed by those. The cornerstones of the Union general data protection law, namely the principles of transparency, accountability, purpose limitation, and the grounds for processing constitute another layer, the controller and processor duties and data subject rights another one, and so on. While figuring out what constitutes the right as a whole –even if this could be precisely pinned down, which I doubt—is not the purpose of this research; what is meant to be conveyed with this visual comparison is that from an instruments perspective the closer to the core, the higher the need for protection, and thus the stronger the instruments to protect it.[9] By stronger, it is meant those instruments with more procedural and substantial safeguards and democratic legitimacy and acceptance, enforcement power, hierarchically higher than other instruments in the Union legal order. From a content perspective, standardization is relevant to different layers that may extend to aspects of the core, ie the data security rationale of the right of art 8 CFREU.[10]

The main and first point of this book can be summarized in simple terms as being that if standardization, as an instrument, has some role to play in data

[8] Brkan M, 'The Concept of Essence of Fundamental Rights in the EU Legal Order: Peeling the Onion to Its Core' (2018) 14 European Constitutional Law Review, 332. Read also: Brkan M, 'The Essence of the Fundamental Rights to Privacy and Data Protection: Finding the Way Through the Maze of the CJEU's Constitutional Reasoning' (2019) 20 German Law Journal, 864.

[9] The comparison is a simplification tailored to the scope of the book. The GDPR and the ePrivacy legislation aim at protecting more than the right of art 8 CFREU, so one could speak of intersecting circles or other, but this lies beyond my research question.

[10] Judgment of 8 April 2014, *Digital Rights Ireland*, Joined Cases C 293/12 and C 594/12, EU:C:2014:238para 40.

protection, this role is to be found primarily in the outer concentric circles of data protection and its regulation. This role, even in the outer layers of data protection, still has relevance to the inner layers such as the rationales and even the core.

The question that this book further sought to answer was which are those outer concentric circles or more broadly framed 'aspects' of data protection law that allow and even invite standardization. What are the components and elements of those outer layers of data protection that may be supplemented with standards, under which conditions and for what purposes?[11]

The analysis on the instruments of the Union data protection law, the General Data Protection Regulation (GDPR) and its *lex specialis* in the electronic communications sector (the ePrivacy Directive, studied together with the 2017 ePrivacy Regulation Proposal), revealed three main themes creating space for additional regulation measures in view of the aforementioned challenges of the secondary data protection law. First, the GDPR establishes general responsibility for data controllers to ensure compliance with the Regulation and to demonstrate the measures taken towards that goal. In addition, several duties of controllers, but also processors, require assessment of a range of factors such as the state of the art, the risks to rights and freedoms of individuals, the purposes of processing and others, to determine what are the appropriate measures to comply with the given duty. The decisional competence of controllers, as described by Quelle,[12] urges them to operationalize their accountability obligations, including by means of private regulation. Second, the analysed data protection laws are human centric and technology neutral, yet technology aware and certainly affected by the deployment of various *technologies*. Several provisions invite technology-specific measures in order to be complied with or enabled. The right to data portability is dependent on structured machine readable formats to be meaningful for the data subject;[13] verification of the age of a child in information society services is possible only with technological means;[14] obtaining consent for the processing of electronic communications data via software attaches legal significance on how the software is designed.[15] Thus, instruments to specify those aspects are necessary for carrying out or enabling the controller and processor to comply with duties stemming from the GDPR and the ePrivacy legislation. A third theme, which concerns only the GDPR, is the omnibus nature of the law applying to entities independently of sector and public or private

[11] The possibility for standardization, perhaps with other private regulation instruments, to constitute its own layer, was excluded from the scope of this book from the outset, for the reasons explained in the Introduction Chapter, including that such a claim of an autonomous standing in protecting the fundamental right to data protection does not have a legal basis in the Union and is a matter heavily addressed in scholarship. See Introduction Chapter 1 in this book.

[12] Quelle C, 'Privacy, proceduralism and self-regulation in data protection law.' [2017] 14 Teoria Critica della Regolazione Sociale, 104.

[13] GDPR art 20.

[14] GDPR art 8(1).

[15] Proposal for ePrivacy Regulation art 10(1).

legal nature. The GDPR suggests the use of private regulation instruments to calibrate obligations of controllers and processors 'taking account of the specific characteristics of the processing carried out in certain sectors.'[16]

Against this backdrop, the second point of the book is that private regulation and in particular standardization as a private regulation instrument, may have a role in addressing issues generated by the increased responsibility and decisional competence of controllers as prescribed in the analysed data protection law, and the technology- and sector- neutral character of the GDPR.

9.3 The Use for Public Goals Following the Identity Shift of Standardization

The book also sought to provide an understanding of the concept of standards in the EU legal order, the development modes of standards in the Union and their effects.

Standards were from their inception instruments of coordination and interoperability in the production of goods. As Murphy and Yates frame it, standards were originally used for specifying requirements for nuts and bolts.[17] Despite their prominent originally technical character, development of standards in social (as opposed to economic) regulation has been expanding,[18] and the Union laws and policies are not an exception. The EU policy makers took note of the identity shift of standardization, as most notably shown with the New Approach legislation; a regulatory technique which relies on standardization bodies to delineate the essential requirements of the law; standardization bodies have taken on a role in providing for example what is a safe toy,[19] radio equipment that ensures health of individuals,[20] what constitutes an effective and safe medical device.[21]

The growing (need for) association of standardization to fields pertaining to public interest led the public regulator in the Union to establish rules for several aspects of standardization such as the 2008 New Legislative Framework on the conditions for placing products in the Union and conformity assessment, and in 2012 Regulation 1025/2012 ('Standardization Regulation'). The Standardization

[16] Recital 98 GDPR.

[17] Murphy CN and Yates J, *The International Organization for Standardization (ISO): Global Governance Through Voluntary Consensus* (Routledge 2009), 20ff.

[18] Yates J and Murphy CN, *Engineering Rules: Global Standard Setting since 1880* (JHU Press 2019).

[19] Directive 2009/48/EC of the European Parliament and of the Council of 18 June 2009 on the safety of toys, [2009]OJ L 170/1.

[20] Directive 2014/53/EU of the European Parliament and of the Council of 16 April 2014 on the harmonization of the laws of the Member States relating to the making available on the market of radio equipment and repealing Directive 1999/5/EC, [104] OJ L 153/62.

[21] Regulation (EU) 2017/745 of the European Parliament and of the Council of 5 April 2017 on medical devices, amending Directive 2001/83/EC, Regulation (EC) No 178/2002 and Regulation (EC) No 1223/2009 and repealing Council Directives 90/385/EEC and 93/42/EEC, [2017] OJ L 117/1, Annex I.

Regulation provides a general framework on European standardization in support of Union legislation and policies, and the cooperation of international, European, and standardization bodies with the European Commission. European harmonized standards may be an outcome of a co-development process, where the Commission and the European Standardization Organizations collaborate, each actor with different powers and responsibilities, to develop standards in support of Union legislation or policy. International standards or European standards developed without any involvement from the Commission, may also find their way into being recognized in the Union legal order. Those standards which are developed on the basis of the internal regulations of the standardization bodies may be *ex post facto* referenced in EU binding or non-binding acts.

Chapter 4 identified four main streams of standards which find their way into the Union legal order; European harmonized standards, general and under the New Approach (Stream 1), committee-based (Stream 2), market-based (Stream 3), and mixed, whereby published committee-based standards are introduced in the co-development standardization process (Stream 4).

The Standardization Regulation requires that standards are voluntary, adopted only by 'recognized standardization bodies', and are sustainable through time. However, practice[22] has shown that standards may become *de facto* binding and/or considered part of EU law. Especially harmonized standards 'grounded on the New Approach are often viewed as delegated private regulation[23] bearing more significant legal consequences than their private nature implies.

A third finding is that the mode of development and integration of standards in the EU legal order impacts their legal effects and the application of good governance principles such as transparency, openness, participation.

9.4 Standardization and a Role in Supplementing Data Protection Law

Rubinstein has argued, private and public regulation is a false dichotomy, in that they should not be seen as mutually exclusive.[24] While this book took a strong stance from the outset[25] in favour of the necessity of public regulation by means of primary and secondary law in data protection, it is true that private regulation and public regulation are not mutually exclusive. The research for this book showed

[22] Judgment of 27 October 2016, *James Elliot*, Case C-613/14, EU:C:2016:821; Judgment of 14 December 2017, *Anstar Oy*, Case C-630/16, EU:C:2017:971.

[23] Medzmariashvili M, 'Delegation of Rulemaking Power to European Standards Organizations: Reconsidered' (2017) 44 Legal Issues of Economic Integration, 353.

[24] Rubinstein IS, 'Regulating privacy by design.' (2011) 26 Berkeley Tech. LJ, 1409, 1445ff.

[25] See Introduction Chapter 1 in this book.

that standards may assume a supplementary role to data protection, as regards data subjects' rights, and controllers' and processors' compliance with their legal duties.

The value of standardization in terms of helping individuals to exercise control over their personal data and hold controllers accountable for respecting the rules of those instruments is a narrative encountered in international instruments on data protection. The GDPR and ePrivacy Directive and its reform refer to technical standards (or technical norms) in the context of data protection. The novelty of introducing standards in those texts but also attributing a greater role to private regulation in general seems to correspond to the modern practice followed by companies of implementing data protection rules, with a set of organizational and technical measures. These include standards for implementation of technical aspects of the rules and privacy management programmes that foster accountability of the persons responsible for processing personal data.[26] Motivation to follow private regulation instruments often includes reputation and enhancing the confidence of individuals, developing a level playing field, or public regulation.[27]

In terms of the regulatees, that is data controllers and processors, standards may assist companies in their general responsibility to comply with their legal duties and demonstrate the measures undertaken to that end. Standards in that matter hold a facilitating and an enabling function. The facilitating function regards aspects of legal duties with a prominent organizational component. Standards, as *facilitators*, are a useful, but not necessary,[28] tool to achieve compliance with a duty laid down in data protection law. The usefulness of standards stems from the expert knowledge they embody, as they are developed in a multi-stakeholder environment with high expertise.[29] Examples include maintaining data processing records,[30] setting data protection policies and notices,[31] and collecting evidence for the authorities. In this type of function one can find also standards providing risk assessment methodologies for adopting data security measures or conducting impact assessment[32] and in general concretizing assessment criteria and assisting controllers and processors calibrate the measures to their data processing operations.

[26] The debates and negotiations for the revision of the OECD Guidelines and the Convention 108+ took place in a parallel course to the reform process of the Union secondary data protection legislation, and there is evidence of mutual influence between the two in terms of how standardization should be regarded in data protection seems a very plausible scenario.

[27] OECD 'Industry self-regulation: role and use in supporting consumer interests' OECD Publication Office (23 March 2015) p.11.

[28] Standards in this role are not necessary since the data protection duty may be carried out without the need for controllers or processors in relying on standards.

[29] Cafaggi F, 'New foundations of transnational private regulation.' (2011) 38 Journal of law and society, 20.

[30] GDPR art 30.

[31] GDPR art 12.

[32] GDPR art 35.

The *enabling* nature of standards usually concerns aspects of duties or compliance measures with a strong technical component, such as pseudonymization and encryption of personal data,[33] responding to data subjects' exercise of the right to data portability,[34] designing terminal equipment including software, and taking into account data protection principles.[35] The characteristics and quality of standards setting benchmarks on the state of the art and allowing for interoperability of systems are pivotal in ensuring that a legal duty is complied with. In those cases, standards may become *de facto* binding. Ensuring interoperability with the aim to comply with a data portability request is not possible if both controllers are not making use of the same standards. And in theory a controller or processor might develop their own pseudonymization technique, other than those prescribed in well-accepted technical standards, but this is rather unlikely for the majority of controllers and processors, and processing operations.

As regards data subjects, when specifications and standards are technically implemented they have an enabling nature. This is the case for example for objections to processing of personal data by means of Internet browser specifications. Such specifications in essence communicate the wishes and preferences of data subjects (Internet users) to website providers acting as controllers.[36] The enabling function in case of data subjects' rights however is hampered by a serious constraint, in that its realization is dependent on data controllers, as explained in the following section.

Beyond looking at standards as a self-standing private regulation instruments, the research showed that when standards are part of other—more elaborately regulated in data protection legislation–private regulation instruments assume a role of providing criteria and requirements.

Following the above, a fourth key finding of the research was identifying and framing the types of supplementary functions of standards: a meta-rule function, a compliance function as regards data controllers' accountability, and a data subjects' rights function.

9.5 Data Protection Standardization: Suitable for Whom?

The analysis showed that data protection has the potential to contribute to the goals of data protection law, as described in the previous section. However, the

33 GDPR art 32.
34 GDPR art 20.
35 GDPR art 25 and EC Proposal for ePrivacy Regulation art 10.
36 The exercise of the right is also possible with other means, for example submitting a request via email or by post, but with a considerable administrative burden in comparison to technical specifications.

materialization of this potential stumbles upon power imbalances of the different actors that could benefit from the use of standards.

For the rights of data subjects, the voluntary nature of standards is problematic due to the uneven balance of power between controllers/processors and data subjects,[37] and results in a paradox: the content of some standards in the field could in theory enable data subject empowerment, but whether this role will materialize depends on the very entities against which the data subject needs to be empowered; data controllers and processors. For this reason, the data subject rights function should be seen with a critical eye. When standards are incorporated in other private regulation instruments such as the data protection certification mechanisms, a monitoring and review role is assigned to certification bodies or other monitoring private regulators in the cases of other instruments. However, it is doubtful this is sufficient to ensure that the wishes of data subjects as expressed via a technical specification, or a standard are respected.

The materialization of such a function for standards would necessitate explicit public regulatory power with oversight and enforcement powers. Such public regulatory intervention is closer to reality than it seems. The Radio Equipment Directive already provides a legal basis for adopting New Approach harmonized standards with data protection requirements. This means that standards that are developed based on the RED are European harmonized standards, subject to the procedural safeguards of the New Approach.

In summary, a fifth finding of the book is that unless standards are vested with technical or legal enforceability, the function of data protection standards as an empowerment instrument cannot materialize, since data subjects are dependent on the choices of controllers and processors to voluntarily adhere to standards and respect their choices. The role of standards would be then limited to *communication of the preferences* of data subjects, without any guarantee that those will be respected.

When it comes to controllers and processors, the situation differs. Controllers bear a general responsibility to take organizational and technical measures to ensure the data protection law is not violated and to be able to demonstrate that processing is conducted according to those rules. Controllers are accountable to comply and demonstrate compliance with the data protection principles. Processors also bear enhanced duties under the GDPR, and may be directly confronted with liability claims in some cases. Thus, the motivation to conform to voluntary standards, that is perhaps lacking for controllers and processors in the data subject empowerment role/function,[38] is accountability and general responsibility

[37] Among many: Gutwirth S and De Hert P, 'Privacy, Data Protection and Law Enforcement. Opacity of the Individual and Transparency of Power' (2022) 18 Direito Público; Kosta E, *Consent in European Data Protection Law* (Brill 2013), 178.

[38] Data subject rights are also within the framework of responsibilities of the controller, which needs to facilitate the exercise of the rights as prescribed in art 12(1) GDPR. Yet—unfortunately so–facilitation of the rights by taking measures is not one-to-one to making sure that, on the ground, even

to ensure and demonstrate compliance with the GDPR. The duty to carry out an assessment of the impact of processing operations per art 35 GDPR may motivate the controller to go the extra step towards compliance, beyond what is strictly required, by conforming for example to voluntary standards, which provide a well-accepted impact assessment methodology.

Besides, those additional voluntary measures, such as conformity to technical standards, may play a role in cases of violations, liability, and fines, as has also been stressed by other scholars for private regulation instruments in data protection.[39] Standards are routinely used as benchmarks for the duty of care of actors or providing the state of the art,[40] and helping with such assessments. In parallel, where a stronger case could be made, is in terms of administrative fines by supervisory authorities. Conformity to technical standards may have added value when for example supervisory authorities view positively an organization that follows the ISO/IEC 27001 standard.

A distinction however concerning the regulatees is in order. The WP29, in its Opinion on the principle of accountability, referred to a 'data deluge' when depicting the growing amount of personal data processing taking place worldwide.[41] The processing is taking place in all types of forms and contexts, and different types of controllers and processors. The acknowledgment of this diversity is important *inter alia* for the determination of a role for standards in the field. That is because as shown in this study, a voluntary measure such as standardization, without teeth of its own and not formally linked to the enforcement mechanisms of the Union data protection law, can go as far as the controllers or processors allow it to go; that is by voluntarily undertaking to conform to one or more data protection related standards and respecting its conditions.

While it is true, as argued by Ausloos and others that data protection legislation is largely intent-agnostic,[42] for voluntary private regulation instruments supporting data protection law such as standards, the intentions of the regulatees are

uninterested data subjects, would be made truly aware of their rights and make conscious choices. The type of obligation for controllers however is stronger when data subject rights are not expressed only as entitlements ('The data subject shall have the right to [...]') but also as an explicit obligation for controllers ('and the controller shall have the obligation to [...]'), such as in art 17(1) GDPR.

[39] Papakonstantinou V, *Self-Regulation and the Protection of Privacy* (Nomos-Verlag-Ges., 2002).

[40] Moore for example argues that standards are capable of raising software quality and that the use of standards may be useful to establish liability for defective software. Moore R, 'Standardisation: A Tool for Addressing Market Failure within the Software Industry' (2013) 29 Computer Law & Security Review 413.

[41] WP29, Opinion 3/2010, 4.

[42] Ausloos J, Veale M, and Mahieu R, 'Getting Data Subject Rights Right: A submission to the European Data Protection Board from international data rights academics, to inform regulatory guidance.' Journal of Intellectual Property, Information Technology and Electronic Commerce Law 10 (2019); See also chapter 5 on the matter of strict liability imposed to controllers in the GDPR. See however art 83(2)(b) GDPR: the supervisory authority assesses the intentional or negligent character of an infringement to determine whether to impose a fine and the amount of the fine.

significant. The reality is, as explained above, that there are controllers and processors that design their business models to harvest and exploit personal data. Standardization linked to data protection is a weak instrument to support the right to protection of personal data with regard to the data processing by those companies.[43] This inherent characteristic of standards should not necessarily be viewed as a weakness of data protection standardization, as long as it is acknowledged and accounted for by all parties, including entities tasked to comply with the data protection legislation, supervisory authorities, but also data subjects.[44]

Standardization could be helpful to controllers and processors that process personal data in the course of their business, using personal data for example to improve services, personalize content, and others, but not at the scale and intensity of the Facebooks of this world. While coming up with criteria on how to apply such a distinction in practice is not in the scope of the book, it is still useful to clarify that this distinction *matters* for the materialization of the supportive functions of standardization in data protection (sixth finding).[45]

A last remark in this regard is that those companies that engage in data intensive and abusive practices that are not the target audience of any voluntary compliance measure such as standardization, they may well influence the standard-setting process and most importantly the content of those standards, and thus indirectly the practices of companies that voluntarily adhere to them. Neither of the two analysed data protection laws requires heightened participation safeguards for the private regulation instruments it addresses. An answer cannot be found in the Standardization Regulation either, since the Regulation does not differentiate its participation requirements when fundamental rights are at stake. Those are cases where extra care of participation, representation, and interest balance is more than necessary. The book does not share the optimistic view that any gatekeeping role can be played by standardization organizations,[46] since having open and transparent procedures in place is far from ensuring representation and preventing capture by some interests. This crucial aspect essentially calls for solutions such as

[43] Perhaps even laws can do little about those companies and the mishandling of information and abusive practices, unless there is proper supervision that is always one step ahead the infringing behaviour and strict enforcement by public authorities. There are however some bright exceptions of cases by supervisory authorities such as the Italian DPA fine to Facebook on Cambridge Analytica 'Cambridge Analytica: Facebook fined 1 million Euro by the Italian Dpa' Press Release Garante 28.06.2019 https://www.garanteprivacy.it/web/guest/home/docweb/-/docweb-display/docweb/9121506 [accessed 20 August 2024].

[44] Information should become available to data subjects as per what an ISO conforming processing/company stands for in broad terms.

[45] It should be noted that controllers and processors not belonging in the data intensive business described above are not to be seen as good Samaritans that do not infringe the law. Quite the opposite, they might breach their duties, and this is exactly why this study *inter alia* explored how law works on the ground, by looking at one of the available supporting instruments, standardization.

[46] Rachovitsa A, 'Rethinking Privacy Online and Human Rights: The Internet's Standardisation Bodies as the Guardians of Privacy Online in the Face of Mass Surveillance' In European Society of International Law (ESIL) 2016 Research Forum (Istanbul). 2017.

public regulatory intervention, by means of scrutiny of substantial and procedural guarantees and approval by supervisory authorities following the art 42 GDPR certification mechanism paradigm. Another preventing–less interventionist–form of oversight is the establishment of common rules among standardization bodies on standardization pertaining to fundamental rights, including data protection, and mutual peer review of the application of those rules among standardization bodies.

9.6 The Perils of the Weak Introduction of Standards in Union Data Protection Law

The analysis shows that while *travaux préparatoires* of the GDPR, contained numerous references to standardization, the final text has reduced those to a handful of direct references in relation to accreditation, certification, right to object, and standardized icons. The ePrivacy Directive refers to standardization mainly in relation to the terminal equipment of users, while the EC Proposal for an ePrivacy Regulation relates standards to the same matter with a broader scope. Those references are on the one hand acknowledgments of standards by the public regulator, but admittedly weak, in that they are limited in scope and they largely leave choices on content, requirements, design, purpose of standards to the Commission or the standardization bodies.

The weak endorsement is perhaps a signal by the EU data protection legislator about the difficulty to control (by regulating in the data protection law) standardization in the field and set rules and conditions for the development of standards in data protection. Unlike other private regulation instruments, standardization is a private regulation instrument with a heavy load related to the semi-autonomy of standardization as a private ordering; that is a network of private actors with its own procedures and internal regulations, the Standardization Regulation which addresses aspects of European standardization, a strong history of use of standards for public interest in the New Approach legislation and the growing CJEU jurisprudence on the nature and effects of standards. This 'heavy load', on the one hand offers a framework of procedural legitimacy guarantees, but on the other hand it can allow (data protection) standards to take their own shape and become a different instrument than the one the public regulator originally envisaged by including standards in eg the data protection law. By different is meant both in terms of content, given the flexibility for example of the ESO to determine the content of mandated harmonized standards, and effects, as harmonizsed standards may have *de facto* binding effects and considered part of EU law.[47] Especially in terms of effects, the GDPR assigns very specific—limited admittedly—effects to certifications

[47] CJEU, Case C-613/14 *James Elliot* (n 22).

and codes of conduct,[48] which it thoroughly regulates, something that could possibly escape the control of the public regulator when including more systematic references to standardization in the data protection law and a different legal significance to standards.

Standards may be developed autonomously and used by controllers and processors independently of their introduction in the data protection legislation. As a result, the weak endorsement of standardization in the EU data protection law has a negative influence on the potential uptake and usefulness of standards in data protection law, and the legal certainty and clarity with regard to their value (seventh finding).

First, the weak introduction in the data protection law allowed authorities to continue to try to fill in a gap into leveraging benefits of standards, without however being competent to formally endorse, or scrutinize and directly approve those standards.[49] Through its Opinions and recommendations, the EDPB for example in that sense, is an authoritative source, carrying *de facto* weight in controller's and processor's compliance, the impact of which is often unaccounted for.[50] Supervisory authorities speak with two voices, as regards standards in data protection law. This stance, as has also recently been acknowledged by Christofi and others, is problematic.[51] On the one hand (some) EU DPAs participate in the development of standards, for example in the ISO/IEC JTC1/SC27 with which the EDPB has a formal liaison relationship (as did its predecessor the WP29).[52] On the other hand, in its guidelines and opinions the EDPB makes elusive references to some specific standards, pointing at the direction of standardization as *a* solution, coupled however with disclaimers, generally empty of guidance or content.[53]

[48] See art 42(4) GDPR for example. The responsibility of controllers or processors to comply with the GDPR is unaffected by their adherence to a data protection certification mechanism. One regulated benefit is found in art 83 GDPR whereby adherence to codes of conduct and certifications is a factor to be considered by the supervisory authorities when imposing fines.

[49] Supervisory authorities may review standards if those are incorporated in a data protection certification mechanism of art 42 GDPR. However, there is no obligation for standards to be included in those certification mechanisms, and it is not certain how far the supervisory authorities will proceed in assessing the merits of such standard.

[50] See discussion on scientific opinions of EU agencies and bodies carrying a hidden source of power, often elevating those agencies to decision-makers on crucial issues of interpretation and application of EU law. Busuioc M, *European Agencies: Law and Practices of Accountability* (OUP Oxford 2013).

[51] However, the author does not agree with the statement that supervisory authorities give a 'blank cheque' to standardization bodies, as put forward in the article, as the WP29 and the EDPB often introduce disclaimers about the alignment with the data protection law together with endorsing statements. Christofi A and others, 'Erosion by Standardisation: Is ISO/IEC 29134: 2017 on Privacy Impact Assessment Up to (GDPR) Standard?' in Gupta M (ed), *Advances in Information Security, Privacy, and Ethics* (IGI Global 2020), 140ff.

[52] See ISO website https://www.iso.org/organization/617298.html [accessed 20 August 2024]. The type of formal liaison is Type C, which means that the EDPB can make technical contributions and actively participate in a working group.

[53] Some exceptions in that matter exist where supervisory authorities provided specific points of attention with regard to the misalignment of standards with data protection provisions they aim to cover, such as the in the case of the DNT standard. See WP29, WP29 comments in response to W3C's public

An assessment would be useful in terms of clarity, aspects of alignment and misalignment with the goals and provisions of data protection law. Alternatively, if such assessment is not in place, supervisory authorities should avoid those hesitant pointers towards standardization, which lend themselves to misinterpretation about the value of conformity to data protection standards.

This is linked to the second peril. The lack of expectation management and a clear stance in the data protection law primarily, and the supervisory authorities secondarily, has given rise to a range of misperceptions about the role of standards in data protection law. Those range from false perceptions by practitioners relating to the value for example of ISO/IEC 27701 to address surveillance from third countries in data transfers, to literature superficially looking to at standards as means to comply with the data protection law.[54]

9.7 A Coordinated Standardization Activity or a Maze of Standards?

The systematic analysis of the emergence and current development of standards in the field of data protection showed an increase in the activity of standardization bodies.

The first standards developed in mid-1990s, performed a pre-law function in that they prepared the ground for the adoption of data protection legislation in some non-EU countries. The activities in international standardization bodies evolved at a slow pace until the first decade of the 21st century. The slow pace reflects *inter alia* the disagreements of different countries[55] and their industry representatives on matters of approach regarding standards, their auditability, comprehensiveness and overall scope. In parallel, the European Standardization Organizations (ESO) and the Commission initiated some first exploratory efforts with a standardization 'mandate' to identify any areas for standardization,[56] the Initiative for Privacy Standardization in Europe (IPSE) a multi-stakeholder platform hosted by CEN,

consultation on the W3C Last Call Working Draft, 24 April 2014, Tracking Preference Expression (DNT) (6 June 2014).

[54] Tzolov T, 'One model for implementation GDPR based on ISO standards.' in *2018 International Conference on Information Technologies (InfoTech)*, 1–3. (IEEE, 2018). While such literature may have its own value, especially in providing practical guidance to regulatees, it misses one essential step: an in-depth assessment of the various data protection related standards in relation to the GDPR, or else the limitations of standardization stemming from the data protection law as its legal basis. Without this essential assessment, the outcomes of analyses contained in literature of such type is disconnected from the goals and substance of the data protection framework.

[55] This refers to standardization organizations that are based on the national delegation principle, such as ISO and IEC, the members of which are the national standardization organizations of countries.

[56] Mandate addressed to CEN, CENELEC and ETSI in support of the European Directive on the protection of individuals with regard to the processing of personal data and the free movement of such data, Mandate/289, (1999).

and a number of standardization deliverables in early 2000.[57] Standards related to privacy and data protection were treated (and to a significant extent until today) as an information security issue, focusing on the data, instead of the individual whose data are processed. Some significant efforts took place in international consortia and fora, such as the W3C and its Privacy Preferences Platform (P3P) and the Do Not Track (DNT) specifications, which related to processing on the Internet.

In the period from 2010 onwards, standardization organizations showed a heightened interest in the broader fields of data protection and (informational) privacy. The fundamental standard ISO/IEC 29100 providing a common vocabulary and privacy principles was adopted in 2011. Shortly after, the ISO/IEC Working Group on privacy and identity[58] started more coordinated work on standardization in the field developing several standards such as the Cloud Computing standard for Personally Identifiable Information processing by Processors and most recently the international standard on Privacy Information Management Systems.[59] New Technical Committees were established such as the ISO/PC 317 on consumer protection and privacy by design for consumer goods and services. In Europe, CEN and CENELEC established a new dedicated Cybersecurity and Data Protection Technical Committee, which *inter alia*, carries out the work for the 2015 Commission standardization request on privacy by design and by default.[60] International fora and consortia also developed ICT specifications on matters relevant to data protection such as the 2016 W3C Data Privacy Vocabulary.

All this interest and activity of standardization organizations on data protection has led to the development of a multitude of new (mainly) international and European standards which are both vertical and horizontal. Examples of vertical standardization include biometrics, RFID, and smart transportation. Horizontal standards can be broadly grouped into three categories depending on their focus and relevance to data protection; that is framework standards, data protection focused standards, and information security standards with a data protection relevance. Those standards vary on their scope and type; eg some providing a) requirements and controls, b) guidance and recommendations c) specific techniques and aim at the technical implementation of requirements, while others focus on a) quality management, and b) the information security management system of organizations.

The question is whether those standards should be viewed as providing a wide variety of options for controllers and processors in the framework of the discussed enabling and facilitating functions, or as a jungle of standards, as the Commission

[57] Those standardization deliverables, that did not have the status of a European standard, were CEN Workshop Agreements.
[58] ISO/IEC JTC1 SC 27 WG5.
[59] ISO/IEC 27018 and ISO/IEC 27701.
[60] M/530(2015).

had famously suggested in an older 2012 Communication.[61] Formal standardization organizations, and in particular ISO and CEN, have protocols and procedures embedded in the standardization process to avoid overlap in the scope of standards, and hierarchy rules ('primacy of international standardization'). However, increasing complexity[62] and the growing number of standards might undermine the function of data protection standards as meta-rules, the aim to provide homogenous rules and facilitate data protection.[63] Furthermore, differences in the regulatory nexus between existing standards in data protection and the data protection legislation, as manifested by definitional discrepancies and material scope, create a risk of excluding aspects of processing from the scope of standards, in a non-transparent manner.[64] The issue therefore is not the lack of standards, but the lack of tailored or at least tailored modules of standards for data protection law in combination with the multiple 'more or less' but not exactly relevant standards.

Thus, another finding of the analysis is the multitude of (partially) overlapping standards and the discrepancies within the data protection law should be flagged for standards aspiring to or *de facto* being used to fulfil a supportive role towards a data protection legal duty (eighth finding).

9.8 Legitimacy Questions and a Need for Taming Data Protection Standardization?

The volume of the ongoing standardization activity and the growing use of standards by data controllers and processors raises questions about the power of the private actors involved in those activities. Although standardization (and standards) and the regulation of data protection law, including its purpose to protect rights and freedoms, and in particular the right of art 8 CFREU, are not incompatible or problematic in principle, there are issues that present significant and less significant challenges.

These issues stem from the predominantly private nature of data protection standardization and its actors. As suggested by Senden and other experts along the same lines, there are two main reasons to address legitimacy issues of

[61] Communication from the Commission to the European Parliament, the Council, the European Economic and Social Committee and the Committee of the Regions 'Unleashing the Potential of Cloud Computing in Europe', COM/2012/0529 final.

[62] This is not a risk only for standards, but also other private regulation instruments in data protection such as data protection certification mechanisms as highlighted by Hornung and Bauer. Hornung G and Bauer S, 'Privacy Through Certification?: The New Certification Scheme of the General Data Protection Regulation.' in Rott P (ed), *Certification–Trust, Accountability, Liability* (Springer 2019), 109.

[63] Gleeson NC and Walden I, 'It's a Jungle Out There'?: Cloud Computing, Standards and the Law' (2014) 5 European Journal of Law and Technology, 2.

[64] The lack of transparency could be due to the exclusion of aspects as a matter of non-identical or equivalent definitions, and thus not outlined in for example in the 'scope' clause of a data protection standard.

standardization.[65] The first is the public dimension of the use of standards in support of public policy goals such as the protection of health, environment, safety, and data protection. Second, standards, although generally voluntary and in the realm of soft law, may have *de facto* binding results, when companies have no viable alternative than to conform to a standard.

European harmonized standards (Stream 1), especially those under the New Approach, are subject to a richer network of safeguards than committee-based standards (Stream 2) that are *ex post* facto integrated in the EU legal order. European harmonized standards are subject to several procedural safeguards imposed by the Standardization Regulation, the internal regulations of the European Standardization Organizations, but also the specific laws which prescribe the development and use of standards, such as the New Approach legislation. Committee-based standards, and especially the ones from international standardization bodies have incorporated good governance principles in their internal regulations and codes of conduct or ethics. As regards market-based standards (Stream 3), those are not developed by what the Standardization Regulation lists as recognized standardization bodies, which presumably abide by principles such as openness, transparency, and consensus via their internal regulations. As a result, the Standardization Regulation offers limited recognition to Stream 3 specifications and thus offers a few channels into entering the EU legal order. The analysis however showed that even though in principle Stream 3 activity is considered as offering fewer procedural safeguards, it actually depends on a specific body. Some of those in fact, such as the W3C example analysed in this book, while falling short in terms of several aspects in comparison to procedures of recognized standardization bodies (eg consultation rounds and complaints mechanisms), they might offer good examples in terms of other aspects. In the case of W3C, transparency of the procedure and privacy review of every W3C specification were such good examples.[66] An interesting case is the mixed Stream 4 standards, whereby a committee-based standard is introduced in the formalized co-development mode and becomes a harmonized standard. Such standards are not subject to the Standardization Regulation during their development. When however, they are adopted as a European standard by the ESO and they are put forward in fulfilment of a standardization request, these standards are subject to the scrutiny mechanism of the Standardization Regulation.[67]

[65] Senden L, 'Towards a More Holistic Legitimacy Approach to Technical Standardisation in the EU,' in Eliantonio M and Cauffman C (eds), *The Legitimacy of Standardisation as a Regulatory Technique* (Edward Elgar Publishing 2020).

[66] The latter point, namely introducing privacy or data protection related reviews in the standardization processes, has been recommended by Danezis and others in an ENISA Report already since 2014, Danezis G and others 'Privacy and data protection by design-from policy to engineering.' arXiv preprint arXiv:1501.03726 (2015).

[67] Standardization Regulation art 10(5).

In data protection, the General Data Protection Regulation includes a direct dated reference to the international conformity assessment standard EN ISO/IEC 17065 (Stream 2), which is developed outside the auspices of the Commission and the Standardization Regulation. This standard, before being referenced in the GDPR, was adopted as European,[68] not by the Union regulator, but by the ESO on the basis of inter-organizational collaboration agreements between ISO and its European counterpart, CEN. Thus, without being part of the co-development mode under Stream 1 or 4, which essentially means without a public regulator assessing aspects of its throughput legitimacy, the standard became part of the GDPR and a mandatory part of any accreditation assessment of art 43(2) GDPR.

For standardization in data protection, the threshold was set by the safeguards the GDPR requires for other private regulation instruments such as certifications, codes of conduct, and Binding Corporate Rules. The GDPR procedural safeguards for private regulation instruments are not one-to-one met by European harmonized standards and international standards integrated in the EU legal order. Overall harmonized standards provide a stronger framework of guarantees than international standards. Another distinction is relevant. As mentioned, under the GDPR, standards may operate as self-standing private regulation instruments or be embedded in one of the other regulated private instruments such as certifications. This distinction is important because in the first case, standards as a self-standing instrument suffer from lack of scrutiny from data protection supervisory authorities and the other safeguards of the GDPR, such as administrative and judicial redress. On the other hand, standards embedded in a data protection certification mechanism per art 42 GDPR or code of conduct per art 40 GDPR, are indirectly subjected to the GDPR system of safeguards. In parallel, those other private regulation mechanisms attach a soft enforcement effect on standards.[69]

Despite those challenges, one cannot speak of incompatibility of standardization with the attainment of data protection goals, prescribed in the Union data protection law. But there is certainly a need for *framing* and regulating the scope, agenda, alignment, and other aspects co-determining the result, and influencing the role of standards in data protection, its materialization and the legitimacy of the standardization process and outcomes (ninth finding). The need for *framing* is becoming more prominent for two reasons. First, the work of standardization bodies in the field is rapidly evolving and the Union regulator (the Commission in this case) continues to issue standardization requests linked to data protection and the Union legislation, as recent examples show.[70] Second, the mix of mechanisms

[68] The standard was adopted as European, thus EN, but not harmonized standard, since it did not go through the co-development mode.

[69] Terpan F, 'Soft Law in the European Union—The Changing Nature of EU Law' (2014) 21 European Law Journal 68.

[70] A Commission Implementing Decision requesting the development of harmonized standards for drones based on the relevant New Approach legislation makes explicit reference to the GDPR 'principles'

for integration in the Union order, the different development modes and degrees of the involvement of public regulator, and the variety of binding and non-binding instruments which provide the basis for the recognition of standards, raise questions of legal certainty, foreseeability, and ultimately conferral of powers to private regulators.

Another finding of this research is that standardization efforts, structures, and activities should not be treated as one whole; speaking of standardization as a homogenous ordering disregards pluralism *within* the ordering. Standardization linked to data protection comes in a variety of scopes, procedures, safeguards, as indicated by the identified Streams and legal bases/forms of incorporation in the Union law, which ultimately attribute a different meaning to the concept of standard, despite shared characteristics such as voluntary character. The study shed light to those distinctions by analysing the standardization activities and different types of existing data protection standards that may obtain legal significance for the Union legal order.

The analysis of the work of the European Standardization Organization's technical work on data protection standards through the Joint Technical Committee 13 showed that in the field of data protection, the ESO largely operate in the shadow of international standardization bodies. The capacity of the newly established CEN/CLC/JTC13 to grow apart, if necessary, from its ISO sibling, still needs to be proven in practice. This is highlighted by the fact that until today the European Technical Committee JTC13 has only published standards which are adoptions of existing international standards, even though recent developments show that this situation might change.[71] In principle, the Technical Committees of CEN/CENELEC and the relevant ISO/IEC are only linked with a liaison connection,

of data protection by design and by default which however is not New Approach legislation. The problem here is that there is no obligation of the ESO to consider the full spectrum of the requirements and principles underlying art 25 GDPR. Besides, the data protection references in the Commission Implementing Decision are admittedly confusing, as they combine potentially conflicting goals, namely identification for 'security and law enforcement needs' with the 'respect for privacy' and protection of personal data'. Any standards to be developed based on this request, should the request be accepted by the ESO, would implicitly enforce data protection requirements, for all the entities conforming to those harmonized standards, introduced with incomplete references, under uncertain legal status, due to the New Approach and non-New Approach legislation to which the request refers. The Standardization request based on New Approach legislation on drones (Unmanned Aircraft Systems) requires the standards to be developed to 'the design of the technical solutions proposed shall take into account the principles of privacy by design and by default outlined in Article 25 of Regulation 2016/679'. Commission Implementing Decision of 11.9.2020 on a standardization request to the European Committee for Standardization as regards unmanned aircraft systems intended to be operated in the 'open' category of operations in support of Commission Delegated Regulation (EU) 2019/945 ('M/567').

[71] See website of the JTC13 https://standards.cen.eu/dyn/www/f?p=204:32:0::::FSP_ORG_ID,FSP_LANG_ID:2307986,25&cs=1F4A71C19873519CC81C4B2C031CF3CF5 [accessed 20 August 2024]. Recently, the JTC13 announced plans for the adoption of an EU specific standard (work item JT013033) specifying 'baseline requirements for demonstrating compliance with the European personal data protection normative framework'.

where in broad terms one follows each other's ongoing and plans for future work. However, it is logical that members of both committees would be comprised of the same entities, namely national standardization bodies of EU Member States. The international Technical Committees obviously enlist members from standardization bodies worldwide, including bodies with a strong standard-setting history such as the US ANSI[72] and the Japanese JISC.[73] It was clearly beyond of the scope of the book to explore the mechanics of the interrelationship between recognized standardization organizations. However, those observations flag that standard setting is multidimensional and complex, and prior to using standards for regulatory purposes, such issues should be considered and in due course regulated with public regulation. An example of such an issue which could be regulated is the criteria with which the ESOs adopt as European standards, standards from other recognized standardization organizations.

A last point on this matter, is a distinction that should be made, and deserves dedicated exploration in future empirical research, between a) the standardization body as an organization responsible for accepting standardization requests, holding the secretariat of Technical Committees, but not actually intervening in terms of content discussions in the development of standards, and b) the experts of the Technical Committees drafting the standards, appointed by various stakeholders and mainly the industry. It should be explored to what extent standardization organizations are able (in terms of expertise) and should be able to monitor and perform some sort of quality control over the work of Technical Committee experts, and are in the position to filter unsuitable or inappropriate input.

9.9 Additional Thoughts and Future Research Outlook

Throughout this book, standards being a private regulation instrument necessitated a look at the recognition rules and whether and to what extent standards are compatible with and integrated in data protection law or soft law guidance from the public regulator. The research showed that standards as an outcome of a private regulation process are extra-legal, *transplants* in Union law,[74] in that they are developed by private normative orderings which interact, and intertwine but are not dependent on the Union public regulator. When integrated in the Union

[72] The American National Standards Institute (ANSI) was established in 1918 and holds the secretariat of the Information Technology Joint Technical Committee of ISO and IEC ISO/IEC/JTC1.

[73] The Japanese Engineering Standards Committee was established in 1921 and is a participating member of the ISO/IEC/JTC1/SC27 committee on information security, cybersecurity and privacy protection. See https://www.iso.org/member/1835.html [20 August 2024]

[74] The term 'legal transplant' in terms of self-regulation was used by Van Gestel in the context of environmental law. Van Gestel examined certification of emissions trading as a 'transplantation of economic principles' to legislation providing rules for emissions trading. Van Gestel R, 'Self-regulation and environmental law.' [2005] 9 Electronic Journal of Comparative Law 1, fn.12.

public legal order however, conceptually standards are deployed as *instruments* to serve the goals of Union law or policy. Standards are instruments used for shaping, improving, operationalizing legislation or policy, as examined in this book. They are used primarily as a market instrument, but they may perform regulatory functions for data protection, independently of any (parallel) market function.

Even if standards are to be construed as extra-legal instruments, the data protection law, ie the GDPR, ePrivacy legislation, and additionally the Radio Equipment Directive, have formally invited standards to be integrated in data protection, and become part of the regulatory toolbox. The plurality of this integration is manifested in the different integration modes of standards in support of data protection law, as part of Commission acts, approved certifications, directly, or other means.

Nevertheless, the integration, the roles assigned to standards by the data protection legislation and the roles claimed by standardization bodies themselves expressed with the ongoing expansive agenda covering different aspects of data protection rules, is one step towards speaking of a supplementary role of standards to data protection legislation in the Union.

To make standards as a private regulation instrument work *for* data protection law, there are still essential steps to be taken, by regulators, supervisory authorities, standardization organizations, experts participating in technical committees, and the civil society.

First, the alignment of data protection standards with the EU data protection law is quintessential. Simply put, there cannot be an instrument aiming at helping controllers and processors comply with the law, if it is not specifically designed to do so. The research for this book showed for example that often standards interpret concepts differently than EU data protection law, such as corporate risks as opposed to risks of the rights and freedoms of persons. These differences need to be flattened out by designing European data protection standards tailored to the Union data protection law. *De minimis* the differences should be made visible and transparent. In general, not only data protection focused standards but all standards should be reviewed from a data protection perspective, following the example of W3C.

Second, given the non-compulsory nature of compliance to standards in data protection, there needs to be a clear reason for controllers/processors and/or data subjects to deviate from the existence and implementation of those standards. One reason to follow standards is the actual added value of standards for regulatees, their enabling and facilitating nature and different functions. Providing the state of the art, techniques for data security measures, methodologies for risk and impact assessment are useful for controllers and processors. Especially taking into account the importance of data security for the fundamental right to protection of personal data, as put forward by the CJEU, the relevance of standards is prominent.

Another reason would be an incentive due to a *regulated benefit* stemming from the data protection law; standards enjoying *de jure* legal effects, instead of practical or coincidental *de facto* effects. One such effect would be similar to the one foreseen for approved data protection certification mechanism, the adherence to which may be a mitigating factor for administrative fines per art 83 GDPR. Another possibility would be a presumption of conformity with the legal requirements in case of harmonized standards following the New Approach. Currently, however, the current data protection law does not prescribe such benefits. Especially in the case of the presumption of conformity with the data protection law there are substantial differences with the New Approach rationale and style of Directives: the data protection law regulates behaviour instead of products; the law is prescriptive and it is rightly *not* reduced to a minimum of vague essential requirements like the New Approach legislation; the data protection law does not concern entry conditions to the Internal Market but primarily the protection of the rights and freedoms of individuals.

Third, supervisory authorities currently often speak with two voices, as explained in the previous section. This intermediate stance sends mixed signals to controllers and processors. One first step is to provide a clear explanation of any value of using those standards, point out specific points of attention or deviation from the legal requirements, and clarify whether and how standards play a role in the audits of controllers and processors performed by supervisory authorities. At an institutional level, the liaisons are indeed ensuring that the EDPB is up to date when it comes new developments in data protection standardization; and vice-versa, the Technical Committees have the tremendous opportunity to receive feedback and comments by the supervisory authorities. The desirability and conditions of intensification of such a relationship could be further explored in future research. For example, the UK Information Commissioner has set up a Regulatory Sandbox, a programme aimed at helping companies working with personal data as their core business, to develop their technologies in a manner compliant to the data protection legislation.[75] Such type of Public Private Partnerships is interesting to be further explored as a framework for standardization. Other approaches could be a *sui generis* membership with voting rights for supervisory authorities, thus going beyond the national delegation principle in CEN and CENELEC, redesigning relevant laws to accommodate an oversight role of supervisory authorities over data protection standardization activity that has the EU data protection law as its legal basis, or a dedicated EU standardization institution[76] are possibilities to be further explored. Issues of function creep for the supervisory authorities, competence and expansion of their current mandate should also be part of such explorations.

[75] See ICO https://ico.org.uk/for-organizations/the-guide-to-the-sandbox/ [accessed 20 August 2024].

[76] This was proposed in the legislative process of the Standardization Regulation.

Fourth, the implementation of specifications and their enforceability is an issue to be further explored. Default technical implementations of (ICT) standards would probably change the voluntary character of standards, which is their inherent characteristic. However, voluntary adherence but with enforceable effects seems to be a promising model.

Fifth, to enable societal participation, financial barriers for societal stakeholders, such as civil rights associations, academia, supervisory authorities should be waived. Accessibility to documentation under confidentiality agreements and to meetings (via exploring alternative methods such as remote participation) should be enabled for such participants.

As regards further research, this book shows the range of development modes that standardization brings to the forefront of regulation.[77] From theoretical perspective, political scientists, economists, or other disciplines could further test the findings of this book by looking into other theories and economic efficiency as a motivation of the public regulator to use standardization in the regulation of data protection, or for example nudge theory to explore the facilitating and enabling functions of data protection standardization.[78]

The aspect of how the debate on legitimacy of standardization impacts public regulation and invites rethinking the legitimacy aspects of public regulation is an interesting topic for further research using the findings of this research as a starting point. Such aspects could include the Commission's decision to fund standardization activity that might not be aligned with its standardization requests, the passive acceptance of the public regulator that standards are available for a fee, the foundations and the use of the decisional power of the Commission to adopt or not binding acts on the basis of (data protection) secondary Union law, and the decision of supervisory authorities to spend resources actively participating in international standardization activity that bears no clear connection with Union or Member State legislation within their competence. A second issue to be explored building on this research and other efforts is to explore the external dimension of this topic, namely the role of standards as data protection bridges[79] between the EU and third countries. This aspect is also closely linked to the transnational character of international standards, as standardization offers a forum which is not confined by geographical borders. The analysed standardization activity in fact showed that international standardization organizations and fora are particularly active in the field of data protection and produce standards that incorporate concepts and requirements found in regional legislation (e.g. GDPR).

[77] Marsden CT, *Internet Co-Regulation: European law, regulatory governance and legitimacy in cyberspace* (Cambridge University Press 2011), 242.
[78] Acquisti A, 'Nudging privacy: The behavioral economics of personal information.' (2009) 7IEEE Security & Privacy, 82.
[79] Abramatic J-F, Bellamy B, Callahan ME, and others, *Privacy Bridges: EU and US Privacy Experts In Search of Transatlantic Privacy Solutions* (2015).

9.10 Final Remarks

To conclude, standardization in the field of data protection in the Union is emerging and assigned a spot in the regulatory landscape by the Union data protection law, alongside regulators such as the Commission and the public supervisory authorities. Standards as a private regulation instrument supplement the Union data protection law by enabling and facilitating controllers' and processors' duties, as communication vehicles for the preferences of data subjects with regard to the processing of their personal data, and as meta-rules for the implementation of the law. However, data protection standardization does not remain unaffected by the procedural legitimacy issues of standardization, largely attributed to its (semi-) autonomous nature and independence from the Union legal order, and its private nature. Ultimately, the value of standardization in the field of data protection will be judged on the ground, by the uptake of standards, the development of new standards, the public regulators' position, and future case law on judicial reviewability of technical standards.

Bibliography

Books, Book Chapters, Journal Articles

Abbott KW and Snidal D, 'International "standards" and International Governance' (2001) 8 Journal of European Public Policy, 345

Abramatic J-F and others, 'Privacy Bridges: EU and US Privacy Experts In Search of Transatlantic Privacy Solutions' (2015)

Acquisti A, 'Nudging Privacy: The Behavioral Economics of Personal Information' (2009) 7 IEEE Security & Privacy, 82

Alhadeff J, Van Alsenoy B, and Dumortier J, 'The Accountability Principle in Data Protection Regulation: Origin, Development and Future Directions' in Ilten C and others (eds) *Managing Privacy through Accountability* (Palgrave Macmillan 2012)

Ausloos J, The *Right to Erasure in EU Data Protection Law* (OUP 2020)

Aziz MAB and Wilson C, 'Johnny Still Can't Opt-out: Assessing the IAB CCPA Compliance Framework' (2024) 2024 Proceedings on Privacy Enhancing Technologies, 349

Barber NW, 'Legal Pluralism and the European Union' (2006) 12 European Law Journal, 306

Barnard FM, *Democratic Legitimacy: Plural Values and Political Power*, vol 34 (McGill-Queen's Press-MQUP 2001)

Beisheim M and Dingwerth K, Procedural Legitimacy and Private Transnational Governance: Are the Good Ones Doing Better? Berlin DFG-Sonderforschungsbereich 700, Governance in Räumen begrenzter Staatlichkeit 2008

Beniger J, *The Control Revolution: Technological and Economic Origins of the Information Society* (Harvard University Press 2009)

Bennett C and Mulligan DK, 'The Governance of Privacy Through Codes of Conduct: International Lessons for U.S. Privacy Policy' [2012] SSRN Electronic Journal

Bennett CJ, 'International privacy standards: Can accountability ever be adequate?' [2010] Privacy Laws & Business International Newsletter

Bennett CJ, 'An International Standard for Privacy Protection,' *Proceedings of the tenth conference on Computers, freedom and privacy: challenging the assumptions* (ACM 2000)

Bennett CJ, 'Arguments for the Standardization of Privacy Protection Policy: Canadian Initiatives and American and International Responses' (1997) 14 Government Information Quarterly, 351

Bennett CJ, *Regulating Privacy* (Cornell University Press 1992)

Bennett CJ, 'Un historique de la normalisation dans le domaine de protection de la vie privée: document d' information', Background paper prepared for the Canadian Standards Council, 2007

Bennett CJ and Bayley R, 'Privacy Protection in the Era of 'Big Data': Regulatory Challenges and Social Assessments' in Van der Sloot B, Broeders D, and Schrijvers E (eds) *Exploring the Boundaries of Big Data* (WWR and Amsterdam UP 2016) 205

Bennett CJ and Raab C, *The Governance of Privacy: Policy Instruments in Global Perspective* (MIT Press 2006)

Bennett CJ and Raab C, 'The Adequacy of Privacy: The European Union Data Protection Directive and the North American Response' (1997) 13 The Information Society, 245

Bennett ML, 'Recurring Dilemmas: The Law's Race to Keep Up with Technological Change' (2007) 2 University of Illinois Journal of Law, Technology, & Policy, 239

Bennett ML, 'How to Think about Law, Regulation and Technology: Problems with 'Technology' as a Regulatory Target' (2013) 5 Law, Innovation and Technology, 1

Benoliel D, 'Technological Standards, Inc.: Rethinking Cyberspace Regulatory Epistemology' (2004) 92 California Law Review, 1069

Berman PS, 'The Evolution of Global Legal Pluralism' (2017) 42 GWU Law School Public Law Research Paper

Bernstein S and Hannah E, 'Non-State Global Standard Setting and the WTO: Legitimacy and the Need for Regulatory Space' (2008) 11 Journal of International Economic Law, 575

Bialous SA and Yach D, 'Whose Standard Is It, Anyway? How the Tobacco Industry Determines the International Organization for Standardization (ISO) Standards for Tobacco and Tobacco Products' (2001) 10 Tobacco Control, 96

Bijlmakers S and van Calster G, 'You'd Be Surprised How Much It Costs to Look This Cheap! A Case Study of ISO 26000 on Social Responsibility,' in Delimatsis P, (ed) *The Law, Economics and Politics of International Standardisation* (Cambridge University Press 2015)

Binns R, 'Data Protection Impact Assessments: A Meta-Regulatory Approach' (2017) 7 International Data Privacy Law, 22

Binns RD, Millard D, and Harris L, 'Data Havens, or Privacy sans Frontières?' *Proceedings of the 2014 ACM conference on Web science* (ACM 2014), 273

Black J, 'Constructing and Contesting Legitimacy and Accountability in Polycentric Regulatory Regimes' (2008) 2 Regulation & Governance, 137

Black J and Murray AD, 'Regulating AI and Machine Learning: Setting the Regulatory Agenda' (2019) 10 European Journal of Law and Technology, 3

Blind K, 'The impact of standardization and standards on innovation: compendium of evidence on the effectiveness of innovation policy intervention' Nesta Working Paper No 13/15, *Manchester Institute of Innovation Research, Manchester, UK* (2013)

Bonnici JPM, *Self-Regulation in Cyberspace* (TMC Asser Press 2008)

Braithwaite J, 'Enforced Self-Regulation: A New Strategy for Corporate Crime Control' (1982) 80 Michigan Law Review, 1466

Bremer ES, 'Government Use of Standards in the United States and Abroad,' in Contreras JL (ed) *The Cambridge Handbook of Technical Standardization Law* (Cambridge University Press 2019)

Brkan M, 'The Concept of Essence of Fundamental Rights in the EU Legal Order: Peeling the Onion to Its Core' (2018) 14 European Constitutional Law Review, 332

Brkan M, 'The Essence of the Fundamental Rights to Privacy and Data Protection: Finding the Way Through the Maze of the CJEU's Constitutional Reasoning' (2019) 20 German Law Journal, 864

Brkan M, 'The Unstoppable Expansion of the EU Fundamental Right to Data Protection: Little shop of horrors?' (2016) 23 Maastricht Journal of European and Comparative Law, 812

Brownsword R,'What the World Needs Now: Techno-Regulation, Human Rights and Human Dignity' in *Global governance and the quest for justice* (Hart Publishing 2004)

Brownsword R, *Rights, Regulation, and The Technological Revolution* (OUP 2008)

Brownsword R and Goodwin MA, 'A Look at Procedural Legitimacy: The Role of Public Participation in Technology Regulation' in Brownsword R and Goodwin MA (eds) *Law and the Technologies of the Twenty-First Century* (Cambridge University Press 2012)

Bronwen M and Yeung K, *An Introduction to Law and Regulation: Text and Materials* (Cambridge University Press 2007)

Büchi M and others 'The Chilling Effects of Algorithmic Profiling: Mapping the Issues' (2020) 36 Computer Law & Security Review, 105367

Burkert H, 'Four Myths about regulating in the Information Society - A Comment' in Koops BJ and others (eds) *Starting Points for ICT Regulation. Deconstructing Prevalent Policy One-liners* (Cambridge University Press 2006)

Burton C, 'Article 32 Security of Processing,' in Kuner C, Bygrave LA, and Docksey C (eds) *The EU General Data Protection Regulation (GDPR)* (OUP New York 2020)

Busch C, 'Towards a New Approach in European Consumer Law: Standardisation and Co-Regulation in the Digital Single Market' (2016) 5 Journal of European Consumer and Market Law, 197

Busch L and Bain C, 'New! Improved? The Transformation of the Global Agrifood System' (2004) 69 Rural Sociology, 321

Busuioc M, *European Agencies: Law and Practices of Accountability* (OUP Oxford 2013)

Büthe T and Mattli W, 'Standards for Global Markets: Domestic and International Institutions,' in Enderlein H, Wälti S, Zürn M (eds) *Handbook on Multi-level Governance* (Edward Elgar Publishing 2010)

Büthe T and Mattli W, *The New Global Rulers: The Privatization of Regulation in the World Economy* (Princeton University Press 2011)

Bygrave LA, *Data Protection Law* (Wolters Kluwer Law & Business 2002)

Bygrave LA, 'Privacy and Data Protection in An International Perspective' (2010) 56 Scandinavian Studies in Law, 165

Bygrave LA and Luca T, 'Article 4(1) Personal Data' in Kuner C, Bygrave LA and Docksey C (eds) *The EU General Data Protection Regulation (GDPR): A Commentary* (OUP 2020)

Cafaggi F 'A Comparative Analysis of Transnational Private Regulation: Legitimacy, Quality, Effectiveness and Enforcement' *Quality, Effectiveness and Enforcement, EUI LAW*, 2014/15 (2014)

Cafaggi F, 'The architecture of transnational private regulation' [2011] *EUI Department of Law Working Papers* 2011/12

Cafaggi F 'The Many Features of Transnational Private Rule-Making: Unexplored Relationships between Custom, Jura Mercatorum and Gloval Private Regulation' (2015) 36 University of Pennsylvania Journal of International Law, 875

Cafaggi F, 'New Foundations of Transnational Private Regulation' (2011) 38 *Journal of Law and Society*, 20

Cafaggi F 'Transnational Private Regulation: Regulating Global Private Regulators' in Cassese S (ed) *Research Handbook on Global Administrative Law* (Edward Elgar Publishing 2016)

Cafaggi F and Janczuk A, 'Private Regulation and Legal Integration: The European Example' (2010) 12 Business and Politics, 1

Cafaggi F and Watt HM (eds), *The Regulatory Function of European Private Law* (Edward Elgar Publishing 2009)

Calliess G-P and Peer Z, *Rough Consensus and Running Code: A Theory of Transnational Private Law* (Hart Publishing 2010)

Cane P and Kritzer H, *The Oxford Handbook of Empirical Legal Research* (OUP Oxford 2010)

Cantero Gamito M, 'The Legitimacy of Standardisation as a Regulatory Technique in Telecommunications,' in Eliantonio M and Cauffman C (eds) *The Legitimacy of Standardisation as a Regulatory Technique* (Edward Elgar Publishing 2020)

Cassese S, D'Alterio E, and De Bellis M, 'The Enforcement of Transnational Private Regulation: A Fictitious Oxymoron,' in Cafaggi F (ed) *Enforcement of Transnational Regulation* (Edward Elgar Publishing 2012)

Chander A, Kaminski ME, and McGeveran W, 'Catalyzing Privacy Law' (2021) 105 Minnesota Law Review, 1733

Charatan J and Birrell E, 'Two Steps Forward and One Step Back: The Right to Opt-out of Sale under CPRA' (2024) 2024 Proceedings on Privacy Enhancing Technologies, 91

Chowdhury N and Wessel RA, 'Conceptualising Multilevel Regulation in the EU: A Legal Translation of Multilevel Governance?' (2012) 18 European Law Journal, 335

Christofi A and others, 'Erosion by Standardisation: Is ISO/IEC 29134: 2017 on Privacy Impact Assessment Up to (GDPR) Standard?' in Gupta M (ed) *Advances in Information Security, Privacy, and Ethics* (IGI Global 2020), 140

Clifford D and Ausloos J, 'Data Protection and the Role of Fairness' (2018) 37 Yearbook of European Law, 130

Clifford D, *Data Protection Law and Emotion* (OUP 2024)

Coglianese C, 'Standards and the Law' (2023) 2 Standardization: Journal of Research and Innovation, 15

Coglianese C, 'The Limits of Performance-Based Regulation' (2016) 50 University of Michigan Journal of Law Reform, 525

Colombo C and Eliantonio M, 'Harmonized Technical Standards as Part of EU Law: Juridification with a Number of Unresolved Legitimacy Concerns?' (2017) 24 Maastricht Journal of European and Comparative Law, 323

Company B, 'A Public Law Approach to Internet Standard Setting' Goettingen Journal of International Law 7 (2016) 49.

Cordeiro AM, 'Civil Liability for Processing of Personal Data in the GDPR' (2019) 5 European Data Protection Law Review, 492

Crepax T, 'Global Privacy Control and Portability of Privacy Preferences Through Browser Settings: A Comparative Study of Techno-Legal Challenges Under the Ccpa/Cpra and the Gdpr' Available at SSRN: https://ssrn.com/abstract = 4710372 (accessed 20 August 2024)

Creutz K, 'Law versus Codes of Conduct: Between Convergence and Conflict,' in Klabbers J and Piiparinen T (eds) *Normative Pluralism and International Law* (Cambridge University Press 2013)

Cuccuru P, 'Interest Representation in European Standardisation: The Case of CEN and CENELEC' Amsterdam Law School Research Paper 2019-52 (2019)

Cuccuru P, 'Regulating by Request: On the Role and Status of the Standardisation Mandate under the New Approach,' in Eliantonio M and Cauffman C (eds) *The Legitimacy of Standardisation as a Regulatory Technique* (Edward Elgar Publishing 2020)

Damian G, Reutimann K and Tamò-Larrieux A, 'GDPR Bypass by Design? Transient Processing of Data Under the GDPR' (2019) 9 International Data Privacy Law (2019), 285

Danezis G and others 'Privacy and Data Protection by Design-from Policy to Engineering' arXiv preprint arXiv:1501.03726 (2015)

Dalla Corte L, 'On Proportionality in the Data Protection Jurisprudence of the CJEU' (2022) 12 International Data Privacy Law 12, 259

Davies M 'Legal Pluralism' in Cane P and Kritzer H (eds), *The Oxford Handbook of Empirical Legal Research* (OUP 2010)

De Hert P, 'The Right to Protection of Personal Data. Incapable of Autonomous Standing in the Basic EU Constituting Documents?' (2015) 31 Utrecht Journal of International and European Law, 1

De Hert P and Gutwirth S, 'Data Protection in the Case Law of Strasbourg and Luxemburg: Constitutionalisation in Action,' in Gutwirth S and others (eds) *Reinventing Data Protection?* (Springer Netherlands 2009)

De Hert P and Gutwirth S 'Privacy, Data Protection and Law Enforcement. Opacity of the Individual and Transparency of Power' in Claes E, Duff A, and Gutwirth S (eds) *Privacy and the criminal law* (Intersentia 2006)

De Hert P and others, 'The Right to Data Portability in the GDPR: Towards User-Centric Interoperability of Digital Services' (2018) 34 Computer Law & Security Review, 193

De Hert P and Papakonstantinou V, 'Three Scenarios for International Governance of Data Privacy: Towards an International Data Privacy Organization, Preferably a UN agency' (2013) 9 *ISJLP*, 271

De Hert P and Papakonstantinou V, 'The New General Data Protection Regulation: Still a Sound System for the Protection of Individuals?' (2016) 32 Computer Law & Security Review, 179

De Hert P, Papakonstantinou V, and Kamara I, 'The Cloud Computing Standard ISO/IEC 27018 through the Lens of the EU Legislation on Data Protection' (2016) 32 Computer Law & Security Review, 16

De Terwagne C, 'Article Right to Rectification' in Kuner C, Bygrave LA, and Docksey C (eds) *The EU General Data Protection Regulation (GDPR): A Commentary* (OUP 2020)

De Vries HJ, *Standardization: A Business Approach to the Role of National Standardization Organizations* (Springer 1999)

De Vries K and van Dijk N, 'A Bump in the Road. Ruling Out Law from Technology,' in *Ius Gentium: Comparative Perspectives on Law and Justice* (Springer 2013)

De Vries SA, 'Balancing Fundamental Rights with Economic Freedoms According to the European Court of Justice' (2013) 9 Utrecht Law Review, 169

Delimatsis P, 'Introduction: Continuity and Change in International Standardisation' in Delimatsis P (ed) *The Law, Economics and Politics of International Standardisation* (Cambridge University Press 2015)
Delimatsis P, 'Into the abyss of standard-setting: an analysis of procedural and substantive guarantees within the International Organization for Standardization (ISO)' EUI RSCAS, 2015/35, Global Governance Programme-170, Global Economics (2015)
Delimatsis P, '"Relevant International Standards" and "Recognised Standardisation Bodies" under the TBT Agreement,' in Delimatsis P (ed) *The Law, Economics and Politics of International Standardisation* (Cambridge University Press 2015)
Demetzou K, 'Data Protection Impact Assessment: A Tool for Accountability and the Unclarified Concept of 'High Risk' in the General Data Protection Regulation' (2019) 35 Computer Law & Security Review 105342
DiMaggio PJ and Powell W, 'The Iron Cage Revisited: Institutional Isomorphism and Collective Rationality in Organizational Fields' in Powell W and DiMaggio PJ (eds), T*he New Institutionalism in Organizational Analysis* (The University of Chicago Press 1991)
Dingermann K and Kottmann M, 'Legal Opinion on the European System of Harmonised Standards' Commissioned by the German Federal Ministry for Economic Affairs and Energy (BMWi) 2020
Doty N, and Mulligan D, 'Internet Multistakeholder Processes and Techno-Policy Standards: Initial Reflections on Privacy at the World Wide Web Consortium' (2013) 11 Journal on Telecommunications and High Technology Law, 11, 135
Doty N, 'Reviewing for privacy in Internet and Web standard-setting' (2015) IEEE Security and Privacy Workshops, 185
Drechsler L and Kamara I, 'Essential Equivalence as a Benchmark for International Data Transfers after Schrems II,' in Kosta E and Leenes (eds) *Research Handbook on EU Data Protection Law* (Edward Elgar Publishing 2022)
Drechsler L, 'What Is Equivalent? A Probe into GDPR Adequacy Based on EU Fundamental Rights' (21 February 2019), Jusletter IT 21
Eijlander P, 'Possibilities and constraints in the use of self-regulation and co-regulation in legislative policy: Experiences in the Netherlands-Lessons to be learned for the EU?' *European Journal of Comparative Law* 9, 1 (2005)
Eliantonio M, 'Judicial Control of the EU Harmonized Standards: Entering a Black Hole?' (2017) 44 Legal Issues of Economic Integration, 395
Engel A, *The Choice of Legal Basis for Acts of the European Union* (Springer International Publishing 2018)
Engle Merry S, 'Legal Pluralism' (1988) 22 Law & Society Review, 869
Esty DC, 'Good Governance at the Supranational Scale: Globalizing Administrative Law' (2006) 115 The Yale Law Journal, 1490
Evans DS, 'The Online Advertising Industry: Economics, Evolution, and Privacy' (2009) 23 Journal of Economic Perspectives, 37
Frantziou E, 'The Horizontal Effect of the Charter of Fundamental Rights of the EU: Rediscovering the Reasons for Horizontality' (2015) 21 European Law Journal, 657
Friedman B (ed) *Human values and the design of computer technology* (vol 72 (Center for the Study of Language and Inf 2004).
Garcia DL, 'Standard Setting in the United States: Public and Private Sector Roles' (1992) 43 Journal of the American Society for Information Science, 531
Gellert R, *The Risk-Based Approach to Data Protection* (OUP 2020)
Gellman R and Dixon P, 'Failures of Privacy Self-Regulation in the United States,' in Wright D and De Hert P, (eds) *Enforcing Privacy: Regulatory, Legal and Technological Approaches* (Springer 2016)
Georgieva L and Schmidl M, 'Article Powers' in Kuner C, Bygrave LA, and Docksey C (eds) *The EU General Data Protection Regulation (GDPR): A Commentary* (OUP 2020)
Gezinski LB and Gonzalez-Pons KM, 'Sex Trafficking and Technology: A Systematic Review of Recruitment and Exploitation' (2022) 10 Journal of Human Trafficking, 497

Gleeson NC and Walden I, 'It's a Jungle Out There?: Cloud Computing, Standards and the Law' (2014) 5 European Journal of Law and Technology, 2

Glinski C and Rott P, 'Deficient Standards by European Standardisation Organisations: Between State Liability and Tort Liability,' in Eliantonio M and Cauffman C (eds) *The Legitimacy of Standardisation as a Regulatory Technique* (Edward Elgar Publishing 2020)

Glinski C and Rott P, 'Regulating Certification Bodies in the Field of Medical Devices: The PIP Breast Implants Litigation and Beyond' (2019) 27 *European Review of Private Law*

González EG, De Hert P and Papakonstantinou V, 'The Proposed ePrivacy Regulation: The Commission's and The Parliament's Drafts At A Crossroads?' in Hallinan D, Leenes R, Gutwirth S, De Hert P (eds) D*ata Protection and Privacy. Data Protection and Democracy* (Hart Publishing 2020)

González Fuster G, 'Fighting for Your Right to What Exactly-The Convoluted Case Law of the EU Court of Justice on Privacy and/Or Personal Data Protection' (2014) 2 Birkbeck Law Review, 263

González Fuster G, 'How Uninformed is the average data subject? A quest for Benchmarks in EU Personal Data Protection' (2014) 19 *IDP.* Revista de Internet, Derecho y Política, 92

González Fuster G, *The Emergence of Personal Data Protection as a Fundamental Right of the EU* (vol 16 Springer 2014)

Graef I, Husovec M, and Purtova N, 'Data Portability and Data Control: Lessons for an Emerging Concept in EU Law' (2018) 19 German Law Journal, 1359

Graz J-C, and Nölke A, 'The Limits of Transnational Private Governance,' in Guzzini S and Neumann I (eds) *The Diffusion of Power in Global Governance: International Political Economy Meets Foucault* (Springer 2012)

Greenleaf G, and Waters N, 'APEC's CBPRs in Operation for Two Years: Low Take-Up, and Credibility Issues' Privacy Laws & Business International Report, 129

Griffiths J, 'What Is Legal Pluralism?' (1986) 18 The Journal of Legal Pluralism and Unofficial Law, 1

Gutwirth S and De Hert P, 'Privacy, Data Protection and Law Enforcement. Opacity of the Individual and Transparency of Power' (2022) 18 Direito Público

Gutwirth S, De Hert P, and De Sutter L, 'The Trouble with Technology Regulation : Why Lessig's 'Optimal Mix' Will Not Work,' in Brownsword R and Yeung K (eds) *Regulating Technologies: Legal Futures, Regulatory Frames and Technological Fixes* (Hart Publishing 2008)

Hallstrom KT, *Organizing International Standardization: ISO and the IASC in Quest of Authority* (Edward Elgar Publishing 2004)

Hameleers M, 'My Reality Is More Truthful Than Yours: Radical Right-Wing Politicians' and Citizens' Construction of "Fake" and "Truthfulness" on Social Media—Evidence From the United States and The Netherlands' (2020) 14 *International Journal of Communication*, 18

Harcourt A, Christou G, and Simpson S, *Global Standard Setting in Internet Governance* (OUP 2020)

Henson S and Reardon T, 'Private Agri-Food Standards: Implications for Food Policy and the Agri-Food System' (2005) 30 Food Policy, 241

Heyvaert V, 'The Transnationalization of Law: Rethinking Law Through Transnational Environmental Regulation' (2017) 6 Transnational Environmental Law, 205

Hijmans H, 'Article Subject Matter and Scope' in Kuner C, Bygrave LA, and Docksey C (eds) *The EU General Data Protection Regulation (GDPR): A Commentary* (OUP 2020)

Hijmans H, *The European Union as Guardian of Internet Privacy: The Story of Art 16 TFEU* (Springer 2016)

Hildebrandt M and Tielemans L, 'Data Protection by Design and Technology Neutral Law' (2013) 29 Computer Law & Security Review, 509

Hirsch D, 'The Law and Policy of Online Privacy: Regulation, Self-regulation, or Co-regulation' (2010) 34 *Seattle University Law Review*, 439

Hirsch, D 'Going Dutch: Collaborative Dutch Privacy Regulation and the Lessons It Holds for US Privacy Law' (2013) Michigan State Law Review 83

Hon WK, Millard C, and Walden I, 'Negotiating Cloud Contracts - Looking at Clouds from Both Sides Now' (2012) 16 Stanford Technology Law Review, 107

Hoofnagle CJ, 'Do Not Track Dilemma DNT ~= Do Not Advertise' Technology Academics Policy TAP (10 February 2011)

Hoofnagle CJ, 'Designing for consent' (2008) 7 Journal of European Consumer and Market Law, 162

Hoofnagle CJ, 'Privacy Self-Regulation: A Decade of Disappointment,' in Winn J (ed) *Consumer Protection in the Age of the Information Economy* (Routledge 2006)

Hoofnagle C, 'Should Regulation Be "Technology Neutral"?' (2 February 2018) https://hoofnagle.berkeley.edu/2018/02/02/should-regulation-be-technology-neutral/ (accessed 20 August 2024).

Hoofnagle CJ, van der Sloot B, and Borgesius FZ, 'The European Union General Data Protection Regulation: What It Is and What It Means' (2019) 28 Information and Communications Technology Law, 65

Hornung G and Bauer S, 'Privacy Through Certification?: The New Certification Scheme of the General Data Protection Regulation', in Rott P (ed) *Certification–Trust, Accountability, Liability* (Springer 2019)

Human S and others, 'Data Protection and Consenting Communication Mechanisms: Current Open Proposals and Challenges' *2022 IEEE European Symposium on Security and Privacy Workshops* (IEEE 2022)

Hustinx P, 'The role of self-regulation in the scheme of data protection' 13th Conference of Data Protection Commissioners, Strasbourg 1991

Hustinx P, 'Co-regulation or Self-regulation by Public and Private Bodies – The Case of Data Protection' [2002] Freundesgabe Büllesbach, 283

Hustinx P, *EU Data Protection Law: The Review of Directive 95/46/EC and the General Data Protection Regulation* (2014) https://www.statewatch.org/media/documents/news/2014/sep/eu-2014-09-edps-data-protection-article.pdf (accessed 20 August 2024)

Iversen EJ, Vedel T, and Werle R, 'Standardization and the Democratic Design of Information and Communication Technology' (2004) 17 Knowledge, Technology & Policy, 104

Jakobi T and others, 'Web Tracking Under the New Data Protection Law: Design Potentials at the Intersection of Jurisprudence and HCI' (2020) 19 i-com, 31

Jakobs K and Blind K, 'ICT Standardisation Policy in Europe - Recent Past, Presence, and Future(?),' *2011 7th International Conference on Standardization and Innovation in Information Technology (SIIT)* (IEEE 2011)

Jasmontaite L, Kamara I, Zanfir-Fortuna G, and Leucci S, 'Data Protection by Design and by Default' (2018) 4 European Data Protection Law Review, 168

Joerges C, Schepel H, and Vos E, 'The law's problems with the involvement of non-governmental actors in Europe's legislative processes: the case of standardisation under the "New Approach" '. Working Paper, EUI LAW, 1999/09 (1999)

Kallestrup M, 'Stakeholder Participation in European Standardization: A Mapping and an Assessment of Three Categories of Regulation' (2017) 44 Legal Issues of Economic Integration 381

Kamara I, 'Article 40 Commentary' in Kuner C, Bygrave LA, and Docksey C (eds) *The EU General Data Protection Regulation (GDPR): A Commentary* (OUP 2020)

Kamara I, 'Article 41 Commentary' in Kuner C, Bygrave LA, and Docksey C (eds) The EU General Data Protection Regulation (GDPR): A Commentary (OUP 2020)

Kamara I, 'Behavioural profiling in the post-constitutionalisation data protection regime,' in Human rights as a basis for reevaluating and reconstructing the law: Acts of the 4th ACCA Conference held in Louvain-la-Neuve on May 29th, 2015 (Bruylant 2016)

Kamara I, 'Co-regulation in EU Personal Data Protection: The Case of Technical Standards and The Privacy by Design Standardisation 'Mandate' (2017) 8 European Journal of Law and Technology, 1

Kamara I, 'Misaligned Union Laws? A Comparative Analysis of Certification in the Cybersecurity Act and the General Data Protection Regulation,' in Hallinan D, Leenes R, and De Hert P, *Privacy and data protection: Artificial intelligence* (Hart 2021)

Kamara I and De Hert P, 'Data Protection Certification in the EU: Possibilities, Actors and Building Blocks in a Reformed Landscape,' in Rodrigues R and Papakonstantinou E (eds) *Privacy and data protection seals* (TMC Asser Press 2018)

Kamara I and De Hert P, 'Understanding the Balancing Act behind the Legitimate Interest of the Controller Ground,' in Selinger E, Polonetsky J, and Tene O (eds) *The Cambridge Handbook of Consumer Privacy* (Cambridge University Press)

Kamara I and Kosta E, 'Do Not Track Initiatives: Regaining the Lost User Control'(2016) 6 *International Data Privacy Law*, 276

Kamara I, 'European Cybersecurity Standardisation: A Tale of Two Solitudes in View of Europe's Cyber Resilience' (2024) Innovation: The European Journal of Social Science Research 1

Kamara I, 'Exam Scripts Are Personal Data According to AG Kokott' (2017) 3 European Data Protection Law Review, 402

Kamara I, 'General Court EU: Commercial Interests Block the Right to Access European Harmonised Standards' [2022] 1 Journal of Standardisation

Kamara I, 'Art. 42 Certification' in Spiecker gen. Döhmann I, Papakonstantinou E, Hornung G, and De Hert P (eds) *General Data Protection Regulation* (Nomos Verlagsgesellschaft mbH & Co KG 2023)

Kamara I, 'Article 43 Certification Bodies' in Spiecker gen. Döhmann I, Papakonstantinou E, Hornung G, and De Hert P (eds) *General Data Protection Regulation* (Nomos Verlagsgesellschaft mbH & Co KG 2023)

Kanevskaia Whitaker O, 'Technology Standard-Setting Under the Lens of Global Administrative Law: Accountability, Participation and Transparency of Standard-Setting Organizations' TILEC Working Paper (2016)

Kanevskaia Whitaker O, 'Disciplining Standard-Setting: Which Approach to Choose (If Any)?' TILEC Discussion Paper No 2017-036

Kanevskaia Whitaker O, *The Law and Practice of Global ICT Standardization* (Cambridge University Press 2023)

King E and Fuson JH, 'An overview of Canadian Privacy Law for Pharmaceutical and Device Manufacturers Operating in Canada' (2005) 57 Food *and Drug Law Journal*, 205

Kingsbury B, Krisch N, and Stewart RB, 'The Emergence of Global Administrative Law' (2005) 68 *Law and Contemporary Problems*, 15

Kirby M, 'The History, Achievement and Future of the 1980 OECD Guidelines on Privacy' (2010) 1 International Data Privacy Law, 6

Klamert M, *The Principle of Loyalty in EU Law* (OUP 2014)

Kokott J and Sobotta C, 'The Distinction between Privacy and Data Protection in the Jurisprudence of the CJEU and the ECtHR' (2013) 3 International Data Privacy Law, 222

Koops B-J and Leenes R, 'Privacy Regulation Cannot Be Hardcoded. A Critical Comment on the "Privacy by Design' Provision in Data-Protection Law"' (2013) 28 International Review of Law, Computers and Technology, 159

Koops B-J, 'Should ICT Regulation Be Technology-Neutral?' in Koops B-J, Lips M, Prins C, and Schellekens M (eds) *Starting Points for ICT Regulation. Deconstructing Prevalent Policy One-liners* (TMC Asser Press 2006)

Koops B-J, 'The Trouble with European Data Protection Law' (2014) 4 International Data Privacy Law, 250

Koops B-J and others, 'Should self-regulation be the starting point?' in Koops B-J, Lips M, Prins C, and Schellekens M (eds), *Starting Points for ICT Regulation. Deconstructing Prevalent Policy One-liners* (TMC Asser Press 2006)

Korenhof P and others, 'Timing the Right to Be Forgotten: A Study into "Time" as a Factor in Deciding About Retention or Erasure of Data' in Gutwirth S, Leenes R, and De Hert P, (eds) *Reforming European Data Protection Law* (Springer 2014)

Kosta E, 'Article 7,' in Kuner C, Bygrave LA, and Docksey C (eds) *The EU General Data Protection Regulation (GDPR): A Commentary* (OUP 2020)

Kosta E and Stuurman K, 'Technical Standards and the Draft General Data Protection Regulation,' in Delimatsis P (ed) *The Law, Economics and Politics of International Standardisation* (Cambridge University Press 2015)

Kosta E, *Consent in European Data Protection Law* (Brill 2013)

Kosta E, 'Peeking into the Cookie Jar: The European Approach towards the Regulation of Cookies' (2013) 21 International Journal of Law and Information Technology, 380

Kosta V, *Fundamental Rights in EU Internal Market Legislation* (Bloomsbury Publishing 2015)
Kranenborg H, 'Article 8 – Protection of Personal Data,' in Peers, Stephen and others (eds) *The EU Charter of Fundamental Rights* (Nomos 2014)
Kuner C, *Transborder Data Flows and Data Privacy Law* (OUP 2013)
Lachaud E, 'ISO/IEC 27701 Standard: Threats and Opportunities for GDPR Certification' (2020) 6 European Data Protection Law Review, 194
Lachaud, E, 'Quelle peut être la contribution de la certification a la protection des données personnelles?' (2017) 20 Trinity CL Rev, 212
Lachaud E, 'Third-Party Certification and Cross-Border Flows in the GDPR: Which Workable Option?' *Available at SSRN 3686132* (2020).
Leenes R and Lucivero F, 'Laws on Robots, Laws by Robots, Laws in Robots: Regulating Robot Behaviour by Design' (2014) 6 Law, Innovation and Technology, 193
Leenes R, 'Commentary Article 42 GDPR,' in Kuner C, Bygrave LA, and Docksey C (eds) *The EU General Data Protection Regulation (GDPR): A Commentary* (OUP 2020)
Leenes R, 'Framing Techno-Regulation: An Exploration of State and Non-State Regulation by Technology' (2011) 5 Legisprudence, 143
Lenaerts K, 'Limits on Limitations: The Essence of Fundamental Rights in the EU' (2019) 20 German Law Journal, 779
Lerner J and Tirole J, 'Standard-Essential Patents' (2015) 123 Journal of Political Economy, 547
Lessig L, *Code: and Other Laws of Cyberspace, 2.0* (Basic Book 2006)
Lindahl H, 'ISO standards and Authoritative Collective Action,' in Delimatsis P (ed) *The Law, Economics and Politics of International Standardisation* (Cambridge University Press 2015)
Lynskey O, 'Deconstructing Data Protection: The 'Added-Value' of a Right to Data Protection in the EU Legal Order' (2014) 63 International & Comparative Law Quarterly, 569
Lynskey O, *The Foundations of EU Data Protection Law* (OUP 2015)
Mahieu R, Van Hoboken J, and Asghari H, 'Responsibility for Data Protection in a Networked World: On the Question of the Controller, Effective and Complete Protection and Its Application to Data Access Rights in Europe' (2019) 10 JIPITEC, 84.
Mak V, 'Pluralism in European Private Law,' in Kenneth A (ed) (2018) 20 Cambridge Yearbook of European Legal Studies, 202
Mak V, 'Standards of Protection: In Search of the "Average Consumer" of EU Law in the Proposal for a Consumer Rights Directive' (2011) 19 European Review of Private Law, 25
Mak V, *Legal Pluralism in European Contract Law* (OUP 2020)
Malgieri G and Niklas J, 'Vulnerable Data Subjects' (2020) 37 Computer Law & Security Review 105415
Malgieri G, *Vulnerability and Data Protection Law* (OUP 2023)
Mann M and Matzner T, 'Challenging Algorithmic Profiling: The Limits of Data Protection and Anti-Discrimination in Responding to Emergent Discrimination' (2019) 6 Big Data & Society 205395171989580
Markoska E, Chorbev I, Ristov S, and Gusev M, 'Cloud portability standardization overview,' in *2015 38th International Convention on Information and Communication Technology, Electronics and Microelectronics (MIPRO)*, IEEE, 286
Marsden CT, *Internet Co-Regulation: European Law, Regulatory Governance and Legitimacy in Cyberspace* (Cambridge University Press 2011)
McDonald AM, 'Stakeholders and High Stakes,' in Sellinger E, Polonetsky J, and Tene O (eds), *The Cambridge Handbook of Consumer Privacy* (Cambridge University Press 2018)
Medzmariashvili M, 'Delegation of Rulemaking Power to European Standards Organizations: Reconsidered' (2017) 44 Legal Issues of Economic Integration 353
Melissaris E, 'The More the Merrier? A New Take on Legal Pluralism' (2004) 13 Social & Legal Studies 57
Mendoza I and Bygrave LA, 'The Right Not to Be Subject to Automated Decisions Based on Profiling' in Synodinou T-E, and others (eds) *Internet Law* (Springer International Publishing 2017)
Meuwese A and Senden L, 'European Impact Assessment And The Choice Of Alternative Regulatory Instruments,' in Verschuuren J (ed) *The Impact of Legislation* (Brill | Nijhoff 2009)

Meuwese A, *Impact assessment in EU lawmaking* (Kluwer Law International 2008)
Michaels R, 'Global Legal Pluralism' (2009) 5 Annual Review of Law and Social Science, 243
Michaels R, 'Law and Recognition – Towards a Relational Concept of Law,' in Roughan N and Halpin A (eds) *Pursuit of Pluralist Jurisprudence* (Cambridge University Press 2017)
Micklitz H-W, 'Soft Law, Technical Standards and European Private Law,' in Eliantonio M, Korkea-aho E, and Mörth U (eds), *Research Handbook on Soft Law* (Edward Elgar Publishing 2023)
Miscenic E and Hoffmann A-L, 'The Role of Opening Clauses in Harmonization of EU Law: Example of the EU's General Data Protection Regulation (GDPR)' (2020) 4 EU and Comparative Law Issues and Challenges Series, 44
Mitrou L, 'Data Protection, Artificial Intelligence and Cognitive Services: Is the General Data Protection Regulation (GDPR) "Artificial Intelligence-Proof"?' [2018] SSRN Electronic Journal
Mitrou L, 'The General Data Protection Regulation: A Law for the Digital Age?,' in Synodinou T-E and others (eds), *EU Internet Law: Regulation and Enforcement* (Springer 2017)
Mitrou L, 'Communications Data Retention: A Pandora's Box for Rights and Liberties,' in Acquisti A and others (eds), *Digital Privacy: Theory, Technologies, and Practices* (CRC Press 2008)
Moerel L, *Binding Corporate Rules: Corporate Self-Regulation of Global Data Transfers* (Oxford University Press 2012)
Moore R, 'Standardisation: A Tool for Addressing Market Failure within the Software Industry' (2013) 29 Computer Law & Security Review 413
Moore SF, 'Legal Pluralism as Omnium Gatherum' (2014) 10 FIU Law Review
Muir E, 'The Fundamental Rights Implications of EU Legislation: Some Constitutional Challenges' (2014) 51 Common Market Law Review 219
Murphy CN and Yates J, *The International Organization for Standardization (ISO): Global Governance Through Voluntary Consensus* (Routledge 2009)
Nadvi K and Wältring F, 'Making Sense of Global Standards,' *in* Schmitz H (ed) *Local Enterprises in the Global Economy: Issues of Governance and Upgrading* (Edward Elgar Pub 2004)
Nissenbaum H, 'From Preemption to Circumvention: If Technology Regulates, Why Do We Need Regulation (and Vice Versa)' (2011) 26 Berkeley Technology Law Journal, 1367
O'Connor S and others, '(Un)Clear and (In)Conspicuous,' *Proceedings of the 20th Workshop on Privacy in the Electronic Society* (ACM 2021)
Olshan MA, 'Standards-Making Organizations and the Rationalization of American Life' (1993) 34 The Sociological Quarterly, 319
Pandit HJ and others, 'Standardisation, Data Interoperability, and GDPR,' in Jacobs K (ed) *Advances in Standardization Research* (IGI Global 2020)
Papakonstantinou V, *Self-Regulation and the Protection of Privacy* (Nomos-Verlag-Ges. 2002)
Partiti E, Bijlmakers S, and Delimatsis P, 'Evolutionary Dynamics of Transnational Private Regulation' (2022) 13 Transnational Legal Theory, 431
Pelkmans J and De Brito A, *Enforcement in the EU Single Market*, Centre for European Policy Studies (2012)
Pelkmans J, 'The New Approach to Technical Harmonization and Standardization' (1987) 25 JCMS: Journal of Common Market Studies, 249
Peters A, Förster T, and Koechlin L, 'Towards Non-State Actors as Effective, Legitimate, and Accountable Standard Setters,' in Peters A and others (eds), *Non-State Actors as Standard Setters* (Cambridge University Press 2009)
Pohlmann TC, 'The Evolution of ICT Standards Consortia' (2014) 95 Communications & Strategies, Quarter, 3
Porcedda MG, 'On Boundaries – Finding the Essence of the Right to the Protection of Personal Data,' in Leenes R, Van Brakel R, De Hert P, and Gutwirth S (eds) *Data Protection and Privacy* (Hart Publishing 2019)
Purtova N, 'The Law of Everything. Broad Concept of Personal Data and Future of EU Data Protection Law' (2018) 10 Law, Innovation and Technology, 40

Quelle C, 'Privacy, Proceduralism and Self-regulation in Data Protection Law' (2017) 14 Teoria Critica della Regolazione Sociale, 89
Quelle C, 'Enhancing Compliance under the General Data Protection Regulation: The Risky Upshot of the Accountability- and Risk-Based Approach' (2018) 9 European Journal of Risk Regulation, 502
Quelle C, 'Not Just User Control in the General Data Protection Regulation, *IFIP Advances in Information and Communication Technology* (Springer 2016)
Rachovitsa A, 'Rethinking Privacy Online and Human Rights: The Internet's Standardisation Bodies as the Guardians of Privacy Online in the Face of Mass Surveillance,' in *European Society of International Law (ESIL) 2016 Research Forum (Istanbul)*, 2017
Reed C, 'Taking Sides on Technology Neutrality' (2007) 4 SCRIPT-ed, 263
Reidenberg JR, 'Lex informatica: The Formulation of Information Policy Rules Through Technology' (1997) 56 Texas Law Review, 553
Rodotà S, 'Data Protection as a Fundamental Right,' in Gutwirth S and others (eds) *Reinventing Data Protection?* (Springer Netherlands 2009)
Rotondo E, 'The Legal Effect of EU Regulations' (2013) 29 Computer Law & Security Review, 437
Rubinstein IS, 'Regulating Privacy by DESIGN' (2011) 26 Berkeley Technology Law Journal, 1409
Rubinstein IS, 'Big Data: The End of Privacy or a New Beginning?' (2013) 3 International Data Privacy Law, 74
Ryngaert C, 'Transnational Private Regulation and Human Rights: The Limitations of Stateless Law and the Re-entry of the State,' in Cernic JL and Van Ho T (eds) *Direct Human Rights Obligations of Multinational Corporations* (Wolf Legal Publishers 2015)
Santos C, Bielova N, and Matte C, 'Are Cookie Banners Indeed Compliant with The Law? Deciphering EU Legal Requirements on Consent and Technical Means to Verify Compliance of Cookie Banners' [2020] Technology and Regulation, 91
Schepel H, 'Between Standards and Regulation,' in Delimatsis P (ed) *The Law, Economics and Politics of International Standardisation* (Cambridge University Press 2015)
Schepel H, 'The New Approach to the New Approach: The Juridification of Harmonized Standards in EU Law' (2013) 20 Maastricht Journal of European and Comparative Law 521
Schepel H, 'Case C-171/11 Fra.Bo SpA v Deutsche Vereinigung Des Gas- Und Wasserfaches' (2013) 9 European Review of Contract Law
Schepel H, 'Rules of Recognition: A Legal Constructivist Approach to Transnational Private Regulation,' in Ys PJ, Kjaer PF, and Yatsunami R (eds) *Regulatory Hybridization in the Transnational Sphere* (Martinus Nijhoff Publishers 2013)
Schepel H, *The Constitution of Private Governance: Product Standards in the Regulation of Integrating Markets* (Hart Publishing 2005)
Schmidt V and Wood M, 'Conceptualizing Throughput Legitimacy: Procedural Mechanisms of Accountability, Transparency, Inclusiveness and Openness in EU Governance' (2019) 97 Public Administration, 727
Schmidt VA, 'Democracy and Legitimacy in the European Union Revisited: Input, Output and "Throughput"' (2012) 61 Political Studies, 2
Schmidt VA, 'Is There a Deficit of Throughput Legitimacy in the EU?' [2019] Critical Reflections on Constitutional Democracy in the European Union, 127
Schmidt, VA, 'Democracy and legitimacy in the European Union revisited: Input, output and "throughput"' (2013) 61(1) Political Studies, 2
Scott C, 'Standard-Setting in Regulatory Regimes,' in Baldwin R, Cave M, and Lodge M (eds) *The Oxford Handbook of Regulation* (Oxford University Press 2010)
Scott C, Cafaggi F and Senden L, 'The Conceptual and Constitutional Challenge of Transnational Private Regulation' (2011) 38 Journal of Law and Society, 1
Senden L and Van den Brink T, 'Checks and Balances of Soft EU Rule-Making' *Policy Department C: Citizens' Rights and Constitutional Affairs* (2012)
Senden L, 'Soft law, Self-regulation and Co-regulation in European Law: Where Do They Meet?' (2005) 9 Electronic Journal of Comparative Law, 1

Senden L, 'Soft Post-Legislative Rulemaking: A Time for More Stringent Control' (2012) 19 European Law Journal, 57

Senden L, 'The Constitutional Fit of European Standardization Put to the Test' (2017) 44 Legal Issues of Economic Integration, 337

Senden L, 'Towards a More Holistic Legitimacy Approach to Technical Standardisation in the EU,' in Eliantonio M and Cauffman C (eds) *The Legitimacy of Standardisation as a Regulatory Technique* (Edward Elgar Publishing 2020)

Senden L, *Soft Law in European Community Law* (Hart Publishing 2004)

Sheffner DJ, 'Integrating Technical Standards into Federal Regulations: Incorporation by Reference,' in Contreras, Jorge L (ed) *The Cambridge Handbook of Technical Standardization Law: Volume 2: Further Intersections of Public and Private Law* (Cambridge University Press 2019)

Simitis S, 'Privacy—An Endless Debate?' (2010) California Law Review, 1989

Simitis S, 'From the Market to the Polis: The EU Directive on the Protection of Personal Data' (1995) 80 Iowa Law Review 80, 445

Solove, D, 'The Limitations of Privacy Rights' (2023) 98 Notre Dame L Rev, 975

Spindler G, 'Market Processes, Standardisation, and Tort Law' (1998) 4 European Law Journal, 316

Stuurman K, 'IT Standards Regulation' (1992) 8 Computer Law & Security Review, 2

Stuurman K, 'Annotatie bij Rechtbank Den Haag 31 december 2008 (Knooble/Staat en NNI)' *AMI/Tijdschrift voor auteurs-, media en informatierecht* (2009) 2

Stuurman K, 'Legal Aspects of Standardization of Information Technology and Telecommunications: An Overview' (1992) 8 Computer Law Security Review

Sunstein CR and Thaler RH, 'Libertarian Paternalism Is Not an Oxymoron' (2003) 70 The University of Chicago Law Review, 1159

Suttmeier RP, Yao X, and Zixiang Tan A, 'Standards of power? Technology, institutions, and politics in the development of China's national standards strategy' (2009) Geopolitics, History, and International Relations, 46

Swenson G, 'Legal Pluralism in Theory and Practice' (2018) 20 International Studies Review, 438

Taekema S, 'Theoretical and Normative Frameworks for Legal Research: Putting Theory into Practice' [2018] Law and Method, 1

Tamanaha BZ, 'Understanding Legal Pluralism: Past to Present, Local to Global' (2008) 30 Sydney Law Review, 375

Tamò-Larrieux A, *Designing for Privacy and Its Legal Framework: Data Protection by Design and Default for the Internet of Things* (Springer 2018)

Terpan F, 'Soft Law in the European Union—The Changing Nature of EU Law' (2014) 21 European Law Journal 68

Teubner G, 'The Corporate Codes of Multinationals: Company Constitutions Beyond Corporate Governance and Co-determination,' in Nickel R, *Conflict of Laws and Laws of Conflict in Europe and Beyond: Patterns of Supranational and Transnational Juridification* (Intersentia Uitgevers 2010)

Thürer D, 'The Role of Soft Law in the Actual Process of European Integration,' in Jacot Guillarmod O (ed) L'avenir du libre-échange en Europe: vers un Espace économique européen (Sculthess Zürich 1990)

Tosoni L, 'Article 4(20)' in Kuner C, Bygrave LA, and Docksey C (eds) *The EU General Data Protection Regulation (GDPR): A Commentary* (OUP 2020)

Tovo C, 'Judicial Review of Harmonized Standards: Changing the Paradigms of Legality and Legitimacy of Private Rulemaking under EU Law' (2018) 55 Common Market Law Review 1187

Trakman L, Walters R, and Zeller B, 'Tort and Data Protection Law' (2019) 5 European Data Protection Law Review, 500

Twining W, 'Normative and Legal Pluralism: A Global Perspective' (2010) 20 Duke Journal of Comparative & International Law, 473

Ursic H, 'Unfolding the New-Born Right to Data Portability: Four Gateways to Data Subject Control' (2018) 15 SCRIPT-ed, 42

Van Alsenoy B, 'Reconciling the (Extra) Territorial Reach of the GDPR with Public International Law,' in Vermeulen G and Lievens E (eds) *Data Protection and Privacy Under Pressure: Transatlantic Tensions, EU Surveillance, and Big Data* (Maklu 2017)

Van Alsenoy B, 'Liability under EU Data Protection Law: From Directive 95/46 to the General Data Protection Regulation' 7 (2016) JIPITEC, 271

Van Alsenoy, *Data Protection Law in the EU: Roles, Responsibilities and Liability* (Intersentia 2019)

van de Kooij AC, 'The Private Effect of the Free Movement of Goods: Examining Private-Law Bodies Activities under the Scope of Article 34 of the Treaty of the Functioning of the European Union' (2013) 40 Legal Issues of Economic Integration, 363

van den Hoogen T and Nowak T, 'The Emergence and Use of Self-Regulation in the European Decision-Making Process: Does It Make a Difference?' (2010) 4 Legisprudence, 343

van der Hof S and Ouburg S, '"We Take Your Word For It"—A Review of Methods of Age Verification and Parental Consent in Digital Services' (2022) 8 European Data Protection Law Review, 61

van Eecke P and Truyens M, 'Standardization in the European Information and Technology Sector: Official Procedures on the Verge of Being Overhauled' (2009) 5 Washington Journal of Law, Technology & Arts

Van Gestel R, 'Self-regulation and Environmental Law' (2005) 9 Electronic Journal of Comparative Law, 1

van Gestel R and van Lochem P, 'Private Standards as a Replacement for Public Lawmaking?' in Gamito MC and Micklitz HW (eds) *The Role of the EU in Transnational Legal Ordering* (Edward Elgar Publishing 2020)

Van Gestel R and Micklitz H-W, 'European Integration through Standardization: How Judicial Review Is Breaking Down the Club House of Private Standardization Bodies' (2013) 50 Common Market Law Review, 145

Van Harten H and Nauta T, 'Towards horizontal direct effect for the free movement of goods? Comment on Fra. Bo.' (2013) 5 European Law Review, 677

Van Leeuwen B, 'From Status to Impact, and the Role of National Legislation: The Application of Article 34 TFEU to a Private Certification Organisation in Fra.Bo' (2013) 4 European Journal of Risk Regulation, 405

Van Leeuwen B, *European Standardisation of Services and Its Impact on Private Law: Paradoxes of Convergence* (Bloomsbury Publishing 2017)

Van Nortwick M and Wilson C, 'Setting the Bar Low: Are Websites Complying with the Minimum Requirements of the CCPA?' (2021) 2022 Proceedings on Privacy Enhancing Technologies, 608

Van Ooijen I and Vrabec HU, 'Does the GDPR Enhance Consumers' Control over Personal Data? An Analysis from a Behavioural Perspective' (2018) 42 Journal of Consumer Policy, 91

Van Schendel S, 'The Challenges of Risk Profiling Used by Law Enforcement: Examining the Cases of COMPAS and SyRI,' in Reins L (ed) *Regulating New Technologies in Uncertain Times* (TMC Asser Press 2019)

Van Waeyenberge A and Restrepo AA, 'James Elliott Construction: A New (ish) Approach to Judicial Review of Standardisation' (2017) 6 European Law Review, 882

Vanderlinden J, 'Return to Legal Pluralism: Twenty Years Later' (1989) 28 The Journal of Legal Pluralism and Unofficial Law, 149

Verbruggen P, '"Private Regulation in EU Better Regulation": Past Performance and Future Promises' (2017) 19 European Journal of Law Reform, 121

Verbruggen P, 'Tort Liability for Standards Development in the United States and European Union,' in Contreras JL (ed), *The Cambridge Handbook of Technical Standardization Law: Volume 2: Further Intersections of Public and Private Law* (Cambridge University Press 2019)

Verbruggen P and Paiement P, 'Transnational Private Regulation' in *Oxford Bibliographies in Political Science* (OUP 2017)
Verbruggen P and Van Leeuwen B, 'The Liability of Notified Bodies Under The EU's New Approach: The Implications of the PIP Breast Implants Case' (2018) 43 European Law Review, 394
Volpato A and Eliantonio M, 'The Contradictory Approach of the CJEU to the Judicial Review of Standards: A Love–Hate Relationship?' in Eliantonio M and Cauffman C (eds) *The Legitimacy of Standardisation as a Regulatory Technique* (Edward Elgar Publishing 2020)
Volpato A and Eliantonio M, 'The Participation of Civil Society in ETSI from the Perspective of Throughput Legitimacy' (2024) 37(5) Innovation: The European Journal of Social Science Research 1375
Von Benda-Beckmann F, 'Who's Afraid of Legal Pluralism?' (2002) 34 The Journal of Legal Pluralism and Unofficial Law, 37
Wallerman A, 'Pie in the Sky When You Die? Civil Liability of Notified Bodies under the Medical Devices Directive: Schmitt' (2018) 55 Common Market Law Review, 265
Weatherill S, 'Compulsory Notification of Draft Technical Regulations: The Contribution of Directive 83/189 to the Management of the Internal Market' (1996) 16 Yearbook of European Law, 129
Weber RH, 'Transborder Data Transfers: Concepts, Regulatory Approaches and New Legislative Initiatives' (2013) 3 International Data Privacy Law, 117
Webley L, 'Qualitative Approaches To Empirical Legal Research,' in Cane P and Kritser HM (eds) *The Oxford Handbook of Empirical Legal Research* (OUP 2010)
Weiler JHH, 'In the Face of Crisis: Input Legitimacy, Output Legitimacy and the Political Messianism of European Integration' (2012) 34 Journal of European Integration, 825
Werle, E, and Iversen EJ, 'Promoting Legitimacy in Technical Standardization' (2006) 2 Science, Technology & Innovation Studies, 19
Wilson CS, 'A Defining Moment for Privacy: The Time is Ripe for Federal Privacy Legislation,' in *Speech at Future of Privacy Forum by Commissioner of US Federal Trade Commission (FTC)*, vol 6. 2020, https://www.ftc.gov/system/files/documents/public_statements/1566337/commissioner_wilson_privacy_forum_speech_02-06-2020.pdf (accessed 20 August 2024)
Winn JK, 'Technical Standards as Data Protection Regulation,' in Gutwirth S and others (eds), *Reinventing Data Protection?* (Springer 2009)
Winn JK, 'Globalization and Standards: the Logic of Two-Level Games' (2009) 5 I/S: A Journal of Law and Policy for the Information Society, 185.
Wolters PTJ, 'The Security of Personal Data under the GDPR: A Harmonized Duty or a Shared Responsibility?' (2017) 7 International Data Privacy Law, 165
Woodman GR, 'Ideological Combat and Social Observation' (1998) 30 The Journal of Legal Pluralism and Unofficial Law, 21
Yasunori F and others, 'Personal Data Sensitivity in Japan' (2017) 1 The ORBIT Journal 1
Yates J and Murphy CN, *Engineering Rules: Global Standard Setting since 1880* (JHU Press 2019)
Yeung K, 'Towards an understanding of regulation by design,' in Brownsword R and Yeung K, *Regulating Technologies: Legal Futures, Regulatory Frames and Technological Fixes* (Bloomsbury Publishing 2008)
Zanfir-Fortuna G, 'Article 82 GDPR' in Kuner C, Bygrave LA, and Docksey C (eds) *The EU General Data Protection Regulation (GDPR): A Commentary* (OUP 2020)
Zimmeck S and Alicki K, 'Standardizing and Implementing Do Not Sell,' *Proceedings of the 19th Workshop on Privacy in the Electronic Society* (ACM 2020)
Zimmeck S and others, 'Usability and Enforceability of Global Privacy Control' (2023) 2023 Proceedings on Privacy Enhancing Technologies, 265
Zuiderveen Borgesius F, 'Singling out People without Knowing Their Names – Behavioural Targeting, Pseudonymous Data, and the New Data Protection Regulation' (2016) 32 Computer Law & Security Review, 256

Treaties, Legislation, Preparatory works and Explanatory Memoranda

CAL. Civ. CODE §§ 1798.100-199 (2018)

Charter of Fundamental Rights of the European Union, OJ C 326, 26.10.2012

Colorado Privacy Act. § 6-1-1301

Commission 'Technical harmonisation and standards: a New Approach' (1) COM(85)19P/85/12)

Commission Decision of 26 July 2000 pursuant to Directive 95/46/EC of the European Parliament and of the Council on the adequacy of the protection provided by the safe harbour privacy principles and related frequently asked questions issued by the US Department of Commerce (notified under document number C(2000) 2441) *Official Journal L 215, 25/08/2000*

Commission Implementing Decision (EU) 2016/650 of 25 April 2016 laying down standards for the security assessment of qualified signature and seal creation devices pursuant to Articles 30(3) and 39(2) of Regulation (EU) No 910/2014 of the European Parliament and of the Council on electronic identification and trust services for electronic transactions in the internal market, OJ L 109/40, 26.4.2016

Commission Implementing Decision (EU) 2019/1729 of 15 October 2019 on the harmonised standard for conformity assessment drafted in support of Regulations (EC) No 765/2008 and (EC) No 1221/2009 of the European Parliament and of the Council, Directive 2006/42/ EC of the European Parliament and of the Council and Union acts incorporating the reference provisions of Decision No 768/2008/EC of the European Parliament and of the Council, OJ L 263/36, 16.10.2019

Communication from the Commission to the European Parliament, the Council, the European Economic and Social Committee and the Committee of the Regions the Annual Union Work programme for European standardisation for 2019, SWD (2018) 434 final

Connecticut Data Privacy Act: Senate Bill 6: An Act Concerning Personal Data Privacy and Online Monitoring

Consumer Product Safety Act, Pub. L. No. 92-573 (Oct. 28, 1972), 15 U.S.C.A. §§ 2051-81 (Supp. 1973)

Corrigendum to Regulation 2016/679 of the European Parliament and of the Council of 27 April 2016 on the protection of natural persons with regard to the processing of personal data and on the free movement of such data, and repealing Directive 95/46/EC (General Data Protection Regulation) (OJ L 119, 4.5.2016) *OJ L 127, 23.5.2018*

Council Decision 87/95/EEC of 22 December 1986 on standardization in the field of information technology and telecommunications OJ L 036, 07.02.1987

Council Directive 83/189/EEC of 28 March 1983 laying down a procedure for the provision of information in the field of technical standards and regulations L 109/8 26.04. 1983

Council Directive 85/374/EEC of 25 July 1985 on the approximation of the laws, regulations and administrative provisions of the Member States concerning liability for defective products OJ L 210/29, 7.8.1985

Directive 1999/34/EC of the European Parliament and of the Council of 10 May 1999 amending Council Directive 85/374/EEC on the approximation of the laws, regulations and administrative provisions of the Member States concerning liability for defective products, OJ L 141/20

Council of Europe, Additional Protocol to Convention 108 regarding supervisory authorities and transborder data flows, ETS No. 181 (2001)

Council of Europe, Additional Protocol to Convention 108 regarding supervisory authorities and transborder data flows, ETS No. 181 (2001)

Council of Europe, Amending Protocol for the modernisation of the Convention 108, CETS No. 223 (2018). Explanatory Report to the Protocol amending the Convention for the Protection of Individuals with regard to Automatic Processing of Personal Data (Strasbourg, 10.X.2018)

Council of Europe, Convention for the Protection of Human Rights and Fundamental Freedoms (ETS No.005)

Council of Europe, Explanatory Report to the Protocol amending the Convention for the Protection of Individuals with regard to Automatic Processing of Personal Data (Strasbourg, 10.X.2018)

Council Resolution of 7 May 1985 on a new approach to technical harmonization and standards, OJ C 136, 4.6.1985

Decision 768/2008/EC of the European Parliament and of the Council of 9 July 2008 on a common framework for the marketing of products, and repealing Council Decision 93/465/EEC, OJ L 218, 13.8.2008

Directive (EU) 2016/1148 of the European Parliament and of the Council of 6 July 2016 concerning measures for a high common level of security of network and information systems across the Union, OJ L 194, 19.7.2016

Directive (EU) 2016/680 of the European Parliament and of the Council of 27 April 2016 on the protection of natural persons with regard to the processing of personal data by competent authorities for the purposes of the prevention, investigation, detection or prosecution of criminal offences or the execution of criminal penalties, and on the free movement of such data, and repealing Council Framework Decision 2008/977/JHA, OJ L 119, 4.5.2016

Directive 1999/5/EC of the European Parliament and of the Council of 9 March 1999 on radio equipment and telecommunications terminal equipment and the mutual recognition of their conformity, OJ L 91, 7.4.1999

Directive 2005/29/EC of the European Parliament and of the Council of 11 May 2005 concerning unfair business-to-consumer commercial practices in the internal market and amending Council Directive 84/450/EEC, Directives 97/7/EC, 98/27/EC and 2002/65/EC of the European Parliament and of the Council and Regulation (EC) No 2006/2004 of the European Parliament and of the Council ('Unfair Commercial Practices Directive') OJ L 149, 11.6.2005, p. 22–39

Directive 2006/42/EC of the European Parliament and of the Council of 17 May 2006 on machinery, and amending Directive 95/16/EC, OJ L 157, 9.6.2006

Directive 2009/48/EC of the European Parliament and of the Council of 18 June 2009 on the safety of toys, OJ L 170, 30.6.2009

Directive 2014/53/EU of the European Parliament and of the Council of 16 April 2014 on the harmonisation of the laws of the Member States relating to the making available on the market of radio equipment and repealing Directive 1999/5/EC, OJ L 153/62, 22.5.2014

Directive 2015/1535 of the European Parliament and of the Council of 9 September 2015 laying down a procedure for the provision of information in the field of technical regulations and of rules on Information Society services, OJ L 241/1, 17.9.2015

Directive 2018/1972 of the European Parliament and of the Council of 11 December 2018 establishing the European Electronic Communications Code OJ L 321, 17.12.2018 as amended by the Corrigendum to Directive (EU) 2018/1972 of the European Parliament and of the Council of 11 December 2018 establishing the European Electronic Communications Code OJ L 334, 27.12.2019

Directive 83/189/EEC laying down a procedure for the provision of information in the field of technical regulations and standards, (1983) OJ L 109/8

Directive 94/10/EC of the European Parliament and the Council of 23 March 1994 materially amending for the second time Directive 83/189/EEC laying down a procedure for the provision of information in the field of technical standards and regulations OJ L 100/30 19. 4. 94

Directive 98/34/EC of the European Parliament and of the Council of 22 June 1998 laying down a procedure for the provision of information in the field of technical standards and regulations and of rules on information society services, OJ L 91, 7.4.1999

European Commission, Commission Delegated Regulation (EU) 2022/30 of 29 October 2021 supplementing Directive 2014/53/EU of the European Parliament and of the Council with regard to the application of the essential requirements referred to in Article 3(3), points (d), (e) and (f), of that Directive, OJ L 7/6, 12.1.2022

European Commission, M/530 Commission Implementing Decision C(2015) 102 final of 20.1.2015 on a standardisation request to the European standardisation organisations as regards European standards and European standardisation deliverables for privacy and personal data protection management pursuant to Article 10(1) of Regulation (EU) No 1025/2012 of the European Parliament and of the Council in support of Directive 95/46/EC of the European Parliament and of the Council and in support of Union's security industrial policy

European Commission, Proposal for a Regulation of the European Parliament and of the Council on the protection of individuals with regard to the processing of personal data and on the free movement of such data (General Data Protection Regulation), COM (2012) 11 final, 25th January 2012

European Commission, Proposal for a Regulation of the European Parliament and of the Council on European Standardisation and amending Council Directives 89/686/EEC and 93/15/EEC and Directives 94/9/EC, 94/25/EC, 95/16/EC, 97/23/EC, 98/34/EC, 2004/22/EC, 2007/23/EC, 2009/105/EC and 2009/23/EC of the European Parliament and the Council', COM (2011) 315 final

European Commission, Proposal for a Regulation of the European Parliament and of the Council concerning the respect for private life and the protection of personal data in electronic communications and repealing Directive 2002/58/EC (Regulation on Privacy and Electronic Communications), COM/2017/010 final, (proposal for ePrivacy Regulation)

European Commission, Proposal for a Regulation of the European Parliament and of the Council laying down harmonised rules on artificial intelligence (Artificial Intelligence Act) and amending certain Union legislative acts, COM/2021/206 final

European Commission, The 2024 annual Union work programme for European standardisation, Commission notice, C/2024/1364, OJ 15.2.2024

European Commission, The 2024 annual Union work programme for European standardisation, Commission notice, C/2024/1364, OJ 15.2.2024

European Parliament legislative resolution of 12 March 2014 on the proposal for a regulation of the European Parliament and of the Council on the protection of individuals with regard to the processing of personal data and on the free movement of such data (General Data Protection Regulation) (COM(2012)0011 - C7-0025/2012 - 2012/0011(COD))

European Parliament legislative resolution of 13 March 2024 on the proposal for a regulation of the European Parliament and of the Council on laying down harmonised rules on Artificial Intelligence (Artificial Intelligence Act) and amending certain Union Legislative Acts (COM(2021)0206 – C9-0146/2021 – 2021/0106(COD))

European Parliament, ***I REPORT on the proposal for a regulation of the European Parliament and of the Council concerning the respect for private life and the protection of personal data in electronic communications and repealing Directive 2002/58/EC (Regulation on Privacy and Electronic Communications) (COM (2017)0010 – C8-0009/2017 – 2017/0003(COD)) Committee on Civil Liberties, Justice and Home Affairs, 20.10.2017

European Parliament, Council of the European Union and the Commission of the European Communities, Interinstitutional Agreement on better law-making, OJ C 321.1, 31.12.2003

European Parliament, Council of the European Union and the European Commission, Interinstitutional Agreement of 13 April 2016 on Better Law-Making, OJ L 123/1, 12. 5.2016

Explanations Relating to the Charter of Fundamental Rights (2007/C 303/02), C 303/17, 14.12.2007

Directive (EU) 2016/1148 of the European Parliament and of the Council of 6 July 2016. L 194/1 19.7.2016

OECD Guidelines on the Protection of Privacy and Transborder Flows of Personal Data (23 September 1980)

OECD, Supplementary Explanatory Memorandum to the Revised OECD Privacy Guidelines (2013)

OECD, The OECD Privacy Framework. Guidelines governing the protection of privacy and transborder flows of personal data (2013)

Office of Management and Budget (OMB) Circular No. A-119 -- Federal Register (Federal Participation in the Development and Use of Voluntary Consensus Standards and in Conformity Assessment Activities), February 10, 1998, revised in 2016 (Revision of OMB Circular No. A-119, 'Federal Participation in the Development and Use of Voluntary Consensus Standards and in Conformity Assessment Activities' 81 FR 4673 (2016))

Personal Information Protection and Electronic Documents Act, S.C. 2000, c. 5 (Last amended on 23 June 2015)

Public Law 104-113, the National Technology Transfer Act of 1995 (P.L. 104-113)

Privacy Protection Act of 1980 (Public Law 95-540)

Recommendation No R (81) 1 on regulations for automated medical data banks (1981)

Regulation (EC) No 45/2001 of the European Parliament and of the Council of 18 December 2000 on the protection of individuals with regard to the processing of personal data by the Community institutions and bodies and on the free movement of such data OJ 008, 12.01.2001

Regulation (EC) No 764/2008 of the European Parliament and of the Council of 9 July 2008 laying down procedures relating to the application of certain national technical rules to products lawfully marketed in another Member State and repealing Decision No 3052/95/EC, OJ L 218, 13.8.2008

Regulation (EC) No 765/2008 of the European Parliament and of the Council of 9 July 2008 setting out the requirements for accreditation and market surveillance relating to the marketing of products and repealing Regulation (EEC) No 339/93, COM (2017) 789 final, OJ L 218/30

Regulation (EU) 1025/2012 of the European Parliament and of the Council of 25 October 2012 on European Standardisation, amending Council Directives 89/686/EEC and 93/15/EEC and Directives 94/9/EC, 94/25/EC, 95/16/EC, 97/23/EC, 98/34/EC, 2004/22/EC, 2007/23/EC, 2009/23/EC and 2009/105/EC of the European Parliament and of the Council and repealing Council Decision 87/95/EEC and Decision No 1673/2006/EC of the European Parliament and of the Council, L 316/12, 14.11.2012

Regulation (EU) 2016/679 of the European Parliament and of the Council of 27 April 2016 on the protection of natural persons with regard to the processing of personal data and on the free movement of such data, and repealing Directive 95/46/EC (General Data Protection Regulation) OJ L 119, 4.5.2016,

Regulation (EU) 2017/745 of the European Parliament and of the Council of 5 April 2017 on medical devices, amending Directive 2001/83/EC, Regulation (EC) No 178/2002 and Regulation (EC) No 1223/2009 and repealing Council Directives 90/385/EEC and 93/42/EEC, OJ L 117/1

Regulation (EU) 2022/2480 of the European Parliament and of the Council of 14 December 2022 amending Regulation (EU) No 1025/2012 as regards decisions of European standardisation organisations concerning European standards and European standardisation deliverables, OJ L 323/1, 19.12.2022

Regulation (EU) 2024/1689 of the European Parliament and of the Council of 13 June 2024 laying down harmonised rules on artificial intelligence and amending Regulations (EC) No 300/2008, (EU) No 167/2013, (EU) No 168/2013, (EU) 2018/858, (EU) 2018/1139 and (EU) 2019/2144 and Directives 2014/90/EU, (EU) 2016/797 and (EU) 2020/1828 (Artificial Intelligence Act), OJ L/1, 12.7.2024

Regulation (EU) 2024/2847 of the European Parliament and of the Council of 23 October 2024 on horizontal cybersecurity requirements for products with digital elements and amending Regulations (EU) No 168/2013 and (EU) 2019/1020 and Directive (EU) 2020/1828 (Cyber Resilience Act), OJ L/1, 20.11.2024

Treaty establishing the European Community Official Journal C 340, 10/11/1997 - Consolidated version

Treaty of Lisbon Amending the Treaty on European Union and the Treaty Establishing the European Communities, Dec. 13, 2007, 2007 OJ (C 306)

Treaty on the Functioning of the European Union, OJC 326, 26 October 2012

Universal Declaration of Human Rights, United Nations General Assembly Resolution 217A, (1948)

Policy documents and commissioned studies

2626th International Conference on Privacy and Personal Data Protection 'Resolution on a Draft ISO Privacy Framework Standard' (2004)

35th International Conference of Data Protection and Privacy Commissioners, 'Resolution on web tracking and privacy' (2013)

APEC, APEC Cross Border Privacy Rules System, 2011

APEC, APEC Privacy Framework, 2005

Article 29 Data Protection Working Party 'Guidelines on Data Protection Impact Assessment (DPIA) and determining whether processing is "likely to result in a high risk" for the purposes of Regulation 2016/679' (adopted 4 April 2017, rev. 4 October 2017WP 248 rev.01., endorsed by the EDPB)

Article 29 Data Protection Working Party 'Guidelines on the right to data portability' (adopted 13 December 2016, rev. 5 April 2017), WP 242 rev.01

Article 29 Data Protection Working Party 'Opinion 03/2013 on purpose limitation', WP203 (2013)

Article 29 Data Protection Working Party 'Opinion 1/2002 on the CEN/ISSS Report on Privacy Standardisation in Europe', WP57 (2002)

Article 29 Data Protection Working Party 'Opinion 4/2007 on the concept of personal data' WP136 (2007)

Article 29 Data Protection Working Party 'Request to publish free of charge the ISO 17065 standard' Letter to the President of ISO (2018)

Article 29 Data Protection Working Party 'Guidelines on Automated individual decision-making and Profiling for the purposes of Regulation 2016/679' WP251 rev.01, adopted 2017, last revised 6 February 2018

Article 29 Data Protection Working Party 'Guidelines on Data Protection Impact Assessment (DPIA) and determining whether processing is "likely to result in a high risk" for the purposes of Regulation 2016/679' WP 248 rev.01 (adopted April 2017, revised October 2017)

Article 29 Data Protection Working Party 'Opinion 08/2012 providing further input on the data protection reform discussions' WP199 (2012):9

Article 29 Data Protection Working Party 'Opinion 3/2010 on the principle of accountability' WP173 (2010)

Article 29 Data Protection Working Party 'Opinion 4/2007 on the concept of personal data' WP136, (2007European Commission, Guide to the Radio Equipment Directive 2014/53/EU, v. of 19 December 2018

Article 29 Data Protection Working Party 'Working Document 01/2016 on the justification of interferences with the fundamental rights to privacy and data protection through surveillance measures when transferring personal data (European Essential Guarantees)' WP237 (2016)

Article 29 Data Protection Working Party 'Working Document 2/2013 providing guidance on obtaining consent for cookies' WP208

Article 29 Data Protection Working Party, 'Guidelines on Data Protection Impact Assessment (DPIA) and determining whether processing is "likely to result in a high risk" for the purposes of Regulation 2016/679' WP 248 rev 1 (2017)

Article 29 Data Protection Working Party, 'Opinion 02/2015 on C-SIG Code of Conduct on Cloud Computing', WP232 (2015)

Article 29 Data Protection Working Party, 'Opinion 03/2016 on the Evaluation and Review of the ePrivacy Directive (2002/58/EC)' (2016)

Article 29 Data Protection Working Party, 'Opinion 04/2014 on Surveillance of Electronic Communications for Intelligence and National Security Purposes' WP 215 (2014)

Article 29 Data Protection Working Party, 'Opinion 1/2008 on Data Protection Issues Related to Search Engines' (2008)

Article 29 Data Protection Working Party, 'Opinion 3/2010 on the principle of Accountability' WP173

Article 29 Data Protection Working Party, Opinion 02/2015 on C-SIG Code of Conduct on Cloud Computing, 2588/15/EN WP232, 22 September 2015

Article 29 Data Protection Working Party, Opinion 05/2014 on Anonymisation Techniques WP216 (2014)

Article 29 Data Protection Working Party, Opinion 1/2010 on the concepts of 'controller' and 'processor' WP169 (adopted 16 February 2010)

Article 29 Data Protection Working Party, Opinion 2/2010 on online behavioural advertising, WP171 (22 June 2010)

Autoriteit Persoonsgegevens 'Besluitinzake de verklaring omtrent Gedragscode Data Pro Code van Nederland ICT1; z2018-11482

Baron, Justus, Jorge L. Contreras, Martin Husovec, Pierre Larouche, and Nikolaus Thumm. 'Making the Rules: The Governance of Standard Development Organizations and their Policies on Intellectual Property Rights'. JRC Science for Policy Report, (2019)

Cloud Select Industry Group (C-SIG) 'Cloud Service Level Agreement Standardisation Guidelines' (2014)

College Bescherming Persoonsgegevens 'Draft International Standard ISO/SEC 20886 ISTPA Privacy Framework', (2004)

Commission Communication, A Strategic Vision for European Standards: Moving Forward to Enhance and Accelerate the Sustainable Growth of the European Economy by 2020, COM 2011/311 final

Commission Decision of 15 July 1992 amending the lists of standards institutions annexed to Council Directive 89/189/EEC [1992] OJ L221/55

Commission Decision, General Guidelines for the co-operation between CEN, CENELEC and ETSI and the European Commission (EC) and the European Free Trade Association (EFTA). 28 March 2003 OJ C 91, 16.4.2003

Commission Implementing Decision of 11.9.2020 on a standardisation request to the European Committee for Standardisation as regards unmanned aircraft systems intended to be operated in the 'open' category of operations in support of Commission Delegated Regulation (EU) 2019/945 ('M/567')

Commission Implementing Decision of 23.8.2023 amending Implementing Decision C(2022) 5637 on a standardisation request to the European Committee for Standardisation and the European Committee for Electrotechnical Standardisation as regards radio equipment in support of Directive 2014/53/EU of the European Parliament and of the Council and Commission Delegated Regulation (EU) 2022/30, C(2023) 5624 final

Commission Implementing Decision of 5.8.2022 on a standardisation request to the European Committee for Standardisation and the European Committee for Electrotechnical Standardisation as regards radio equipment in support of Directive 2014/53/EU of the European Parliament and of the Council and Commission Delegated Regulation (EU) 2022/30, C(2022) 5637 final

Commission notice The 'Blue Guide' on the implementation of EU product rules 2022) 2022/C 247/01, C/2022/3637, OJ C 247, 29.6.2022.

Commission of the European Communities, 'Communication from the Commission to the European Parliament and the Council. An area of freedom, security and justice serving the citizen', COM (2009) 262 final

Commission of the European Communities, 'White Paper. Modernising ICT Standardisation in the EU – The way forward', COM (2009) 324 final

Commission staff working document - Instruments for a modernised single market policy - Accompanying document to the Communication from the Commission to the European Parliament, the Council, the European Economic and Social Committee and the Committee of the Regions - A single market for 21st century Europe {COM(2007) 724 final} {SEC(2007) 1517} {SEC(2007) 1519} {SEC(2007) 1520} {SEC(2007) 1521} /* SEC/2007/1518 final

Commission, Accompanying document to the Communication from the Commission to the European Parliament, the Council, the European Economic and Social Committee and the Committee of the Regions - A single market for 21st century Europe {COM(2007) 724 final} {SEC(2007) 1517} {SEC(2007) 1519} {SEC(2007) 1520} {SEC(2007) 1521} /* SEC/2007/1518 final

Communication from the Commission to the European Parliament, the Council, the European Economic and Social Committee and the Committee of the Regions 'Unleashing the Potential of Cloud Computing in Europe', COM/2012/0529 final
Council and the European Economic and Social Committee on the implementation of Regulation (EC) No 765/2008 of the European Parliament and of the Council of 9 July 2008 setting out the requirements for accreditation and market surveillance relating to the marketing of products and repealing Regulation (EEC) No 339/93, COM (2017) 789 final
Council, Council Resolution of 28 October 1999 on the role of standardisation in Europe, OJ C 141/1, May 2000
Degallaix L, 'The use of standards in legislation and policies: How to ensure a legally-sound and socially acceptable use of standards by policy-makers in view of the CJEU James Elliot ruling and other court cases', European Environmental Citizens Organisation for Standardisation (ECOS) [no date]
Der Landesbeauftragte für den Datenschutz und die Informationsfreiheit Baden-Württemberg Orientierungshilfe Videoüberwachung durch nicht-öffentliche Stellen (2020)
Dumortier J, Kosta E, 'ePrivacy Directive: assessment of transposition, effectiveness and compatibility with proposed Data Protection Regulation' (2015) European Publications Office
EDPB 'Guidelines 3/2018 on the territorial scope of the GDPR. (Article 3)' v. 2.1 (2019)
EDPB 'Guidelines 4/2019 on Article 25 Data Protection by Design and by Default' (version 2.0 adopted on 20 October 2020)
EDPB 'Opinion 3/2015 (with addendum). Europe's big opportunity EDPS recommendations on the EU's options for data protection reform' (2015)
EDPB 'Opinion 5/2019 on the interplay between the ePrivacy Directive and the GDPR, in particular regarding the competence, tasks and powers of data protection authorities' (2019)
EDPB Guidelines 05/2020 on consent under Regulation 2016/679 (Version 1.1 Adopted on 4 May 2020)
EDPB Guidelines on Accreditation 4/2018 v.3 (2019)
EDPB Recommendations 01/2020 on measures that supplement transfer tools to ensure compliance with the EU level of protection of personal data (version for public consultation, adopted on 10 November 2020)
EDPB, 'Guidelines 07/2020 on the concepts of controller and processor in the GDPR' (2020) v.1
EDPB, Guidelines 1/2018 on certification and identifying certification criteria in accordance with Articles 42 and 43 of the Regulation - version adopted after public consultation, v. 3.0 (2019)
EDPB, Opinion 16/2019 on the draft decision of the Belgian Supervisory Authority regarding the Binding Corporate Rules of ExxonMobil Corporation (2019)
EDPS 'Guidelines on the Rights of Individuals with regard to the Processing of Personal Data' (2014)
EDPS 'Opinion of the European Data Protection Supervisor on the data protection reform package' (2012)
EDPS 'EDPS Opinion on the Proposal for a Regulation on Privacy and Electronic Communications (ePrivacy Regulation)' Opinion 6/2017
EDPS 'Opinion on Personal Information Management Systems. Towards more user empowerment in managing and processing personal data' Opinion 9/2016 (2016)
EDPS 'Preliminary EDPS Opinion on the review of the ePrivacy Directive (2002/58/EC)' Opinion 5/2016
EDPS 'Preliminary Opinion on privacy by design' Preliminary Opinion 5/2018 (31 May 2018)
EDPS Guidelines on the concepts of controller, processor and joint controllership under Regulation (EU) 2018/1725 (2019)
Egyedi TM. 'Beyond Consortia, Beyond Standardisation? New Case Material and Policy Threads–Final Report for the European Commission.' (2001)
ENISA 'Guidance and gap analysis for European standardisation: Privacy standards in the information security context' (2019)
ENISA 'Recommendations on European Data Protection Certification' Report for ENISA (2017)
ENISA 'Handbook on Security of Personal Data Processing' (December 2017)

ENISA *Privacy and data protection by design – From policy to engineering*, 2014, https://data.europa.eu/doi/10.2824/38623
European Commission 'A comprehensive approach on personal data protection in the European Union'. COM (2010) 609 final
European Commission 'Communication from the Commission to the European Parliament, The Council, the Economic and Social Committee and the Committee of the Regions. A comprehensive approach on personal data protection in the European Union' COM(2010) 609 final
European Commission 'Communication from the Commission to the European Parliament, the Council and the European Economic and Social Committee. A strategic vision for European standards: Moving forward to enhance and accelerate the sustainable growth of the European economy by 2020' COM (2011) 311 final
European Commission 'Communication from the Commission to the European Parliament, the Council, the European Economic and Social Committee and the Committee of the Regions, An EU Strategy on Standardisation, Setting global standards in support of a resilient, green and digital EU single market' COM(2022) 31 final
European Commission 'Methods of referencing standards in legislation with an emphasis on European legislation' Entreprise Publications (2002)
European Commission 'Communication from the Commission to the European Parliament and the Council Data protection as a pillar of citizens' empowerment and the EU's approach to the digital transition -two years of application of the General Data Protection Regulation' COM (2020) 264 final (June 2020)
European Commission 'Guide to application of the Machinery Directive 2006/42/EC' ed.2.2 (October 2019)
European Commission, 'Communication from the Commission to the European Parliament, the Council, the Economic and Social Committee and the Committee of the Regions Single Market Act. Twelve levers to boost growth and strengthen confidence. Working together to create new growth.' COM (2011) 206 final
European Commission, 'Communication from the Commission to the European Parliament, the Council, the European Economic and Social Committee and the committee of the Regions: Unleashing the Potential of Cloud Computing in Europe' COM (2012) 529 final
European Commission, 'Report from the Commission to the European Parliament and the Council on the implementation of the Regulation (EU) No 1025/2012 from 2016 to 2020', COM(2022) 30 final
European Commission, A comprehensive approach on personal data protection in the European Union, OJ C 181/01, 22.06.2011
European Commission, Commission Staff Working Document, Better Regulation Guidelines, SWS (2017) 350
European Commission, Commission Staff Working Document, Vademecum on European standardisation in support of Union legislation and policies, PART II, Preparation and adoption of the Commission's standardisation requests to the European standardisation organisations, SWD (2015) 205 final
European Commission, Communication on the role of European standardisation in the framework of European policies and legislation, COM (2004) 674 final
European Commission, European Parliament and Council, Inter-Institutional Agreement on Better Lawmaking, OJ C 321/01 (2003)
European Commission, Report from the Commission to the European Parliament, the European Commission, Rolling Plan for ICT Standardisation 2020
European Commission: Directorate-General for Communications Networks, Content and Technology, Raiz Shaffique, M. and van der Hof, S., *Mapping age assurance typologies and requirements – Research report*, Publications Office of the European Union, 2024
European Parliament, 'Report on the future of European Standardisation', October 2010
European Parliament, Council and Commission, Interinstitutional Agreement on Better LawMaking, 2003/C 321/01, OJ C 321, 31 December 2013
EY 'Independent Review of the European Standardisation System Final Report' (2015)

https://www.unicef.org/media/113731/file/Ending%20Online%20Sexual%20Exploitation%20and%20Abuse.pdf
International Working Group on Data Protection in Telecommunications 'Working Paper on Biometrics in Online Authentication' (2016)
International Working Group on Data Protection in Telecommunications, 'Working Paper on Web Tracking and Privacy: Respect for context, transparency and control remains essential' (2013)
Jenkins R 'Corporate Codes of Conduct: Self-Regulation in a Global Economy' United Nations Research Institute for Social Development, Paper Number 2 (2001)
Kamara I and others, 'Data protection certification mechanisms: Study on Articles 42 and 43 of the Regulation (EU) 2016/679' 1 ed. Brussels: European Commission - DG Justice & Consumers (2019)
Kamara I, Sveinsdottir T and Wurster S. (2015). Raising Trust in Security Products and Systems through Standardisation and Certification: The CRISP Approach, In *ITU Kaleidoscope 2015 - Trust in the Information Society* (2015). IEEE, 57-63
Korff D 'EC Study on the Implementation of Data Protection Directive 95/46/EC' Study for the European Commission (2002)
Larouche P and others, 'Consumer privacy in network industries. A CERRE Policy Report' Centre on Regulation in Europe (2016)
Lauth M 'Thematic Legal Study on assessment of data protection measures and relevant institutions. Report on Germany' Study for the Fundamental Rights Agency (2009)
Mańko R 'EU competence in private law: the Treaty framework for a European private law and challenges for coherence' European Parliamentary Research Service, (2015)
Monti M 'A New Strategy for the Single Market: At the Service of Europe's Economy and Society. Report to the President of the European Commission José Manuel Barroso by Mario Monti' European Union (2010)
OECD 'Codes of Corporate Conduct: Expanded Review of their Contents', OECD Working Papers on International Investment, 2001/06, (2001) OECD Publishing
OECD 'Industry self-regulation: role and use in supporting consumer interests' OECD Publication Office (23 March 2015)
Office of the Privacy Commissioner of Canada, 'Annual Report to Parliament 1994-1995', Canada Communications Group, (1995)
Prins C et. al. 'Vorebereiden op Digitale Ontwricthing' WRR, 2019
Recommendation No R (81) 1 on regulations for automated medical data banks (1981)
Recommendation No R (83) 10 on the Protection of Personal Data used for Scientific Research and Statistics (1983)
Recommendation No R (86) 1 on Protection of Personal Data Used for Social Security Purposes1 (1986)
Report from the Commission to the European Parliament and the Council on the third annual review of the functioning of the EU-U.S. Privacy Shield, COM (2019) 495 final
Schepel H and Falke J 'Legal Aspects of Standardisation in the Member States of the EC and EFTA' (2000) vol 1, Office for official publications of the European communities
Schepel H, and Falke J 'Legal Aspects of Standardisation in the Member States of the EC and EFTA' (2000) vol 2, Office for official publications of the European communities
Senden L, Kica E, Klinger K, and Hiemstra MI 'Mapping Self-and Co-regulation Approaches in the EU Context": Explorative Study for the European Commission, DG Connect' (2015)
UNICEF, Ending Online Child Sexual Exploitation and Abuse, Lessons Learned and Promising Practices in Low- and Middle- Income Countries (2021)
Working Party on the Protection of Individuals with regard to the processing of personal data 'Opinion 1/97 on Canadian initiatives relating to standardisation in the field of protection of privacy', WP2 (1997)
Working Party on the Protection of Individuals with regard to the Processing of Personal data Working Document: Judging industry self-regulation: when does it make a meaningful contribution to the level of data protection in a third country? DG XV D/5057/97 final WP 7 (1998)

Working Party on the Protection of Individuals with regard to the Processing of Personal data 'Future work on codes of conduct: Working Document on the procedure for the consideration by the Working Party of Community codes of conduct' DG XV D/5004/98 WP 13 (1998)
Working Party on the Protection of Individuals with regard to the Processing of Personal data 'Future work on codes of conduct: Working Document on the procedure for the consideration by the Working Party of Community codes of conduct' DG XV D/5004/98 WP 13 (1998)
Wurster S and others (2015). *Consolidated report on security standards, certification and accreditation – best practice and lessons learnt: Deliverable 2.2 for the CRISP project*, FP7 CRISP project
Zuiderveen Borgesius F, and others. 'An Assessment of the Commission's Proposal on Privacy and Electronic Communications' *Directorate-General for Internal Policies, Policy Department C: Citizen's Rights and Constitutional Affairs* (2017) 23

Standards, standardisation reports, SDO statutes and agreements

<no author> CSA Model Guide' (2010) https://www.cippguide.org/2010/06/29/csa-model-code/ (accessed 20 August 2024)
AS/NZS ISO/IEC 17799:2001, Information technology—Code of practice for information security management
BS 10012 Personal Information Management
BSI PAS 1296: 2018 Online age checking – provision and use of online age checks services – code of practice
Canadian Standards Association, 'PLUS 8300. Making the CSA Privacy Code Work for You. A workbook on applying the CSA Model Code for the Protection of Personal Information (CAN/CSA-Q830) to your organisation' (1996)
Canadian Standards Association, Model Code for the Protection of Personal Information, approved by Standards Council of Canada, CAN/CSA-830-96, March 1996, ISSN 0317-5669
CEN – CENELEC, Internal Regulations Part 2: Common Rules for Standardisation Work, July 2023
CEN 'The Statutes of CEN', July 2018
CEN CENELEC 'Code of conduct for delegates, experts and observers participating in the technical work of CEN/CENELEC' (2018)
CEN CENELEC 'The concept of affiliation with CEN and CENELEC' Guide 12, ed.4 (2016)
CEN CENELEC 'The concept of Companion Standardisation Body with CEN and CENELEC' Guide 13, ed. 4 (2016)
CEN CENELEC 'Guide 18 concerning the execution of Specific Agreements issued to CEN and CENELEC in accordance with the EC and EFTA Framework Partnership Agreements 2009 (FPA 2009) covering the tasks to be assigned to CEN and CENELEC relating to European standardisation' 2010
CEN CENELEC 'Guide 4 General Guidelines for the Cooperation between CEN, CENELEC and ETSI and the European Commission and the European Free Trade Association' 2003 (ed.2)
CEN CENELEC BTWG 12 'Harmonised standards and the European regulatory framework. HAS system for BOSS', draft proposal for the new process HAS contractor/consultants system interaction with the CEN-CENELEC process, published on the website of CEN-CENELC
CEN CENELEC Guide 2 'Consumer interests and the preparation of European Standards; (ed. 1 2001)
CEN Workshop Agreement Inventory of Data Protection Auditing Practices, CWA 15262 (2005)
CEN Workshop Agreement, CWA 15263 Analysis of Privacy Protection Technologies, Privacy-Enhancing Technologies (PET), Privacy Management Systems (PMS) and Identity Management systems (IMS), the Drivers thereof and the need for standardisation (2005)
CEN Workshop Agreement, CWA 15292 Standard form contract to assist compliance with obligations imposed by article 17 of the Data Protection Directive 95/46/EC (2005)

CEN Workshop Agreement, CWA 15499-1 Personal Data Protection Audit Framework (EU Directive EC 95/46) - Part I: Baseline Framework and CWA 15499-2 Part II: Checklists, questionnaires and templates for users of the framework - The protection of Personal Data in the EU (2005)
CEN-CENELEC 'The concept of affiliation with CEN and CENELEC' Guide 12, ed.4 (2016)
CEN-CENELEC 'The concept of Partnership with European Organizations and other stakeholders' Guide 25, v.3 (2021) updated version in January 2024
CEN/ISSS Workshop Data Protection and Privacy, 'Business plan for CEN/ISSS Workshop Data Protection and Privacy' v. 2 (adopted in 2003)
Dumortier Jos, Goemans Caroline 'Data Privacy and Standardization. Discussion paper prepared for the CEN/ISSS Open Seminar on Data Protection', (2000)
ETSI Cloud Standards Coordination Phase 2; Interoperability and Security in Cloud Computing ETSI SR 003 391 (2016)
ETSI Directives, version 47 (2023)
ETSI EN 302 537-1 V1.1.2 (2007-12), Electromagnetic compatibility and Radio spectrum Matters (ERM); Short Range Devices (SRD); Ultra Low Power Medical Data Service Systems operating in the frequency range 401 MHz to 402 MHz and 405 MHz to 406 MHz; Part 1: Technical characteristics and test methods
ETSI EN 303 645 V2.1.1 (2020-06) Cyber Security for Consumer Internet of Things: Baseline Requirements
ETSI TR 103 370 V1.1.1 (2019-01) Personally Identifiable Information (PII) Protection in mobile and cloud services
ETSI TR 103 657 V1.2.1 (2011-12) Lawful Interception (LI); Retained data handling; System Architecture and Internal Interfaces
ETSI TS 118 103 'oneM2M; Security solutions'
ETSI TS 187 016 V3.1.1 (2010-06) Telecommunications and Internet converged Services and Protocols for Advanced Networking (TISPAN); NGN Security; Identity Protection (Protection Profile)
IEC and CENELEC, 'Agreement on IEC - CENELEC Agreement on Common planning of new work and parallel voting (Frankfurt Agreement)' (2016)
IEC ITU, Agreement for Mutual Cooperation and Exchange of Documentation between the International Telecommunication Union and the International Electrotechnical Commission. October 2005
ILNAS and ANEC, Standards analysis. ICT Sector, Luxembourg, v. 3 (2014)
ISO 'ISO Code of Ethics and Conduct' (as approved under Council Resolution 11/2023, adopted on 23 February 2023) (2023)
ISO 9001 Quality management systems – Requirements
ISO and CEN 'Agreement on technical co-operation between ISO and CEN (Vienna Agreement)', Version 3.3 (2001)
ISO and ITU: Agreement for Mutual Cooperation and Exchange of Documentation between the International Telecommunication Union and the International Organisation for Standardisation, August 2005
ISO CEN, Agreement on Technical Co-operation between ISO and CEN (Vienna Agreement), 2001, codified, v. 3.3
ISO Publication on Good Standardization Practices (2019) ed.1
ISO 31700-1:2023 Consumer protection—Privacy by design for consumer goods and services
ISO/IEC 'Using and referencing ISO and IEC standards to support public policy' (2014)
ISO/IEC (PAS) Draft International Standard (DIS) 20886 for a Privacy Framework
ISO/IEC 17000: 2004 – Conformity assessment vocabulary and general principles
ISO/IEC 17065:2012: Conformity assessment – Requirements for bodies certifying products, processes, and services
ISO/IEC 17067:2013 Conformity assessment – Fundamentals of product certification and guidelines for product certification schemes
ISO/IEC 17788:2014 and Rec. ITU-T Y.3500 (08/2014)

ISO/IEC 20546:2019 Information technology – Big Data - Overview and Vocabulary
ISO/IEC 20889:2018 'Privacy enhancing data de-identification terminology and classification of techniques
ISO/IEC 27001:2022, Information technology — Security techniques — Information security management systems — Requirements
ISO/IEC 27002:2022, Information technology — Security techniques — Code of practice for information security controls.
ISO/IEC 27018 Information technology - Security techniques - Code of practice for protection of personally identifiable information (PII) in public clouds acting as PII processors. Japanese Privacy Mark JIS Q 15001:1999 'Requirements for companies' program on personal information protection'
ISO/IEC 29100:2024 Information technology — Security techniques — Privacy framework.
ISO/IEC 29151:2017 Information technology — Security techniques — Code of practice for personally identifiable information protection
ISO/IEC 29184:2020 Information technology — Online privacy notices and consent
ISO/IEC 31000:2018 on Risk management - Principles and guidelines
ISO/IEC Directives Part 1 and Consolidated ISO Supplement, Procedures specific to ISO, V01/2024
ISO/IEC Directives Part 2, Principles and Rules for the structure and drafting of ISO and IEC documents, 9th edition, 2021
ISO/IEC ISO/IEC 29134:2017 Information technology — Security techniques — Guidelines for privacy impact assessment
ISO/IEC TS 29003:2018 Information technology — Security techniques — Identity proofing
ITU-T X.1058 – Supplement on code of practice for personally identifiable information (PII) protection for telecommunication organizations
ITU-T X.1058 (2017)/ ISO/IEC 29151:2017, Information technology – Security techniques – Code of practice for personally identifiable information protection
ITU-T X.srfb Recommendation: Security Requirements and Framework for Big Data Analytics in Mobile Internet Services
JIS Q 15001 'Personal information protection management systems - requirements'
Kantara initiative User-Managed Access (UMA) 2.0 Grant for OAuth 2.0 Authorization, v.2 (2018)
Lipton P, C Lauwers, and D Tamburri, 'Oasis Topology and Orchestration Specification for Cloud Applications (tosca) tc' (2017)
NEN 7510 - Informatiebeveiliging in de zorg
NISTIR 8062, 'An Introduction to Privacy Engineering and Risk Management in Federal Systems' *Information Technology Laboratory, National Institute of Standards and Technology* (2017)
NIST Special Publication 800-63A, Digital Identity Guidelines, Enrollment and Identity Proofing Requirements, June 2017 (updated in 2020), https://doi.org/10.6028/NIST.SP.800-63a
NIST Special Publication 800-63A Digital Identity Guidelines 'Enrollment and Identity Proofing Requirements' (2017)
OASIS Privacy by Design Documentation for Software Engineers (PbD-SE)
OASIS, Privacy Management Reference Model and Methodology (PMRM) Version 1.0 Committee Specification 02, 17 May 2016
EN 17529:2020 Data protection and privacy by design and by default
Standards Council of Canada, Annual Report 1997-1998, (1998)
Tracking Compliance and Scope W3C Working Group Note (22 January 2019)
UNINFO - Feasibility study for standardization in support of article 42 of the GDPR European Data Protection Seal candidate scheme, CEN/CLC/JTC 8 N 164
W3C, Data Privacy Vocabulary (DPV) version 1, Final Community Group Report 05 December 2022
W3C, DPV-GDPR: GDPR Extension for DPV version 1 Final Community Group Report 05 December 2022
W3C, The Platform for Privacy Preferences 1.1 (P3P 1.1) Specification, W3C Working Group Note 13 November 2006 (Retired 30 August 2018)

Doctoral dissertations

Lachaud EMT, 'What could be the contribution of certification to data protection regulation?' Doctoral dissertation, Tilburg University, 2019

Medzmariashvili M, Regulating European Standardisation through Law: The Interplay between Harmonised European Standards and EU Law. Doctoral dissertation, Lund University, 2019

Volpato A, Towards a legal framework for the delegation of powers in the EU legal system. PhD dissertation, Padova University and Maastricht University (2018). https://www.research.unipd.it/retrieve/e14fb26f-b45e-3de1-e053-1705fe0ac030/volpato_annalisa_tesi.pdf (accessed 10 August 2024)

Other (blogs, online publications)

Cavoukian A, 'Understanding How to Implement Privacy by Design, One Step at a Time' *IEEE Consumer Electronics Magazine* 9, no. 2 (2020): 78–82

Centre for Information Policy Leadership, Organisational Accountability – Past, Present and Future, White paper (30 October 2019)

EDRi (author Douwe Korff) Letter to A29 Working Party- Comments on the Draft Guidelines on the Accreditation of Certification Bodies (WP261)' (April 2018)

EDRi (under guest author) 'Are GDPR certification schemes the next data transfer disaster?' 2 May 2018

EDRi Initial Comments on the Proposal for a Data Protection Regulation (January 2017)

Goel V, 'Facebook tinkers with users' emotions in news feed experiment, stirring outcry.' *The New York Times* 29 (2014)

Hofman C, 'Why Enabling Do Not Track does not help you from being tracked' (16 October 2020)

Hoofnagle C, 'Do Not Track Dilemma DNT ~= Do Not Advertise' Technology Academics Policy TAP (10 February 2011)

Hoofnagle C, 'Should Regulation Be "Technology Neutral"?' (2 February 2018)

Kuner C, 'Schrems II reexamined' Verfassungsblog (25 August 2020)

MacAskill E andDance G, 'Files Decoded NSA. Edward Snowden's surveillance revelations explained' *The Guardian* 1 (2013)

Volpato A and Mariolina E, 'The Butterfly Effect of Publishing References to Harmonised Standards in the L series,' European Law Blog (7 March 2019)

Index

For the benefit of digital users, indexed terms that span two pages (e.g., 52–53) may, on occasion, appear on only one of those pages.

Tables are indicated by an italic *t* following the page number.